AMI VOLANSKY

THE PENDULUM SYNDROME
Centralisation and Decentralisation of Education in England and Wales

Ramot Publishing - Tel Aviv University

Ramot Publishing - Tel Aviv University

Design & Layout: Tal Pockard Tzalel
Cover Design: Notelstudio

© All rights reserved. Ramot Publishing - Tel Aviv University.
No part of this publication may be reproduced or transmitted
in any form or by any means, electronic or mechanical, including
photocopying, recording or any information storage or retrieval
system, without written permission from the publishers.

ISBN 965-274-366-6

Published in Israel, 2003

This book is dedicated to my wife Tsvia
In gratitude for her love, support, wisdom and cheerfulness

CONTENTS

Preface 8

Acknowledgements 10

Abbreviations 11

Chapter 1: Introduction 13
1.1: Main issues 13
1.2: Theoretical perspectives 21
1.3: The nature of the study 29

PHASE ONE: ESTABLISHING NATIONAL ORDER 35
Chapter 2: Historical Background 37
2.1: Towards a state system: The establishment of popular education 37
2.2: The development of secondary education 41
2.3: The failure of attempts to establish a new administrative order 46
2.4: Further attempts to achieve equality 49
2.5: Conclusions 51

**Chapter 3: The Construction Of A New Order:
The 1944 Education Act** 57
3.1: Voluntary schools come under control 58
3.2: Towards equal opportunities: Secondary education for all 68
3.3: Towards a new administrative order 72
3.4: Conclusions 77

**PHASE TWO: MOVING AWAY FROM THE NEW ORDER:
THE DECENTRALISATION PROCESS** 87

    **Chapter 4: Local Interaction Blurs the Structure
of the New Order** 89

        4.1:   Central specifications for local organisations 90
        4.2:   Community interaction and transformation
             towards a new structure 95
        4.3:   Blurring the uniqueness of the grammar schools 108
        4.4:   The government's defence of the grammar schools 114
        4.5:   Conclusions 120

    **Chapter 5: The LEAs Face Further Complexity:
The Interaction Between Sub-groups** 127

        5.1:   Parental concerns with status 128
        5.2:   Teachers' status 132
        5.3:   Politicians and their motives 140
        5.4:   Conclusions 144

    **Chapter 6: The Collapse of the Tripartite System:
The Emergence of a New Order** 151

        6.1:   The modern school: Searching for significance 153
        6.2:   The technical schools: Shattering an illusion 164
        6.3:   The selection problem 169
        6.4:   The new structural order: The comprehensive
             school 175
        6.5:   Conclusions 183

**PHASE THREE: RESTORING ORDER: TOWARDS A NEW
SYSTEM STRUCTURE** 193

    **Chapter 7: From Criticism of Standards to the
Core Curriculum** 195

        7.1:   Streaming, mixed ability and progressive methods 196
        7.2:   The Black Papers 202

7.3:	The media campaign	207
7.4:	Towards a national core curriculum	211
7.5:	Conclusions	215

Chapter 8: From Human Capital to Market Economy Values in Education ... 221

8.1:	The human capital approach	222
8.2:	The rise of the "New Right": Towards centralisation and decentralisation under the same umbrella	229
8.3:	Market values penetrate the education system	235
8.4:	Conclusions	243

Chapter 9: Old Values, New Structure: From the Education Reform Act 1988 to the Policies of the 1990s ... 251

9.1:	The national curriculum	254
9.2:	National assessment	268
9.3:	Choice for parents: Open enrolment	282
9.4:	Efficiency through decentralisation: Towards the establishment of an "enterprise culture"	289
9.5:	Conclusions	298

Chapter 10: Conclusions ... 313

10.1:	The initial position of the pendulum	313
10.2:	The swing of the pendulum: The decentralisation process	317
10.3:	Restoring order: Correcting the swing of the pendulum	323
10.4:	Between theory and practical reality	329

Bibliography ... 341

Appendices ... 359

Index ... 363

• PREFACE

This book aims to explain the "pendulum syndrome" characterising the movement of the education system in England and Wales along the centralisation-decentralisation axis. The analysis of this syndrome is principally a description of the structural elaboration and transformation that took place as a result of dialectical interplay between the interests, needs and perceptions of subordinate systems – the periphery – and the interests of the central authority – the government. The dualism at issue is between local tradition and specific attempts made by subsystems (LEAs, divisions, schools, teachers, parents) to meet their own interests and goals by evading central control and the need to curb freedom to some extent in order to effect the implementation of a particular and desired central policy.

The analysis is comprised of three phases, corresponding to three periods. The first concerns the uniform order established by the 1944 Education Act, which aimed to institute secondary education for all and unify the disconnected, isolated, overlapping subsystems under the LEAs – as a single type of administrative control. It also sought to implement a policy of exclusion and differentiation between schools based on the tripartite system, by means of strict government intervention. The second phase examines the *eroding factors*, from the mid-1950s to the end of the 1970s, that led to abuse, neglect, distortion and blurring of the uniform order and the government's exclusion policy. These factors were characterised by: a move towards particularisation on the basis of local interests; implementation of secondary reform on the basis of local needs and local tradition; increased involvement of subsystems, with a concomitant increase in complexity; levelling-up elements as a result of self-determination and the search for significant certification on the part of modern schools; and organisational factors. All these led to a radical *structural transformation* and a gap between the government's vision, aspirations, philosophy and planning, and the extant reality.

The reduced significance of distinctions between schools that transpired during this second period stimulated counter-forces that aimed to restore the elitist tradition, called for a return to the "good old days" and the high standards of the grammar school era; this trend constitutes the main focus of the third phase (which lasted from the mid-1970s to the beginning of 2000s). The economic decline of the 1970s accelerated the contrivance of a *new order* based on market principles of competition, choice and inequality of school resources. The aim was to create differentiation between schools, a goal which the strong central intervention policy of the 1940s had failed to achieve.

The constant trend towards disorder; the mechanisms that foster disorder; the counter-forces working towards stability, correcting deviation and increasing order – all of which contribute to explaining the "pendulum syndrome" – are the main propositions of system theories. Such theories, which guide the observations presented here, shed light on the interplay between individual actions and the mechanisms that aim to control such actions. They carry some explanatory weight in the analysis of factors influencing structural change, and offer considerable enlightenment in understanding the factors that affected the pendular movement and cyclical trend, from centralisation towards decentralisation and vice versa.

The research and data presented in this book were conducted, collected and analysed during three different periods. The first took place in the late 1980s while I was pursuing my doctoral studies at the University of Oxford. The second was towards the end of the 1990s, at which point my research turned to the study of governmental documents and policy analyses using, inter alia, advancements in Information Technology to learn about later policy developments in the UK. The last stage took place when I returned to Oxford in 2002 for further observation and data collection, which enabled me to update and finalise the book. The periods that the book covers, especially the last decade, were very intensive and raised complex questions in the field of educational policies and tendencies. During this time, developments and policies in this field were disputed and contradicted, and extensive education legislation was enacted. Hence, these periods have been extremely interesting from the point of view of researchers and educators, particularly for a foreigner. The findings and observations in this book are an attempt to present the dynamism of educational policies and tendencies, from the early 1940s to the beginning of the 21st century.

ACKNOWLEDGEMENTS

My thanks are due to many individuals who were associated with the completion of this book. Their support, contributions and assistance are what made it possible.

Prof. David Phillips from the University of Oxford provided valuable guidance during my D.Phil. studies and was a great supporter of the publication of the book. Professor A.H. Halsey not only read the manuscript and encouraged me to publish it, but was a source of valuable advice at various stages of the research. I also wish to thank Professor Richard Pring, the director of the Department of Educational Studies, who read part of the study and provided many helpful comments and suggestions. Dr. Vivian Williams, whose interest in this study throughout the decade provided incentive as well as academic enlightenment, deserves many thanks and my greatest appreciation.

Moving to the other side of the globe, I wish to express my gratitude to Professor Dan Brown of the University of British Columbia for his useful comments on the manuscript as well as his encouragement to pursue publication.

Wolfson College at the University of Oxford became my second home during the research. I am deeply grateful to everyone at the College who assisted me throughout our association.

On the Israeli side, Mrs. Miri Chernilas, the head of Tel Aviv University Publishing House (Ramot) and Mrs. Aya Darel treated the book with professionalism and dedication.

All this helpful assistance and genuine interest made it possible to bring this book to press. Thank you all.

ABBREVIATIONS

APS	Assisted Places Scheme
APU	Assessment of Performance Unit
ASSP	Australian Studies in Student Performance
CCCS	Centre for Contemporary Cultural Studies
DES	Department of Education and Science
DfEE	Department for Education and Employment
DP	Development Plan
CTC	City Technology College
FEVER	Friends of the Education Voucher Experiment in Representative Regions
GCE	General Certificate of Education
GCSE	General Certificate of Secondary Education
GM	Grant Maintained
HMI	Her/His Majesty's Inspector(ate)
IEA	Institute of Economic Affairs
ILEA	Inner London Education Authority
LEA	Local Education Authority
LMS	Local Management of Schools
MSC	Manpower Services Commission
NFER	National Foundation for Educational Research
OECD	Organisation for Economic Co-operation and Development
NVQ	National Vocational Qualification
GNVQ	General National Vocational Qualification
NUT	National Union of Teachers
QCA	Qualification and Curriculum and Authority
RSA	Royal Society of Art
SSEC	Secondary School Examinations Committee
TVEI	Technical and Vocational Education Initiative
TGAT	Task Group on Assessment and Testing

• C H A P T E R   1

INTRODUCTION

1.1: MAIN ISSUES

Over the past three decades, the issue of centralisation and decentralisation in education has attracted increasing attention. The focus has centred primarily on two areas: first, the involvement of several levels and subsystems in the education process, and second, the reallocation and redefinition of power, responsibility and decision-making with respect to various times, aspects and forms of that participation. Factors that influence this redefinition and reallocation of power constitute our main research interest, while the primary aim is to identify the forces at work along the centralisation-decentralisation axis.

The term "centralisation" is here used mainly in reference to the governmental level and to attempts by central government to exert greater authority over educational matters. It implies a displacement of power from subordinate systems on the periphery towards the centre, or the formation of new rules and a new order that operates from the centre outwards. Decentralisation, on the other hand, involves devolution of decision-making from the centre to peripheral subsystems such as local authorities, schools, parents and community, from superior to inferior agencies, or a movement towards "reorganis[ation] into smaller, more autonomous units."[1]

Observation of events in other industrial countries throws light on the shifting of power along the decentralisation-centralisation axis.

The Australian education system – to take one example of developments in other countries – has been operated as a highly centralised state system based on two separately financed subsystems: public and private schools.[2] Popular dissatisfaction with the public system and greater support for the private system stimulated the government to shift power in such a way as to "bring [the characteristics of private schools] to the public schools."[3] This was accomplished by decentralising decision-making on budgetary and personnel questions and on responsibility for curriculum matters. But this power-shifting process faced major opposition from bureaucrats who did not "wish to share their power."[4] On the other hand an attempt – arising from concern over low standards – to establish a national assessment system and national performance data failed; schools opposed it or ignored it, eventually forcing the government to abandon it at the national level while continuing to support the idea of assessment (Power, 1984). Nevertheless, in 1988 the Minister of Education announced the government's wish to establish a national curriculum framework and again attempted to institute a national testing programme (OECD, 1989). Although the "Government clearly reserves the right to intervene where it believes it is necessary to ensure the appropriate levels of outcomes,"[5] there has been a steady shift toward self-management in all Australian states over the last 30 years (Caldwell, 2003; Caldwell and Spinks, 1998; Kenway, 1995).

The United States, on the other hand, has historically espoused a decentralised system of education. Gross inequalities and a decline in academic performance and standards of discipline prompted the federal government to embark on educational reforms. However, the results of central reforms and intervention have been "particularly disappointing."[6] Swanson's explanation is that the government "failed when it attempted to specify the organisation and implementation of educational programs."[7] It might be concluded that the need to take proper account of individual schools, classrooms and teachers, was the most significant factor in the failure of central attempts to bring about change.

In another analysis of federal action in the US, Power (1984) describes the result of a central government initiative to establish a national assessment system, aimed at achieving greater accountability of teachers. This initiative was completely disregarded by schools. Power explains this in terms of the "long tradition of local control over the curriculum [which] meant that, in the end, the testing program became general and bland."[8] It appears to have been unfeasible to demand that any particular state, district, school or programme, account for its performance through central intervention.

Michael Kirst (2003) describes a wide swing towards decentralisation and shifting of power to schools. According to him, school-based management (SBM) has taken a back seat to district-wide concerns, and the many attempts to introduce SBM have had "marginal impact and…little to do with improving classroom instruction. The nature of district governance and management is such that they resist school-based management."[9] As of 2001, 95,000 school board members in 14,500 districts were still formally in charge of local elements of the public school system. SBM reformers attempted to overcome district-wide policies, such as union contracts, but often met with resistance.

The interplay between cycles of decentralisation and centralisation in the USA education system during two decades of reforms has been described by Finn and Rebarber (1992) and Volansky (1995). The first wave of reform occurred in the mid-1980s, "when states became the main engines of change in education policymaking."[10] The second wave moved towards increasing the school burden on local school managers and the third wave was greater federal intervention and a new federal leadership standard in the early 1990s.

A shift in the other direction is described by Martin Schiff (1976) in his explanation of the failure of an attempt made to transfer power from the centre to the community in the inner city of New York. The main assumptions behind this move were that community control would improve the educational achievements of children from minority groups, increase parental participation and raise teachers' accountability and expectations. In practice, the process resulted in the emergence of militant elements that encouraged violence, and many of the leaders of the 32 autonomous school districts behaved in a manner that was "financially irresponsible, educationally incompetent, and patronage oriented."[11] Consequently, the educational aims were far from met, and the disappointingly poor results provoked a counter-move, again shifting power in the opposite direction.

The French education system's long tradition of high levels of control and centralisation underwent a shift of power with the attempt to move towards a more decentralised system, away from bureaucratic control over school assessment towards internal control conducted by teachers and based on teachers' evaluations (Broadfoot, in Lauglo, 1985). The shift of power included schools taking control over administrative and financial matters and attempts to decentralise decisions related to the curriculum and instruction. An OECD Report (1989) explained this in terms of loss of power at the national level and the minister's difficulty ensuring "the full implementation of national policies through a central control mechanism."[12]

Over the last three decades the highly controlled Israeli system has experienced frequent movements toward and away from decentralisation. In the mid-1970s, the Ministry of Education initiated a sophisticated reform of matriculation examinations, which allowed for differentiation of the level of examinations in elective subjects on school initiative (with Ministry approval).[13] This meant that in some cases a national examination was prepared for a group of only 30 pupils. This central initiative was quickly matched by head teachers' initiatives, which a decade later would exceed public tolerance and become an open scandal. The accumulation of subject combinations at the optional level had risen beyond the administration's capacity to cope. Moreover, the universities accused the Ministry of Education of lowering student performance by the matriculation examinations reform. Media attacks and parliamentary intervention led the Minister of Education to establish two committees to sort out what appeared to be a state of utter disorder over the examinations. The result was reallocation of power from schools to the centre and a redefinition of the matriculation examination curriculum that restricted subject options and the discretionary power of schools.

Centralisation in Israel is motivated by a deep sense of equality that has sustained political consensus regarding the necessity of a highly interventionist state. Sharp cuts in the education budget during the 1980s affected the national curriculum, including core subjects, and the school day has been shortened. The counter-process saw the emergence of parents' organisations, which had been encouraged to take a more active part in the education process for many years. These aimed to increase school working hours and enrich the curriculum by means of private funds. The curriculum of 38% of schools,[14] particularly in middle-class areas, has consequently been enriched – including in core subjects. The process has exposed the government's inability to assist schools catering to "socio-economically disadvantaged population groups"[15] and also endangered the highly sensitive principle of equality. The situation has politically explosive potential. From this point on, the two impulses – the government's desire to pursue equality by controlling the curriculum and encouraging parental participation in the education process – were revealed as contradictory, a political trap. When the government proved unable to fully finance the national curriculum, it was in parents' interests to compensate for the shortfall at their own expense. Eventually, the conflict of interests and the resulting disorder led to government intervention aimed at restoring order. New legislation was laid down in 1997 that sought to effect equality between schools by extending the school day for all.[16]

Two cycles of change can be identified in Sweden. The first, moving towards a centralised, integrated and comprehensive system, was gradually developed between 1940 and 1970, driven by the need to offer uniform opportunity and a modern curriculum. But the contrasting need for differentiation, prompted by local communities, led to the second cycle of change – a movement towards decentralisation which has been in evidence since 1970 (OECD, 1989). The motives for the second wave are the desire to respond to local needs and to set broader curriculum goals. These result in "differences among schools."[17] In research on the development and the direction of the decentralisation process in Sweden, many indications were found that central reforms had "not . . . made much impression on teaching"[18] and that despite central control at the political level of resources, teacher appointments and curriculum, it is impossible to control and to steer the profession.

Lauglo (1985), in explanation of this point, argues that schools are slow to change, and behave and develop according to intrinsic rather than extrinsic goals because they have a commitment to the society they serve. This commitment could be one of the explanations for the deliberate shift of power by the government, and its desire to go "along [with] the current teaching tradition rather than seeking to bring about radical change,"[19] for the nature of that tradition is one of autonomy and decentralisation rather than of central authority.

Japan's highly uniform education system took steps towards reducing rigidity and uniformity by declaring reform and reorganisation of schools towards the year 2002, on the basis of respect for the autonomy of individual schools. The Ministry of Education explained the change in the following terms: "overemphasis on egalitarianism and uniformity of school education derives from problems in educational systems and operations, reforms have been made for the purpose of decentralising the administrative systems that support school education."[20]

The education system in England and Wales, which is the subject of the present research, has experienced three periods of shifting power: central dominance from the end of the Second World War until the mid-1950s; local dominance from then until the 1970s; and the present period, which can be regarded as one of accelerated centralisation of curriculum and assessment matters and decentralisation of administrative issues (Lowe 1989; Phillips and Furling 2001; Ranson 1985; Whitty, Power and Halpin, 1998).

This short review of some developments in the education systems of seven countries demonstrates the phenomenon of repeated shifts of power along the axis of centralisation and decentralisation. This might be called a "pendulum syndrome." Some of the countries experienced a shift in one direction alone, from the centre to the periphery (France, Sweden); others a double shift from the centre to the periphery and vice versa (Israel, England, Australia); or a shift from the decentralised system (US) towards central intervention in some elements (assessment, finance) and then a further shift towards decreasing government intervention.

It is important to mention at this stage that in the cases reviewed the terms "centralisation," "decentralisation," and "shift of power," refer to parts of the education system at any given time. For example, in England the move towards centralisation during the 1940s by and large affected administrative elements but not curriculum matters, while the reallocation of power during the 1980s had exactly the opposite impact: centralisation of curriculum and assessment and decentralisation of management. Thus, when we mention shifts that occurred at any particular time, we are referring to particular elements within the education system, and not to a revolutionary process involving the entire system.

The brief description presented above brings us to the main question of this research: if the "pendulum syndrome" may be said to characterise some education systems, what are the factors that propel the system in either direction – towards centralisation or towards decentralisation – in a cyclical process? A review of the literature sheds some light on this question.

In a comparative study covering structural changes in four countries,[21] Margaret Archer (1979, 1984) distinguishes between the pattern of change in centralised and decentralised systems. Centralised systems are compelled to reduce their "standardisation and to meet a multiplicity of demands with greater precision, by introducing more differentiation and specialisation."[22] In decentralised systems, characterised by a pattern of internal initiation and incremental change in many small local parts of the system, the integrative role of the central authorities is to connect and co-ordinate these "anarchic changes."[23] Archer's conclusions generate arguments for the existence of a dialectic, a dualism between the rights of individuals and minorities on the one hand and central attempts to reduce internal chaos and to increase coherence, unification and standardisation on the other. Broadfoot (in Lauglo & McLean, 1985), explains this dialectic and the support for decentralisation as a "growing awareness of the rights and needs of minorities; the concept of decentralised control of education tends to be associated with a policy provision for minority, local and individual interests against the lumbering impersonality of a huge central bureaucracy."[24]

If so, does the decentralisation process, which is associated with a policy of devolution of power, bring about greater satisfaction, reduce pressure from subordinate groups and establish a greater balance within the system? McGlinn & Street (1986) argue that governments harbour the illusion that decentralisation will reduce dissatisfaction and solve education problems. McGlinn & Street claim instead, that "not only is there little positive evidence that policies of decentralisation 'work' or can be made to work, but there is considerable evidence that they do not work, that they do not increase effectiveness, administrative efficiency, or local participation."[25] If decentralisation is evidently failing, they ask, "why do governments persist in promotion of policies of decentralisation?"[26]

But in Lauglo's view (1985) the contrary system of bureaucratic centralism does not "work" either. In the Scandinavian countries of Sweden, Norway and Denmark there has been a tendency "to relax control from the centre in the hope that greater scope for local and school level decision-making would elicit local initiatives for pedagogic renewal in order to make the new structure 'work better'."[27] Lauglo has argued that central attempts to redefine the structure or status of institutions that threaten occupational identities have been resisted by those who might be affected, while schools' intrinsic goals and their commitment to fulfilling internal and local needs are more powerful than any external demands. Swanson comes to a similar conclusion, arguing that no reform could be achieved without taking classroom circumstances into account.

But the brief review of the cases of Israel, the inner city of New York and England presented above gives some indication that even when fulfilment of particular needs of minorities, communities or individuals has been achieved and greater autonomy allowed, this autonomy eventually begins to diminish and a new cycle of setting up new rules – in order to reduce autonomy and increase standardisation – takes place.

This brings us to the heart of the theoretical question. A review of the literature on the shift of power between the two poles of centralisation and decentralisation shows repeated attempts to establish a new or improved order, either by centralising or decentralising a particular aspect of the education system. On the other hand, some of the cases reviewed also show consistent abuse, neglect and distortion of any new order (whether characterised by centralisation or decentralisation). This prompts further attempts to take corrective measures (to establish a new order), this time in the opposite direction, thus resulting in a "pendulum movement." In Swanson's view such reform results from a degree of imbalance within the system that can no longer be tolerated; the system is in substantial disequilibrium and deliberate attempts are made to correct it.

Robert Slavin (1999) offers a major insight to understanding the "pendulum syndrome." According to Slavin, one of the major factors contributing to the permanent motion of the pendulum is a "lack of respect for research and development in the change process…in education, we rarely wait for or demand hard evidence before we adopt new practices."[28] Thus, every aspect of school life became legitimate grounds for dispute, for moving back and forth, for a quick departure from the old educational line and fostering of a new and always "modern" one, while "every innovator claims research support for his or her methods."[29]

Therefore, if the "pendulum syndrome" that occurs along the centralisation-decentralisation axis is attributable to the correction of a previous order as a result of instability and disequilibrium, we should seek a theoretical explanation for the propositions of order and disorder. Such propositions are associated with the desire for greater autonomy and freedom versus the desire to maintain central control; particular attempts of individuals, minorities, communities and other subsystems to fulfil their interests and goals that contradict central rules and bureaucracy; the centrifugal forces associated with individuals' tendency to fly out of control and to pursue their own goals versus the need for some curbing of individual freedom and to maintain a certain level of unification and standardisation. Such theoretical considerations are the main concern of the following discussion.

1.2: THEORETICAL PERSPECTIVES

Structural changes along the centralisation-decentralisation axis lead to the search for a theoretical explanation for the dualism between central attempts to impose or restore order and counter-forces resisting and departing from such order. This search involves consideration of three types of theoretical explanation: the macro-sociological view; social systems theories; and motivation theories.

In Max Weber's view the dualism behind structural transformation is the result of tension and conflict between classes, status groups and parties over privileges such as improved income, political monopoly, hierarchical domination and status dependent on education; therefore, "man and groups in society act with and against each other on the basis of their material interests and ideal interests."[30] Theoretical explanations on the basis of this conflict theory of macro-sociology have proved unhelpful in explaining the full range of the actual changes and structural transformations in the education systems that have been reviewed. Thus, the "macro-question" does not equip us with analytical tools for understanding the events that led, in the case of the US, to government intervention in the establishment of a national assessment system as a result of decline in academic performance, nor does it have explanatory power in addressing the shift in power either in the case of the inner city of New York or in the case of the double shift of power in the Israeli education system. This theory also throws little light on attempts in the Swedish and French education systems to devolve power from the centre to the teachers, or the difficulties experienced in exerting central policy in these countries. It is therefore inadequate as a theoretical base for explaining the "pendulum syndrome"; a more sensitive theoretical explanation is needed.

Systems theories offers more explanatory power for the dialectic between the centre and the periphery, between holism and individualism – the interplay between individual actions and a mechanism aimed at controlling and curbing such actions. First let us concentrate on those factors that affect mainly centrifugal forces (of decentralisation) by prompting deviation from a prescribed path and escape from central control.

Parsons examines a social system's leaning towards instability and disorder in his General Theory of Action. According to this theory, the individual selects, or commits himself to, objectives or goals "with respect to their potentialities for gratification; he also selects from among the modes of their possible significance to him."[31] The "personality system" is therefore the major element in the trend towards a state of disorder. The basic frame of reference of the theory is individual striving for attainment of "states of gratification or goals within a situation. The polarity of gratification and deprivation, and hence of the two fundamental tendencies of action – seeking and avoidance – are inherent in this conception."[32] Such individual motivation needs further explanation and this point will be further examined and clarified below.

The involvement of individuals, the community and other subsystems, is another factor in explaining deviation and disorder within a system. A social system is defined as a living system which is "engaged in processes of interchange (or input-output relations) with its environment."[33] This definition, which represents the actual reality of the education system as an open system deeply engaged with its environment in the form of such groups as parents, employers, local education authorities and communities, raises the theoretical question of the effect of such involvement.

Bertalanffy (1968) argues, in his General System Theory, that such involvement is necessary in order to maintain a state of balance and protect a system from destruction. According to the Theory, the trend towards disorder (entropy) is the basic rule of an open (social) system. Interaction with the environment aims to prevent such destructive damage, and to decrease the level of disorder by importing energy and materials from the environment. Thus, it could be argued that parents' response to the shortening of the school day by direct financing of the curriculum, as in the Israeli case, meets the General System Theory's proposition that such involvement is aimed at preventing the system's (the schools) destruction. Lauglo's (1985) description of headteachers' struggles for reliable supplies of materials, finance, staff and students in terms of their reliance on their own ability and initiative in the environment is an explanation of the relationship between school and its environment in modern education according to the perspective of General System Theory. But Bertalanffy's propositions do not illuminate how such environmental involvement affects structural transformation, a change which must be at the centre of an understanding of the interplay between centralisation and decentralisation, and the dualism at issue.

The Dissipative Structure Paradigm offers further explanation of the question at hand. According to this theory, a system's involvement with its environment results in a continuous process of instability and entropy (disorder) production,[34] which has a direct effect on structural change, and increases deviation from a given reference point. This instability is due partly to the nature of an hierarchical organisation, such as an education system, in which the potential for disorder increases:

> ...each level includes all lower levels – there are systems within systems within systems... within the total system in question... evolution leads to differentiation in multilevels, hierarchic systems.[35]

Prigogine (1976) discusses this point in relation to the social system and argues that the more functioning elements in the interaction between system and environment, the greater the complexity of that system. As long as an open system continues to exchange energy with the environment, the production of disorder (entropy) increases, forcing the system over the threshold of instability and through it to the formation of a new structure and a new order.

If this is so, one might argue that district involvement in the case of the inner-city of New York, which culminated in the emergence of militant elements that "encouraged violence,"[36] was the formation of a new structure. Or, in the Israeli case, that the involvement of headteachers and schools, and the minimal freedom given to them over the matriculation examinations, increased disorder and instability and hence brought about structural changes in secondary education.

The Dissipative Structure Paradigm contributes to a discussion of the characteristics of open systems that might be able to explain the link between policies of greater freedom, greater autonomy and greater involvement for teachers, schools and communities, and cycles of instability, disorder, and the need for some corrective measures and structural changes. The theory attributes the evolution of systems and structural changes to a dynamic of self-organisation, self-renewal and self-production.[37] Such a theoretical proposition would explain the development of independent parental organisation and action in the Israeli system, aimed at raising private money to enrich the curriculum – either in terms of Carlson's description of school development as "domesticated organisations"[38] or Lauglo's (1985) view that that schools are slow to change and develop according to intrinsic rather than extrinsic goals.[39]

The terms "intrinsic," "self-conduct," and "self-renewal," bring our discussion to focus on a further type of theory and question the nature of the "intrinsic" factors that affect structural changes within an organisation. This question leads us to an extension of Parsons' view of the role of the individual and to motivation theories. These theories fall into two main types – theories of *avoidance* of participation in activity on the one hand, and theories of *seeking* participation and *involvement* on the other. Both types of theories are concerned with change, disorder, failure and success.

Argyris (1982), Srivastva (1988) and Meyer & Zucker (1989) concentrate on elements of individual motivation to avoid taking part in action, which undermine and subvert order or organisational goals. Argyris argues that mistrust, uncertainty, inter-group rivalry, invalid information and parochial interests result from miscommunication and misinformation. He claims that people become defensive and do not tend towards fruitful co-operation because "unilateral control does not usually produce valid feedback."[40] Srivastva takes a similar view in addressing the unseen and unconscious factors that affect individual behaviour in terms of a chain of conflicts within an organisation. Thus, different perceptions of reality result "from members' telling different stories, selecting different relevant details, using different methods of expert analysis."[41] In Srivastva's view, people create convoluted rationalisations that justify their perceptions, their views and behaviour, and their overriding principles. The force most destructive to the integrity of a system, is "protecting one's turf."[42]

The Theory of Permanent Failure draws on the dependency approach in psychology, arguing that those who have few alternatives have greater motivation to "maintain the organisation regardless of its performance."[43] In propounding this theory, Meyer & Zucker make two key assumptions about organisations. The first is that over time organisations tend "toward sustained low performance, insofar as performance measures reflect the interest of owners."[44] The second is that multiple actors, whose interests "sometimes correspond but sometimes conflict"[45] with the organisation's goals, constitute a permanent source of tension between motivations that are not easily aligned, especially when "external conditions cause performance to decline."[46] So, those who are seeking change, even if they have formal authority, are confronted by others "whose interests are served best by nonchange."[47]

The psychological term *perception*, which refers to the understanding of *reality* when things look different to different people, is the common ground for the cluster of theories dealing with *avoidance* and *obstruction* of particular developments within an organisation.

It could be argued that in the US and Australian education systems, in spite of the governments' formal authority to impose a central assessment system, schools resisted simply because the teachers' interests were best served by "nonchange." Or it might be claimed that the conservative forces within the Swedish system hindered innovative forces[48] because the changes did not correspond with their interests. Avoidance theories of motivation reinforce the view that forces of delay resist and ignore changes because they are acting on behalf of different interests, different needs, and based on a different perception of reality.

The second cluster of motivation theories takes the opposite tack in attempting to explain change and evolution within the organisation from the point of view of individual needs or drives. These theories emphasise the image of a human being seeking rather than avoiding participation in significant action. This might elucidate the terms "self-conduct" and "self-renewal." Maslow, in his Motivation Theory, suggests the existence of a hierarchy of human needs.[49] The need for esteem, in Maslow's theory, is reflected in people's desire for "high evaluation of themselves, for self-respect or self-esteem, and for the esteem of others"; in pursuit of this end people seek "strength, achievement, adequacy, mastery and competence, confidence in the face of the world, and independence and freedom."[50] In this view, the desire for reputation and prestige, "status, fame and glory, dominance, recognition, attention, importance, dignity, or appreciation"[51] is central to human activity. Handy posits an approach based on the idea that man is a self-activating organism who can "control his own destiny . . . can select his goals and choose the paths towards them."[52] Handy's view is that each individual has a set of needs and desired results which he strives to reach.[53]

At the centre of McGregor's Theory Y is the image of a human individual who seeks responsibility, considers work a source of satisfaction, and commits himself to objectives in order to gain rewards. Commitment to objectives, in McGregor's view, is a "function of the rewards associated with their achievement."[54]

The theories reviewed thus far have a certain capacity to analyse the factors influencing structural change. There are two main propositions that affect such change or deviation from a reference order: the involvement of subsystems, the environment and humans; and secondary factors related to the individual that are conducive to either avoidance of a particular order (policy) or achievement of a particular goal. It could be argued that disorder, or departure from the type of order that a government attempts to impose, is mainly a result of the combination of these two factors. Such factors could explain the difficulties of the Swedish and French governments in implementing a national policy through a central control mechanism and their consequent moves towards greater decentralisation.

This brief description of the interplay between centralisation and decentralisation raises some evidence (in the cases of the US, Australia, England and Israel) that subsequent to a period when subgroups are given more freedom and authority, an attempt is made to introduce corrective measures or to impose new central rules. The following discussion will concentrate on the concept of a "control mechanism" in the reviewed theories, which might explain the reverse movement of the pendulum and a new cycle of structural transformation towards a new order or towards certain measures of centralisation.

Parsons' view is that when the stability of the social system is in question as a result of departure from normative standards, there are certain "'control mechanisms' which serve to keep the potential dispersion of the actor's reaction within limits narrower than would be produced by the combination of the total situation and the actor's personality."[55]

We could hence regard the structural change in the cases of Australia and the US as attempts to establish a "control mechanism" that will prevent a decline in standards. We could say that the new measures taken by the Israeli government to diminish schools' discretion with respect to matriculation examinations was an attempt that got out of control to introduce a "control mechanism" into the secondary school curriculum.

Kurt Lewin's (1947) view on "control mechanisms" is that a social structure maintains divergent forces and whenever a strong force seeks change in a particular direction, a counter-force emerges to maintain or restore the previous situation. The result is that "quasi-stationary processes are not perfectly constant but show fluctuation around an average level."[56] Prigogine argues for the existence of a metastable state, rather than equilibrium, which results from subsystems being quick to "damp smaller and medium fluctuation and to maintain the system in a state of metastability,"[57] which actually delays evolution.

Buckley's view is that the nature of a social system fosters spontaneous behaviour which leads to social unrest; there is a tendency towards breakdown or rejection of institutional control and various forms of spontaneous collective behaviour "culminating in some cases in the institutionalisation of a new order."[58] There is hence no chain of events with clear-cut antecedents and consequences; instead, institutional structures help to create and recreate themselves in an ongoing process, or a circular process containing elements of stability and rigidity (control mechanism) and elements of increasing disorganisation (see Appendix 1).

According to Bertalanffy's General System Theory, Kurt Lewin's model of social change and group dynamics and Parsons' General Theory of Action, there is an equilibrium[59] between the forces that preserve stability by means of control or feedback mechanisms.[60] The interplay between forces attempting to impose uniform standards, stabilisation and a level of inflexibility, and counter-forces attempting to increase flexibility and disorganisation, to reduce standardisation and increase particularisation, might explain the "pendulum syndrome" as a continuous and cyclical movement along the centralisation-decentralisation axis.

The theoretical review suggests two primary propositions: first a constant trend towards disorder; second, counter-forces moving towards correction of deviation and increased order and stability. These propositions are the core of the dualism between micro and macro, between particular needs, motives and behaviour of groups, minorities, communities, and individuals, and complex kinds of social interactions, versus the interests of a central authority in imposing a particular order. Such dualism is the basis of our attempt to explain the "pendulum syndrome" in education, which occurs along the axis of centralisation and decentralisation.

Several questions arise from this attempt: can we discover the factors, the facts, the events and the processes leading towards disorganisation and motivated by "particular needs," that subverted the national or government-defined order? Can we find evidence for the theoretical view that subsystem involvement increases the potential for complexity and disorder and actually creates a qualitatively new structure by blurring and undermining the previous order? Would we find any evidence for the theoretical proposition that destruction, transformation and distortion of order result from attempts by teachers, LEAs, parents and other subsystem groups to avoid the fulfilment of actions that have negative meaning or are not significant for them? Is there demonstrable evidence that the desire of schools, LEAs and parents to achieve objectives that are significant for them has any effect on structural order? Could we identify the counter-forces, facts and events that led towards a corrective process and towards an attempt to preserve the previous order? These questions will be at the centre of the observation and description of events, decision-making and implementation of decisions, the interaction of different levels, centrifugal and spontaneous (or organised) forces away from order and the counter-steps of control mechanisms to curb these forces – all in an attempt to explain the "pendulum syndrome" in the English and Welsh education system.

The social scientist is not satisfied with simply describing a process; it has to be understood. Theories are therefore needed, which may or may not prove useful in answering the above questions.

1.3: THE NATURE OF THE STUDY

Initially, the research was designed as a comparative study of Israel and England. The discrepancy between the two systems was the initial trigger for comparative research into the question at hand – the "pendulum movement" along the axis of centralisation and decentralisation.

The complexity of changes in the English education system, the endless factors to be taken into account, the complexity of decision making, and the numerous documents to be assessed, make proper assessment of material and the in-depth study of structural changes an enormous enterprise. The present discussion therefore focuses on one education system – that of England and Wales – with a view to developing a theoretical tool adequate to examining and explaining the "pendulum syndrome."

This study is based on a comparative method, and elucidates the evolution, reconstruction and transformation of an education system, the multiplicity and complexity of factors affecting changes in structure and influencing decision making. Comparative methods require analysis of the interplay between different factors, which in this case means the factors that have affected structural changes in the direction of either centralisation or decentralisation.

The complexity of such changes and of the elements of human behaviour that affect change, is a central concern in a comparative study. An interdisciplinary approach based on a broad theoretical perspective is therefore essential in the planning of such research, alongside a qualitative and more holistic approach that brings together various governmental, management, social and economic factors. As Edmund King puts it: "nothing is really static in society, and education to-day is one of society's least static elements. Therefore, no quantity of 'snapshots' will portray the living whole."[61] The present discussion therefore uses social science theory, which deals with such complexity, providing "relevant information, clarifying some issues and suggesting possible causes of events or decisions, suggesting hypotheses or areas for further enquiry, and giving an overall picture of local complexity."[62]

The discussion is aimed in the main at explaining the complexity of structural transformation or system evolution and arriving at an explanation for similar movements along the axis of centralisation and decentralisation. This approach lends itself to further investigation of the issue at hand by decision makers and planners alike, with regard to *"what are thought to be the outcomes of various decisions."*[63] In this sense it borrows from the methods of comparative education.

The book focuses on secondary education in particular, a field that experienced major changes, events and decisions during the period in question. Little attention is paid to the other tiers of the system (pre-school, primary, further education and higher education). Furthermore, even within the secondary level, attention is devoted to the most influential committees, official documents and Acts, while other important documents or Acts are ignored. The investigation concentrates on the state system (maintained schools) rather than the independent sector.

The analysis is restricted to government, local authorities, divisions within the local authorities and, in a few particular cases, schools; the class level is not addressed. Particular reference is made to the period 1941-2002, a period long enough to observe the nature of the "pendulum syndrome" manifest in forces towards centralisation or decentralisation. A historical background is provided in order to explain the factors that led to the structure of the 1944 Education Act.

The exploration of trends in the education system along the centralisation-decentralisation axis is based on educational documents in the Public Record Office,[64] parliamentary legislation, DES/DfEE documents, and analysis of commentaries and case studies, in addition to interviews undertaken to illuminate the evidence.

The structure of this study has three phases. The first is the establishment of a *new order*, an effort which came to an end in the legislation of the 1944 Education Act. This phase, starting with government intervention in education in 1833, is addressed in two chapters. The main government effort was dedicated to establishing a national education system by means of legislation on three main fronts: primary education for all; secondary education for all; and a unification of all sorts of schools – secular as well as voluntary – under a single type of administrative control, the LEAs. These attempts came to fruition in the 1944 Education Act, which constructed a new educational order.

The second phase is covered by three chapters that examine the interplay between the government and subsystems and elements that balked, distorted, deformed, neglected and abused the new central order. This process was partly a result of the involvement of three different levels in the education system, each with its own tradition, its own goals, and its own perceptions. Thus, the LEAs at first, and then parents, local politicians and teachers, widened the gap between central ideas and the Ministry of Education's outlook, in order to construct a new reality and a new education order; this could be regarded as a decentralising effect.

The third phase deals with the counter-movements towards centralisation, or the "control mechanism," motivated by what was seen as a failure of standards and performance resulting from the distortion of the old order. This counter-process took the form of calls for greater government intervention, tighter control over education issues and a return to some of the old values and teaching methods. Such forces gathered momentum with the formulation of the 1988 Education Reform Act and the policies of the 1990s, which shifted power over the main educational issues from schools to central government.

These three phases, which constitute a process and an era, explain the factors behind the "pendulum syndrome" of centralisation and decentralisation in the education system of England and Wales.

Notes:

1. OECD (1989). *Decentralisation and School Improvement: New Perspectives and Conditions for Change*. Paris: OECD, 4.
2. Most of these were Roman Catholic schools that served the working class.
3. Austin D. Swanson (1988). *The Bureaucratisation of Education: A Comparative Perspective*. Unpublished document. Buffalo: State University of New York, 8.
4. Ibid.
5. Brian J. Caldwell (2003). "A Theory of Learning in the Self-Managing School." In A. Volansky and I. Friedman (eds.), *School-Based Management — An International Perspective*. Jerusalem: Ministry of Education.
   Brian J. Caldwell and J. M. Spinks (1998). *Beyond the Self-Managing School*. London: Falmer.
6. Swanson (1988), 10.
7. Ibid.
8. Colin Power (1984). "National Assessment: A Review of Programs in Australia, the United Kingdom, and the United States." *Comparative Education Review*, 28(3), 362.
9. Michael W. Kirst (2003). "School-Based Management: The United States Experience." In A. Volansky and I. Friedman (eds.), *School-Based Management – An International Perspective*, Jerusalem: Ministry of Education.
10. Chester E. Finn Jr. and Theodor Rebarber (1992). "The Changing Politics of Education Reform." In Chester E. Finn, Jr., and Theodor Rebarber (eds.), *Education Reform in the 1990s*. New York: Macmillan.
11. Martin Schiff (1976). "The Educational Failure of Community Control on Inner-City New York." *Phi Delta Kappa*, February, 378.
12. OECD (1989), p.24.
13. Ministry of Education and Culture (Israel) (1977). The General Director's Circular, A. 70. (Hebrew)
14. Shoshana Langerman & Ronit Bar Siman-Tov (1989). *Additional Studies Programme Financed by Parents in Primary School*. Jerusalem: Szold Institute, 7. (Hebrew)
15. Ministry of Education (1988). *Facts and Figures on the Education and Culture System in Israel*. Jerusalem. Foreword by the Minister.
16. Ministry of Education and Culture (1991). The General Director's Circular, I. (Hebrew)
17. OECD (1989), p.25.
18. Swedish National Board of Education (1989). *Effects of Decentralisation in the School Sector*. Lund: University of Lund, 4.
19. Jon Lauglo & Martin McLean (eds.) (1985). *The Control of Education*. London: Heinemann, 141.
20. Ministry of Education, Culture, Sports, Science and Technology - Mext (Japan) (2001), 18.
21. The French, Russian, English and Danish education systems.
22. Margaret S. Archer (1984). *Social Origins of Educational Systems*. London: Sage, 198.
23. Ibid., 199.
24. Patricia Broadfoot (1985). "Towards Conformity: Educational Control and the Growth of Corporate Management in England and France." In Lauglo & McLean (1985), 105.

25. Noel McGinn & Susan Street (1986). "Educational Decentralisation: Weak State or Strong State?" *Comparative Education Review*, 30(4), 473.
26. Ibid.
27. Lauglo & McLean, (1985). 129.
28. Robert E. Slavin (1999). "The Pendulum Revisited: Faddism in Education and its Alternatives." In Gregory J. Cizek (ed.). *Handbook of Educational Policy*, NY: Academic Press, 374.
29. Ibid, 375
30. Reinhard Bendix (1960). *Max Weber*. London: Heinemann, 290.
31. Talcott Parsons & Edward A. Shils (eds.) (1962). *Towards a General Theory of Action*. New York: Harper, 11.
32. Ibid. 234.
33. Talcott Parsons (1977). *Social System and Evolution of Action Theory*. New York: Macmillan, 180.
34. A view that contradicts General System Theory.
35. Erich Jantsch (1980). *The Self-Organising Universe*. Oxford: Pergamon, 33. The new ordering principle of dissipative structure theory is defined as order through fluctuation.
36. Schiff (1976), 374.
37. Such theoretical perspectives matches research findings on "second order change" (Knight 1967; Watzlawick 1974) as well as the so-called the "new naturalism-new science of chaos," (Gleick, 1988; Sungaila, 1990).
38. Quoted by Lauglo in Lauglo & McLean (1985), 140.
39. Such a theoretical perspective is analogous to the "effective schools" approach.
40. Chris Argyris (1982), *Reasoning, Learning and Action – Individual and Organisational*. London: Jossey-Bass, 86.
41. Suresh Srivastva & Frank J. Barrett (1988). "Foundations for Executive Integrity: Dialogue, Diversity, Development." In S. Srivastva, *Executive Integrity*, London: Jossey Bass, 317.
42. Ibid., 315.
43. Marshall W. Meyer and Lynne G. Zucker (1989). *Permanently Failing Organisations*. London: Sage, 92.
44. Ibid., 22.
45. Ibid.
46. Ibid., 150.
47. Ibid., 24.
48. Swedish National Board of Education, 1989. *Effects of Decentralistrom in the School Sector*. Lund: University of Lund.
49. These are, from the lowest upwards: psychological needs, needs for safety, the need to belong and the need for love and self-actualisation. In Maslow's view, the higher needs and lower needs have different properties, but are fundamental to human nature. The lower needs are dominant until they are satisfied, at which point a higher need comes into operation.

50. Abraham H. Maslow (1987). *Motivation and Personality*. New York: Harper, 21.
51. Ibid., 21.
52. Charles B. Handy (1988). *Understanding Organisations*. London: Penguin, 33.
53. At the heart of Handy's model is the image of an individual as a calculating being, deciding how much energy to expend on any particular activity or set of activities in order to achieve his desired result.
54. Douglas McGregor (1985). *The Human Side of Enterprise*. New York: McGraw-Hill, 48. The author claims that avoidance of responsibility and lack of ambition are "generally consequences of experience, not inherent human characteristics" (p.65).
55. Parsons & Shils (1962), 22.
56. Kurt Lewin (1947). "Frontiers in Group Dynamics." *Human Relations* 1, 16.
57. Quoted by Jantsch (1980), 255.
58. Walter Buckley (1967). *Sociology and Modern Systems Theory*. New Jersey: Prentice Hall, 137. In Buckley's view, the organisational complexity of an institution results in ambiguity within a range of alternative norms, both random and structured deviation, social and cultural differentiation, and stressful situations; new perspectives, new symbols, norms and values are "collectively generated in a more or less spontaneous" manner (p.137).
59. Prigogine argues for the existing of a metastable state, not one of equilibrium.
60. Parsons uses the term "moving equilibrium" while Lewin's term is "quasi-stationary." Ibid., 51.
61. Edmund J. King (1968). *Comparative Studies and Educational Decision*. London: Methuen, 50.
62. Ibid., 51.
63. Ibid.
64. Up to 1959.

PHASE ONE: ESTABLISHING NATIONAL ORDER

INTRODUCTION

The 1944 Education Reform Act concluded an era that had lasted more than a century, during which the government had attempted to establish a national education system for the elementary and secondary levels.

Since the beginning of central intervention in education, which can be dated back to 1833, government dedicated itself to the construction of compulsory elementary education. This was achieved by the 1870 Elementary Education Act. The establishment of a national primary system was soon followed by initiatives and attempts on the part of school boards to improve the quality of instruction by exerting pressure for higher grades, thus sowing the seeds of popular secondary education. The emergence of left-wing groups calling for equal opportunity and expressing dissatisfaction at the social injustice and lack of privilege suffered by the working class led to greater state intervention in education when the government addressed itself to supplying unlimited places in secondary education towards the end of the nineteenth century. The influence of the First World War and a deep-rooted sense of injustice led to a further attempt to introduce even greater equality in the form of the 1918 Education Act, which in principle raised the leaving age to 15 and abolished fees in public elementary schools.

The rapid growth of educational institutions led to unsuccessful government initiatives to establish a rational organisation linking schools together. At the crux of the problem was the co-existence of two separate and unconnected systems: those schools controlled by the local authorities and those controlled by the Church. The Balfour Act of 1902 aimed to authorise the LEAs as a single machinery to control all types of schools, but failed to unify the Church schools under the LEAs' jurisdiction.

The 1944 Act did construct a national order and brought to an end the previous series of attempts to do so since the beginning of the twentieth century. The success of the Act lay in the achievement of two main goals that earlier Acts had failed to realise: first, the quest for justice and the trend towards greater equal opportunity by raising the leaving age to 15 and establishing secondary education for all; and second, the move towards a higher degree of control and connection between the different organisations and levels within the education system by bringing the voluntary schools under LEA control.

• CHAPTER 2

HISTORICAL BACKGROUND

2.1: TOWARDS A STATE SYSTEM:
THE ESTABLISHMENT OF POPULAR EDUCATION

From the beginning of the nineteenth century attempts were made to establish a general system of popular education for the purpose of giving instruction to poor children in exchange for a small fee. This was done by raising private subscriptions, most notably to the National Society and the British and Foreign Schools Society, both of which were Church organisations[1] aiming to provide elementary instruction along with some teaching of the Christian faith. However, the income from voluntary subscriptions and school fees quickly proved insufficient for the enormous task the societies had undertaken and in 1833 the State came to their aid for the first time with an annual grant, which was to become the cornerstone of State intervention in education. This first annual grant of £20,000 was intended to provide for adequate means of instruction for the young with the "aid of private Subscription for the erection of Schools for the Education of Children,"[2] particularly in the great towns and manufacturing districts. The Chancellor of the Exchequer, representing the Government in this matter, laid down six basic principles which became the first guidelines of public interest in and government control of education. The fifth principle explained the meaning of control thus:

> That the applicants, whose cases are favourably entertained, be required to bind themselves to submit to any audit of their accounts which this Board may direct, as well as to such periodical Report respecting the state of their schools, and the number of Scholars educated, as may be called for.[3]

In 1839, six years after the first State grant for education, the Committee of Council for Education was set up, with James Kay as its first president. The committee symbolised the State's official status as a leader of education organisations. One of its primary tasks was to be "the foundation of the national college for the training of teachers."[4] This was the predecessor, in structure and name, of what later became the Board of Education (1899), the Ministry of Education (1944) and the Department of Education and Science (1964). In the same year H.M. Inspectors emerged in embryonic form as part of the apparatus used by the State in exercising its responsibilities in the field of education, and so as a means of State control. The Committee of Council for Education appointed these Inspectors and published a paper that declared their main duties as follows:

> ...visiting, from time to time, schools aided by grant of public money made by the authority of the Committee, in order to ascertain that the grant has in each case been duly applied, and to enable you to furnish accurate information as to the discipline, management, and methods of instruction pursued in your schools, your appointment is intended to embrace a more comprehensive sphere of duty.[5]

Concern for the education of the poor was the motivation behind the new Education Acts of 1844 and 1849. Accordingly, in 1844, the purpose of the State grant was precisely defined as "promoting the Education of the Poor in Great Britain."[6] The 1849 Act was even more specific in defining its aim as to facilitate the erection of school buildings, especially for the poor.

The increasing use of public money for elementary schools, on the one hand, and the inability of most of the poor to provide schooling for their children on the other, led to the establishment in 1861 of a Commission to

Inquire into the Present State of Popular Education in England. The Commission's Report, known as the Newcastle Report, raised two main questions: how to extend elementary education for the poor and how to exercise control over school management. The Report began with the statement: "it is only within comparatively modern times, that the importance of providing elementary instruction for all classes of the population has been recognised."[7] This recognition led to a recommendation that control over education be tightened, but without any suggestion that the chief features of the old system be modified to the advantage and on behalf of the poor children. With the new monitoring system of "payment by results" that was adopted by the Government, a significant amount of power was transferred to H.M. Inspectors. From now on, each school would receive funds according to the scholastic achievement of each of its pupils, based on rigid instruction. The Inspectors were given the power to make the final decision regarding the amount of money that a school would receive. This was based on the Inspectors' reports, which would cover examination results, attendance of pupils at school, discipline and the state of the school buildings.

The Newcastle Report revealed that 8-10 year olds were the age group most widely attending school, and that the majority of pupils left school at 11, with just 5.4 per cent remaining after 13. It stated that "the attendance of the children who go to school at all is distributed with more or less regularity over about four years."[8] Despite this discovery the Committee did not recommend any modification of the system towards universal compulsory education because parents were "not prepared to sacrifice the earnings of their children for this purpose, and . . . they accordingly remove them from school as soon as they have an opportunity of earning wages . . . which adds to . . . the family income."[9]

Annual reports presented to Parliament by the Committee of Council for Education repeatedly confirmed what was already well known from the Newcastle Committee Report: that many children did not attend school at all, and some children were registered at unaided and uninspected schools, which were acknowledged to be the worst. These reports led to the 1870 Act, which aimed to fill the gap by means of voluntary effort. Foster, the Vice-President of the Committee of Council who introduced the Act in Parliament, explained its motivation thus:

> Only two-fifths of the children of the working classes between the ages of six and ten years are on the registers of the Government schools, [10] and only one-third of those between the ages of ten and twelve. Consequently, of those between six and ten, we have left unhelped 1,000,000... ; but it so happens – and we cannot blame them for it – that the schools which do not receive Government assistance are, generally speaking, the worst schools, and those least fitted to give a good education to the working classes. That is the effect of the present system. [11]

Foster provided some examples to illustrate his arguments, among them the following:

> In Liverpool the number of children between five and thirteen who ought to receive an elementary education is 80,000; but as far as we can ascertain, 20,000 of them attend schools where they get an education not worth having.[12]

The 1870 Act is remarkable in that it represents a state move away from reliance on the initiative of volunteer organisations towards providing a complete national system of education according to central instruction and established by law. The establishment of a state education system was achieved by defining the roles and duties of four main participants: central government, school districts, managers and parents.[13]

Under the 1870 Act the government had the task of paying out monies provided by Parliament as an aid grant, and of requiring that school boards be formed where necessary. School boards in the school districts were entitled to frame by-laws requiring compulsory school attendance of all children aged five to thirteen within the district. It was the boards' duty to provide a "sufficient amount of accommodation in public elementary schools available for all the children resident in such districts."[14] The school boards were authorised and entrusted with providing this public school accommodation by means of compulsory purchase of land where necessary, appointing a body of managers, paying school fees in full or in part, establishing and building industrial schools, and as has already been noted, instituting a by-law that required parents to send their children to school.[15] It thus became the parents' duty to see that their children attended school.

But the new state system was still comprised of two sorts of schools: those owned by the churches and those owned by the school boards. The new national system was hence organised as a partnership between church schools on the one hand and the new school boards on the other. There were two major problems inherent in this situation. The first, which was reflected in the 1870 Act, was the rivalry between those who wanted the Church to have control over education and those who aspired to a completely secular system. A compromise was reached, on the basis of a formula devised by Cowper and Temple, in which religious instruction in schools supported by means of local rates should consist of "simple Bible teaching without reference to the formularies of any religious body."[16] The "dual system" of Church schools and board schools was established on the basis of this formula. The second problem was that the Church system was at a financial disadvantage compared with the board system. While the school boards were entitled to raise rates in order to finance their schools and activities, voluntary schools only received a 50% grant from the Education Department and building grants disappeared altogether. This policy caused a deep rift between the two sorts of schools, which became one of the central issues in both the 1902 and 1944 Acts.

The 1870 Act concluded an era that had begun in 1833 by establishing compulsory elementary education for the first time. The Act allocated powers and responsibilities and defined the duties of the main parties towards the education system: central government, local authorities, managers[17] and parents. From then on, central government duties included the definition of payment scales and curriculum guidelines. School boards and parents now had official duties laid down in law. This Act gave the national system its first form.

2.2: THE DEVELOPMENT OF SECONDARY EDUCATION

The establishment of a national primary system was soon followed by the development of secondary education. During the last quarter of the nineteenth century three major processes led towards greater state intervention in education generally and the development of secondary education in particular. The former was a direct result of the 1870 Act;[18] at the point when the sixth grade came to be taken for granted, recurrent pressure for higher grades and standards was exerted by the elementary schools (Dent, 1949). The Secondary Education Commission Report of 1895 reveals the influence of the Act in this respect:

> For some years the work of erecting and organising schools, to meet the needs of the vast mass of children whom it was their duty to provide for, fully occupied the school boards; but after a time they found themselves drawn on to attempt to improve the range and quality of the instruction given. Thus subjects which had been deemed luxuries for children who were to leave school at twelve, soon began to be classed as necessaries. The pressure of the boards upwards brought about an extension of the parliamentary grant to a new Standard, now called the Seventh…some school boards undertook to carry on the education of children beyond the limits which the parliamentary grant had fixed and instituted what are called "ex-standard classes".… These schools, though they have received the name of "higher grade elementary," are really *secondary* in their character [present writer's emphasis].[19]

The improvement in the quality of primary education raised the general level of achievement among the older pupils in the elementary schools, thus strengthening the foundations upon which further education could be built. The initiatives taken by the schools and school boards in pursuit of higher standards was one factor leading both to the development of secondary education and to deeper State involvement in education.

The internal schools' attempt to improve their range by establishing higher grades in the elementary school was backed up by the emergence of numerous left-wing groups calling for a "new Liberalism," by which they meant a more just distribution of resources and equality of opportunity (Brennan, 1975; Dent, 1949; Halsey, 1980; Hee-Chun, 1982). These groups sprang, in the main, out of a growing sense of dissatisfaction that sections of the educated classes expressed with the social injustice and lack of legal privilege suffered by the working classes. For example, Clay estimated that in 1920/1, 64 percent of the wealth of the nation was in the hands of 8 percent of the population, while the remaining 92 percent of the people held only 36 percent.[20] The attack on these social and economic inequalities was led by the Fabian Society, founded in 1884, an organisation that aspired to social reconstruction. Patricia Pugh describes the atmosphere prevailing among such groups at the time; according to her they were "dissatisfied with materialist attitudes, suspecting the inventions of their expanding world were not being used for the benefit of the many but for the enrichment of the few."[21] Their aim was to secure the general welfare of society by reconstructing the law, not by revolutionary means but by permeating the Liberal and Conservative parties with socialist ideas. The basic Fabian belief in the importance of the "national minimum" in areas such as factory legislation, sanitation, housing and local government, as well as education, was justified not only in terms of individual happiness but also in terms of the welfare of the state. In the field of education this principle was to be applied to ensure that education beyond the elementary level would not be the prerogative of the more privileged social classes alone, but rather accessible to all social strata.[22] According to Sidney Webb, one of the most influential and inspirational forces in the Fabian Society for over more than thirty years, the main task of reconstruction in the educational field was to press[23] "for an increase in the number of their higher grade schools, schools which were in fact providing a new sort of secondary education for the people, and demand an extension of the free meals service."

R.H. Tawney (1924), expressing his views on social welfare in education in the early years of the twentieth century, did not ignore the need for the expansion of secondary education but claimed that the first and main aim of reconstruction should be to promote the health of the children. Accordingly Tawney, who was one of the main figures in shaping the 1918 Act, averred that the main task of the schools was as much to improve the level of "physical well-being" as to see to "intellectual attainment." Among the developments he suggested in this area were nursery schools, special schools, special classes for the mentally retarded, school meals, and medical inspection performed by the Local Education Authorities.[24]

The third factor was increasing industrial and commercial competition with other nations. During the early decades of the nineteenth century

Britain's industrial supremacy was taken for granted. Britain was producing about two-thirds of the world's coal, half its iron, half its cotton cloth and five-sevenths of its steel (Brennan, 1975; Cruickshank, 1963). An increase in both prosperity and commercial competition with European countries such as Germany, France and Switzerland led to an 1840 inquiry into the state of schools of design in these countries.[25] In the same year state intervention had been extended to the grammar school curriculum, aimed at extending instruction in other branches of literature and science, besides Greek and Latin, in order to prepare pupils for the "superior trades and mercantile business."[26] This legislation was intended to improve the conditions and increase the benefits of grammar schools, with the needs of the state in mind. The growing concern with the state of schools of design and reports submitted by five different committees during the 1840s led to the establishment of the Department of Practical Art in 1853. A year later this became the Department of Science and Art. The objective was to improve manufacture by lending "encouragement to local institutions for practical science, similar to that already commenced in the Department of Practical Art."[27] Between the years 1864 and 1885 there was further pressure to modify the curriculum in the direction of more scientific and technical instruction at all levels of education. Five different reports were submitted to Parliament as a result of widespread concern about English industry's capacity to stand up to European competition.[28] The introduction of the Technical Education Report (1867) opened with the following statement:

> Our attention has been incidentally called to the evidence considered to be afforded by the International Exhibition at Paris, of the inferior rate of progress recently made in manufacturing and mechanical industry in England compared with that made in other European countries.[29]

Lord Taunton, the Chairman of the commission added: "I am sorry to say that, with very few exceptions, a singular accordance of opinion prevailed that our country had shown little inventiveness and made but little progress in the peaceful arts of industry."

The inadequacy of the system of technical education in Britain was clearly evident in the urgent need to train skilled workers for industry. "New liberals" like Matthew Arnold claimed that the answer could lie only in the provision of more technical education.

The significance of the processes described above lies mainly in the trend they fostered towards greater state intervention in education. The last decades of the nineteenth century and the first quarter of the twentieth century were a remarkable period during which the state attempted to supply unlimited places in secondary education, set up more technical schools and technical classes, and to provide welfare services at all levels of the system. These attempts marked the demise of the laissez-faire principle which had been dominant until the last quarter of the nineteenth century, in order to meet the challenges of the education system as described above, particularly through secondary education.

Thus, "Continuation Schools" appear for the first time in an amendment to the Elementary Education Act in 1888 which gave the county councils an additional duty, to "provide and maintain schools or classes for the continuation of the education of such children as are either wholly or partially exempted from attendance at elementary day schools"[30] so that any child of the age of thirteen years might attend a continuation school until he or she attained the age of fifteen, should their parents wish them to. The Act required the Education Department to give grants to continuation schools to facilitate giving instruction to every scholar in at least three compulsory subjects and other optional subjects, and with much emphasis on science and technical instruction.[31] One year later, the 1889 Act further defined the duty of the school board as follows:

> [The] School Boards may make provision for giving technical education in any school under their management, and either by day or evening classes... if the local authority by special resolution determines that provision or further provision ought to be made, they may themselves make such provision.[32]

2.3: THE FAILURE OF ATTEMPTS TO ESTABLISH A NEW ADMINISTRATIVE ORDER

The rapid growth of new institutions for secondary education, which could not survive without funds from national resources, led to a report issued by the Commissioners on Secondary Education in 1895, which is known as the Bryce Report. The Committee's main recommendation was the establishment of a central authority for secondary education headed by a Minister who was accountable to Parliament, in order "to bring about among the various agencies which provide that education harmony and co-operation."[33] This central authority was implemented by the 1899 Act which set up the Board of Education, a body that incorporated the existing Education Department and the Science and Art Department. The following description by the Committee explains its principal recommendation:

> The growth has not been either continuous or coherent; i.e., it does not represent a series of logical or even connected sequences. Each one of the agencies whose origin has been described was called into being, not merely independently of the others, but with little or no regard to their existence. Each has remained in its working isolated and unconnected with the rest.... This isolation and this independence ... will nevertheless prepare the observer to expect the usual results of dispersed and unconnected forces, needless competition between the different agencies, and a frequent overlapping competition of effort, with much consequent waste of money, of time, and of labour.[34]

What was described by the Committee on Secondary Education as disorder, overlapping of resources and virtual chaos, was described in much more bitter terms by Prime Minister Balfour when he introduced the 1902 Bill in Parliament. According to Balfour there were three main reasons for this Bill, all resulting from omissions in previous Acts, particularly on the part of those who had formulated the 1870 Act. The first was that there was no organisation of voluntary schools, and these "were isolated and unconnected."[35] The second omission was the lack of teaching staff in the growing education system; and the third was the lack of "any kind of rational or organic connection"[36] between primary and secondary education, and secondary education through university education.

The Bill recommended redistribution of power and subordination of the voluntary schools to local authorities. Voluntary schools made up half of the system, comprising 13,197 schools with 2,833,000 pupils; the council schools numbered 6,003, with 2,870,000 pupils.[37] The main problem however, was the condition of the schools. The condition of the voluntary schools in towns was grave, and many were in imminent danger of extinction. The Bishop of Rochester wrote frankly to the Prime Minister in December 1901 that "if the schools are not in some way relieved many will go within the year."[38] The position of Church schools and board schools in rural areas was the same: low standards and low expenditure. Representatives of the denominational schools consequently requested rate aid and were prepared, in return, to have a minority of their managers appointed by the local authorities.

The implementation of the Balfour Act therefore required further development of the existing power of the counties and county boroughs, which became the Local Education Authorities (LEAs), in order to allow them to meet their responsibilities by unifying the education system and reducing the dislocation between the different school organisations. The Prime Minister explained this as follows:

> ...the local education authority which we create will be absolute master of the whole scheme of secular school education in every elementary school in its district, voluntary or otherwise . . . as regards the voluntary schools, they obtain it partly by the explicit mandate contained in the Bill . . . partly by the right given them in the Bill of appointing one-third of the managers; partly by the power of the purse.[39]

According to the new administrative arrangement effected by the Bill, grants for voluntary schools would no longer be distributed by the Board of Education, but by the Local Education Authority. Moreover, the responsibilities of the LEAs were extended to cover other levels of the system and to "supply or aid the supply of education other than elementary."[40]

The 1902 Act determined that the provision and repair of church school buildings remained the responsibility of the denomination, while the school maintenance costs, including teachers' salaries, were expected to come from the local rate. But many authorities refused to fulfil their obligation to the Church schools until they received their government grant (Bell, 1958). The immediate result of the Act is described thus by Marjorie Cruickshank:

> In England and Wales passive resisters launched a rate war as an organised campaign against the 1902 Act.... Here it was the new local education authorities who defied the Government by collecting the new education rate but leaving the denominational schools exactly as they had been before the Act.[41]

It soon became clear that the aim of unifying the Church schools under the LEAs' power was far from being achieved and that they remained outside public control despite the new legislation. An unsuccessful attempt to abolish the abiding dual system was made by means of a new Bill introduced in 1906. According to this Bill, a new system of total public control was to be achieved by empowering the local authorities to take over all existing Church schools and divide them into two types: "the moderate denominational schools and the extreme denominational or 'atmosphere' schools."[42]

Meanwhile, the absence of any national resolution of the denominational issue led some local authorities to take the initiative in arriving at their own accommodation with the churches. This initiative met with a willingness on the part of the Anglicans to transfer their schools to the local authorities by giving the authorities control of the management and organisation of the schools and getting additional grants of public money as a *quid pro quo*. These agreements included provision for compulsory religious instruction in council schools and denominational teaching in church schools that transferred their management to the local authority (Butler, 1971; Cruickshank, 1963).[43]

2.4: FURTHER ATTEMPTS TO ACHIEVE EQUALITY

Another prominent Act, in 1918, left the denominational issue unmodified. It was drafted under the influence of the First World War and a deep-rooted sense of injustice on the part of the British people concerning educational provision. Its goal was enhanced societal cohesion by means of new measures towards equality, and particularly by means of new legislation on behalf of the working class. Fisher, the President of the Board of Education, explained the motivation for the Act when he said:

> When you get Conscription, when you get a state of affairs under which the poor are asked to pour out their blood and to be mulcted in the high cost of living for large international policies, then every just mind begins to realise that the boundaries of citizenship are not determined by wealth.... There is a growing sense not only in England ... that the industrial workers of the country are entitled to be considered primarily as citizens and as fit subjects for any form of education.[44]

The main aims of the Act were: abolition of fees in public elementary schools; raising of the leaving age to 15;[45] continued part-time education for all school leavers aged 14 to 16; extension of the range of ancillary services, including those for disabled or retarded children; and extension of medical services and health control.

The school medical and health service was perceived as the only way to control and monitor children's health. The service was established in 1907 and the 1918 Act extended the LEAs' remit to cover the health of the children. The importance of this service was explained by Fisher when he introduced the 1918 Bill before Parliament:

> One of the great dates in our social history is the establishment of the school medical service in 1907. We now know...how greatly the value of our educational system is impaired by the low physical condition of vast numbers of the children...and how imperative is the necessity of raising the general standard of physical health.[46]

The rising interest in the attendance rates of children between the ages of 14 and 15 or 16 was not new. But the 1918 Education Act was significant in establishing the principle that the education of adolescents was a necessary public concern that should be compulsory up to the age of 15, and in obliging all the LEAs to provide education facilities, regardless of their financial circumstances (Hee-Chun, 1982).

Another of Fisher's intentions was to merge some authorities, particularly those of small urban areas, because of the deep differences in the education services and facilities provided by them. Strong opposition from the LEAs forced him to drop this plan. Thus, both the denominational problem and the inequality of educational services between authorities remained unsolved.

The raising of the age for compulsory school attendance was followed by an increase in the number of children remaining at school beyond the age when they were legally obliged to do so. But the system was still a long way from achieving either the principal goal of a school leaving age of 15, or equal access to schooling. The latter now included a call for "secondary education for all." A report published by the Hadow Committee in 1926 revealed that the number of children attending school full time, five years after the 1918 Act, fell off very rapidly after age 14. Between 13 and 14 it was 88% (compulsory education up to 14 became law in 1900); between 14 and 15 it was only 31%, between 15 and 16 it was 9.9%. The proportion of children at school between ages 14 and 16 was just over one in five or 20.5%. One of the Committee's explanations for low attendance rates was the wide diversity of educational provision between the regions: "The proportion of the total school population over 11 which is found in secondary schools varied from as low as 6.9% to as high as 42.5%."[47]

During the 1920s and the 1930s several attempts were made to raise the leaving age to 15 by means of administrative arrangements, legislation and suggestions for varying the types of secondary education and curriculum. The Hadow Committee proposed that "progress must take place… along several different paths" and "if the system of post-primary education is to be successful, it must correspond to the needs of the pupils, and if it is to correspond to their needs, it must embrace schools of varying types and free places in secondary education."[48] This recommendation was in line with developments that had already taken place. The Committee described it as a result of the 1918 Act:

> The Act left very wide discretion to Local Authorities in this matter, and no attempt was made by the Board to suggest, still less to prescribe, the lines upon which courses of advanced instruction should be organised. Local Authorities have accordingly been free to develop the methods which they consider best suited to their local circumstances and needs.[49]

This recommendation laid down the concept of the tripartite system which was accepted by the Board of Education in the 1944 Act.

The expectation of a major improvement in the field of education during the 1920s and 1930s soon dwindled to lip service. The economic crisis of 1931 forced new cutbacks in the education service, and only a small number of able individuals could get through to the top levels of the system. Kogan (1978) gives some illustrative figures: "between 1918 and 1939 public expenditure on education was meagre.... The Board of Education estimates in 1922-3 were £45 million. They rose to £51 million by 1938, representing a 3 percent increase at constant prices."[50]

The last attempt to raise the school age was made in July 1936, when a new bill passed by Parliament promised that the school age would be raised from 1 September 1939. However, the outbreak of the Second World War put an end to the new Act.

2.5: CONCLUSIONS

Five main processes influenced the chief organisational and administrative factors in the field of education: (a) the need to truly establish elementary education for all; (b) the recurrent school pressure for "higher grades"; (c) the unsuccessful attempt to establish the LEAs as a sole and absolute power by unifying the voluntary schools under their control; (d) the constant tendency towards a higher degree of order within the education system, specifically the attempt to tighten the connections between elementary, secondary and university levels; (e) more intervention by the State in the secondary school curriculum, prompted by increasing commercial and trade competition with European nations.

These processes led to a steady increase of state intervention in the education system by means of legislation and administrative rules with regard to such matters as curriculum guidelines, standards of achievement, standards of facilities, salary scales and financial support. But what appeared to be a trend towards increased centralisation was simultaneously a trend towards decentralisation, with the LEAs regarded by the government as a major means of implementing national values in the educational field. Devolution of responsibilities established the LEAs as the main power creating by-laws in order to fulfil central government's goals, and requiring parents to ensure that their children attend school.

One general point worth mentioning at this stage is that some of the major modifications that were purportedly government initiatives were originally local initiatives, subsequently adopted by the government. For example, the demand for "higher grades" – that were to be the embryo of universal secondary education – was the result of pressure for finance from the school boards and managers; and the basic formula and administrative arrangement between the Church and the local authorities was achieved after the failure of central government's attempts to impose an effective solution upon the LEAs. Finally, the tripartite system that had been recommended as a way to raise the rate of attendance of children at schools was put forward by government long after it was adopted in practice by the LEAs.

Four main problems remained unsolved however, and these became the main issues for "Education Reconstruction" after the war. The first three fall under the umbrella of equal opportunities: (1) the state of the Church schools and the denominational problem; (2) the deep differences between educational services offered by the various LEAs; (3) the provision of secondary education for all; (4) unification of the different parts of the system in order to achieve a higher degree of control and order. These unsolved problems became the prime focus of the 1944 Education Act which aimed to produce a definite order after the war.

Notes:

1. The National Society was founded by the Anglican Church in 1811 to promote the education of the poor and teach the Church's doctrine; the British and Foreign School Society was established in 1808 by the Royal Lancastrian Society to advocate simple Bible teaching.
2. House of Commons: *Estimates and Accounts*. Vol. XLII, 1834, 525.
3. Ibid.
4. Stuart J. Maclure (1986). *Educational Documents*. London: Methuen, 42.
5. House of Commons: *Accounts and Papers*, Vol.XX, 1841, 99.
6. House of Commons: *Bills*, Vol.II, 1844, 1. Implementation of the Act was left to the Minister of each parish in co-operation with the Churchwardens.
7. Report of the Commissioners: *The State of Popular Education In England*, Vol.I, 1861, 15.
8. Ibid., 172.
9. Ibid., 15.
10. Hansard's Parliamentary Debates Third Series, Vol. CXCIX, 17 February 1870, 441.
11. *Government schools* were those schools receiving government grants and being inspected by HMI.
12. Hansard's Parliamentary Debates, 1870, 442.
13. The country was divided into districts; this term was changed to "country districts" in the 1899 Act.
14. House of Commons, *Bills*, Vol.I, 1870, 2.
15. The Act set out a long list of exceptions.
16. Moberly E. Bell (1958). *A History of the Church Schools Company 1883-1958*. London: SPCK, 5. Cowper was a Cabinet member and Dr Temple the incumbent Bishop of London.
17. Today these functionaries are known as governors.
18. Indeed, public interest in secondary education had begun, with the appointment of the Royal Commission in 1864, to inquire into the condition of recognised "public schools," which were known as endowed schools. H.C. Dent (1949) describes the result of the inquiry as "generally depressing" and says that "individual schools were in a scandalous condition." The inquiry led to the Public Schools Act 1868 and later to three successive Acts and the establishment of a body called "The Endowed Schools Commission." The latter became an integral part of the public system of education, and aimed to promote the efficiency, management and academic quality of these schools.
19. House of Commons: *Secondary Education - Report of the Commission on Secondary Education*, Vol. XLIII, 1895, 10.
20. H.R. Tawney (1964). *Equality*. London: George Allen, 68.
21. Patricia Pugh (1984). *Educate, Agitate, Organise: 100 Years of Fabian Socialism*. London: Methuen, 1.
22. According to Dent (1949). in 1868 secondary education was available to 1 percent of the total population and less than 2 percent of all the endowments for secondary education were for girls' schools.

23. E.J.T. Brennan (1975). *Education for National Efficiency: The Contribution of Sidney and Beatrice Webb*. London: Athlone 1975, 18.
24. Ibid., 3-5. Tawney concluded his views on the need of reconstruction and justice in the education field bitterly: "A nation which can spend £100,000,000 in expeditions against Russia, and £14,000,000 on a dock at Singapore, £400,000,000 on drink, £20,000,000 on the owners of land in London, and £6,000,000 on the owners of royalties …may prefer not to attend to the welfare of its children, but it is stopped from arguing that it cannot *afford* to do so [original emphasis]," 56-7.
25. House of Commons: *Schools of Design, Accounts and Papers*. Vol.XXIX, 1840.
26. House of Commons: *Bills*. Vol.II, 1840, 4.
27. House of Commons: *First Report of the Department of Science and Art*. Reports of the Commissioners, Vol.XXVIII, 1854, 277.
28. The reports are: Select Committee on Schools of Art, 1864; Schools Inquiry Commission Report Technical Education, 1867; Report from the Select Committee on Scientific Instruction, 1867-8; Report of the Royal Commission on Scientific Instruction and the Advancement of Science, 1871-5; and Report of the Royal Commission on Technical Instruction, 1882-4.
29. House of Commons: *Schools Inquiry Commission Technical Education*. Report of Commissioners, Vol.XXVI, 1867, 263-6.
30. House of Commons: *Bills: Elementary Education (Continuation Schools)*. Vol.I, 1888, 580.
31. The compulsory subjects were: commercial and applied arithmetic, elementary mathematics, mechanical drawing, book-keeping, shorthand, French, German, elements of agricultural science.
32. House of Commons: *A Bill to Provide Technical Education in England and Wales*. 1889, 205.
33. Reports from Commissioners, Inspectors, and others: *Secondary Education; Report of the Commissioners on Secondary Education*. Vol.I, 1895, 257.
34. Ibid., 17-18.
35. Hansard, 24 March 1902, Vol.CV, 849.
36. Ibid.
37. The data referred to the year 1903 and was taken from Marjorie Cruickshank (1963). *Church and State in English Education: 1870 to the Present Time*. London:Macmillan, 191.
38. Ibid., 70.
39. Ibid., 191.
40. House of Commons: *Education Bill*. Vol.I, 1902, 455.
    The counties and the county boroughs became the LEAs; boroughs with populations of 10,000 and urban districts with populations of 20,000 became authorities for elementary education only.
41. Cruickshank (1963), 87. The Act was followed by two other sorts of opposition: on the one hand nonconformist extremists launched a movement of "passive resistance" against

the payment of rate aid to denominational schools under the slogan "No control, no cash." On the other hand, among a minority of Churchmen, especially Methodist leaders, there was massive protest and resistance to the new administrative arrangements.

42. Cruickshank, 1963, 93.
43. Cambridgeshire was the first county to reach this agreement, which was called the "agreed syllabus," and eight other counties followed during the 1920s.
44. Hansard, Vol.XCVII, 1917, 800.
45. The legislation for raising the leaving age included a large number of exemptions, particularly for children between the ages of 14 and 15.
46. Hansard, Vol.XCVII, 1917, 799.
47. Board of Education (1926). *The Education of the Adolescent*. Consultative Report, London: HMSO, 52-3, 55.
48. Ibid., 52.
49. Ibid.
50. Maurice Kogan (1978). *The Politics of Educational Change*. Manchester: Manchester University Press, 23.

• CHAPTER 3

THE CONSTRUCTION OF A NEW ORDER: THE 1944 EDUCATION ACT

The series of unsuccessful attempts to establish a new educational order that punctuated the early decades of the twentieth century came to an end in 1944. The new Education Act, which was formulated during the Second World War, emerged as a radical change. The new system it embodied aimed to tackle three major issues that had been on the education agenda for more than four decades. These were: secondary education for all; LEAs as a single type of administration over educational matters; and voluntary schools under the control of LEAs.

During the year 1941 a provisional scheme for educational reform directed at achieving these goals was drawn up by the Board of Education under the leadership of Herwald Ramsbotham. The vision underlying his memorandum entitled "Education After the War" (the "Green Book"), was expressed by the Prime Minister, Winston Churchill, as "establishing a state of society where the advantages and privileges, which hitherto have been enjoyed only by the few, shall be far more widely shared by the men and the youth of the nation as a whole."[1] The main aim of this chapter is to follow the events, the arguments and the considerations that created and shaped the new order of the education system of England and Wales during the War period.

3.1: VOLUNTARY SCHOOLS COME UNDER CONTROL

The desire to alter the system in order to subordinate their schools to the LEAs was not new to the Church leaders. Since the 1902 Act, Church leaders had been aware of further attempts to modify the dual system so that the voluntary schools would be under the control of the LEAs, and they feared that increased state interference and greater bureaucratic control would lead to loss of independence. In pursuit of more explicit recognition of religion in schools, the Anglican and Free Church leaders had united in launching a public appeal in February 1941. The appeal read as follows:

> There is an ever deepening conviction that in this present struggle we are fighting to preserve those elements in human civilisation and in our own national tradition which owe their origin to the Christian faith.... There is evidently an urgent need to strengthen our foundations by securing that effective Christian education should be given in all schools.[2]

This declaration was the starting point for a bitter struggle between the Church and the Board of Education. It was a fundamental tenet of the Church that true education must be religious in its basis and texture, and that religious instruction should be the basis and foundation of the entire curriculum in all types of schools.[3] This concept found expression in a set of demands known as the "Five Points," which stated that a Christian education should be given in all schools, to all pupils, by teachers willing and competent to give it; and that an act of worship would take place at the beginning of the school day, in all schools, for all the pupils.[4]

In July 1941 R.A. Butler became President of the Board of Education and took the "Green Book" as a basis for preliminary talks and ideas on the content and methods of educational reform that he held with all the main bodies involved in the education system. Immediately after his arrival at the Board, Butler asked to meet a deputation from the Anglican Church and the Free Churches. These representatives, headed by the Archbishop of Canterbury, came in support of the "Five Points." The President, in reply, assured them of his complete sympathy with the objective of securing effective

Christian teaching which would be given in all schools, to all pupils, "by teachers competent and willing to give it... when the time came for legislation."[5] The President promised to consider the proposal that religious instruction should be overseen by HM Inspectors, but he mentioned that it did not appear to him to be easy to divorce the inspection of methods from the inspection of the content. For Butler it was important at this stage to achieve a basis of trust and to create an atmosphere of goodwill with the Churches before embarking on further discussions. His long diplomatic experience made him very well aware that there is no substitute for good personal relations and basic trust in conducting negotiations effectively. For this reason he did not ignore any of the Church's demands.

In the early stages of his Presidency of the Board he declared in the House of Commons that educational reform was necessary. He defined the main aims of this reform, in a letter to the Prime Minister of 12 September 1941, as a need for settlement with the Churches about their schools and about religious instruction, and a need for industrial and technical training (Butler, 1971). For Butler the state of the voluntary schools lay at the core of his efforts to achieve equality of opportunity, and the "Green Book" laid out the main features of the reforms that were needed for progress in this direction. But Butler's letter to the Prime Minister informing him of the main areas calling for reforms met with an unexpected and nervous response. Churchill replied as follows on 13 September 1941:

> It would be the greatest mistake to raise the 1902 controversy during the war, and I certainly cannot contemplate a new Education Bill. I think it would also be a great mistake to stir up the public school question at the present time . . . . Your main task at present is to get the schools working as well as possible under all the difficulties of the air attack, evacuation, etc. If you can add to this industrial and technical training, enabling men not required for the Army to take their places promptly in munitions industry or radio work, this would be most useful. We cannot have any party politics in wartime, and both your second and third points raise these in a most acute and dangerous form.[6]

In Winston Churchill's mind the religious issue could split the nation. The virulent debates over the 1902 Bill, which had lasted for fifty-seven days in the House of Commons, were still fresh in his memory; as was the collapse of the Government and the overwhelming electoral victory of the Liberals in the January 1906 election as a result of the 1902 Education Act (Butler, 1982). Butler accepted Churchill's fears about imposing any legislative modification of the system upon the Church schools as evidence of his anxiety that such legislation could have terrible results for the Conservative Party. Butler did not ignore the warning but believed nevertheless that he could find a solution which would suit all parties. He decided to go forward, but cautiously; in his own words: "I decided to disregard what he said and go straight ahead."[7]

The reason for the demand for such revision by the Board was the fact that lack of funds and lack of control over the organisation of voluntary schools meant that 541 voluntary (non-provided) schools out of 753 still remained on the Board's black list of schools with defective and out-of-date premises. Some 62% of the children of 11 years of age and over in council (provided) schools were in senior schools while the corresponding figure for voluntary schools was only 16%.[8] The Local Education Authorities had no power to spend money on repairs, alterations and improvements to voluntary schools; this was the responsibility of the managers, except in respect of wear and tear. Moreover, the divided responsibility of the dual system had given rise to endless administrative complications leading to problems of economy and efficiency; for example, a non-provided school with 30 pupils could not be closed; a teacher from a council school could not be transferred to a voluntary school; a voluntary school might be set up even if there were enough places for the area's children in the council school. There were 10,533 non-provided schools with a total attendance of 1,374,000 pupils; and the 10,363 council schools catered for 3,151,000. And so, while the LEAs had control over secular instruction, they had no power to alter the organisation or to institute a system based on efficiency and equality of opportunity applying to all the children in a given area.[9]

Moreover, it was obvious to Butler that most of the churches could not pay for the reconstruction of their substandard schools: "When I took over at the Board, I noted that the dual system was in a dangerous and muddled state after seventy years of political and religious rivalry."[10] The state of the Church schools was juxtaposed with that of the council schools and during the preceding forty years had made it more and more difficult for the Church school managers to raise the funds needed for alteration and improvements to the premises of their schools: "Only 582 of 10,553 Voluntary schools were new since 1902 whilst only 288 had been rebuilt since that date; this meant that 9,683 were at least 40 years old."[11] In addition to the managers' lack of sufficient funds to enable them to discharge their statutory duties, over 4,000 schools, particularly Anglican schools, were in rural areas. Most of these schools were small, with a wide age-range of pupils and a limited number of teachers (sometimes only one). They were "built with the Squire's money and taught the parson's catechism."[12] These "single school" areas were sources of resentment and dissatisfaction on the part of parents who had no effective choice of schools, especially when the local parson took part both in the control of the school and in the religious instruction, whereas local authority schools gave religious instruction based on the Bible and not connected with any particular Church.

In April 1942 a document called "The Dual System and the Archbishop's Five Points" had been put together by the Board of Education and sent by Butler to the leaders of the Anglican Church with the aim of testing their reactions. The scheme, which was based on the Green Book's ideas, proposed to modify the Dual System, basically extending financial assistance to voluntary schools but also extending public control over them by transferring power to the LEAs. From now on, according to this scheme, the LEAs would have the duties of upkeep and repair and the duty to cease to maintain unnecessary schools. They would have the power to appoint and dismiss teachers in primary schools. In secondary schools, existing arrangements were to continue except where managers were unable to bear the cost of structural improvement.[13]

Responses to Butler's scheme voiced particular reservations as to the proposal to transfer the single school areas to LEA control. William Eloy, the Archbishop of York, wrote the following to Butler on 4 April 1942: "I have been very carefully reading the scheme… my present feeling is that clause 5 in the scheme as drafted would be a source of very great difficulty."[14] A similar answer was sent by the Bishop of Winchester:

> I have read it with a great interest and it undoubtedly makes a very great advance on anything which has been proposed in the past... if I understand it rightly Section 5 and Section 4 taken together would mean the extinction of all non-provided schools in single school areas. I fully recognise that there is much to be said for this, but the proposal would undoubtedly be met by very strong opposition'.[15]

The Archbishop of Canterbury, in a forceful letter of 14 May 1942 addressing not only the scheme but also Butler's tactics, wrote to Butler:

> (1) I seemed to trace a suggestion that because the "five points programme" is so largely accepted, the church should be ready to make concessions.[16]

When Butler realised that the element of compulsion in the Green Book scheme could prevent him from obtaining any settlement with Church leaders, he ordered his officials at the Board of Education to prepare another proposal based on the principle of voluntary transfer of single schools in rural area to the LEAs. In a letter dated 24 April 1942 he directed his officials as follows:

> The other great difficulty which presents itself to my mind is that the beauty of our scheme has been that it is *voluntary*.... It would ease my mind were we to introduce a little less spirit of compulsion into the rather staccato of present B.5. There is something in the suggestion put forward by the Bishop of London, through the mouth of the Archbishop of Canterbury, that schools which are unable to fulfil their obligations should automatically be taken to have the declaration that is described in our paper. *The area of compulsion should be limited* [my emphasis].[17]

In a further attempt to dispel the Church leaders' suspicions, Butler explained that his desire to reform the Dual System was based on two principles, "first, that all schools should reach a minimum standard of accommodation; and secondly, that the...school leaving age is raised to fifteen."[18] His strategy was to stick to his main goal of equality of opportunity, but to make a real attempt to respond positively to the Churches' demands whenever he deemed them commensurate with his main aim. Hence, the "Five Points" were accepted by the Board of Education.

Meanwhile, a new scheme known as the "White Memorandum" was proposed by Parliamentary Secretary, Chuter Ede. According to this scheme, managers of voluntary schools, whether primary or secondary, would have two alternatives: a Church school could choose to be either "controlled" or "aided." If such a school were unable or unwilling to meet half the cost of alterations and improvements needed to bring the building up to standard, it would become "controlled," and all financial obligations would be transferred to the Local Authority, including the power to appoint and dismiss teachers; and the majority of the managers would be appointed by public bodies. In an "aided" school, the managers would have to meet half of the cost of alterations and improvements and the remaining half would be met by a direct grant from the Exchequer; the school's Church would have majority representation on the managing body and the managers would retain the right to appoint and dismiss teachers and to control religious instruction, while the Local Education Authority would be responsible for the teachers' salaries and the running expenses of the school.

An immediate response to this scheme came from Lord Selborne, who telephoned the president and warned him that the National Society would put up strong resistance. "The Church had got only five mingy points and was being made to give up all her schools."[19] Dr Temple responded to the new suggestion at the Annual Meeting of the National Society in June, 1942, saying:

> There is an inherent and inevitable tendency in any bureaucratic control towards mechanical uniformity; with the best will in the world the administration cannot prevent it increasing ... the importance of regaining the real independence of the several schools ought, surely, to be obvious to all of us. If we wish to avoid Totalitarianism, there is a merit in the very duality of the dual system.[20]

However, when Dr Temple realised that the full cost of retaining independence as aided schools would be £42,000,000 – as a direct result of the two main tasks of the reform (raising the leaving age to 15 and bringing school accommodation up to council school standards) – he responded that most of the parishes would find that staying independent as aided schools was beyond their means and so opt to be controlled. In a private note dated 14 July 1942 Butler recorded his impression of Dr Temple's response after a meeting with him, during which the full financial implications of the reform became clear to the Archbishop:

> I had read to him figures which had opened his eyes to the real state of the voluntary schools. I then asked the Archbishop whether the Church of England expected a grant for new building …. He said that he thought the National Society were desirous of accepting public money in return for a measure of control.[21]

A few weeks later Dr Temple suggested a compromise to Butler: that instruction on the agreed syllabus should be given in all kinds of Church schools and not only in single school areas.[22] This suggestion became the basis for an agreement that enabled the Church of England to give its own religious teaching two days a week and made it possible to include the "controlled" option in the White Paper and later in the Bill.

The fact that a large proportion of the voluntary schools would have to opt for controlled status was a key point in the transfer of power to the LEAs. Butler explains this as follows:[23]

> The Roman Catholics felt that the 50 per cent grant was not enough. But we knew that if it were raised, and if many Anglican schools were involved, this would continue the Dual System of Church-local authority schools under slightly different terms. For the plan to succeed Anglican schools would have to opt for controlled status in large numbers. This insistence was a key to the whole success of the plan.[24]

But the amendments to the scheme suggested by the Anglican leaders still had not been confirmed by the Church Assembly. At this critical stage, during heated discussions in the Church Assembly, the Archbishop of Canterbury explained the reasons for supporting the scheme after pointing out some of the weaknesses of the Church school system:

> It is useless to go back over the past and point [out] what might have happened if at critical moments a different attitude had been adopted by one party or another; but it's of course a fact that by 1900 there was a state of acute bitterness, poisoning the whole atmosphere of educational enterprise. This came to fullest expression in 1902 … . There is no doubt that free churchmen feel a genuine grievance with regard to their position in the single school areas … . [J]ust because these families have no remedy they must send their children to a school where they receive teaching and sometimes treatment which is bound to cause resentment in the parents. There is therefore good reason why in our administration of our trust we should do everything possible to avoid creating that sense of grievance…. I am always saddened when, in reports upon a parish received through visitation returns or the like, I find that there is a Church school but that the parson in fact does not go into it, either to teach or to show friendly interest.[25]

Then he turned to the advantages that the new scheme would have for the Church, emphasising the second option whereby Anglican schools could retain their independence:[26]

> The Church shall retain complete control of its schools if it can find 50 per cent of the cost of their readjustment and maintenance; whereas under the present law they can only retain that control if they find the whole cost … we certainly shall not be able to retain them all, though I hope that in a very great many cases what are at present junior schools, if they cannot be retained for that function, may still be retained as nursery and infant schools … above all let us not give the impression that our concern as Church people is only with the adjustment of the dual system;

> we ought as Christians to be concerned about the whole of educational progress. I am quite sure that the raising of the school age will of itself do more to make permanent the religious influence of the school than anything that can be done with a directly denominational purpose.[27]

The Archbishop announced that the proposed reform was both "a glorious opportunity" and a challenge. He called on the Assembly to accept the policy and the challenge, and concluded with an appeal to the members to support the scheme.[28]

The Anglicans did confirm the scheme, thus leaving the Roman Catholics completely isolated in their demand for independence. Their objections were mainly on financial grounds, claiming that the criteria for remaining "aided" rather than becoming "controlled" were too harsh. In May 1943 the Roman Catholic Bishops of England and Wales announced: "We shall not give up our schools, no matter what sacrifice we may be called upon to make for them."[29] The statement continued with an appeal to the group "to protest with all our energy, and to oppose by all lawful means any proposals which would threaten the existence of our schools."[30]

Meanwhile, it became apparent that the issue of the agreed syllabus could render all the efforts that had been made in achieving the complicated settlement with the Church futile. In a meeting with the National Union of Teachers (NUT) on 11 December 1942, the President of the Board was attacked on the grounds of his supposed intention that syllabuses should be framed to suit the Churches.[31] At the annual meeting of the Incorporated Association of Headmasters in January 1943 a warning was conveyed to Butler in the form of the exhortation that headmasters "must be alert and prepared to defend against all comers their ideals and their freedom."[32] At the same meeting John Murray, the Principal of the University College of the South-West in Exeter, suggested that headmasters take the lead in forming a strong opposition by joining forces with other organisations which shared their fears of losing autonomy. The Joint Committee of the Four Secondary Associations took a more extreme stance in their resolutions to prohibit denominational religious instruction in all schools wholly or partly financed by public funds, and to make all religious instruction optional. When Miss

Cantnach, the Headmistress of Putney School and one of the influential figures on the Joint Committee, published her statement against the agreed syllabus, Butler told her that she bore partial responsibility for the success or failure of the reform, and asked for her support in the Joint Committee:[33]

> The statutory requirement is an essential part of the religious settlement which I hope to secure, and without it I could not count with any certainty on the support of the Churches.[34]

In reply she wrote the following to the President on 21 June 1943:

> I should just like to say that I myself will represent your views with the utmost sympathy and that the last note you wrote to me will be of great assistance to me in so doing. My own Association is prepared to face up to the statutory requirements, I think, although we do not like it, but it is difficult to change the feeling of the other three.[35]

This was the last obstacle standing in the way of bringing the voluntary schools under state control through LEA administration. In December 1942 the memorandum on Educational Reform was laid before the War Cabinet. The memorandum proposed three main steps "to put the system on a satisfactory footing." They included:[36]

> The revision of the Dual System, with a view to enabling the voluntary schools to play their part in education reform, while at the same time ensuring the provision of religious instruction in schools of all types.[37]

The Cabinet's approval of the Memorandum marked the end of a stage and a new departure for relationships within the national education system that was being constructed.

3.2: TOWARDS EQUAL OPPORTUNITIES: SECONDARY EDUCATION FOR ALL

In Butler's view, the primary aim of the Reform was to secure real equality of opportunity for all children, as he explained to the Cabinet:

> The full-time schooling of the children of our country is in many respects seriously defective. It ends for some 90 per cent of them far too soon (fourteen). It is conducted in many cases in premises which are scandalously bad. It is imparted in the case of some schools by persons who need have no qualifications to teach anybody anything. It is conducted under statute and regulations which emphasise social distinctions and which in general make the educational future of the child more dependent on his place of residence and the financial circumstances of his parents than on his own capacity and promise.[38]

For this reason the President of the Board of Education suggested: (a) raising the school leaving age with no exceptions to 15, and as soon as possible to 16; (b) reorganising the system to provide separate schools and advanced instruction for all children over 11.[39] Butler strengthened his argument regarding "social distinctions" by giving a few examples:[40]

> Under section 37 of the Education Act 1921, the charging of fees in Elementary Schools is prohibited. There is no such prohibition in schools of Higher Education. What is the result? When the parting of the ways comes at the age of 11+ many a boy and girl is compelled to proceed to Senior School (which is in the elementary field) because his parents cannot afford to pay a fee for him to attend a Secondary School (which is in the higher field). It is true that if the child is clever enough he will get a "Special" place at the Secondary School, in which case this fee will be remitted or reduced according to the means of his parents, but it is undoubtedly true there is many a child in a Senior School of greater ability and promise than many a fee paying pupil in a Secondary School.[41]

Butler's philosophy was that the reform should include equal opportunity for all children, irrespective of economic or social conditions. For him the ideal was full democracy, in the sense of a society free from injustice, but he acknowledged the anomalies of the pre-war period when he said that "the 'two nations' still existed in England a century after Disraeli had used the phrase."[42]

These anomalies had been highlighted by the war. Soldiers of all classes fought together in the battlefield: "Several who could never previously have aspired to it were given social status and personal resources through commissioned or non-commissioned rank."[43] The sacrifice of wartime was based on a spirit of national solidarity and stimulated a highly emotional consensus to abolish social deprivation and to unite the nation through social reforms and the breaking down of social and economic privilege. The social implications were vast, with reforms planned in most of the public services: housing policy, health services, pensions, sickness and unemployment benefits, as well as education. But education was seen as "the agency through which people, pupils and parents would move towards participation in the benefits of a richer, fairer and more civilised society"[44] (Butler, 1971; Hee-Chun, 1982; Kogan, 1978; Lowe, 1988; Tawney, 1964).

In the education realm, the establishment of equal opportunities for all was based on two principles: (a) that secondary education should be available to all children; and (b) the establishment of further education and extension of the health services. The main alteration in the system required by the former was an extension of the concept of secondary education beyond the type of academic course given in grammar schools, in order to enable children of different abilities to take part in secondary schooling. This idea, which arose from a combination of three reports (Hadow, Spens and Norwood) was influenced by psychological evidence that "equality of opportunity" did not mean that all children should receive the same form of education: "It is accordingly evident that different children from the age of 11, if justice is to be done to their varying capacities, require types of education varying in certain important respects."[45] And so at the secondary level there must be a variety of educational opportunities and curricula in order to meet the "very varying requirements and capacities of the children,"[46] if the system was to involve large numbers of children.[47] Accordingly, the first paragraph of the

White Paper of 1943 opened with a definition of the main aim of the reform:

> To ensure a fuller measure of education and opportunity for young people and to provide means for all of developing the various talents with which they are endowed and so enriching the inheritance of the country whose citizens they are. The new educational opportunities must not, therefore, be of a single pattern. It is just as important to achieve diversity as it is to ensure equality of opportunity.[48]

The White Paper outlined the new policy that was needed by reference to the traditional form of secondary education, bound to the grammar school curriculum and designed for a limited group of pupils:

> The traditional curriculum has been widened and adapted to meet the ever-increasing variety of demands and, helped by the introduction in 1917 of the School Examinations system, an education has been evolved which in the main meets the needs of the more promising pupils. But in spite of this success, the schools are facing an impossible task. An academic training is ill-suited for many of the pupils who find themselves moving along a narrow educational path bounded by the School Certificate and leading into a limited field of opportunity. Further, too many of the nation's abler children are attracted into a type of education which prepares primarily for the University and for the administrative and clerical professions; too few find their way into schools from which the design and craftsmanship sides of industry are recruited. If education is to serve the interests both of the child and of the nation, some means must be found of correcting this bias and of directing ability into the field where it will find its best realisation.[49]

The second principle in the pursuit of equal opportunity was the establishment of "further education," primarily in the form of proposed compulsory part-time education. The perceived need for further education lay in the fact that most of the children who ceased full-time education at the age of 14 "do not pursue any formal education and much of the work of schools inevitably runs to waste." Moreover, "hundreds of thousands of boys and girls are left without the supervision and help that they need during the most critical years in the formation of character."[50]

The President of the Board of Education was determined to break what appeared to him to be a pattern in young people's lives. Announcing that "boys no longer automatically follow father into the pit or mill,"[51] he made the development of diverse kinds of schools, including "further" education, central in his reforms. Nor was the development of individuals' careers and scholastic abilities the sole aim. Butler's vision of the meaning of equal opportunity extended to the lack of medical supervision hitherto suffered by thousands of children above the age of 14. The attendance of school by the young, even in part-time education, was a means of providing all forms of medical treatment. As Butler said, "under such a system the health and physical well being of the adolescent could be supervised."[52] The extension of this health service and the provision of colleges for the further education for pupils up to 18 years of age, became one of the duties of many of the Local Education Authorities.

In order fully to achieve the goal of "secondary education for all," parents were now regarded as partners with their own responsibility in accomplishing the aims of the Act. Parental responsibilities had changed, and were now defined as "to cause every child of compulsory school age to receive efficient full-time education suitable to his age, ability and aptitude."[53] But the main change was not in this new definition of parents' duties, but in their new options as *customers*. From now on, there would no longer only be grammar schools or public schools with limited numbers of places, but a large variety of types of schools for different abilities and aptitudes. Supplying these options became the LEAs' duty towards the customers of the education system, the parents. Butler defined this choice thus:

> The parents get very little consideration in our education and it was suggested that they should be brought in on making the choice for secondary opportunities... . The secondary choices were –

first, the new senior school... second, the ancient grammar school... and third, the junior technical school, of which there were far too few in this country. These choices were originally recommended in the Spens Report . . . all three schools – senior, grammar and junior technical – would be equally accessible.[54]

3.3: TOWARDS A NEW ADMINISTRATIVE ORDER

The move towards the establishment of secondary education for all was tied up with a new administrative order. The White Paper proposed an education system based on three stages: primary education, secondary education and further education. The secondary schools would be of three main types, which would be known as grammar, modern and technical schools.[55]

The principle of "secondary education for all" was both raised and implemented by administrative and legislative action, in particular by revision of the local administration of education. The 1902 Act provided two separate types of Local Education Authority: elementary education authorities, of which there were 315, and higher education authorities, of which there were 146. Thus, for example, the "modern school," which was recommended by the Hadow Committee as a form of post-primary education, was in fact provided for and administered under the powers of the Authority for elementary education. The difficulties of such a system were explained in the following description:

> In those areas which, so far as elementary education is concerned, are administered as autonomous areas, there is the possibility of unprofitable competition or overlapping between the Part II and Part III Authorities in the supply of post-primary education.[56]

Moreover, since the 1902 Act, "body after body has recommended that the proper arrangement would be to have a system whereby all Local Education Authorities are charged with all educational functions."[57] In 1927 the Permanent Secretary of the Board of Education delivered a warning on this matter:

> In view of the past history of this matter it would be hazardous to prophesy how or how soon the obstacle to educational organisation presented by the incoherence of administrative area will be overcome. It is to be hoped that realisation of the great and increasing inconveniences of the present arrangements will lead, whether by way of central or local action, to real effort to overcome them.⁵⁸

This conclusion inevitably led to the suggestion that "suitable arrangements for the transfer of a child from the primary to either a modern school or a grammar school or technical school can only be made if the same Authority is responsible for all three types of education."⁵⁹ The repercussions of this would include the abolition of 169 out of 315 Local Education Authorities for elementary education. Another obstacle to the implementation of "secondary education for all" was the differences between the Authorities both in size and in financial resources. Dent (1947) describes this situation as follows:

> Previously it was the duty of the local authorities to provide elementary education only, though Part II authorities had powers to provide or aid the provision of secondary and other higher education. How adequately those powers were exercised depended upon the attitude towards education of a local authority or upon the financial resources at its command, and, as everyone knows, the provision of higher education was *extremely unequal and nowhere sufficient* [original emphasis]. ⁶⁰

A similar explanation had been given by the Health Minister in a letter to Butler of 13 March 1943:

> In any event, if re-allocation of functions is essential for efficient administration, some shifting of the burden as between various groups of ratepayers is inevitable and must be faced as the price of reform. ⁶¹

Responses to the proposals varied. On the one hand there were those who said that only compulsory measures imposed on the counties would work, and that a re-distribution of the powers of the LEAs should be made if the real aim was to be achieved.[62] On the other hand several responses warned the President of the Board of Education not to take compulsory steps. For example, a secret document with the title "Questionnaire on Local Government: Answers of the Board of Education" raised some hypothetical options concerning the transfer of educational administration. Four such options were examined, including the "transference of the education services to the central government," which was immediately dismissed as "unrealistic undesirable and impracticable." The practical route, according to this document, was to follow a process already adopted voluntarily by some Authorities:

> Arrangements by which the functions of a major Authority are exercised in part by a minor Authority by voluntary delegation are familiar in local educational administration... Local Education Authorities which decentralise the administration of higher (especially secondary) education through District Committees... where the major Authority is interested and competent, and there is a satisfactory local tradition also in existence, as in Lancashire, these arrangements have worked on the whole smoothly and effectively but, in the absence of these precedent conditions, they have not left such a favourable impression. The principle, however, of such voluntary delegation runs right through the system of educational administration.[63]

Meanwhile, William A. Jowitt, the Chairman of the County Council Association of Municipal Corporations, responded to the Board of Education's scheme in a letter to Butler:

> The first point to be noted is that under your proposals the units of local educational administration must in any case be re-defined, since the continuance of Authorities for elementary education will not be possible when that term ceases to have any statutory significance.[64]

In order to avoid a re-definition that could destroy local interest in education and might provoke a great many conflicts, Jowitt made the following suggestions:

> The new Local Education Authorities should be confined to Counties and County Boroughs, subject to the possible merger of some of the smaller County areas. I regret it, however, as of the greatest importance, that local interest in education matters should be lost.... I recommend, therefore, that the county authority should be empowered to delegate to the council of any borough or urban district within its area.... It may well be that some of these Authorities will, of their own motion, seek amalgamation for educational purposes with other Authorities within their area.[65]

But in order to ensure that such amalgamation would be implemented, rather than leave the matter wholly to local initiative, Jowitt suggested that the Board of Education might "make an order" to combine the areas of the councils.

In response to this proposal the Permanent Secretary of the Board of Education, M.G. Holmes, wrote to the Parliamentary Secretary saying:

> A further study of your Paper on Local Educational Administration leaves me with an uneasy feeling that adoption of a scheme on the lines there set out would greatly complicate the work of the Board as a *central authority* and, in a lesser degree, the work of the County Local Education Authorities [present writer's emphasis].[66]

Thus, opinions were divided between those who thought that only compulsory means would achieve the re-definition of powers required and those who believed that only LEA initiatives on the basis of the Board of Education's rules and orders would achieve this aim. Butler regarded a comprehensive inquiry into a new structure and re-definition of the local authorities as a waste of time; he wanted the Act in operation quickly. In

July 1943, just before the publication of the White Paper, he wrote to the Prime Minister:

> The Authorities for elementary education only will disappear, but, in order to mitigate their sorrow, an elaborate scheme of devolution is proposed, following upon the model of counties such as Lancashire, the West Riding and Essex, which should result in the expansion of local interest in education, where it exists, and its creation, where it does not.[67]

The compromise that had been arrived at empowered the Minister to constitute a "Joint Education Board"[68] for the area of two or more counties or county boroughs judged too small or poor to carry the full burden of the new education service by themselves, on condition that the population of the county district was no less than 70,000.[69]

What this meant from the administrative point of view was that on 1 April 1945, when this part of the Act came into operation, 169 Local Education Authorities ceased to exist (Dent, 1947). At the same time, a higher degree of coherence between the two educational levels, primary and secondary, was anticipated. Local Authorities not able to carry the full financing burden of the old as well as the new education service by themselves amalgamated with other Authorities. Butler explained how the new administrative order would aid the quest for more equality by raising the school leaving age to Parliament: "The extension of education up to the age of 18 will involve such a vast scope of educational provision that it is not sensible to rely on very restricted areas to give all these facilities."[70]

The extension of the LEAs' duties under the 1944 Act was based on the guiding principle of the reform that the system should retain a diversity of choice while attempting at the same time to fuse the parts and weld them into an organic whole which would include all three types: primary, secondary and further education. Consequently, the LEAs' duties were widened and made more comprehensive, the principal one being to secure places and "to afford for all pupils, opportunities for education offering such variety of instruction and training as may be desirable in view of their different ages, abilities and aptitudes."[71]

The LEAs now had not only the administrative responsibility for providing a large range of types of schools, but also, and most significantly the power to decide on the content of instruction because they were now empowered to revise the school curriculum – particularly in the secondary schools as a result of the amendment of the secondary structure and fulfilment of the aim of secondary education for all.

3.4: CONCLUSIONS

The 1944 Education Act set out a new radical order, superseding several previous attempts made since the beginning of the century, to achieve two main goals. The first one was the quest for justice and the trend towards a higher degree of equal opportunity; and the second the move towards a higher degree of control and connection between the different organisations and levels within the education system. These two factors apply similarly to its predecessors, the Acts of 1870, 1902 and 1918, which accomplished a gradual shift in the direction of equal opportunities and greater unification of the education system. But, while the 1870 Act was significant in establishing *elementary* education, the 1944 Act established *secondary* education for all. The 1902 Act was an attempt to establish a rational connection between primary and secondary education and to unify the voluntary schools under the LEAs; the 1944 Act succeeded in implementing this aim. Raising the leaving age was among the aims of the 1918 Act, but only came about as a result of the 1944 Act.

The 1944 Act created two main forces in the educational field: central government, which determined the main values and directions of the education system, and the LEAs which were delegated absolute power to implement those values and directions[72] (Ranson & Tomlinson, 1986; Wells & Taylor, 1949).[73] Moreover, the LEAs had wide discretionary powers and a high degree of freedom to decide about the best way of implementing the Act according to "local interest in education."[74] While the achievement of goals such as equality of opportunity and a higher degree of order required central intervention and new rules and legislation, the implementation of that new legislation required that the LEAs have absolute power to execute the Act[75] (Liell & Sounders, 1989). And so the extension of state intervention in education increased the power of the two forces of central government and local government, the first being identified with decisions on *where to go* and the second with decisions on *how to get there*. The LEAs became the main operational power as a result of the devolution of power by central government.

But what is also significant in the 1944 Act is the process by which settlements were reached with the main organisations concerned. An atmosphere of co-operation and even optimism among all participants in the negotiations was maintained even though the result would be a loss of power for some of them. What had been a feeling of neglect and alienation at the beginning of the negotiations, by the end was transformed into announcements and declarations by the leaders of the various organisations involved, stating that the Act was desirable and represented progress in the education system. Thus, for example, Temple said:

> Above all let us not give the impression that our concern as Church people is only with the adjustment of the dual system; we ought as Christians to be concerned about the whole of educational progress. I am quite sure that the raising of the school age will of itself do more to make permanent the religious influence.[76]

A resolution by the Association of Education Committees announced that "individually [LEAs] would have to give up something they hoped for and they might have to accept some things which offended their sense of justice and fair play; that was the price to be paid for a broad, general advance . . . in the future interests of the children of the country."[77] The Education Committee of London County Council declared that "the Council should welcome the publication of the White Paper as a substantial contribution towards educational progress,"[78] and a special national assembly of the National Union of Teachers declared that the "Education Bill established a national system of education with equality of opportunity for all children."[79]

The 1944 Act dealt more successfully with some of the issues that had occupied a central position in the 1902 and 1918 Acts. As has been described already, equality of opportunity was the main inspiration of the 1944 Act and it had been achieved by re-allocation and re-definition of powers. This re-distribution involved the same organisations that had fought against such re-definition in previous Acts. Set against the background of these former Acts the success of the 1944 Act seems to be unique. This leads us to the question: What was unique in the process of framing the 1944 Act that enabled the accomplishment of re-distribution of power for the purpose of achieving more equality of opportunity? What was the new element in the process that fostered the co-operation and accommodation of the organisations in accepting the Act? What were the factors that enabled these organisations, at the same time as they relinquished power, to announce that the Act represented progress in the education system? Could it be explained simply as a typical process of cognitive dissonance? In answering these questions, four main points must be considered.

The first is the introduction of an option giving the schools more than one choice and so some degree of freedom in the implementation of the Act. As Butler said, "the beauty of our scheme has been that it is voluntary."[80] In practice, all parties to the negotiation had more than one choice open to them; there was a definite attempt to avoid any sense of compulsion. The Church schools could retain independence as "aided" schools if they could improve their premises up to Council standards, but would be controlled if they could not afford to do this. The meaning and the message were clear: "more public money – more control",[81] but the options remained available. This was accepted by the Church leaders as giving them a genuine choice based on their own ability to raise the money that was needed in order to retain independence. The re-distribution of the power of the LEAs was achieved in a similar way. The government laid down the principle that no population smaller than 70,000 could have its own Local Education Authority, but did not decide who would be merged with whom, leaving a wide degree of freedom for negotiations between the local authorities about the conditions of amalgamation and the distribution of powers between them.

The second point is that the government accepted many of the demands of their negotiating partners that did not confuse or obstruct the main aims of the Act. For example, most of the Churches' Five Points were accepted and included in the Bill. In the matter of the Local Authorities the government accepted William Jowitt's suggestions that they should seek amalgamation with other Authorities of their own accord, and that the county Authority should be empowered to delegate some power to any borough urban district. This negotiating tactic of accepting the organisations' demands where possible, enabled the government to reach an agreement without conceding its main goals, and without succumbing to obstacles which had caused previous attempts to founder.

The third reason for this Act's success was the adaptation of solutions and formulas that were self-organised and self-conducted at the local level, and had already had been proved a success, to the national level. For example, the "agreed syllabus" had been arrived at in Cambridgeshire in 1924 and was in use by over 100 local education authorities by 1942.[82] Another example is the successful amalgamation of many voluntary schools through negotiation with local authorities, especially for the maintenance of a secondary school, without any intervention by the government. Following this principle, Butler decided: "What is important, I think, is to work out a method of delegation which will be satisfactory, and allow time for local agreements to be made."[83] He saw that any central intervention in and attempt to negotiate details could take several years; a formula that had already proved workable could provide a much more practical basis. In fact the government laid down only one sanction as to the achievement of its aims: a time limit. The choice of methods and the negotiations were left entirely to the local level.

The fourth reason was a common identification with and shared belief in the value of the fundamental concept of equal opportunity. This consensus as to the just aims of the Act in the face of the existing injustice and inequality within the education system was shared by all those who took part in the negotiations, especially those leaders who were close to Butler. The Archbishop of Canterbury, Dr Temple, was deeply committed to the Act's aim, as the following passage demonstrates:

> The school leaving age was still 14 at a time when the sons of wealthy parents went to public schools… the sons and daughters of poorer parents were thrown out into the rough and tumble of the labour market to find what jobs they could. They were members of no community; they did not belong to anything or

anybody. That was the great evil. The early influence of home, school and church was largely neglected by the experience of the years between 14 and 20.[84]

Butler explained Temple's motivation thus: "Temple was so keen on the provisions of the Act itself that he was determined not to allow a religious quarrel to hold up educational advance."[85] Miss Cantnach, one of the main figures on the Joint Committee for the Four Secondary Associations, wrote to Butler saying: "I should just like to say that I myself will represent your views with the utmost sympathy."[86] At the same time the reform proposal had considerable political support, including that of the Chancellor of the Exchequer.[87]

Notes:
1. Board of Education (1941). *Education After the War*, (the Green Paper), 5.
2. PRO ed. 136/228 (12 February 1941).
3. Ibid. In fact the Church of England was divided between two opinions; there were those who felt that a truly Christian atmosphere and teaching could only occur in Church schools, and others who thought that an "agreed syllabus," which would also include Christian instruction in Council schools, was sufficient.
4. The three other demands in the Archbishop's Document were that religious instruction should be an "optional subject" in teacher training and not an "additional option," that only qualified teachers give Christian teaching and that the methods, not the content, should be inspected by HM Inspectors.
5. PRO ed. 136/228.
6. R.A. Butler (1971). *The Art of the Possible*. London: Hamish Hamilton, 94.
7. R.A. Butler (1982). *The Art of Memory*. London: Hodder and Stoughton, 149.
8. PRO ed. 136/228.
9. Board of Education (1941), 55.
10. Butler (1982), 152.
11. PRO ed. 136/228.
12. A quotation from Halevy cited by Butler, 1971, 98.
13. The proposal included general acceptance of the Archbishop's "Five Points."
14. PRO ed. 136/228. Section 5 contains a suggestion for transfer of the single school area to the LEAs.
15. Ibid.
16. Ibid.
17. Ibid.
18. PRO ed. 136/229. At this stage Butler decided to change tactics and to ask the Church leaders to plan a new proposal. The Archbishop of Canterbury replied that this was the task of the Board and not the Church.
19. Marjorie Cruickshank (1963). *Church and State in English Education*. London: Macmillan, 150-1.
20. PRO ed. 136/228. Our Trust and Our Task. 1942, 8.
21. PRO ed. 136/229. The figures include the cost of raising the learning age in order to deal with 208,772 children over 11, 69,591 and children between the ages of 14 and 15, at a total cost of £22,000,000. The cost of raising accommodation to council school standards would be about £19,000,000.
22. "Agreed syllabus" is a term born as a result of the failure of the 1902 Act. During the 1920s eight counties followed Cambridgeshire in creating an agreed syllabus with the denominational parties and about 100 counties were practising it by 1942. This settlement facilitated religious instruction in council schools. And so, Temple's proposal was based on a settlement that had already been achieved at the local level.
23. Butler (1971), 101.
24. Fifteen years after the Act about half of the voluntary schools were "aided" and about half "controlled." Among the half that remained aided, 3,378 belonged to the Church

of England and 1,946 to the Roman Catholic Church. (Cruickshank, 1963, 191).
25. *The Times*, 26.10.43.
26. Ibid.
27. In fact Temple knew very well that the Anglican Church could not raise the money to retain all "aided" schools. In a meeting with Butler in the summer of 1942 he had said "The Church schools would opt for controlled status" (Butler, 1971). But the Church of England insisted on making "aided" status the first alternative and "controlled" the second option (Howard, 1986).
28. Cruickshank describes the atmosphere of this Assembly in terms of suspicion among members of the National Society and a feeling of "selling the past." There was no question of a secret arrangement.
29. *The Times*, 8.5.43.
30. *The Times*, 8.5.43.
31. PRO ed. 136/235.
32. *The Times*, 2.1.43.
33. PRO ed. 136/224.
34. Butler's own opinion on the whole question of state intervention in the school curriculum was revealed in a meeting with Miss Cantnach in which he said that "he was, however, in favour of all reasonable freedom for teachers, and he thought some use might be made of the suggestion that the syllabuses should be in the form of handbooks of suggestion" (PRO ed. 136/224). This comment, along with the unions' stance on this issue, indicates what might have happened if the issue at stake had been not just the religious syllabus but wider government intervention in the curriculum.
35. Ibid.
36. PRO ed. 136/382.
37. The two others steps were (a) "A general recasting of the existing education system so as to secure a longer school life and a more equal educational chance for all children," and (b) "The institution of a system of compulsory continued education and training for young people after they leave school."
38. PRO ed. 136/382.
39. The Butler Memorandum included much more administrative details, such as (a) the replacement of the terms "elementary" and "higher" education with the terms "primary education," covering full-time education up to 11+, "secondary education," covering full-time education of all types between 11+ and 18+, and "further," education covering other full-time or part-time education; (b) a common code of regulations for secondary schools of all types in order to raise the standard of school accommodation; (c) simplification of the system of local education administration for the provision of elementary and secondary education.
40. PRO ed. 136/377.
41. Butler was blamed by John Simon in the House of Lords for supplying the Labour Party with arguments that could damage the Conservatives. For years, Lord Simon argued, the Conservatives had been blamed by Socialists who constantly informed their audiences

that the education system provided a "preserve for the rich" and the Butler Memorandum supported this argument in its use of the phrase "social distinction," which "would give our Labour colleagues… a handle for repeating this" (PRO ed. 136/377).

42. Butler (1971), 92.
43. Maurice Kogan (1978). *The Politics of Educational Change.* Manchester: Manchester University Press, 24.
44. Ibid., 25.
45. Board of Education (1938). *Report of the Consultative Committee of the Board of Education on Secondary Education with Special Reference to Grammar Schools and Technical High Schools.* Quoted in Stuart J. Maclure (1986), *Educational Documents*, New York: Methuen, 195.
46. Board of Education (1941), 7.
47. The structure of the education system in that period was as follows: compulsory education begins at the age of 5, the child moves to junior school at the age of 7-8 where he stays until 11. At the age of 11 every child can take an examination on the basis of which selection is made for secondary school. A quarter of the children who pass the examinations enter secondary school on payment of a fee that varies according to their parents' income (from full fee to nothing). At secondary school they prepare for a school certificate at about 16. About 10% remain at school after 16 for advanced courses in preparation for university or other institutions of higher education. In fact, about 25% leave the secondary school before 16 and about 40% do not take the School Certificate. About three quarters, the remainder at elementary school after the 11+ Examinations (1.5 million pupils out of 2 million do not pass the Special Place Examination) continue into senior elementary school in the same building in which they started unless they are selected (27,000 pupils) for junior technical, junior commercial or junior art schools until 14, the age at which compulsory education ceases.
48. Board of Education (1943). *Educational Reconstruction*, 3.
49. Ibid., 9.
50. Board of Education (1943), 18. The fact that most of the English-speaking countries had a higher leaving age than 14 was another trigger for Butler's argument for raising the leaving age and establishing further education. In 1943-48 states in the United States had a leaving age of 16 or over. In Canada and South Africa the age varied between 15 and 16. In the United States as a whole nearly 90% of the children of 14 and 15 years of age were attending school full-time. In England and Wales it was estimated that in all not more than about 60,000 young workers were attending day continuation or day time classes – i.e. about 2.5% of the total number of young people between 14 and 18.
51. *The Times*, 25.3.43.
52. Ibid. The health services were extended under this Act to all the forms of treatment for all children and young persons attending schools.
53. This clause was substituted by the parents' obligation "to cause their children to attend school" according to the 1870 Act. In fact the latter legislation mentioned the need for parents to be aware and responsible as to the "suitable school" for their child and not

only to cause him to attend.
54. *The Times*, 30.7.43. The parents could make their choice after receiving advice from teachers.
55. The White Paper mentioned the option of combining the three different types in one building, similar to the idea of the comprehensive school which was raised immediately after the war and was the main target of "comprehensive reorganisation" from 1965 onwards.
56. Board of Education (1941), 51. Part II is the legislation for higher education and Part III is the legislation for elementary education.
57. Board of Education (1943). *Educational Reconstruction*, 29.
58. Quoted in Board of Education (1941), 51.
59. Board of Education (1943), 29.
60. H.C. Dent (1947). *The Education Act*. London: University of London Press, 15.
61. PRO ed. 136/354.
62. Ibid.
63. PRO ed. 136/358.
64. PRO ed. 136/354.
65. Ibid.
66. Ibid.
67. PRO ed. 136/377.
68. Hansard, Vol. 396, 8.2.44, 1642.
69. Board of Education (1943), 29.
70. Hansard, Vol. 396, 9.2.44, 1862.
71. 1944 Education Act, Clause 8.
72. The Board of Education became a ministry and the minister was charged with securing effective execution by local authorities throughout England and Wales, under his control and direction, in order to provide a varied and comprehensive education service (Wells, M.M & Taylor, P.S. (1949), 5).
73. Ranson & Tomlinson (1986) mention that the strengthening of central government was designed as a means of "contraction of local decision-making powers and a reduced capacity on the part of the local authorities" (2).
74. Board of Education (1943), 29.
75. The duties of the LEAs included: appointment of managers or governors as local instruments for running the schools; provision of transport; causing parents to send their children to receive efficient full-time, age-appropriate education; securing special educational provision; ensuring that school premises conform to prescribed standards; providing religious education as required; securing medical and dental services; providing board and lodging, milk and meals; providing clothing, including boots and other footwear; providing financial assistance to enable pupils to take advantage of educational facilities; providing financial assistance for any university or university college. All these duties were in addition to the main one: the establishment of nursery, primary, special, secondary and further education schools.

76. *The Times*, 26.6 43.
77. *The Times*, 17.9.43.
78. *The Times*, 19.10.43.
79. *The Times*, 2.11.43.
80. PRO ed. 136/228.
81. This was the basic formula that was declared by Butler as government policy.
82. The local authorities took the initiative by making their own arrangements with the churches according to which many Anglican managers were willing to hand over their schools to the local authorities in return for Christian teaching in provided and transferred schools. The result was an improvement in the quality of religious instruction in council schools and a higher degree of unification of the education system (Butler, 1971; Butler, 1982; Cruickshank, 1963).
83. PRO ed. 136/354.
84. *The Times*, 14.7.43.
85. Butler (1971), 103.
86. PRO ed. 136/224.
87. The political support included some dominant figures in the Labour Party such as Attlee, Bevin and Greenwood.

PHASE TWO: MOVING AWAY FROM THE NEW ORDER: THE DECENTRALIZATION PROCESSS

INTRODUCTION

The 1944 Education Act laid down a fundamental canon that all children should be given education suitable to their age, ability, and aptitude. The principles of reorganisation fostered by the government to implement this canon were based on the Hadow (1926), Spens (1938) and Norwood (1943) Reports, which approved the psychologists' claim that individuals could be differentiated in terms of their intellectual characteristics early in life. Acceptance of these psychological criteria led to the specification by government of a rigid, fixed allocation of places in each of three types of school: grammar, technical and modern.

Each LEA was asked to submit a Development Plan following guidelines set down by the government for the minister's approval. But interaction between local groups, the prominence of local traditions, selection problems, parents' right to choose a school according to their wishes, local perceptions concerning technical schools, organisational problems, and the power given to local divisions (communities) to defend their own education interests, all contributed to the first phase of blurring and undermining the government's concept, principle and vision concerning the structure of secondary education and the tripartite system.

The second phase of this erosion of the new order was the involvement of sub-groups of parents, teachers and local politicians in the implementation of the Development Plans. Each level involving sub-systems that was needed to implement what had already been approved by the Minister after years of discussion and disputes, paralysed and delayed the evolution and the implementation of the secondary reform and introduced a new level of complexity. Discrepancies in interests, needs and perceptions between and within the sub-groups, aspects that could not have been foreseen by the founders of the new order, were among the factors that led to confusion, paralysis of decision making and neutralisation of any attempt to implement the approved plan.

The third phase of distortion and diversion of the principle of the tripartite system and of the government's rigid guidelines centred on the powerful determination of both pupils and teachers in the modern schools to obtain significant and meaningful qualifications and certification, in other words, to gain access to external examinations, despite the government view that only grammar school students should have such access. The vanishing of technical schools, which did not rank high in local priorities for developing secondary schools; the strong research arguments against the validity of selection tests and the low predictive power of such tests; population migration; the rise of the birth rate and the rapid development of the suburbs – all these factors combined to foster the gradual and steady move towards a new structural system based on comprehensive schools, which spelt the end of the government's original policy and the collapse of the tripartite system.

Thus, the LEAs in the first phase, parents, teachers and local politicians in the second, and modern school motivation and other combined factors in the third, widened the gap between the central ideas and vision of the Ministry of Education and local reality, leading to the construction of a new and different order in education.

• CHAPTER 4

LOCAL INTERACTION BLURS THE STRUCTURE OF THE NEW ORDER

The 1944 Education Act was followed by the construction of frameworks of organisational and educational principles. Both of these frameworks, particularly the latter, represented attempts to specify the national allocation of children to three types of schools suitable to their age, ability and aptitude, in definite terms. The Reform was thus directed by the government's attempt to implement reorganisation by dictating – at the level of LEA, district and single-school – definite numbers of places in grammar, technology and modern schools. It did so by keeping a tight control on the LEAs' development plans.

Despite the government's aim to control the reform, LEAs were given the authority to take "local circumstances" and local needs into consideration. This was a policy at cross-purposes with the government's principle of allocating a definite percentage of pupils to each of the three types of schools; it allowed administrative factors, parents' wishes, selection considerations and numerous and unforeseen local interests to transform the government's intention and specifications for the new order and to move towards a different structural organisation. This chapter concentrates on the effect of local traditions, interests, needs and perceptions in carrying the process of change away from the path intended by the government.

4.1: CENTRAL SPECIFICATIONS FOR LOCAL ORGANISATIONS

The Education Act of 1944 required every Local Education Authority to estimate the immediate and prospective needs of its area with regard to primary and secondary education, including proposals for pupils under five years of age and for those who require special educational treatment. The Act therefore required each Local Education Authority to survey the needs of the area as it saw fit, in the light of the new provisions, and to submit a development plan containing proposals for development in each specified branch of education to the minister, together with any other proposals the authority might deem necessary.

The minister gave two main types of guidance to the local authorities in the preparation of their Development Plans: organisational principles and educational principles. The organisational principles included the following, laid down by the minister in November 1944:[1]

> (a) Compulsory school age to be extended from five to fifteen, but provision should be made for raising the upper limit to sixteen.
> (b) The size of classes was to be kept to a maximum of 40 in primary schools and 30 in secondary schools.[2]

These directions were followed in March 1945 by regulations prescribing the minimum standards for school premises. These standards covered minimum areas for playgrounds and classrooms, dining rooms and kitchens, staff rooms, storage provision, heating and ventilation, residential accommodation, cloakrooms, etc. Over and above the minimum standards, the LEAs were encouraged by the Building Regulations to include provision for other, more generous facilities within their development plans – in comparison with the previous principles of 1937 and 1938.[3] For example, the importance of providing swimming pools was mentioned: "a covered bath may be included as part of the premises of a very large secondary school or for use by a group of schools";[4] the needs of pupils staying on for the sixth-form stage were addressed through directions to plan "division rooms, in which small groups of pupils can study"; similarly, "it will be an advantage to have one or more such rooms where music forms part of school activities."[5] Some evidence of the liberality of the new building regulations, approved by the Report of the Committee on School Sites and Building Procedures, may be seen in calculations of the total building expenditure contained in the LEAs' development plans and further education schemes, estimated to be of the order of £1,000 million. The Committee explained this estimate as follows:[6]

> The capital expenditure necessary to implement that Act will obviously be on a very much bigger scale than which any educational administration has ever before had to deal. Under the normal procedure the greatest amount of capital expenditure ever approved in one year was £16.5 million in 1938 and that at a time when the machine was working at full pressure to prepare for the raising of the compulsory school age in 1939 and to secure the urgently needed extension of technical education . . . it would not be unreasonable in our view to fix a maximum of 15 years for the completion of the programme. This means an annual average expenditure of approximately £70 million a year which at present costs is roughly double the programme in 1938.[7]

The differences between the early estimates in 1943, when Parliament was asked to approve the Act, and the later estimates reported by the Committee on School Sites and Building Procedures, was explained in part by Florence Horsburgh, Minister for Education at the time, in a letter to R.A. Butler, who by then was Chancellor of the Exchequer. Horsburgh argues that the freedom and autonomy over administrative aspects that was given to LEAs, particularly the raising of money by rate, were severely affected by central control over educational issues:[8]

> The Education Service...is a well established service almost wholly administered through local education authorities, who are responsible for raising a substantial part of the money that they spend. We could hardly have an inquiry into the Education Service which was largely designed to review the responsibility of local authorities for its administration.[9]

Consequently the capital expenditure deemed necessary to implement the Act in 1946 was much greater than the sum estimated in 1943. This fact raised major financial problems during the 1950s that threatened the continuity and full implementation of the Act (see Chapter 8).

The second type of guidance provided for the LEAs by the Minister took the form of educational principles. The 1944 Education Act laid down, as a fundamental canon, that *all children should be given education suitable to their age, ability and aptitude*. This was accepted by the LEAs as axiomatic, but in many cases their interpretation of it differed from that of the government, leading to several disagreements and disputes with the Ministry of Education during the period of the Act's implementation. At the core of these disputes was the discrepancy between the local notion of what was *suitable* for the children of the area and their educational needs, and what the direction of secondary education should be, according to national needs, from the government's point of view. The contradiction between these two concepts soon gave rise to conflicts between the government and many of the LEAs. These will be discussed later in this chapter.

The principle of reorganisation advocated in the Hadow Report (1926 – the provision of separate schools for all children over 11) was accepted as an "educational axiom"[10] in the 1944 Education Act. The distribution of the three different types of secondary education – the grammar school, the technical school and the modern school – was determined by a percentage formula based on the normal distribution of different kinds of ability. This formula was based on the "psychologists' claim that it is possible at a very early age to predict with some degree of accuracy the ultimate level of a child's general intelligence,"[11] and was justified on the grounds of "individual differences in intellectual and emotional characteristics."[12] The Norwood Report accepted the psychological claim and on this basis recommended a rough grouping in terms of three kinds of curriculum. This Report gave added weight to the secondary education concept and the need to establish a secondary school system based on the differences between individuals. Such a system would on the one hand preserve the tradition of the grammar school and on the other would incorporate secondary schools of "great variety as regards traditions, the aim and destination of pupils."[13]

The 1944 Education Act was followed up with pamphlets and circulars aimed at providing instructions and laying down principles regarding the organisation of secondary schools in order to guide the LEAs in their preparatory work for the development plans. Pamphlet No.1, "The Nation's Schools," clearly stated that "the most urgent reform to which the development plan must be addressed is the completion of 'Hadow' reorganisation,"[14] meaning the provision of different kinds of education within the same age range in order "to meet the differing needs of different pupils."[15] The importance of the grammar schools was asserted from two points of view: from the past perspective, of the "remarkable success in establishing worthy traditions and sound standards of scholarship which it is essential to retain,"[16] and from the future perspective of fulfilling the national duty to educate the nation's most intellectually capable children by continuing their school life up to age 18:

> The war has thrown into sharper relief our shortage of persons with higher qualifications, particularly in science, and from more than one quarter the view has been expressed that in future the requirements of this country will call for a substantial increase in the out-turn of those who have successfully completed courses, in wide variety, of university and comparable standard.[17]

The second type of school, the technical school, was strongly linked to the engineering and building industries and designed "for children of 11-16 selected on the basis of their general intelligence and special interests and aptitudes."[18] The development of these schools was envisaged in order to address other advanced industrial areas, science and craft skills, the needs of agricultural engineering and the rapidly widening field of women's employment.

According to the Hadow Report, the third type, the modern school, was to replace the senior or central school, which had been part of the old statutory field of elementary schools. It was intended to provide secondary education for the majority of the nation's children between the ages of 11 and 16. The diffuseness of the stated aims of the modern school was deliberately emphasised, especially in light of the precise definition and high expectations associated with the grammar schools. The aim of the modern school was thus defined as follows: "Free from the pressures of any external examination, these schools can work out the best and liveliest forms of secondary education suited to their pupils...which will add to the meaning and enjoyment of life."[19]

The rationale for the three main types of school[20] was soon followed by general guidelines on the proportion of accommodation that was to be provided for each of the three types, according to the normal distribution formula of ability and intelligence. It was suggested that "under normal conditions 70 to 75 percent should be of the modern type, the remaining 25 to 30 per cent being allocated to grammar and technical in suitable proportions according to the local circumstances of the area."[21] The phrase *"suitable proportions according to local circumstances"* seems to conflict with the rigid instruction regarding the relative proportions of the three types of schools laid down and published by the Ministry of Education. This is symptomatic of the attempt, which was noticeable in many such government publications at this time, to satisfy two general needs that contradicted one another: the preparation of the development plan according to local needs, and the government's desire to maintain *central control* of the correct proportions between the three different types of school, and especially to preserve the grammar schools. The first reservations about the tripartite system were expressed in the White Paper:

> It would be wrong to suppose that they will necessarily remain separate and apart. Different types may be combined in one building or on one site as considerations of convenience and efficiency may suggest.[22]

The words *convenience and efficiency* fall into the same category as *local circumstances*. An example of the meaning of such terms was given in Pamphlet No.1: "in sparsely populated districts it may well be essential to bring together a variety of types of secondary course in one school unit."[23] In order, however, to avoid the widespread foundation of single school units of this kind, which were defined as multilateral schools and might have threatened the main aim of the tripartite policy – to cater for *the differing needs of different pupils* – the multilateral school would be established only as an experiment and as an "extreme measure of combination" in order to secure the traditional schools:

It would be a mistake to plunge too hastily on a large scale into revolutionary changes…which for this country are perhaps somewhat uncertain. Innovation is not necessarily reform.[24]

Another example of the government's "two voices" – the desire on the one hand to retain the traditional schools and on the other to encourage reform – appears in Circular 73. This document recommends that the LEAs plan a system based on three different types of school according to local circumstances: "inasmuch as in most areas grammar school provision already exists it would be unwise to apply any drastic reduction of the annual intake to such schools."[25] But in special circumstances, and in order to meet local needs, the minister would be prepared to consider proposals for bilateral and multilateral schools.[26]

The LEAs were asked to submit a development plan based on three main sources of guidance: (a) the building regulations; (b) the tripartite system; (c) the local needs and local circumstances, to the minister. In the latter two, the Ministry of Education appears to be taking two different positions: on the one hand stipulating rigid proportions of types of school based on psychological criteria established for categorising pupils into three types, and on the other encouraging the LEAs to take the needs of the area into consideration. These two positions were contradictory. When community needs, local tradition, the effect of the War, and the dispersal of the population were all taken into account as local circumstances requiring consideration, the central order began to crumble. At that point local division and community interaction emerged as more powerful and dominant factors than any external centrally dictated rules.

4.2: COMMUNITY INTERACTION AND TRANSFORMATION TOWARDS A NEW STRUCTURE

The 1944 Education Act, which included the requirement to submit a Development Plan to the minister, met the wishful thinking of many authorities that had long since recognised the need for alterations within their education system, but been prevented from taking the initiative and implementing what they saw as the most urgent alterations by the economic crisis of the 1930s and then the War.

A few LEAs did not wait for ministerial guidance and made their own proposals before the Education Act was approved by Parliament. The initiatives put forward by these pioneering authorities included ideas and plans for urgent and necessary changes in education according to their own local needs and future perspectives. Thus, for example, the London County Council decided in principle, after the publication of the White Paper, to establish a system of comprehensive schools based on US experience. Westmoreland County Education Committee appointed a planning sub-committee in November 1943 to formulate a proposal for the reorganisation of primary and secondary education. This proposal was approved by the County Council and was the basis for the Development Plan submitted to the Minister of Education in 1946. The Oxfordshire Education Committee submitted a report to the County Council in October 1944, raising the problems of a predominantly rural district with a few small urban areas, and suggested solutions that had "occupied their attention over a long period."[27] The outbreak of the War prevented Hampshire from completing schemes for new senior schools at Basingstoke, Fareham, Lymington, Romsey and Havant,[28] while in Birkenhead single schools were organised before 1944 Act became operative under the recommendations of the Hadow Report.[29]

Most of the LEA initiatives, however, occurred as a result of the 1944 Education Act and the requirement that they submit Development Plans to the minister. This requirement, which included the whole field of education from nursery school to adult education, in many cases evoked an enthusiastic response from the LEAs. They set about preparing their Development Plans with great dedication. The general feeling was that the Education Act of 1944 "makes provision for a great advance in public education" and that for the first time the new standards, regulations and legislation embodied the conception that "education is not just 'school'."[30] The preparation of the plan required co-operative work with several elements in the community, such as architects and administrators, as well as consultation with governors and managers of voluntary schools and with county district councils, as required by the Act. This process made preparing the Development Plan more complex and further blurred the government's intentions towards a central order. Local officials in many areas, frustrated with and critical of the disadvantages of the existing system, hoped that many of those disadvantages would disappear under the new system. The generous standards laid down by the Government strengthened the belief of LEA officials that this would be a chance to implement some of their wishes and ideals regarding what was needed in their area, and the right way to achieve justice and a higher degree of organisational order within their education system. Moreover, the Act encouraged the authorities to include any proposals that "the authority [might] think necessary"[31] for their area. This clause encouraged imagination and creativity in those who were involved in the preparation of the Development Plans.

The LEAs took the initiative in two main senses: (a) in contributing their own innovation and enterprise in order to go beyond the minimum standards of buildings required by the minister; and (b) in interpreting the Act according to their own interests, needs and beliefs as to the right reforms for their communities. The LEAs' initiative, in the first sense, arose from optimism directly inspired by the generosity of the standards set down by the ministry, a generosity which encouraged several LEAs to submit lavish Development Plans for the minister's approval.[32] The generosity can be clearly understood from the text of the Bradford Development Plan, which gives us some sense of the high expectations and optimism of many of the LEAs at that time:

> Every new Secondary School, therefore, must have its proper sports organisation, its sports master, its playing fields, and if possible, its swimming bath. As an ancillary to the playing field and swimming bath, every school must be provided with sufficient gymnasium accommodation, properly equipped…. The school must be sited so as to catch all the sunlight and fresh air possible …Every school must have a library…. Every school must have a hall or halls, large enough to take the whole school assembly…. There must also be a cinema screen and projection room… rooms for typewriting, Shorthand teaching, Economics, Geography, Book-keeping, filing, etc, should be features of the accommodation.[33]

Bolton's enthusiasm and initiative may perhaps be attributed to the high standards proposed for bilateral secondary schools:

> Each base is to be sited on the outskirts of the area and will provide a building site of approximately ten acres and a playing field of approximately *forty-two acres*.... The school house will cover all three departments; school societies, orchestras and choirs...a large school hall with stage, a swimming bath [present writer's emphasis].[34]

The area specified for this playing field exceeded by far the minimum laid down in 1945. Blackpool's Plan included an "office" block for the use of youth organisations and community centres in the north and the east of the town, while some other counties and cities included a field study centre as part of their plan. The wording of the London plan, which draws attention to the contrast between the former regulations and the new ones, is a further illustration of the scope allowed by the new regulations:

> The average size of the sites of the Council's former elementary schools is 1 acre and of the non-provided schools 0.25 acre; many of these sites are very inconvenient in shape and many cannot be enlarged. Under the regulations 2 to 3 acres would be required for a primary school and more for a secondary school.[35]

The total cost of the London Development Plan was £187 million. The new building regulations were one of the reasons behind this high total, particularly in a commercialised area like London.

Thus, the initiative taken by the government in passing the Act, not only triggered a wave of enthusiasm and initiative in many of the LEAs, but was also considered to be among the causes of economic and inflationary pressure during the early 1950s, far exceeding the government's plan in the early 1940s.

The second sense in which the LEAs took the initiative was in interpreting the Act according to local needs and circumstances. This resulted in several variations and mixed proposals for the secondary education system. Thus, for example, the London Education Committee Report adapted its suggestions to the City Council on the basis of the government's message, interpreting it as follows:

The White Paper recognised "three main types of secondary schools to be known as grammar, modern and technical schools," but very significantly went on to say that "it would be wrong to suppose that they will remain separate and apart. Different types may be combined in one building as considerations of convenience and efficiency may suggest…." This statement enunciates no educational philosophy or principle and makes no statement of national policy, but it leaves the door open to any suitable combination.[36]

The "*suitable combination*" was understood by the Council as an open door to any future flexible plan that might seem necessary in any divisional area of London.

Oxfordshire took the opportunity to plan for bilateral schools, taking advantage of a loophole in the minister's guidance that was understood as follows:

> It suggested that short-term plans should be based on the existing three-type lay-out of schools which might be modified later. Yet a loophole was left for an alternative organisation when it was stated that "authorities may reach the conclusion that the needs of the locality can best be met by continuing two or more types of secondary education in one school," and went on to say that "indeed in some rural areas this may be the only satisfactory solution."[37]

The loophole was not perceived by the Oxfordshire Education Committee as a chance to make radical change, but rather the opportunity "to propose a lay-out of secondary schools which is flexible and capable of subsequent modification, by variations in the Local Education Order."[38] But what Oxfordshire understood as a loophole was used by many other authorities as grounds for claiming much greater flexibility and autonomy. A confidential letter from Middlesex Education Committee and the Education Development Sub-Committee reads: "many of the new requisites can only be achieved by a radical change of educational orientation."[39] The radical change for

Middlesex was departure from the rigid definition of the tripartite arrangement because:

> ...there is a definite lack of uniformity as regards the provision and organisation of secondary schools and it may be argued that it is not possible to impose a single system on an area so large as Middlesex.[40]

Huntingdonshire based its DP proposals on the main duty of the authority, which was to provide education for all pupils in accordance with their age, ability and aptitude, but stated clearly that "no rigid three-fold system is to be imposed, and there will clearly have to be flexibility and room for experiment."[41] The authority laid claim to flexibility via reference to Circular 73; in its proposal it quoted that document as follows: "[an] authority may, in certain circumstances, reach the conclusion that the needs of the locality can best be met by combining two or more types of secondary education in one school, and the Minister will be prepared to consider such proposals."[42] Hampshire expressed a similar interest in similar terms, and proposed the establishment of bilateral schools.

In analysing the reasons behind this demand for a greater degree of freedom and more scope for community determination of the future organisation of their secondary education, we can observe four main types of argument: organisational reasons, parents' rights, selection problems, and division/community needs.

The organisational reasons were diverse, primarily and fundamentally affected by local circumstances: for example, there were special needs in rural counties, and in metropolitan areas that had suffered heavy damage during the war. County authorities in rural areas claimed that it would be economically desirable to maintain multilateral or bilateral schools. Westmorland's claim was typical of many other counties: "The County of Westmorland presents exceptional problems in the planning of educational reorganisation. The most difficult factor is the small and scattered population in a comparatively large geographical area."[43] This factor raised difficulties of staffing and transport, and the question of whether it was better to provide three different schools or one inclusive establishment under the reorganisation. Oxfordshire County had mentioned that it would be disadvantageous to separate schools into three broad types of secondary education because it would not be possible "to secure the numbers necessary for a proper school life in a sparsely populated area."[44] In Cumberland County the problem was more complicated and "there are areas in the County from which no child can reach Secondary School by daily travel, and the Authority has found it necessary to give some measure of boarding accommodation for each type of Secondary School."[45] These kinds of argument were common to many of the rural areas and were recognised by the ministry as constituting a real problem that justified granting some degree of the freedom demanded by the rural counties.

The second organisational problem was in those cities that had suffered most during the war period. Kent's Development Plan explained this point as follows:

> Kent has suffered far more than most county authorities from the effects of the war. Not only have many schools been destroyed or damaged but in some areas there have been movements of population which have made it difficult to calculate future educational needs upon a reliable estimate of population figures.[46]

For this reason the authority requested that the secondary schools "should not be tied down permanently to a rigid three-fold organisation."[47] The City of Coventry proposed a complete system of comprehensive schools for the same reason: "Enemy action during the war destroyed or seriously damaged the Art School, one Girls' Secondary School, one Boys' endowed School, and eleven of the then Elementary Schools. The position as regards school accommodation is, therefore, serious."[48] Middlesex raised the point that war damage to existing school premises was not the only administrative problem: "the absence of staff on war service, the losses through casualties, and the war-time limitations on the training of new teachers will cause great difficulty in staffing any scheme."[49] This type of difficulty was one of the reasons for the claim that the secondary education scheme "must be elastic enough to provide ... the variations between districts from time to time as the provision of new accommodation catches up with requirement."[50]

The second type of LEA demands for greater freedom was based on Section 76 of the Act. This Section required that local education authorities:

> have regard to the general principle that so far as is compatible with efficient instruction and training and the avoidance of unreasonable public expenditure, *pupils are to be educated in accordance with the wishes of their parents* [present writer's emphasis]. [51]

Section 76 appeared to contradict the guidance of Circular 73, which proposed fixed proportions of the three types of schools, while there was much evidence from the past that parents wished their children to have access to places in grammar schools in particular, in excess of the 15% that was recommended by the Government. The LEAs interpreted this Section as an option to ignore the fixed proportional allocation of places in secondary education. Thus, for example, Middlesex supported its proposal for multilateral schools by raising the argument that the percentage assumed in Circular 73 was mistaken, and that if the grammar school was to be "a separate entity then it should provide for at least 30 percent of the standard age group."[52] Given however that the ministry did not recommend placement of a high percentage of pupils in grammar schools, according to the Middlesex DP, parents would prefer a multilateral school because there "questions of parity of esteem will not arise."[53] Barrow in Furness raised the question of how the overly rigid instruction given by the ministry, was to be balanced with local requirements and the wishes of the parents. Finding that "the Ministry of Education [had given] little or no direct guidance in this matter," they came to the conclusion that "it would appear that in the absence of any other authoritative pronouncement on these questions, a tentative empiricism should be adopted."[54] Birkenhead raised the argument that *equality* was the main motivation of the Education Act, and because secondary education had been the privilege of one group of pupils since the beginning of the century, doubt would be raised among parents as to whether real parity of esteem would be achieved between the three different types of school. As he put it, "…parents may often doubt whether the secondary course recommended by the Education Committee as most appropriate is, in practice, in the best interests of their children." [55] Hence the authority's suggestion was that "the proper solution must inevitably depend on existing local conditions and must be determined by the needs of the area."

The third point the LEAs raised in favour of a larger degree of freedom in implementing the Act concerned the problem of selection and the associated examination. The tripartite system presupposed that children could be selected for a grammar, technical or modern school at about the age of 11, according to their abilities and aptitudes. This assumption, based on the Hadow Report, met with enormous opposition in several local authorities. Cheshire expressed the view that given "immaturity in the development of special aptitudes at about the age of 11 years, it is not possible to select for Technical education at the beginning of the pupil's Secondary School career."[56] Leicestershire raised a similar point, arguing that "no reliable test has yet been invented which can discover at the age of eleven specific technical aptitudes as distinct from general intelligence and capacity for learning."[57] Hampshire raised the possibility of prejudicing the child's future, and the difficulty of measuring intelligence: "it is necessary to take into account not only general intelligence . . . but also a verbal and a practical factor . . . but at the age of eleven it is difficult to determine the type of school which a child should attend."[58] The need to perform selection for two or three types of school raised a lot of confusion within the LEAs, as was expressed by Barrow-in-Furness:

> There is a generous symmetry about nature which would lead to the belief that there are as many children who would profit by an education of technical school type as would profit by that provided by the grammar school.[59]

This kind of confusion led many of the LEAs to adopt bilateral, and in some cases multilateral, schools, which seemed to be more appropriate in light of the problems of selection.

The fourth and apparently most influential factor at work calls for a greater degree of flexibility in the distribution of the community's needs. To understand the origins of these factors we must go back to the formulation of the 1944 Act, when amalgamation and redefinition of the functions of some small counties raised fears that the educational interests of those counties would be destroyed. In order to protect local interests in education, Section 6 and Part III of the first Schedule to the Education Act 1944 set up a new mechanism for the local administration of education – a joint education board. The object of this provision was to "work out in a spirit of the fullest co-operation the administrative organisation best adapted to the varying needs of their areas"[60] under the general control and supervision of the Local Education Authority. Moreover, Circular 5, 1944, strengthened the rights of the divisional executive vis-à-vis the Local Education Authority by announcing that:

> It would be neither desirable nor practicable to attempt to lay down any hard and fast model scheme to which the Authority should be expected to conform. Such uniformity would be irreconcilable with the wide differences in the circumstances and requirements of different areas.[61]

Despite the importance of securing the community's interests, however, the ultimate responsibility remains that of "formulating the educational policy of the area within the national framework."[62] Moreover, the Circular states that "the Local Education Authority must retain the ultimate right to approve such proposals."[63] This Circular raised some measure of confusion and complexity in decision making, because three different authorities were now involved: national policy, the Local Education Authority, and the community's needs. What policy should prevail in case of a conflict of interest between two of the three main authorities? Who should have first decision regarding policy: the local authority or the divisional executive? The divisions (communities) had apparently been given the power to take decisions on the desired future of their secondary education, but subject to the final decision of the local authority within the national framework. This fragmentation of decision making among three different authorities raised the question of whose line of policy the development plan proposals had been based upon. Further observations on the development plans will throw some light on these questions.

Huntingdonshire explained its approach in terms of meeting the needs of the districts: "every effort has been made to ensure by such consultation that provision proposed . . . is soundly based on the needs of the districts, so that the Plan will need a minimum of adjustment."[64] Derbyshire's Development Plan includes all the combinations of secondary education in accordance with the Divisional Executive's recommendations to the Authority:

> It will be observed that no uniform plan has been adopted for the county. Thus unilateral, bilateral and multilateral schools all find their place in the Plan . . . the Divisional Executives were charged with the task of surveying their respective areas . . . . In doing so they had regard to the circumstances affecting their areas, and this is particularly reflected in the proposals for secondary schools.[65]

Hence the suggestion that fourteen of Derbyshire's secondary schools be multilateral schools was based on "careful consideration both of geographical characteristics *of the division* and the optimum size for such communities" [present writer's emphasis].[66] Devon County explained the need for "more room" as follows: "There is plenty of scope for variety within the public system of education... . They have, therefore, considered the needs of each area on its own merits... which may be considerably different in nature and scope from the provision in a neighbouring area."[67] The London Development Plan issued a clear statement that apart from it being to the community's advantage to secure its own interests, it is in the City's interest that each of the divisions should decide on the best shape for its secondary education. This is because "it is impossible to generalise with accuracy about it as a whole ... . The essential feature of that plan is the division of London into community areas."[68] The issue raised by the London statement is that it is impossible to embrace all the necessary local details in planning any reform through the centre.

In fact, the LEAs' proposals were constructed and expressed according to the communities' needs and proposals. LEAs gave full freedom to the divisions in order to achieve quick and easy adjustment to the secondary education reform and avoid conflicts with their communities. For this reason they did not enforce their power to impose a central LEA policy or to implement the tripartite system as it was expected to be fulfilled by the Ministry of Education. This was not a question of ignoring the central policy; it was a result of the communities' interaction and involvement in the process of reforming secondary education according to their local needs and traditions. Thus the fragmentation of the system into Government policy, LEA policy and divisional needs carried the implementation of central government policy far from the original intention of the planners of the Act.

Drawing together of the main findings arising from the local authorities' demand for a greater degree of freedom and for more flexibility in deciding the future of secondary education, shows that the LEAs offered many reasons in support of their claims. The ministry's recognition of the need to plan according to local needs led to several variations, not only across the nation but within many of the LEAs. Some of the arguments were based on organisational and administrative problems, some on parents' rights, some on selection problems, some on the special needs of the community, and above all, on the fragmentation of decision making. In many cases combined arguments based on more than one factor made shaping the future of the education system a complex problem, which explains the variations that were proposed. The result was a move towards a different structure of secondary education which in many cases was a long way from the original scheme and the rigid structure of the tripartite system as defined by the ministry.

Joan Thompson (1947) analysed 54 Development Plans, further illuminating the distribution of schools and entrants according to the LEAs' proposals to the ministry.

Table 4.1: Distribution of schools and entrants

	Schools %	Entrants %
Grammar	17	12
Technical	7	6
Modern	54	41
Grammar + Technical	2	1.5
Technical + Modern	11	10
Grammar + Modern	1	1
Multilateral	10	26.5

Source: Thompson (1947), *Secondary Education For All*, 8.

Thompson mentions that the LEAs had shown a willingness to experiment, and "had not accepted the policy of segregation without misgiving,"[69] but she described those LEAs that accepted the policy of segregation between the grammar, modern and technical schools as still "relying on tradition." Further examination of the Development Plans of another random sample of 34 LEAs gives us more information about the combinations that those LEAs suggested in their proposals for the reorganisation of secondary education. It shows that the overwhelming majority of the authorities rejected a rigid tripartite system and suggested more flexible and varied types of a mixed system. The following table reveals the diversity of the counties' intentions in implementing the Act.

Table 4.2: Variations in counties' DPs for secondary education

Variation of DP	No of counties	in %
Tripartite only	7	20.6
Bilateral only	12	35.3
Comprehensive only	4	11.7
Tripartite + bilateral	1	2.9
Tripartite + comprehensive	5	14.7
Tripartite + comprehensive+bilateral	2	5.8
Bilateral + comprehensive	3	8.8
Total	34	99.9

Source: Thompson (1947), *Secondary Education For All*.

Table 2 shows the general tendency of the LEAs in their proposals, but it does not include the exceptions, for example some "pocket" areas with a single school of one type. The LEAs' proposals were for a pure system but a mixed one; and despite the overall choice in the case of each of them of a unilateral, bilateral, or comprehensive system, space had been left for other additional arrangements according to "local circumstances" and particular needs.

The provision that left room for local arrangements and special needs might explain the variety of suggestions not only at the national but also at the local education authority level. This situation is summarised in the words of the Bolton Development Plan:

> The Authority feel, therefore, that during the initial stages the new secondary schools proposed in the earlier years of the implementation of the Development Plan should be planned to permit of easy adjustment to single type, dual type or comprehensive schools and have decided to experiment with a series of "secondary school bases."[70]

Thus, the government policy of a tripartite system faced enormous obstacles to implementation by the LEAs, among them the special circumstances of rural areas, the effect of the War, the lack of staff, parents' wishes, selection problems, consideration of parity of status, and LEAs' commitment to protecting the interests of districts and communities. Together they worked in favour of a system based on continuity of tradition, previous administrative arrangements, and local needs, which were powerful enough to transform the structure of government plans for secondary education.

4.3: BLURRING THE UNIQUENESS OF THE GRAMMAR SCHOOLS

The tripartite system that was the main plank of the government's policy[71] for the reorganisation of secondary schools specified three types of school: modern, technical and grammar.

The modern school was aimed at the majority of the nation's children.

The name was given by the Hadow Committee in 1926 to what were then called "senior schools" or "central schools" under the Code of Regulations for Public Elementary Schools. The term "modern school" was suggested to apply to both "non-selective central schools" and "selective central schools" and was in both cases of a less academic type than the grammar schools. The pupils in these schools were about three-quarters of those who did not pass the special place examinations at the age of 11 but continued into senior elementary school in the same building in which they had started. The idea of the modern school was to establish a school free from the pressures of any external examination and based on the principle of using the "surroundings to make education alive and interesting, appealing to country boys and girls through their familiarity with nature and to town children through their own special interests."[72] The stimulation of the pupils' interests could be related to practical work and varying degrees of vocational bias, involving such studies as housecraft, handicraft, pre-nursing, catering, dressmaking, technical, agricultural and commercial studies as well as more formal and academic courses like history, geography and social structure in order to raise the pupils' standards of achievement.

The second type, the technology school, was developed from other schools such as junior technical schools, junior commercial schools and junior art school departments. The origin and the purpose of these forms of junior technology school were rooted in two main features: on the one hand, vocational courses of instruction lasting two or three years in subjects such as printing, dressmaking, laundry work, commerce and art which can prepare pupils for a variety of vocations (Spens Report, 1938), and on the other hand junior technical schools, based on the engineering and building courses and regarded as an alternative to the grammar schools and the few technical high schools that were respected as equal to grammar schools. The technical high schools provided a five-year course from the age of 11+, on the basis of selective examination at that age. The aim of expanding the technology schools was defined in Pamphlet No.1:[73]

> Its aim is not to produce little engineers or builders nicely adjusted to strict industrial requirements, but rather, through the interest created by a curriculum with broad relation to future careers, to

send out pupils equipped with a good general education that will stand them in good stead in whatever occupation they may enter.[74]

The third type, with a long tradition in English history, was the grammar school. The term grammar school had been in use since the 14th century and included endowed schools, provided schools and direct grant schools. The curriculum was designed to prepare pupils for advanced courses as candidates for study in universities or other institutions of higher education. Those children judged to be brighter and abler, who passed the 11+ examination, were transferred to secondary grammar schools and directed "primarily to the service of Church and State and to the professions."[75] These schools were highly regarded as having achieved remarkable success, and enjoyed the tradition of serving the country to the full in the past. They were still regarded as having a vital part to play in the future of the state, in fulfilling "the great national duty of educating the nation's most intellectually able children to the limit of their ability."[76] Therefore the grammar school became a symbol of success and was seen as essential in supplying the state with high grade professionals.

The tripartite system aimed to provide for both equal opportunity for secondary education on the one hand and the continuity of the traditional grammar school on the other. Some element of freedom was allowed, according to "local circumstances," the local authorities in experimenting with some multilateral schools, such as more scope for proposing bilateral schools, but the stipulation remained that the *curriculum for three different types of pupils* should be promised and provided. There were, however, three types of LEA proposals that posed some threat to the traditional grammar schools:

(1) The move on the part of some LEAs that accepted the tripartite system in principle but proposed higher proportions in grammar school places, beyond the 15% recommended by the ministry, because of local tradition with respect to the allocation of grammar school places;

(2) Increasing the percentage of the grammar school places by merging them with technical or modern schools;

(3) Blurring the uniqueness of the grammar school by suggesting an LEA system of multilateral schools.

When the Development Plans were sent to the ministry it became clear that some of the authorities had gone far beyond the Government's intention and that their proposals would endanger the achievement of *high standards by the brightest and most able of the nation's children.* The ministry saw this tendency as a threat to the future existence of grammar schools, which it wished to protect and maintain in view of the "future needs of professions such as teaching and medicine and of the need to provide recruits for higher managerial and administrative posts in commerce and industry."[77]

Brighton accepted the tripartite system but suggested a high proportion of places for children in grammar and technical schools; the ministerial response was an instruction to reduce this number in order not to "depress the standards."[78] Derbyshire, which preferred no uniform overall plan, explained its high proportion of grammar school places thus:

> It is necessary to remember that all but one of the eleven Grammar streams included in the Plan are in existence. It would therefore be unrealistic to suggest that any of the proposed Grammar streams at Buxton or Glossop should be eliminated.[79]

Derbyshire's case was simply one of continuing the existing proportion of the grammar school type of education. Cumberland had a similar experience, and brushed aside the ministry's recommended proportion, saying:

> The Authority does not accept anywhere the very common allocation of, say, 15% to Grammar Schools, 10% to Technical Schools and the rest to Modern Schools.... The Authority believes in the maintenance of the Grammar School, and in a constant raising of its intellectual and cultural level.[80]

This approach looked to past experience and powerful local traditions rather than the ministry's policy. It refers to:

> The striking development of Sixth Form work over the *past twenty years.* Where there are no serious fetters, it allocates about 20% of the year group to the Grammar Schools [present writer's emphasis].[81]

The bilateral schools that were mentioned by the ministry as an available policy choice according to local considerations constituted another threat to the existence of the traditional grammar schools. Leicestershire planned to accommodate 25%-30% of pupils in its existing grammar schools by a scheme of bilateral grammar/modern and grammar/technology schools. The reasoning behind this proposal was explained as follows:

> The secondary age groups for the most part are large enough to provide a variety of courses. They may indeed be described, in their present state, as bilateral, in that their pupils proceed, not only to the University and the professions, but to executive posts in industry and commerce, and to clerical posts of all kinds.[82]

This approach met with fear and criticism in the ministry, a reaction that will be explained presently. A similar proposal came to the ministry from Kent, whose Plan provided for turning three of the existing grammar schools into grammar/technical schools simply "because of the educational flexibility that such sites give."[83] Huntingdonshire suggested bilateral schools based on grammar and technical education for two main reasons:

> First that it is only in this way that the numbers necessary for proper school organisation and adequate staffing can be secured; and secondly that in an agricultural area such as this a general technical education . . . appears more appropriate.[84]

Gloucestershire's proposal for six bilateral schools and one multilateral school was aimed in particular at ensuring that schools had sufficient pupils to enable a really high standard of work to be achieved. "The Authority appreciate the need for ensuring that the staffing of these Schools allows for the provision of an adequate range of sixth form courses for the Grammar Schools. As these Schools are in rural areas, the Technical side will, in general, have a rural bias."[85] Berkshire, by comparison, preferred bilateral schools because:

> ...such schools may have some advantage in breaking down the rigid classification into "types" of secondary education ... . But it

was less than the most compelling geographical factors which led them to adoption of two types of curriculum in certain schools.[86]

The main motivation for Cheshire's decision to turn all grammar schools into bilateral schools was the difficulty in establishing a tripartite system based on the presupposition that children can be selected for technical, grammar or modern school at the age of 11. It was claimed that "the Authority does not support this supposition."[87] Because of the disadvantages of both multilateral and bilateral systems, the Authority preferred two types of secondary schools: "the Grammar School and the Modern School. In each type of School, Technical Courses will be provided."[88]

But a more real threat to the existence and status of the grammar schools was posed by the LEAs' proposals for multilateral schools. Here it was clearer than in the case of the bilateral schools, that a real blurring of the uniqueness and purpose of the traditional grammar schools could result.[89] Some authorities, including London, Bradford, Westmorland, Coventry and Birmingham, proposed a secondary system based mainly on comprehensive schools. Westmorland, for example, explained their proposal as follows:

> One effect of the Act has been to give a new meaning to the term "secondary education" which no longer means an academic type of education leading to School Certificate and Higher School Certificate, but now means the second stage of education for every child ... and the question arises whether it is better to provide the different courses in separate schools or under the one school organisation.[90]

Derbyshire's proposal for 14 multilateral schools included a promise to safeguard the academic courses: "It is certainly the intention that full technical and academic courses should be available at all the schools."[91]

Once the LEAs had submitted their Development Plans, each Plan was examined by the ministry's officials and by HM Inspectors before being granted the minister's approval. There were two types of ministerial approval: those authorities that followed wholly or largely the ministry's guidance on the tripartite system and the continued existence of the traditional grammar schools received quick approval, whereas for those authorities whose interpretation of the Act and "local circumstances" carried their proposals away from the ministry's intention and threatened the grammar schools in particular, discussions went on in some cases for years before Ministerial approval was given.[92] The following section concentrates on the government point of view and its responses in defence of the grammar schools.

4.4: THE GOVERNMENT'S DEFENCE OF THE GRAMMAR SCHOOLS

The Ministry of Education had to face three main problems with regard to the submission of the LEAs' Development Plans:
1. The proposal of some LEAs, while basing their plans on the standard tripartite system, to offer a high proportion of places in the grammar schools.
2. The pseudo-bilateral schools which from the minister's point of view were seen as simply a manoeuvre to increase the number of grammar school places.
3. The replacement of grammar schools by multilateral schools with the aim of gaining the prestige and status of the grammar schools for all three types of children instead of only 15% of them.

In tackling these three problems the minister aimed above all to defer any proposal which would reduce the importance and distinction of the traditional grammar school and to preserve, for the same reason, a strict definition of the tripartite system. The minister's intervention involved him in a vast area of detail and numerous questions of implementation in the attempt to specify the organisational reform not only in the LEAs in general, but on the level of every single school. For example, Oxfordshire received a letter in June 1949 on the minister's direction in response to the Authority's provision of grammar school places for 25-27 percent of the age group:

> It is suggested that there could with advantage be some reduction in the amount of the provision for education of the grammar school kind, estimated by the Authority as 18% of the total

secondary provision. I am to ask that the Authority will consider, in particular, whether the Banbury County Grammar School would not be big enough if it were 2 form entry instead of 3 form entry.[93]

For the same reason, the minister asked the Authority not to open a new grammar school at Kidlington. Brighton was asked by the minister in a letter of March 1948 to reduce the number of places in both grammar and technical schools:

> 33.3% will be in schools of Grammar and Technical type. This is a somewhat higher proportion than would normally be expected …. Over-provision of Grammar and Technical places would carry with it the danger of depressing the standards.[94]

Birkenhead's proposal for bilateral grammar/technology schools aroused the suspicions of ministry officials: "15 streams of academic provision are thus balanced against 6 streams of technical provision. I am to enquire whether the Authority are satisfied, on re-consideration, that there should be excess of Grammar over Technical provision."[95] The ministry's letters make it clear that its main concern was to safeguard the grammar schools' quality, with the technical schools being only a second priority for the ministry's priorities. A subsidiary priority was given to the modern schools in the interests of the grammar schools by pushing authorities to extend the modern places in order to reduce the number of pupils in grammar school. A minute on the Cumberland Development Plan noted:

> On the basic age group of 340 + 10 per cent = 374, Secondary Modern requirement is 1404 places and provision is made for 1350 places. Is this sufficient?[96]

The suspicions about Cumberland's plan to introduce pseudo-bilateral schools went further:

> The Secondary Grammar/Technical is 468 places and 450 are being provided in Grammar School which, it is proposed, shall be for 500. Do you consider it better that the new Grammar school

should be a full 4-form entry school? It might then be possible to introduce technical provision – no technical provision is mentioned at all, but *Grammar provision seems over generous at 30 per cent* [present writer's emphasis].[97]

Leicestershire faced a similar response, its proposal for bilateral grammar/technology and grammar/modern schools provoking an anxious reaction from the ministry, fearful of a lack of balance between grammar and the technical provision.

An internal minute about Gloucestershire's DP makes the Ministry's view of the grammar school clear:

> In framing the Secondary Education proposal... of Gloucestershire to provide for the three types in the proportion Modern 6: Grammar 1: Tech. 1, giving percentage figures of 75 : 12.5 : 12.5 .... I do not consider that we should ask the County to increase the 14% Grammar provision, for I regard the figure of 12.5% as too high if the quality of Grammar School academic training is to show any marked improvement under the new conditions of the 1944 Act.... The only hope for the Grammar School of the future is that it must limit its entry closely to those mentally able to profit from the book study technique. Gloucestershire in the past has packed her Secondary Grammar Schools with large numbers and sacrificed quality of instruction and result in the hopeless task of attempting to carry children of the wrong mental type to impossible bookish levels, and in my opinion Gloucestershire has less than the normal percentage of children mentally fitted to face a course of study that is examination controlled. *The County needs not more Grammar Schools of mediocre quality but fewer and finer*, and these too with a clearer conception of the higher standard of attainment that is intended in the Grammar Schools of the 1944 Act [present writer's emphasis].[98]

Gloucestershire's attempt to increase the number of pupils that would enjoy the status and the public esteem of the grammar schools by proposing to merge them in bilateral schools based on two streams of grammar and technical studies met with ministerial resistance:

> He [the Minister] would suggest, for instance, that it will not be possible, in the small Grammar-Technical schools proposed at Thornbury, Coleford, Wootton-under-Edge, Durseley . . . to develop Secondary Technical work of high standard which he has in mind in using that term, and *that to attempt to do so would indeed be likely to affect adversely the education of the Grammar type in them* [present writer's emphasis].[99]

An interview memorandum with Cheshire Local Education Authority stated with respect to the same issue that:

> On the question of Grammar-Technical schools we must go carefully. At the interview in April last we were highly critical of the Authority's intention to base their selective provision on this type of school and tried to persuade them at least to have some separate Technical schools. This they have not done.[100]

Further analysis of the ministry's responses reveals a similar attitude toward the tendency of other LEAs to increase the percentage in grammar schools. The Ministry was strongly in favour of preserving the past achievements of the grammar schools in the future by blocking any authority's attempt to break the set proportion of places laid down by the ministry.

The ministry was likewise determined to block the widespread introduction of multilateral schools because their establishment implied the closure of grammar schools. Twenty-six out of 146 local authorities included such schools in their Development Plans.[101] Despite the fact that multilateral schools formed part of the ministry's policy, restrictions were published (Circular 144) that affected schools in rural areas in particular. The minimum size for these schools was defined as 10-11 form entry (1500-1700 places), providing two grammar, two technical and six or seven modern streams. But in sparsely populated rural areas it was impossible to fulfil these requirements. Nevertheless some experiments were allowed in cases where they would not threaten the grammar schools' existence. In cases where they were seen as a real threat, the response was as in the case of Bradford, when Florence Horsburgh, the Minister of Education, sent the following letter:

> The Minister suggests that in preparing such proposals the Authority should not regard themselves as committed to a comprehensive organisation of secondary education except on an experimental basis and should not expect her to approve such proposals on any other assumption.[102]

Lincolnshire met an impatient response typical of the atmosphere of that time when it proposed a multilateral school of six form entry in Barton-on-Humber: "We don't, as you know, like multilateral and the Authority will have to think again."[103]

Thus, all the types of school development mentioned in the ministry's publications since the White Paper threatened to erode the position of the traditional grammar school by extending the percentage to more than 15% of the existing grammar schools, and in proposing pseudo-bilateral and multilateral schools. The LEAs' inclination to make the prestige and esteem of the grammar school accessible to more children by extending this type of provision was not a new policy. Before the 1944 Act, the proportion of grammar school places in many of the LEAs was far above 15%, reaching up to about 25%; what to them was simply a continuation of their policy and local tradition came across as an attack on the traditional schools to the government.[104] The ministry, on the other hand, was determined to baulk this trend and to protect what the Government saw as the grammar schools' "remarkable success in establishing worthy traditions and sound standards of scholarship which is essential to retain."[105] It achieved this by using ministerial power to approve or reject the authorities' Development Plans, particularly in those cases where grammar schools were under attack.

Both sides, the Ministry of Education and the LEAs, recognised the importance of retaining the atmosphere of optimism and co-operation despite disagreements, disputes and the government's demands for reconsideration or review of some parts of the Development Plans. Consensus and compromise were needed to maintain the momentum of the Act, for the local authorities as well as for the Ministry of Education; neither side wanted to spend years on worthless quarrels. The following paragraph in the minister's letter to the Manchester authority reveals the atmosphere that prevailed:

> The Minister respects the motives which have led the Authority to propose this solution to one, or even some, of the problems affecting the organisation and administration of provision of the Secondary type, which he agrees present problems the solution of which cannot in every case be foreseen at present, but he asks the Authority with all seriousness and earnestness that it may be reconsidered.[106]

A letter to Derbyshire from the Ministry of Education stated:

> The Secondary proposals here are, of course, among the most controversial matters in the Plan, and much thought has been given to them in the Ministry, and by HM Inspectors. They are bold and enterprising, and the Minister appreciates the motives which have inspired them … . The last thing which the Minister wishes to do is to discourage experiment. He would welcome the setting up of one or two Multilateral schools of sufficient size to guarantee the provision of alternative courses in Technical and Grammar streams.[107]

Similarly, Westmorland's letter to the ministry could be considered a typical answer seeking as it does a compromise that would win ministerial approval for their Plan:

> The Authority has given very close attention to the suggestion contained in the Ministry's letter of the 21st November 1947, and especially to the last paragraph of the letter, in which were suggested certain changes in the grammar school provision in the County.[108]

Oxfordshire wrote a similar letter to the ministry:

> The Authority have taken note of the Minister's opinion of secondary schools of Grammar type and have decided to reduce the size of Banbury County Grammar School from three streams to two and to omit for the time being the proposal for a Grammar School at Kidlington.[109]

After years of discussions within the local authorities, divisional authorities and the Ministry of Education, the minister eventually approved the Plans of 146 LEAs. Most of the LEAs now applied themselves to the implementation of the Act according to the terms of the ministerial approval; in a few cases, deviation from the originally approved DP was soon discovered by the ministry. But implementation of the Act after ministerial approval raised new conflicts and disputes, for two main reasons: in the first place the enormous amount of money needed for the implementation of the Act led to Treasury demands for a change in education policy; and secondly bitter conflicts arose among interest groups and political parties within the authorities. Long delays in executing the secondary reorganisation resulted; having achieved ministerial approval after years of discussions, the LEAs were only at the beginning of a long and more complex period of secondary education reform and the continued erosion of the tripartite order.

4.5: CONCLUSIONS

The interaction of the community and divisions at the local level soon prevailed over the Ministry of Education's ambitions to dictate a central order based on rigid allocation of pupils to three different types of schools.

The principles held up by government for defining the exact percentage of each of the school types on the one hand, and allowing consideration of "local circumstances" and local needs in planning the secondary reform on the other, was an attempt to establish uniform order based on different and contradictory principles. Taking local "circumstances" into account was an invitation to raise enormous intervention factors in LEAs and in each authority and division, which blurred and neutralised government definition and order. With each additional interaction, deviation from the allocation proportion determined by the government also increased. The government principle whereby sub-systems within any LEA were allowed to express the needs, according to their own perception of tradition, needs and interests, had a direct effect on increasing disorder and departure from the central order. Thus, parents were given grounds to express their wishes, rural areas raised economic factors, local authorities that had suffered during the War raised their own views, there was acknowledgement of the necessity to maintain the interests of small authorities and divisions, and the involvement of local officials and professionals in the preparation of the Reform. All these were additional forces in the construction of plans that deviated from the government reference-point and initial points of erosion, blurring, and distortion of the government view of secondary reform.

The departure from the tripartite system was not due to disregard of the actual principle of the tripartite system, but was instead the result of power given to the local authorities, divisions (communities) and parents to express their will in the shaping of secondary education. Moreover, secondary education was not virgin ground: the proportion of grammar school places in each authority's area was well defined in local tradition, and it was a naive illusion to think that this could be changed simply to accord with a new ministry requirement of a fixed proportion between the three types of schools.

Attempts by local authorities to ignore or resist the fixed proportions recommended by the Ministry of Education met with equal resistance from a ministry keen to secure the respected traditional grammar school and to fulfil the national duty of educating the nation's most intellectually able children by using its power to approve or reject the local Plans.

The administrative direction was another source of deviation from the initial estimation and the overall cost in implementing the 1944 Education Act. The fact that capital expenditure was greater than the sum estimated in 1943 was due to a definition of minimum standards that gave way to enthusiasm, initiative, imagination and ambition to guide the Development Plan on the one hand and the fact that local education authorities themselves raised, in Horsburgh's words, a "substantial part of the money that they spend."[110] This last fact itself raised control difficulties for the government in ordering a policy of restraint over education spending when inflation pressures hit the economy (see Chapter 7).

Thus tension arose between local needs, circumstances, concepts and traditions on the one hand and the government's aims and concept of how to shape the future of secondary education on the other. Further observation of the process at local level will give us more information about the factors at stake and the development of the system.

Notes:
1. Ministry of Education (1944). *Draft Building Regulations*, Circular 10, 1.
2. In public elementary schools the standard class size had been 50 pupils for juniors and infants and 40 for seniors.
3. These principles were not regulations but included in a "Handbook of Suggestions" (Ministry of Education (1944), Circular 10).
4. Ibid., 3. A very large school would have 1600-1700 pupils.
5. Ibid., 7.
6. Ministry of Education (1946). *Report of the Committee on School Sites and Building Procedures*. London, 2.
7. The total amount of additional expenditure proposed to Parliament by the Board of Education in 1943 for implementation of the Act was £67.4 million over seven years. (Board of Education (1943), *Educational Reconstruction*, 35).
8. PRO ed. 136/889. A letter of 6.2.53.
9. There are two other possible reasons that would explain the differences in the early estimation: (a) the minister defined the standards and building regulations with no reference to the estimated costs submitted to and approved by Parliament; (b) the LEAs were asked to make their surveys and to estimate the total cost of their development plans in relation to the building regulations and the guidelines on educational principles, in isolation from the projected cost of the Act in 1943.
10. Board of Education (1943), London, 6.
11. Board of Education (1938). *Report of the Consultative Committee on Secondary Education*, London, 357.
12. Ibid., 357.
13. Report of the Committees of the Secondary Examination Council Curriculum and Examinations in Secondary Schools (the Norwood Report), 1943, 10.
14. Ministry of Education (1945). *The Nation's Schools: Their Plan and Purpose*, London, 12.
15. Ibid., 13.
16. Ibid., 14.
17. Ibid., 16.
18. Ibid., 19.
19. Ibid., 21
20. Further discussion of the three types of schools appears later in this chapter.
21. Ministry of Education (1945), Circular 73.
22. Board of Education (1943), 10.
23. Ministry of Education (1945). *The Nation's Schools*, 22.
24. Ibid., 24.
25. Circular 73, December, 1945.
26. At that stage Circular 73 defined the technical conditions for ministerial approval of bilateral and multilateral schools. For example: (a) the school's premises must be adequate for its various purposes; (b) the school must be staffed and equipped to provide suitable alternative courses; (c) large schools must be designed to be capable of effective

separation into smaller units. But the ministry's main reservation on the development of multilateral schools would be its desire to keep and maintain the traditional grammar school.
27. PRO ed. 152/130: Oxfordshire. DP, 6.
28. These schools were defined as "secondary modern" schools in the 1944 Education Act.
29. PRO ed. 152/213: Birkenhead. DP, 8.
30. PRO ed. 152/173: Westmorland. DP, 1.
31. Education Act 1944, 11(2)(h).
32. This was one of the reasons for the deviation from the original estimates as to the extra cost of the Act, which caused financial problems during the 1950s. This will be explained in Chapter 7. The other reason was that the central government estimate was made before the LEAs finished their survey. The results of this survey show a huge gap between the early estimates and the real needs that were dictated by minimum standards and the new building regulations.
33. PRO ed. 152/235: Bradford. DP, 5.
34. PRO ed. 152/229: Bolton. DP, 9.
35. PRO ed. 152/107: London. DP, 12.
36. PRO ed. 152/105. Report of the Education Committee to London County Council, July 1944, 4.
37. PRO ed. 152/130. DP, 8.
38. Ibid.
39. PRO ed. 152/110. Letter from Middlesex County Council Education Committee to the Education Development Subcommittee, 9 November 1945.
40. Ibid.
41. PRO ed. 152/61: Huntingdonshire. DP, 2.
42. Ibid., 4.
43. PRO ed. 152/173. In addition to this argument the figures had shown that 44 schools had under 30 children, and that many of the small villages were located in isolated environments.
44. PRO ed. 152/130. DP, 7.
45. PRO ed. 152/21: Cumberland. DP, 3.
46. PRO ed. 152/74: Kent. DP, 1.
47. Ibid.
48. PRO ed. 152/260: Coventry. DP, 1.
49. PRO ed. 152/110: Middlesex County Council, letter of November 1945.
50. Ibid.
51. Education Act 1944, Section 76.
52. PRO ed. 152/110. DP, 150.
53. Ibid.
54. PRO ed. 152/208: Barrow-in-Furness. DP, 20-1.
55. PRO ed. 152/213. DP, 8.
56. PRO ed. 152/13: Cheshire. DP, 3.

57. PRO ed. 152/91: Leicestershire. DP, 3.
58. PRO ed. 152/50: Hampshire. DP, 22.
59. PRO ed. 152/208. DP, 22.
60. Ministry of Education (1944), Circular 5, 3.
61. Ibid.
62. Ibid., 7.
63. Ibid
64. PRO ed. 152/61. DP, 2.
65. PRO ed. 152/24: Derbyshire. DP, 1.
66. Ibid.
67. PRO ed. 152/28: Devon. DP, 3.
68. PRO ed. 152/107.
69. Joan Thompson (1947). *Secondary Education for All*, London (Fabian Publications), 9.
70. PRO ed. 152/229.
71. As already explained, the Ministry allowed combinations of types of secondary school under special circumstances; this will be discussed in the next chapter.
72. Ministry of Education (1945). *The Nation's Schools*, 21.
73. Ibid., p.17.
74. The reader may raise the pertinent question: What is the dividing line between the modern school and the technology school according to ministry definitions? It is clear that there is some similarity between the two types of school. While the aim of the technology school was defined as "to send out pupils equipped with a good general education… in whatever occupation they may enter," the modern school aimed to raise their standards of attainment through general education. Moreover, the modern schools included vocational courses which were a basic feature of the technology schools. This similarity raised some problems in the definition of the technology schools and led to their merging with modern schools in some of the authorities.
75. Ministry of Education (1945). *The Nation's Schools*, 14.
76. PRO ed. 147/206.
77. Ministry of Education, Circular 73, 2.
78. PRO ed. 152/238: Brighton. Letter from the minister to the local authority, 10 March 1948.
79. PRO ed. 152/24. Notes of meeting of 24 July 1947.
80. PRO ed. 152/21. DP, 2-3.
81. Ibid.
82. PRO ed. 152/91. DP, 3.
83. PRO ed. 152/74. DP, 2.
84. PRO ed. 152/61.
85. PRO ed. 152/47: Gloucestershire. This proposal met with a keen and much-criticised response from ministry officials, which will be elaborated upon later.
86. PRO ed. 152/4: Berkshire.
87. PRO ed. 152/13.

88. Ibid.
89. At that stage the difference between multilateral and comprehensive schools was not clear to many of the authorities. Circular 144, published in 1947, aimed to clarify this confusion with the multilateral school being defined as "one which is intended to cater for all the secondary education of all the children in a given area and includes all three elements in clearly defined sides." Comprehensive "means [a school] which is intended to cater for all the secondary education of all the children in a given area without an organisation in three sides" (Ministry of Education (1947), Circular 144, June, 1-2).
90. PRO ed. 152/173. DP, 7.
91. PRO ed. 152/24. DP, 2.
92. Some authorities only received approval for their Development Plan after six or even seven years.
93. PRO ed. 152/130. A letter signed by V. Forman to the Local Education Authority.
94. PRO ed. 152/238. A letter directed by the minister to Brighton on 10 March 1948.
95. PRO ed. 152/213. A draft letter sent by the minister to the Local Authority.
96. PRO ed. 152/21. Minute sheet reference p/57wp/4.
97. Ibid.
98. PRO ed. 152/47. Minutes from 3 March 1948.
99. Ibid. Letter from the minister to the LEA on 27 November 1948.
100. PRO ed. 152/13. Interview memorandum of 8 April 1948.
101. PRO ed. 147/206.
102. PRO ed. 152/235. Letter from the Minister to Bradford of 30 April 1952.
103. PRO ed. 152/102: Lincolnshire: Lindsey. Interview memorandum of 19 May 1948.
104. The variations in different areas according to local traditions and circumstances is clearly demonstrated by the fact that in 1952, 9.3% were in grammar schools in Gateshead, 21.% in Lancashire, 32.4% in Cardiff, 15.1% in Birmingham, 26.3% in Shropshire and 48.4% in Cardiganshire (PRO ed. 147/206).
105. Ibid., 14.
106. PRO ed. 152/328: Manchester.
107. PRO ed. 152/24.
108. PRO ed. 152/173. Letter from E.L. Clarke to the Secretary of the Ministry of Education on 29 April 1949.
109. PRO ed. 152/130. Letter from Oxfordshire Education Committee to the Ministry of Education.
110. PRO ed. 136/889.

• CHAPTER 5

THE LEAs FACE FURTHER COMPLEXITY: INTERACTION BETWEEN SUB-GROUPS

After the LEAs had attained Ministry of Education approval for their Development Plans, they encountered a new set of problems in the shape of resistance from groups – made up of parents, teachers, local politicians and parties – that had become involved in the reform.

It soon became apparent that the years of discussion had only been the beginning, although no one could have foreseen that secondary school reform would require more extensive discussions with interest groups before it could be put into action. Hindsight reveals that the discussions with the Ministry of Education were the soft side of the process, while bitterer and tougher disputes occurred between the local authorities and local sub-groups that became involved in the process after ministerial approval was received. Such involvement delayed or paralysed the implementation of secondary reform for twenty or even thirty years.

The aim of this chapter is to identify the factors that delayed and paralysed the reform, and the principal motives of the major groups that opposed implementation of the LEAs' plans according to the *proposals that had been approved by the minister*. The decision making process pertaining to the reform of secondary education has been described often (Brown, 1978; Fenwick,

1967; Ribbins, 1985; Ribbins & Brown, 1979; Saran, 1973), and the present chapter therefore makes no attempt to introduce a new explanation. Instead it offers observations on various aspects of the complexity of the decision making as it was affected by the perceptions, needs and interests of groups. Brown puts it thus: What was significant to the participants? What were their main objectives? What were their wishes, motives and the factors that raised such confusion? Why did the implementation of the secondary education reform become impossible for so many years? Why, after the ministry had approved the LEAs' proposals, was the decision making mechanism immobilised?

Analysis of case studies can help provide answers to these questions.[1] Particular attention will be paid to interest groups such as parents, teachers and headteachers on the one hand, and local politicians and political parties on the other. The case studies differ in length, depth, detail and period. Moreover, the overwhelming majority of the studies deal with the political and administrative aspects of decision making while the focus of this section is primarily on the motivational, social-psychological and sociological, as well as administrative aspects, of these questions. Analysis of several local case studies and even the process of reforming individual schools will shed some light on the disturbance between centre and periphery in the implementation of secondary reform.[2]

5.1: PARENTAL CONCERNS WITH STATUS

Analysis of the case studies shows two main identifiable strands of parental resistance to the local plan: those parents who wanted to protect their children's existing places in the grammar school, and those parents who wanted to evade the inferior status of the modern school and send their children to a more prestigious school. The common aim of these two groups was the pursuit of status and esteem.

According to Rene Saran, when Middlesex set out to establish the three comprehensive schools that had been approved by the minister, it encountered two main parental responses. The first was opposition from those who believed that they would lose status by sending their children to a comprehensive school instead of a grammar school; the second was approval from those who believed that through reorganisation into comprehensive schools they had the opportunity to improve their status, particularly in areas where there was no grammar school and the modern school was the only option.

> The plan to establish the first comprehensive school in Middlesex was abolished as a result of parental opposition, despite the fact that it had been approved on three levels: by the Minister, the LEA, and the local division committees. The parents' main argument was that until then children who passed the 11+ examinations "were given the choice between comprehensive and grammar school,"[3] while now they would lose their right to choose between schools. Saran claims that the main element of their opposition was "that Keats Grammar School – the only one in this area and one of which local residents were *proud – was threatened*" [present writer's emphasis].[4]

Parents claimed that the grammar school was "their" school and "they were not going to have it merged with 'those gypsies' at the secondary modern the other side of the railway."[5] Although hundreds of residents had signed a petition against the scheme to abolish the grammar school and replace it with a comprehensive school, the LEA was forced to drop the plan in order to secure the continuity of the Keats grammar school.

Contrarily, the second Middlesex proposal according to which Blake Secondary Modern School would become a comprehensive school was welcomed by parents. Saran explains that there was no grammar school in this area and parents had to choose between sending their qualified children to the nearest grammar school five miles away and keeping them in a modern school; therefore the parents supported the move partly because "the area hoped to gain academic opportunities for its children within the comprehensive school."[6] However, when it become known that the authority intended to abolish the 11+ tests and to transfer all the children to the new comprehensive school, parental opposition was not directed at the comprehensive school itself but at compulsory attendance of that school. The feeling was that the comprehensive system would hold bright children back. A new organisation called the Parents' Educational Rights Association published a new letter which claimed "that in the event of parents moving to another district, there would be no certainty of scholastic status."[7]

Despite continuing support for the comprehensive school from local parents, Blake became a bilateral school with a modern/technical curriculum mainly because of middle class parents' "fierce local protests" and because they "eagerly sought grammar school places for their children."[8] Only the third proposal for a comprehensive school, that pertaining to the Eliot School, was put into effect. Until 1954 the school was a magnet for those who had "failed" to obtain a place at a grammar school in the neighbouring area. However, in the years 1954-8 a decision was made to restrict admissions from adjacent areas to qualified pupils that opted for Eliot comprehensive school instead of a grammar school. The support and esteem that Eliot gradually gained resulted in greater demand for places in this school: 6% opted for the school as first choice in 1953, while 27% chose it in 1958.

The three Middlesex cases illustrate parental desire to obtain better educational status for their children. When the comprehensive school appeared to offer higher status in the eyes of those parents who had previously sent their children to modern school, it enjoyed massive support, while among those parents whose children passed the 11+ examination and had the right to attend grammar school, vigorous opposition and resistance to the comprehensive school was raised in order to defend this status. Saran came to the conclusion that the main reason for these parents' attempts to defend the selective system was that "the comprehensive idea was new and that grammar school was accorded a high status in the eyes of parents and teachers."[9]

We can further observe parental concerns in the case of Eastshire and Birkenhead during the 1960s. In Birkenhead, Catholic parents attacked the Authority for its acquiescence to the policy "of placing Catholic children in Catholic secondary modern schools, rather than in County grammar schools."[10] In the case of Brownborough (David, 1977) parental pressure forced the Authority to abandon zoning after 89 appeals from parents who preferred the grammar school to the modern school. Reynold & Sullivan (1987) refer to the grammar school's significance for the parents in Treliw, mentioning that the modern school was of low status and low resources while "the grammar school was held in high esteem as the avenue of social mobility for working class boys and girls."[11] For this reason,

> Many local politicians, pressured by the more activist parents of grammar school pupils, actually did not want to see the grammar schools destroyed, even if the comprehensives were to be grammar schools for all.[12]

Any attempt to change the status of the grammar school by merging it with another type of school encountered vigorous parental opposition that made use of diverse means, including appeals to the court, in order to avoid compromising their status or that of their children. By contrast, parents of lower status supported the changes and reform, provided the new school would enable them to achieve higher status and prestige. In the case of West Riding, Gosden (1978) explains the modern school parents' fight for status during the 1950s, from the point of view of the Chief Education Officer:

> Parental determination to avoid the modern schools was increasing every year, was "almost frantic" . . . and, until they could view the modern schools in a similar light, they would continue the pressure to get their children into the grammar schools.[13]

Parents of modern school pupils seeking to gain higher status were not only in favour of merger with a more prestigious type of school but also against any suggestion of merger with a school of lower status. Philip (1980) mentions that certain parents of modern school pupils in Birmingham resisted reorganisation because their schools "were programmed for integration with notoriously tough schools."[14] Parkinson concludes that in the four cases he examined, parents' groups at particular schools became active "in terms of self-interest rather than from any concern with the general pattern of policy."[15]

Thus far we have identified two main groups of parental response to the secondary reform; those who resisted any change in order to protect their existing status, and those who supported the changes provided that they would thereby gain higher prestige and status. Many of the researchers concur with this view as reflected in the following main statements: (1) as a group the parents played only a subordinate role in the reform (Fenwick, 1967; Jennings, 1977; Kesternard, 1970; Parkinson, 1973; Philip, 1980); and (2) LEAs had no power to compel parents to send their children to a comprehensive school without offering an alternative choice (David, 1977; Fenwick, 1967; Saran, 1973). These two statements may explain the reasons for the nature and complexity of the interference that LEAs encountered in their attempts to lead the reform. Parents did not play a major part in consultation and discussion regarding the reform, but they had the power to ignore and resist any suggestion that in their view harmed their status and threatened to reduce their prestige. Further analysis of the role of the teachers will give us a deeper understanding of the LEAs' difficulties in implementing the secondary reform.

5.2: TEACHERS' STATUS

The teachers' response to reorganisation was much more complicated. The reform threatened four aspects of their status: salary, recognition, qualifications and prestige.[16] On all four counts teachers stood to lose; consequently most of the suggestions that were raised by the local authority lacked credibility among the teachers, who banded together and in most cases resisted the proposals.

The first aspect, salary, was the least complicated. One of the effects of the reform was the amalgamation of schools, and hence the main concern was the loss of posts, particularly heads, deputies and special benefits for those who taught in the sixth form. Particular objection to the scheme came from the Joint Four, i.e. the (principally) grammar school union. Kesternard (1970) describes the Joint Four response, in the case of Birmingham, as "violently opposed to any scheme which may cause this advantage to be lost."[17] Only when the Birmingham Education Authority guaranteed that "salary and status would not suffer"[18] as a result of the reorganisation and introduction of comprehensive schools, was the pressure in this respect eased. Middlesex and Brownborough came to the same conclusion that the first step in reducing pressure from teachers and unions had to be to recognise the need for salary protection (David, 1977; Saran, 1973).

The second aspect of the teachers' status was recognition. Officially it was acknowledged that the classroom was the real battlefield of the education system and that the teachers were on the front lines of this battle. This recognition, however, was soon revealed as mere lip service when the teachers were the last to be informed of the reorganisation that would affect them so closely. In many cases they only learned about changes in their own school through the local media, which underscored their sense of being disregarded by the education system. The minister had directed the LEAs, according to the 1944 Education Act, to give notice to any managers or governors of voluntary schools affected by the plan, but they were not required to give the same notice to governors of maintained schools.[19] In reality, in all the cases that were examined, the teachers did not participate in the early discussions but only those that took place after the publication of the plan. The feeling of being scorned and humiliated was eloquently expressed by Keats Grammar School teachers in the following letter:

> We, the undersigned... wish to record our unanimous protest against the fact that the first official information received by Head or Staff of the contemplated change in the character of this School was the summary notice of dismissal sent to the Headmaster. This was received by him without previous consultation of any kind, and despite his 21 years as Head of school and 36 years in the service of the Education Committee.[20]

A similar feeling was described by Hewiston in the case of Doncaster:

> It did great harm, coming as a particularly nasty jolt to the teachers of the City, who felt justifiably annoyed that their first intimation of a decision which affected them so closely should come through the letter-box with the evening papers.[21]

Parkinson (1973), in the case of Liverpool, Batley (1970), in the case of Gateshead, and David (1977), in the cases of Brownborough and Eastshire, describe similar situations wherein teachers felt they had been disregarded and their place on the front line of the education system not been recognised, despite the fact that they were the ones who had to cope with day-to-day teaching problems and educational principles. The following further illustrates this feeling:

> The present pattern of negotiation under which a scheme is put up in a fair amount of detail without any teacher participation in the early stages of its formulation is not the happiest of arrangements. Teachers' organisations then find themselves in the position of having to "knock it down" to secure acceptance of fundamental educational principles.[22]

The third aspect of teachers' status concerned qualifications, and their fear of losing what they knew best – their teaching expertise. Movement towards a mixed system that included pupils of all types within the comprehensive school, and the idea that teachers qualified for and accustomed to teaching in a specific type of school would teach another kind of pupil in the same school, threatened both the grammar and the modern teachers. Their confidence rested mainly on their qualifications in teaching a specific type of pupil a specific curriculum within a specific type of school culture, and this qualification constituted their power; but now, no one could guarantee that each teacher would continue to teach the same type of pupil the same curriculum in the same way within the same school. This was a source of anxiety for teachers, who experienced a loss of confidence in their professional abilities and a powerlessness in coping with the new situation; consequently, they resisted the changes. Woodward describes the teachers' stress over the new situation as follows:

> The existing grammar school staff were really the problem. I felt it desirable to reassure them that they would not be taken away from the kind of work with grammar stream pupils which they knew how to do, and for which their qualification and experience suited them.[23]

A similar argument is mentioned by Saran in the case of Middlesex, where "grammar school teachers were concerned to preserve the grammar schools and in the particular the type of teaching to which they were accustomed."[24] Batley (1970) found that the younger teachers in the grammar schools tended to be less opposed to the idea of reorganisation while "the older grammar school teachers probably had their opposition moderated by the fact they were relatively secure in their positions . . . and unlikely to wish to prejudice them."[25] This disadvantageous aspect of the changes was also expressed by the teachers of the modern schools; in the case of Doncaster as follows:

> The existing secondary modern schools had now acquired the courses, techniques, activities and teaching staff to give these children suitable instruction of a practical nature. But with reorganisation the courses and specialist staffs of these schools would be split up.[26]

The teachers asked to retain their independence in order not to lose what each of them knew best:

> Full "comprehension" was not possible for twenty or thirty years, and... meantime two things were essential. One was to bind together the secondary modern schools and the grammar schools into a comprehensive cocoon from which they could not escape; the other was to see that they retained sufficient independence to continue doing what each was best suited to doing until they could be united in one big purpose-built comprehensive school.[27]

The teachers' status issue became real, according to David (1977), when the distribution of teachers required more non-specialists for the junior schools in Brownborough while the "problem of status for teachers was ignored."[28] The multilateral plan provoked a strong reaction among the teachers and they "were very angry and worried about their personal prospect," while "the officer managed to avoid making explicit the issue of teacher status."[29] The feeling of powerlessness and the teachers' fear that from now they would have to cope with unknown situations, new types of pupils and new methods, led to fears that they were losing their specific qualifications and position and, as a result, their prestige. This anxiety caused teachers to resist the changes.

The fourth aspect of the teachers' status was prestige. As with the parents, this area manifested two main strands of reaction: from those whom the changes affected by reducing their school's prestige, and from those who were expected to gain higher prestige by amalgamating with schools that were more highly regarded.

> Saran (1973) describes the teachers in Middlesex's response to the suggestion that a grammar school be merged with a modern school in order to establish a comprehensive school. The modern school teachers were not against the idea of merging with the grammar school but were concerned about personal details such as the fate of their headteacher and the inconvenience of transfer. The grammar school teachers' concern was the threat of losing the grammar school's reputation and the "particular type of teaching to which they were accustomed."[30] Moreover, one of the grammar school headteachers who took part in a discussion about Keats Grammar School claimed that "the clever child would be handicapped in a comprehensive school and the other children would not reap any genuine advantage.[31]

In the eyes of this headteacher, the Council decision amounted to the decree: "If all the children could not be swans they should all be geese."[32]

The struggle to defend the status and prestige of the grammar school was described by the headteacher of Tetbury Grammar School in Gloucestershire. In 1946 he was informed that his grammar school, which was founded in 1610 and had a distinguished record, was slated to become a modern school. In order to save the school's long tradition and its high public esteem, he took the initiative and drew up a proposal for a multilateral secondary school. He explained the idea in a letter addressed to the parents of the grammar school pupils:

> We are adding a secondary Modern stream on to the already existing Grammar School. It will be one school with two streams or courses of work – not two separate schools.[33]

The headteacher's initiative was designed to minimise the harm to the school's reputation and the teachers' prestige. After a struggle with the Ministry of Education and the Local Education Authority that lasted five years, approval was granted for a bilateral school. The teachers' prestige was affected, but not to the extent implied by the initial proposal with its suggested modern school.

The grammar school teachers in Darlington opposed the idea of comprehensive schools put forward during the 1950s. One of the headmasters said: "comprehensive schools might never be as good as grammar schools"; moreover, if the plan were implemented the result would be " 'inferior staffs' [and] inferior pupils."[34] Teachers feared damage to their status and prestige as a result of the establishment of comprehensive schools. This disagreement led to escalation of the conflict; teachers from two grammar schools and the Old Student organisation went into action and organised protests ("the local Press was bombed with letters"[35]). One message was a warning to the politicians:

> Those who, with whatever good intent, would sweep away this *heritage* are still, however, subject to one all-powerful deterrent… the power of the ballot box [present writer's emphasis].[36]

"Heritage" related not only to the grammar school as an institution but also to the teachers, and their general feeling was that they were going to lose the prestige connected to the tradition and public esteem enjoyed by the grammar school. The bitter dispute continued through the 1960s until an agreement was reached in 1967 on the basis of shared prestige and status. A plan drawn up in 1963, known as the Peter Plan, suggested three principles: abolition of the 11+ examinations, institution of seven neighbourhood comprehensive schools for pupils between the ages of 11 and 16, and establishment of a sixth-form college. After years of discussions and rifts among supporters of the grammar schools and the modern schools, the plan was accepted by both sides. For the supporters of the grammar schools, the best traditions were to be preserved in the sixth form college, while the supporters of the comprehensive school were promised pupils of a mixed range of ability, including the cream of the grammar school.

Secondary school reform in Birmingham evolved in the direction of the comprehensive idea during the 1950s-60s. Kesternard (1970) mentions that the keen controversy over the organisation of secondary education was apparently focused on the principle of parental choice and the parents' right to 11+ examinations. In reality however, "the only important principle which remained was that of retaining the grammar school."[37] This fact cannot be explained by teacher support for the values of "free choice," but because,

> Teachers in selective schools derive a great advantage over their counterparts in the secondary modern schools in respect of the type of pupils they teach, in status and in salary.[38]

In contrast to the grammar school teachers, who attempted to avoid changes in order to secure their prestige, the modern school teachers were more open to change. This openness was not without its suspicions, but harboured the hope of gaining more prestige through amalgamation with schools enjoying higher public esteem than the modern type, such as bilaterals or comprehensives. The teachers at Blake modern school in Middlesex campaigned for a comprehensive school. In this case teachers initially supported the Local Authority's proposal to establish a comprehensive school in place of the existing modern school. Moreover, teachers and parents joined forces to carry the new proposal through despite difficulties. When a dispute arose with those parents who wished to retain the choice between comprehensive and grammar schools, the "head master for some time feared that the school would revert to secondary modern status."[39] Therefore, in order to secure the change to the new status, the headmaster of Blake School and other teachers "took matters in their own hands and propagated the comprehensive school idea."[40] To counter the activity of the modern school teachers, the grammar school teachers organised anti-comprehensive activities through the Joint Four, the union of (mainly) grammar teachers.[41]

The pursuit of status is illustrated well by the case of Turton modern school in Lancashire (Fenwick, 1967). The school's headmaster had reservations about the proposal for a comprehensive school, but changed his mind and became a supporter of the comprehensive idea when he realised that his school's status would thereby be elevated:

> The Head of Turton Secondary Modern School had come to *favour the comprehensive* principle which would lead to the considerable *expansion of his school* [present writer's emphasis].[42]

To summarise: the secondary reform threatened teachers' status on four counts: salary, recognition, qualification and prestige. Grammar school teachers stood to lose most, while modern school teachers expected to benefit from the changes and consequently had fewer reservations, and in some cases even encouraged the reorganisation. The case studies raise two main points: (1) teachers were disregarded by the local authorities as an important group or partner in discussions and decision making regarding the proposed changes; (2) successful execution of the reform could not be achieved unless teachers were committed to the changes. There seems to be a hierarchy of stages in implementation of the reform and when the basic one is missing – *status* in its broadest sense – it is almost impossible to achieve the second, namely, teachers' commitment to change. When the authority failed to recognise the teachers' status, it could not obtain their commitment; indeed, in most cases invoked their opposition. Only in the second phase, after the authorities became aware of the need to consider the teachers' status by involving them in joint discussions, securing a salary scheme, addressing teacher training, and recognising the need to secure their status by means of several kinds of compromise,[43] was the path to further discussions cleared. This took years, but ensured more teacher commitment to the changes than was likely in the first phase of the secondary education reform process. So, while the LEAs and the Ministry of Education attempted to set a rapid reorganisation in motion, when it came to implementation, the teachers – although they did not play an important role in decision making – nevertheless had the power to resist, ignore and avoid the changes for many years. Expectations of what could be achieved without teacher involvement proved unfounded and caused a long delay until teachers were afforded recognition as an essential group in the reform process and its success. Saran explains the point well:

> Teachers are most closely involved in the detailed implementation of educational policies. It was shown that the enlistment of their

personal sympathies for proposed schemes proved crucial to the successful introduction of change in the schools.[44]

The complete picture of the disturbances that attended implementation of the secondary reform is still not clear, and the teachers' and parents' angles in this process should not be judged until the role of a more influential group in the LEAs, the politicians and the political parties, has been established.

5.3: POLITICIANS AND THEIR MOTIVES

The question regarding the nature of the disturbances that negated the central intention of the reform – or even what had already been suggested by LEAs and had gained ministerial approval – remains to be asked.

Those researchers who have analysed the decision making that took place between the end of the 1940s and the 1960s, when the secondary education reform was implemented in the LEAs, agree that the situation was so complicated that it is difficult to identify how the decision making was carried out, and even difficult to assess the relative weight of the propositions among the interest groups (Fenwick, 1967; Ribbins & Brown, 1979; Saran, 1973). This study aims to explain the intervening factors that disrupted the attempt of a central authority[45] to carry out a policy, rather than provide details of the precise process of decision making. The secondary reorganisation case studies illustrate the politicians' role in some of the difficulties with implementing this reorganisation.

It is important to mention at this stage that during the 1940s and the 1950s both of the main parties, Conservative and Labour, supported the tripartite system and concurred on the importance of retaining the traditional grammar school. Ministers of both parties hence did not approve comprehensive schools, except in cases defined as experimental. During the 1960s Labour Party policy was changed to support the comprehensive idea. In any case, any assumption that the reorganisation was based on consensus during the 1940s and 1950s or on controversy between the two main parties should be examined with some care.

In the case of Darlington the Authority was split between those who supported reform on the principle of comprehensive schools, and those who wanted to secure the old system, including the grammar schools. The issue was only resolved in 1965, after twelve years of disputes (Batley, 1970). The first move towards comprehensive schools had been led by the Labour Party but soon opposition to the comprehensive principle arose within the Labour Party itself, with the older members adopting and committing themselves to the bilateral proposal. Moreover they were "convinced that Darlington had the best possible system of education."[46] Batley explains this by saying that the real struggle was over power in the local Labour Party rather than over the comprehensive issue. During these years attempts by Labour members to remove the old Labour councillors – and even an intervention by the General Secretary of the Labour Party – were unsuccessful, and the issue remained deadlocked until 1960. In that year Labour lost control to the Conservative Party and until 1963, when Labour regained power, no action was taken in the area of secondary reform. Meanwhile, a change in the climate of opinion against selection and test discrimination[47] led to a new proposal based on a scheme for establishing seven comprehensive schools without selection for pupils between the ages of 11 and 16, and a sixth form college. The idea was to abolish the selection system but at the same time preserve the tradition of the grammar school by means of the sixth form college. This was approved by the Education Committee in 1965 and confirmed by the Conservatives when they regained control in 1967. In concluding the case of Darlington it may be said that the split within the Labour party on the issue of securing the old system versus proposals for the comprehensive principle was the main reason for the delay in reforming secondary education.

A similar situation was described by Parkinson (1973) in the case of Birkenhead. A dispute between the old Labour guard and the local Labour Party prevented any move towards reorganisation for eleven years. The old leadership was committed to the grammar schools and reluctant to introduce any major change, but "eventually… the local party pressure could no longer be resisted, and the leadership could not avoid adopting the national party's position on secondary education."[48]

On the contrary, however, in some cases there is clear evidence that local Conservative parties supported the idea of comprehensive schools. In Bootle the Conservative Party favoured the comprehensive idea more than the

Labour Party did. Parkinson's explanation for this is based on the idea that working class Conservative Party members preferred the comprehensive principle to the principle of different opportunities for different types of pupil.

Leicestershire was among the Conservative authorities that proposed some comprehensive schools, while the Conservative opposition in London did not resist the Development Plan proposal to found 103 comprehensive schools. Reynolds (1987) comes to the conclusion that, ironically, some of the pioneering authorities in establishing comprehensive schools were controlled by Conservative councils:

> Paradoxically, while the two major parties' position on comprehensive education became polarised in Parliament, developments were taking place in some LEAs which were completely different to the positions taken by the national parties. Many Labour controlled LEAs were reluctant even to seek permission to establish comprehensive schools.[49]

Parkinson (1973) in the case of Liverpool, and David (1977) in the case of Brownborough, explain the twenty years of discussions and the political swing as a result of both parties' inability to cope with the complicated and practical problems of the reorganisation of secondary education rather than a political dispute about educational principles. Administrative problems and the various combinations that had to be considered paralysed the possibility of moving forward with the secondary reform. Among these problems David mentions the "response to environmental problems, the local and national political pressures . . . responding to wishes of pressure groups."[50] Parkinson came to the same conclusion, saying that the situation "offered far more possible combinations to be considered."[51]

Fenwick (1967) in the case of Division Nine in Lancashire, found that "opposition to reorganisation was structural in terms of the existing schools system."[52] Parkinson (1973) comes to a similar conclusion in terms of the conflict: "Parties, officers, teachers, groups, Catholics, compete to gain advantage."[53] The complexity of that time was explained by the Director of Education for Leicestershire, quoted by Rubinstein and Simon (1969):

> Backed as it was by the Norwood Report and by the Ministry of Education's pamphlet *"The New Secondary Education"*...it was clear that the practice of selection was no longer tenable.[54]

Thus far it is possible to identify four main factors that disrupted and confused LEA policies of secondary education reform from the political point of view, which was among the variables that avoided and delayed implementation of the 1944 Education Act in respect of secondary reform for up to thirty years. The factors are:

1. The attitude and perception of local *individual politicians* as to the future of secondary education with no consideration of the policy of their local or national party.
2. *Local party* policy towards the needs of the authority in shaping secondary education with no consideration of the policy of the national party.
3. The complexity of administrative and selection questions, which paralysed decision making.
4. Attempts to reduce complexity by changing part of a previous proposal were seen as a new move in a new direction and raised opposition on political and professional grounds.

The case studies point to a combination of causes of difficulty on the political level, which could throw some light on the disturbances in decision making on secondary reform. One clear finding is that members of both parties lacked commitment on the local level to the official policy of their national party. Moreover, there were even splits among members of the same party at the local level. This indicates that party members' main motive to act, vote, fight and dissent was their local interests and concepts of the future shape of secondary education. Indeed, there were cases where there was a correlation between national party policy and the local policy, but this seems to have occurred for random reasons rather than as a result of political obedience; national policy simply happened to fit the local needs and interests of the elected members. Conversely, whenever the personal interests of even an individual elected member were incommensurate with his party's beliefs, perceptions or interests, the vote was cast without any commitment to the local or national party. Such behaviour on the part of politicians, as depicted in the case studies, partly explains the two or three decades of disputes, even chaos, that beset the education system.

5.4: CONCLUSIONS

When LEAs were ready to implement their plans after several years of internal discussions and external discussions with the Ministry of Education, they encountered a new difficulty: any interaction between sub-groups involved in the reform process increased the level of complexity. Disputes with these groups paralysed their ability to execute what had already been approved by the minister and the implementation of the reform was postponed for further years.

The three groups examined by the case studies, parents, teachers and political parties, represented different perceptions, needs and interests to such an extent that fast progress towards reorganisation became impossible. Moreover, the keen struggle of each group, in some cases,[55] to secure its own interests and status was among the reasons why the execution of the reform took up to thirty years.

The parents' group was divided between those who wanted to avoid the low status of the modern school by supporting the idea of bilateral or comprehensive schools and those who wanted to secure the high status of the traditional grammar school and were against any proposal for amalgamation with another type of school. Progress in implementation of the reform was blocked by the fact that parents had the power to ignore and resist any suggestion, while the LEAs had no power to compel parents to send their children to a comprehensive or bilateral school without offering an alternative choice of the grammar school type.

The fact that teachers, as a group, were disregarded as an important partner in the discussions and not consulted, was one reason for their resistance to the preliminary proposals. In the first phase the teachers received no recognition of their role on the front line of the educational battlefield and were informed, in many cases, through the media about changes that would affect their schools and their posts. Moreover, many of the changes damaged their status, thus invoking their resistance, suspicion and alienation. When, during the second phase, the teachers were invited to join the local education discussions as partners, they were finally recognised as an essential component of the reform process and its success. This recognition, though it helped by resolving one obstacle pertaining to status, did not greatly accelerate the execution of the reform, since three other status problems remained unsolved: salary, qualification, and prestige. The teacher partnership was a forum in which practical status problems, such as salary and training, could be raised and a route opened for the solution of problems. Prestige problems however, were what prevented rapid execution of the reform, particularly because some of them involved contrary interests of teachers, for example the grammar school teachers' expectations versus those of the modern teachers.

The expectation of quick results without involving teachers proved an illusion. Despite the fact that they played a secondary role in the first phase, it was agreed in the second phase that further progress could only be achieved if the teachers were committed to the reorganisation.

The third group, the politicians, were ostensibly the official bearers of the public responsibility and power, local as well as central, to carry out the reform plan according to local suggestions and ministerial approval. In reality, the four main reasons identified above were among those that counteracted the ministerial approval of the local plan. The main motive of political members was commitment to their local interests without regard or consideration for their local or national party policy. Any correlation between national party policy and local policy was not because of political obedience but simply because the local needs and interests of the elected member(s) coincided with wider party policy. The complexity of administrative and educational problems such as the selection problems, the pressure to merge the traditionally highly regarded grammar schools, and the problems of teachers' resistance and status made up a complicated situation that could not be solved in a short period.

Many studies have noted this complexity (Brown, 1978; Fenwick, 1967; Ribbins, 1985; Ribbins & Brown, 1979; Saran, 1973). As described above, the sub-groups – teachers, parents and politicians – had limited power to implement the secondary reform. There were conflicts of interest and factors that neutralised each other and these, together with the complexity of some administrative and educational questions, caused confusion and paralysed decision making.

Thus, the contradictory forces, the divergent interests, and the unforeseen reasons for supporting or opposing the reform, contributed to the complexity that arose with any intervention of sub-groups in the reform. Such developments support the Dissipative Structure Theory of growing deviation from the reference-point and increasing disorder with any further involvement with the environment. So, if the first stage in the process of blurring and eroding the government order was the initial interaction with the LEAs over the Development Plan, the second phase of this erosion was when the sub-groups became involved in implementation of the government Reform and the LEAs Development Plans.

The conflict of interests and factors that neutralised each other confirm Kurt Levin's (1947) equilibrium model, arguing that the process of change involved groups that seek change and those that resist it and lead to a return to the previous situation. In the case studies reviewed, any decision made raised resistance from a counter-group that regarded the decision as damaging their interests; consequently the decision making process was paralysed. Moreover, resistance to change also confirms the motivation theory which holds that avoidance and conflict in organisations come about when actors' interests do not correspond with a planned reform or change (Handy, 1988; Meyer & Zucker, 1989). Thus, those who were seeking the change and who had the formal authority, either the ministry or the LEAs, were confronted by those with an interest in non-change. But still we have to ask: Where were the guidelines for the further development of the reform? What were the forces that led to the change after ten, twenty or even thirty years of discussions and disputes? What was the direction of these changes?

Notes:

1. The cases include: Rene Saran (1973). *Policy-Making in Secondary Education: A Case Study*. Oxford: Clarendon [referring to Middlesex]; Parkinson, M.H. (1973). *Politics of Urban Education*. Liverpool: University of Liverpool [Birkenhead, Bootle, Liverpool, Wallasey]; Miriam E. David (1977). *Reform, Reaction and Resources: The 3Rs of Educational Planning*. Windsor: NFER [Brownborough, Eastshire, Lightborough]; David Reynolds & Michael Sullivan (1987). *The Comprehensive Experiment*. London: Falmer [Treliw]; P.H.J.H. Gosden & P.R. Sharp (1978). *The Development of an Education Service: The West Riding 1889-1974*. Oxford: Martin Robertson [West Riding]; R.J. Woodward (1970). Sir William Romney's School, Tetbury, Gloucestershire. In Elizabeth Halsall (ed.) (1970). *Becoming Comprehensive: Case Histories*. Oxford: Pergamon [Tetbury in Gloucestershire]; Isaac-Henry Kesternard (1970). *The Politics of Comprehensive Education in Birmingham 1957-67*. unpublished thesis, University of Birmingham [Birmingham]; David Rubinstein & Simon Brian (1969). *The Evolution of the Comprehensive School, 1926-1966*. London: Routledge & Kegan Paul [Leicestershire]; Richard Batley et al.(1970). *Going Comprehensive*. London: Routledge & Kegan Paul [Darlington, Gateshead]; I.G.K. Fenwick (1967). "Organised Opinion and the Comprehensive School, 1944-64: A study of some educational groups and the policy-making process for education in England," unpublished thesis, University of Manchester [Lancashire]; J.N Hewitson (1969). *The Grammar School Tradition in a Comprehensive World*. London: Routledge [Doncaster].
2. Some cases provide single political and administrative details without any sociological or psychological reference.
3. Saran (1973), 144.
4. Ibid., 148-9. Saran gives fictitious names to the institutions examined in the research.
5. Saran (1973), 151.
6. Ibid., 160. The other part of the explanation, according to Saran, is that the chairman of the district education committee supported the establishment of the comprehensive school.
7. Ibid., 165.
8. Ibid., 263.
9. Ibid., 177.
10. Parkinson (1973), 46.
11. Reynolds & Sullivan (1987), 59.
12. Ibid., 60.
13. Gosden & Sharp (1978), 173-4.
14. H. James Philip (1980). *The Reorganisation of Secondary Education*, Windsor: NFER, 49. The author's description is based on Marmion's study of 1967 (unpublished dissertation).
15. Parkinson (1973), 33.
16. The term "status" will be analysed in terms of the above four aspects rather than as a whole.
17. Kesternard (1970), 152.
18. Ibid.
19. Schools under the control of the local authorities.

20. Saran (1973), 152.
21. Hewitson (1969), 69.
22. Ibid., 85.
23. Elizabeth Halsall (ed.) (1970). *Becoming Comprehensive: Case Histories.* Oxford: Pergamon, 6.
24. Saran (1973), 159.
25. Batley (1970), 85.
26. Hewitson (1969), 79.
27. Ibid., 71.
28. David (1977), 70.
29. Ibid., 76.
30. Saran (1973), 159.
31. Ibid., 155.
32. Ibid.
33. Woodward (1970), 9.
34. Batley et al. (1970), 31.
35. Ibid., 34.
36. Ibid., 35.
37. Kesternard (1970), 173.
38. Ibid., 152.
39. Ibid., 170.
40. Ibid., 179.
41. The unions were deeply involved in the dispute. While the grammar school teachers were organised mainly as members of the Joint Four, the majority of teachers were organised as members of the NUT, which represented teachers at primary and modern schools.
42. Fenwick (1967), 414.
43. Such as establishing sixth form colleges and introducing comprehensive schools while retaining the selective system.
44. Saran (1973), 262.
45. In this sense central authority may refer to the LEA level in relation to its divisions as well as to the relation between the central government (Ministry of Education) and LEAs.
46. Batley et al. (1970), 27.
47. The selection issue will be discussed in detail in the next chapter.
48. Parkinson (1973), 46. It should be mentioned that Labour Party policy was only modified towards the comprehensive idea during the 1960s and in the run-up to the 1964 election.
49. Reynolds & Sullivan (1987), 11.
50. David (1977), 87.
51. Parkinson (1973), 40.
52. Fenwick (1967), 416.
53. Parkinson (1973), 57.

54. Rubinstein & Simon (1969), 83.
55. Generalisation of this kind should be qualified by noting that it did not carry the same weight in all cases. The parents, for example, were (in some cases) more apathetic than the teachers or parents in other authorities.

• CHAPTER 6

THE COLLAPSE OF THE TRIPARTITE SYSTEM: THE EMERGENCE OF A NEW ORDER

The aim of this chapter is to identify several more factors that contributed to the widening of the gap between the Ministry of Education's central ideals, vision and intentions with regard to reforming secondary education in England and Wales, and actual practice. Particular emphasis will be placed on tracing this process in ministry documents as an adjunct to the information provided in previous chapters by means of the case study data and the local authorities' development plans.

The government's main policy aim concerning secondary education was secondary education for all according to different ages, abilities, and aptitude. There are two main threads to this definition: (1) education for all; and (2) different types of schools for different types of abilities. Both warrant close examination in relation to the facts. The full effect of the first principle, education for all, was to provide an extra year of education for nearly 400,000 children as a consequence of the school-leaving age having been raised from 14 to 15 in 1947. In January 1947 the number of pupils between 14 and 15 years old was 150,101, in 1948 it went up to 389,900 and in January 1949 it rose even higher to 480,127,[1] This rapid expansion may be considered representative of the success of government policy in this respect.

The application of the second principle, classification of pupils according to the proportion of 70-75% to modern schools and 25-30% to grammar and technical schools, calls for more careful examination. The following table shows the pattern of secondary education in 1948, four years after publication of the Education Act:

Table 3: Distribution of pupils in secondary schools

Type	Total no.	%
Modern	3,063	66.6
Grammar	1,212	26.3
Technical	319	6.9
Total	4,594	99.8%

Source: Education Statistics in 1949

It would seem that the two main aims of government policy for secondary education were achieved to the full extent, with the relative proportions of pupils in three types of schools corresponding closely to the government target. But the second principle of that policy and the figures in the table are representative of existing traditions and the development of the education system up to the post-war period rather than of acceptance or implementation of the 1944 Education Act by local authorities. In this sense these figures are more a reflection of the past than an indication of recent achievements and future developments.

The first signs of resistance, on the part of local authorities, to developing the secondary education system along the lines laid down by the government became apparent soon after the publication of the Act (see Chapters 4 and 5). Further disregard of central policy with respect to the selection, classification and categorisation of the nation's children resulted in a disparity between the reality and the vision of those who planned the 1944 Education Act. The main factors that shaped the new reality, leading to a disregard of and resistance to the policy of classification into three rigid groups, eventually led to the collapse of the tripartite policy and the emergence of a new order.

6.1: THE MODERN SCHOOL: SEARCHING FOR SIGNIFICANCE

The Norwood Report on "Curriculum and Examinations in Secondary Schools," published in 1943, followed the basic assumption laid down by the Hadow Committee with regard to the need for three distinctive curricula in three different types of school for three different types of pupil. The Report proposed increasing teachers' freedom and responsibility by suggesting that the School Certificate be internal to schools, conducted by the teachers and based on pupils' records and performance in internal examinations.[2] The Report, which was accepted by Minister of Education R.A. Butler, distinguished between teachers at grammar schools and those at the technical and modern schools. Lawton (1980), in evaluating this approach, said:

> When the report talks of teachers having more responsibility and control, only the elite of the profession were to be involved. It is quite clear that the idea of handing over control of examinations to secondary modern teachers (mainly ex-elementary teachers) was not part of the Norwood plan.[3]

Lowe (1988) comes to the same conclusion, saying that "the debate on examinations was posited on the assumption that it was only the small minority of pupils who attended grammar schools who were to be involved."[4]

But despite this fact, the Labour Ministers of Education, Ellen Wilkinson and her successor George Tomlinson, supported the idea of abolishing the school examinations according to Norwood's proposals. The universities, however, responded by threatening to set their own entrance examinations, and this led to the rejection of the Norwood Committee's proposal and finally to the creation in 1951 of a new style of examination, the General Certificate of Education (GCE) (Lawton, 1980; Lowe, 1988).

The new examination scheme, first proposed in 1947 by the Secondary School Examinations Committee (SSEC), suggested three levels of examination: Ordinary level, taken at the age of 16+, Advanced level at the age of 18, and Scholarship examinations. This new scheme threw the disadvantageous position of the overwhelming majority of the nation's pupils, almost 70% of whom attended modern schools, into high relief on two main counts: (1) the age limit for the "O" level examination was 16+, and pupils in modern schools left their schools at the end of compulsory education, which at that time was age 15; (2) the new "O" level in some respects demanded higher standards than the previous School Certificate. The distinction between the type of schools embodied in the scheme represented a move towards increased exclusiveness of the grammar schools rather than real consideration of and confrontation with the need for the expansion of secondary education, particularly the needs of the modern schools (Lawton, 1980; Lowe, 1988).

The definition of the modern schools as secondary schools raised the expectations not only of parents but also of teachers and employers. While parents wished their children to gain some concrete recognition in the shape of a formal certificate rather than simply "general education," employers asked for some qualification whereby they could assess young candidates for jobs, and teachers in the modern schools argued that there was enormous ability among their pupils, who could, if given the chance, achieve good grades in the "O" level examination. Moreover, they claimed they were able to lead these pupils towards such achievements. These expectations – of parents, teachers and employers – led to calls for either allowing modern school pupils to take "O" level examinations at the existing standards, before turning 16, or introducing a new and separate inferior examination. Both demands were based on the perceived need to give a significant aim and rationale to the modern school. The Ministry of Education was aware of this theme when it stated the following:

> We are all aware of pressure from several quarters (e.g. employers, parents, teachers, examining bodies, LEAs) for something lower than GCE "O" level. Some of it asked for a lower level in GCE, some for a new and separate exam. It is difficult to measure the volume of it and the less vocal opposition to it. It must be remembered that outside the Ministry pressure groups must inevitably contain vested interests.[5]

The National Union of Teachers (NUT) was split over whether or not to ask for an inferior certificate, but there was consensus regarding the idea that the modern school should have a more explicit aim. This was expressed by Miss H. Drake, a member of the NUT who took part in the discussions: "A special examination for the secondary modern school would supply a sense of purpose…children would stay on at school if they thought there was a better job at the end of it."[6] According to heads and teachers in modern schools, this demand for a purpose and a kind of recognition through a certificate, "centre[s] around the anxiety of and the need for at least the abler modern school pupil to have some sort of certificate on leaving school both relevant to his future career and recording his achievement."[7] Thus, the diffuse definition of the modern school as "free from the pressures of external examination" and aimed at fostering the "enjoyment of life"[8] was rejected by parents and teachers who demanded formal recognition of achievement and for the replacement of these initial aims of the modern schools by higher demands for scholastic attainment, more pressure in study, examinations and finally a recognised certificate of some sort. The *Liverpool Daily Post* responded to these wishes on the part of parents and teachers, saying that "the secondary modern school is drifting along, knowing not at what to aim, and a first essential is the creation of a set of standards upon which to base its work."[9]

The Ministry of Education did consider the possibility of allowing an external examination at a lower level and a lower age. The factors in support of this proposal were:[10]

(a) incentive for children and parents;
(b) incentive for teachers;
(c) usefulness in obtaining suitable jobs and getting placed in suitable further education courses;
(d) purpose for modern schools;
(e) method of assessing schools.

Against these purported advantages, arguments that opposed modification of the examinations claimed that "good teachers find plenty of purpose and incentive in their day-to-day work"[11] and that the more popular the certificate and examinations, the worse the effect on standards would be. The demand for a modern school certificate was seen as something that could weaken the education system as a whole. David Eccles, the Conservative Minister of

Education, said: "Let us keep sights high and resist at all costs any soft option calculated to lower standards or impede the maximum educational progress and development."[12]

When the pressure intensified, with over 1000 modern schools asking for suitable external examinations,[13] the NUT, the AEC, the London Head Teachers Association, the National Association of Divisional Executives and the RSA argued that this justified independent initiatives to establish their own leaving certificates.[14] Eccles could not ignore the public feeling on this point and came to the conclusion that if the ministry did not take the initiative to solve the problem it could result in an undesirable outcome, such as the setting-up of comprehensive schools. He suggested in a letter to his permanent secretary that the way forward was to take a positive line in developing the differences between the types of school, which in practice meant emphasising the practical courses on the modern schools' curriculum. The minister's idea was that such enrichment of the curriculum would reduce the public pressure and that of ambitious pupils, parents and teachers to take an examination:

> I have read the papers about the GCE exam. The demand for a new exam for Secondary Modern Schools strikes me, as does the argument for comprehensive schools, as another of the growing pains of the Butler Act. The true line of development is to expand the special courses in Secondary Modern Schools, and the more this is done the more differences there will be between schools, and therefore, I presume, the less ground for a national exam.[15]

But the minister, in coming to the conclusion that the demands for a modern school certificate represented no real problem, just an egalitarian attempt to spoil the Butler Act, failed to the assess the situation adequately:

> Machiavelli in his Discourses says of Ferdinand of Aragon that "his actions have arisen in such a way one out the other, that men have never been given enough time to work steadily against him". This is how we deal with the levellers and spoilers of the Butler Act.[16]

The LEAs, parents, teachers and employers were more sensitive than the ministry to real needs, and took the initiative by developing their own certificates and examinations. In response to this initiative, the minister insisted that there would be no external examinations other than the GCE; moreover, judging the situation through his own experience, he concluded that certificates were necessary only for the abler pupils within the education system for purpose of entry to the universities: "I cannot for the life of me see why an external examination is needed to do all these desirable things."[17] In his view, the pressure for a new kind of certificate represented a threat "to lower the standards."[18] And so the demand for more significance and purpose for the modern schools was interpreted as an alarming and harmful possibility that the ministry should avoid and resist "at all cost."[19] Indeed the minister, in publishing Circular 289 in July 1955, made an attempt to block the modern schools' wishes by the following instructions:

> Experience has shown that many modern schools can prepare pupils adequately for taking the GCE examination: in the summer of 1954 at least 5500 candidates from 357 modern schools were entered for it. The Minister welcomes this evidence . . . .[20]

But the conclusion went in the opposite direction:

> Schools should, however, be careful not to sacrifice the interests of the majority of their pupils to meeting the needs of the small minority who are entering for the GCE examination. They should not build up "a GCE course" for reasons of prestige when the pupils concerned would be better advised either to transfer to another school or to follow some different course. Teachers will no doubt be well aware of these dangers and know how to avoid them.[21]

Once again the ministry saw the meaning of achievement and high standards in terms of protecting the exclusiveness of the grammar school as the sole type of school having access to the GCE. The needs and the gradual achievements of pupils at modern schools in passing the examinations made no impression on the minister, and the government's aim remained to support and plan the GCE examinations for about 20% of the school population, leaving the rest to a mere "good general education" without providing any recognition of their ability, achievement and ambitions. Moreover, the employers' request for a kind of certificate only met the recommendation "for a closer link between the employers and schools . . . and the more general use of school records."[22] The Circular addressed both of the possibilities that had been raised – lower level examinations and modern school direct access to the GCE – and on both counts blocked the aspirations of the modern school pupils. Apart from the most able individuals who could transfer to other schools, the overwhelming majority of modern school pupils remained at school without any concrete and significant purpose.[23]

The publication of Circular 289 was followed by protests and resistance to the policy, which led to two main developments. The first was further development of local initiatives for the provision of certificates; the second, when it became clear to the minister that the policy was leading to undesirable results, was a gradual change in policy. In Lancashire, the Headmistress of Lipstick County Secondary School for Girls wrote to Charles Panel, MP for Stretford, in response to Circular 289, claiming:

> We know that a tremendous amount of ability – and a tremendous amount of the Nation's money – is being wasted because in the absence of incentives to maximum effort the majority of children are leaving school with a standard of attainment which is well below that of which they are capable.[24]

She asked that there be no prevention by administrative means of the school's attempts to encourage pupils towards a higher level of attainment. Her argument advocated letting modern school pupils stay at school until the age of 16, not because of egalitarian ideas but simply because "the incentive of an examination at 16 has no significance until 16 is the recognised school-leaving age for Secondary Modern as well as Secondary Grammar Schools."[25] The headmistress was convinced that she would be able, if she were allowed, to show over the next few years a steady increase in the quality of attainment based on the recent experience of the school as reflected in the results of the College of Preceptors School Certificate Examination as follows:

Table 6.1: Results of the College of Preceptors School Certificate Examination

	Number entered	Number passed	With distinction
English Language	25	23	2
English Literature	25	19	2
Arithmetic	23	21	1
History	18	2	-
Geography	19	6	-
Scripture	22	17	-
Housecraft	7	7	-
Needlework	10	10	5

Source: Pro.Ed 147/303. Letter from L. Davies (September 1955).

On the basis of this evidence Charles Panel wrote to the minister, protesting at the publication of Circular 289 and the blocking of modern pupils from access to the GCE. He requested that the minister's attention be directed at the potential of pupils in the modern schools. He quoted from the headmistress's letter to show the significance and effect of this option for pupils as well as for parents:

> Parents are pleased and grateful, and the girls have a sense of achievement. There is an enthusiasm and a sense of purpose throughout the school…. . Seven girls have returned to take a 5th year course. The majority of our new 4th year groups have signified their intention of finishing the course instead of leaving, as has been customary, as soon after their 15th birthday as possible.[26]

The result of this case was a total blocking of the modern schools' opportunity to create, and to offer their pupils the chance to study for, any type of certificate. A letter written by Mr A. Part, a Deputy Secretary at the ministry, in response to the MP's letter made a clear statement of the ministry's policy:

> Lancashire Local Education Authority... cannot prevent parents on their own initiative from entering children under 16 for an external examination, but ... *school organisation cannot be used at all in this direction* [present writer's emphasis].[27]

Inevitably, the Local Education Authority blocked the school's initiative and informed the headmistress that the school organisation could not be used at all in preparing pupils for examinations "without running contrary to the minister's policy."[28]

Other responses by Local Education Authorities to Circular 289 included descriptions of the strong parental pressure for some evidence of their children's attainment. For example, the Director of Education of Middlesbrough wrote to the minister not only about the pressure but also about pupils' potential:

> There is evidence that many parents of children attending secondary modern school are willing to let their children stay at school beyond 15 and an examination qualification is an undoubted incentive .... There has been a big expansion of G.C.E. day classes in technical colleges due largely to secondary modern school pupils desiring to proceed to some examination qualification after leaving school at 15.[29]

Middlesex wished to allow secondary modern schools to enter candidates for GCE to "enable the candidates to give full expression to their knowledge and ability."[30]

The ministry's obduracy in the face of the wishes of modern schools and of parents in this respect led to two main types of initiative directed at breaking the deadlock: (a) raising money from the local authority or parents in order to run courses up to the age of 16, on the assumption that if parents would pay the exam fee nothing could stop their children's entry, whatever their age; (b) moves by private organisations to establish external examinations of a general character. Thus, for example, London County Council inquired as to "what would be the Ministry's reaction to the Council wishing to pay the fees for the RSA School Commercial Certificate or other comparable examination of pupils who have reached school leaving age?"[31] But the ministry's answer was that "Circular 289 does not include the loophole which your people thought they saw in it,"[32] and the key position was that "it is, of course, perfectly possible for the Local Education Authority to forbid its teachers to run courses in their schools for under-age candidates on the ground that this is contrary to the spirit of the Regulation."[33] Further pressure from other quarters, such as the National Union of Teachers, reached the ministry with a call for some form of external examination other than the GCE.

The ministry's initial idea that the modern school should not be under the stress of external examinations met, paradoxically, with a keen response from parents, teachers and local authorities. Pressure groups were against diffuse aims and against an investment of effort without significant reward. They asked, in contradiction to the "soft" education approach, for more pressure and more demands on pupils and concrete targets, and were prepared to make greater efforts provided that the pupils could take an examination that would provide them with a certificate representative of their scholastic attainment.

Given the substantial volume of comment in response to Circular 289, the minister could not help but reconsider the issue. David Eccles decided that the "present standards of the ordinary level should be retained,"[34] but also announced that he was prepared to modify his previous policy discouraging the use of a regionally organised external examination, because "I am impressed by some of the letters, etc., asking for freedom to enter Secondary Modern pupils for examinations that would help their progress to Technical Colleges."[35]

The search for practical solutions for the modern schools as a result of public pressure led to measures of four main types being taken:

(1) 5-year courses for children selected on their entry into modern school;
(2) Preparation of "marginal" pupils for transfer to grammar school as soon as they reached the necessary standards;
(3) Establishment of new comprehensive schools provided that they did not involve the closure of grammar schools;
(4) Reclassification of modern schools as comprehensive, multilateral and bilateral schools.

These steps led to a gradual increase in the numbers of modern school pupils entered for the General Certificate of Education, as the following table indicates:

Table 6.2: Secondary modern pupils entering external examinations

Year	O level	A level
1955	7,334	-
1956	8,571	-
1957	10,986	280
1958	16,444	343
1959	19,407	385
1960	21,680	597

Source: Rubinstein & Simon, 1973, p.58.

These figures are evidence of the increasing numbers of modern pupils taking this examination from 1955 on. The figures do not include candidates from nearly 800 secondary modern schools which in "1958 were no longer classified as secondary modern schools."[36]

The results achieved by modern school pupils in the external examinations raised doubt in the Ministry of Education about the validity of their earlier predictions and the assumptions regarding the distribution of intelligence on which the tripartite system was based. Ministry officials identified other factors, not taken into account in the original assumptions, as a source of success: "When imagination is caught, ambition is fired and self-confidence is gained, even the dullest child will surprise his teacher by his progress."[37] Ministry officials had reported to the minister that there were cases of children in the least intelligent quartile who reached standards they would never have been expected to attain in the past. Eccles could not ignore this evidence; he wrote to his secretary concerning the debate on secondary education: "I like the idea of overlapping between GS [Grammar School] and Secondary Modern …Does the variation in ability at a secondary modern dictate a minimum size to a successful staff?"[38]

Constant pressure for change during the mid-1950s led to discussions and reports within the Ministry of Education concerning the future of secondary education and of the tripartite system.[39] One of the reports stated that LEAs could not implement the tripartite system and that "they are more and more taking the view that to draw firm demarcation lines between different 'types' of school is unrealistic."[40] Moreover, it concluded that:

> This blurring of the boundaries altogether fits the picture of children's needs, for children develop and change and what may seem suitable for them at one stage may later cease to be adequate for them. Geese can never become swans *but a surprising number of them can take the GCE* [present writer's emphasis].[41]

The report's conclusion, in keeping with the atmosphere at that time, was that the tripartite system intended by the authors of the 1944 Education Act should be reassessed in view of the fact that "the ideal of a separate curriculum for every child may sound Utopian."[42] The Report of the Central Advisory Council for Education (Crowther Report) came to a similar conclusion in 1959:

> All over the country changes are being made that profoundly modify the previous pattern of education … . There are many variants, and no doubt there will be many more… . All aim at reducing the waste of talent which arises from the overlap in ability…, all aim at giving each individual pupil a better chance of an education… . All the variants try to provide a common social life; none tries to provide a uniform curriculum.[43]

For this reason, the Council came to the conclusion that "we do not now have, and never have had, a tripartite system."[44]

The role played by the modern school in the move away from the tripartite system thus becomes clearer; but we still need to look at the other leg of the tripartite system: the technical schools. What was the role of the technical schools in the attempt to establish the tripartite system? What were the results of the ministry's aim to increase the volume of the technical schools up to 10 or even to 15 percent?

6.2: THE TECHNICAL SCHOOLS: SHATTERING AN ILLUSION

Soon after the publication of the 1944 Education Act, the Ministry of Education published the plan for secondary education. Pamphlet No.1 had mentioned, among the disadvantages of the previous secondary system, that the brighter and most able children were transferred to grammar schools and prepared for clerical and office occupations, while "industry on the production and manufacturing side has to that extent been deprived of its reasonable share of the national talent."[45] The pamphlet went on to explain this phenomenon in sociological terms, saying that "clerical as opposed to industrial employment is commonly held in higher esteem and is more eagerly sought by those who have a choice of their work in life."[46] It was argued that technical schools had difficulty attracting pupils of high ability because of their low image, which affected the development of industry. Moreover, parents expressed their fears of insecurity which in the past had been attached to industrial employment and hence, to the technical schools. The new ministry plan stated that "these disabilities should disappear."[47]

The ministry defined the purpose of the plan, with regard to the technical schools, on two levels: on the public relations level, to undertake "missionary work" among the parents in order to remove the misapprehensions concerning these schools; and on the practical level, to institute technical studies for children from 11 to 16 on a selective basis[48] and to increase the proportion of pupils in technical schools to 10% (as opposed to 4.5% in 1948[49]).

The Ministry of Education proposed no clear solutions to the practical problems faced by local authorities in implementing the government's policy. These included questions such as: What are the new subjects and means to attract brighter pupils to these schools in contrast to the previous means? Who would finance the heavy investment that was needed to establish a technical school system two or three times bigger than the previous one? What would be seen as a new purpose of these schools? What about a sixth form at the age of 16 in technical schools?

These concrete and day-to-day questions were left to the local authorities to answer. The government's policy of conducting this process by leaving such matters to the local authorities was one of the impediments to implementation of the plan according to the ministry's aims. Local authorities, left to decide about practical questions in the absence of central answers, adopted measures according to their own circumstances, such as industrial needs, local perceptions, educational tradition, financial and accommodation means.

Thus, when Northamptonshire submitted its DP to the Ministry of Education, technical schools were not part of the plan, because preparation for: "the Boot and Shoe Trade…can, as a rule, be made more conveniently in the Modern Schools duly equipped with practical rooms than in specially designated Technical High Schools."[50] Another argument against the provision of technical high schools was the interest in enabling the modern schools to gain public status by avoiding "second creaming of the senior children"[51] in technical schools and avoid the pupils of modern schools being thought of as "predestinate hewers of wood and drawers of water."[52]

Blackpool could find no vindication or justification for classifying children, either for academic or technical courses, at the age of eleven. For this reason the Authority proposed bilateral grammar/technical schools after the age of 13, with places in the proportion of two to one in favour of the grammar stream.

Cheshire rejected the separation into a tripartite system for the same reason, saying that "it is not possible to select for Technical education at the beginning of a pupil's Secondary School career."[53] But the Cheshire case revealed that the minister was not only incapable of leading the LEAs' policy towards secondary technical schools, but could hardly have achieved a consistency of opinion among his own officials. When Dr Kellett, Cheshire's Director of Education, proposed that pupils should stay in schools of a technical type up to the age of 18, ministry officials responded that "it is most undesirable to inculcate highly specialised technical knowledge at 16-18."[54] In Buckinghamshire the minister's response pointed in the opposite direction: "it is suggested that the age-range in these schools should be described as 11-18."[55]

Manchester, as a markedly industrial area with 10% of pupils in technical schools, raised several difficulties in implementing the ministry policy, such as: entry to technical schools at the age of 13 is entirely from secondary modern schools; no mention is made of a technical sixth form at the age of 16; the existing accommodation is unsuitable and inadequate; technical education for girls was ignored. Consequently, when the Authority had to solve these complicated problems on its own it came to the conclusion that the most suitable school would be the bilateral grammar/technical type, and dismissed the central policy of the ministry in the following words:

> The Authority in its Development Plan rejected the concept of the tripartite division of the secondary education into grammar, technical and modern types. The use of these labels in the Development Plan had no significance beyond the fact that the forms of plan had been determined by the Ministry of Education.[56]

Cumberland rejected the ministry's allocation of 15% to grammar schools, 10% to technical schools and the rest to modern schools and prepared its technical education "from its own experience."[57] Thus, for example, the junior technical school at Millom was to continue its two year courses with entry at 13+ within the framework of the grammar schools, while the same type of school in Workington, which had provided four year courses for entry at 11+, was to continue unchanged. The Authority evidently preferred to follow its own traditional education system rather than accept the policy of the Ministry of Education.

Barrow-in-Furness also constructed the proposals regarding technical schools in their DP according to their own circumstances and tradition. The fact that Barrow was a town of heavy industry with specific and long-term demands was hence the major factor in planning the DP. Local conditions meant that there was no demand for female labour, and so the Authority resisted the demand for separate technical schools for girls on the argument that:

> In the absence of the need for a specific vocational training, the Authority are of the opinion that girls with high general factors of intelligence... can satisfactorily secure the secondary education ... of a bilateral technical-modern type.[58]

Local circumstances, needs and traditions hence played a major role in shaping the secondary technical school system, and the central policy and rigid instructions of the ministry were correspondingly neglected and rejected.

The ministry had difficulty controlling and monitoring the development of the technical schools for the following reasons: (1) the ministry's main effort during the development plan discussion period (the end of the 1940s to the early 1950s) was directed at defending the grammar schools, and little attention was left for the ministry's aspiration to double the number of pupils in the technical schools; (2) the state of school buildings within a period where the compulsory school leaving age was extended did not allow for further development and financing of separate technical schools; (3) the 1944 Education Act included a huge number of details that the ministry had to approve, and it was impossible to respond to every detail that was not commensurate with central policy without endangering the progress and the implementation of the entire reform. A clearer picture of the trends in the process of development of the secondary technical school was revealed to ministry officials in November 1954:

> Many authorities prefer to try to provide in grammar school the sort of courses which might have been provided in a secondary technical school. Others are experimenting with bilateral grammar/technical schools.[59]

In both cases, in modern and grammar schools, technical courses were means of enriching the curriculum; while in grammar schools these courses were planned for the less able pupils, in the modern schools they were intended to offer career opportunities of a vocational type. And so, not unsurprisingly, when the full extent of the gap between the policy that was to have been carried out and the reality was revealed to David Eccles, the Minister of Education, in 1955, he raised fundamental questions about the future of the technical schools:

> I do not have a clear idea of the importance of these schools.... We need more wisdom in the electorate and greater efficiency in industry.... But wherever we turn we are met with shortages of trained craftsmen, engineers, scientists, etc... what lies behind

> this figure of 5 per cent? If some such proportion was right 25 years ago when industry was less complicated and took in more apprentices, how can it be right to-day? ... Is it a great advantage to give a technical school a separate existence with a Modern secondary school? or with a Grammar school? I see that 53 per cent of 90,000 children now in technical schools went there at 13+. Where were they from 11 to 13?[60]

The minister's response reveals that the number of pupils had not been increased nor the years of study been extended since 1945. Moreover, the low image of the technical schools and the prejudices against them – which were among their genuine problems and had supposedly been removed by "missionary work" in order to attract abler and brighter students – had in fact not been changed; not only in the eyes of the public, but even in the eyes of Eccles, the minister charged with "remov[ing] the misapprehensions."[61] He wrote:

> A good many children from homes poor in letters or in morals might find it easier to take GCE and go to a University via a technical school rather than via a grammar school. 11+ is early to show your paces if you come from a dumb or bad home. But you may have some practical abilities. This is one reason why technical schools attract me.[62]

This letter from the minister to his secretary might partly explain the unattractiveness and poor image of these schools. Instead of trying to define development of the technical schools in terms of industrial and professional national needs, the ministry was defining them according to the order of social stratification; this was among the reasons for the low image of technical studies and for the regression in the development of this type of school.[63]

Thus, inevitably, when the Crowther Report claimed in 1959 that "we do not now have, and never have had, a tripartite system,"[64] the explanation offered with respect to technical schools was that:

> Technical schools as a group are slightly less numerous today than they were in 1947. To justify us in talking of a tripartite

system, we should need as many technical schools as grammar schools. In fact we have four grammar schools to every technical school and six grammar school pupils to every technical school pupil. Over 40 per cent of the local education authorities do not provide technical schools.

The report constituted official recognition of the fact that the government had not succeeded in implementing the policy of a tripartite system. The Report went on to characterise what existed in its place:

> Instead of a tripartite system we have...a two-sided system, based on the assumption, where maintained schools are concerned, that all boys and girls alike go to undifferentiated primary schools, and that from the age of 11 onwards all go to a modern school unless they can show cause to the contrary and there is a place for them in a school giving a different kind of education. The secondary modern school is the school for the great majority of the population from the age of 11.[65]

Thus, towards the beginning of the 1960s, the Ministry of Education's aim of having 10% of pupils attend technical schools was far from being achieved. Moreover, between the years 1948 and 1964, the number of technical schools was reduced from 6.9% to 3.3%.

There are several other factors that played a major part in eroding the assumptions and intentions underlying the tripartite system and contributed to the final collapse of the separation and classification approach that had governed the English education system for almost half a century.

6.3: THE SELECTION PROBLEM

Under the provisions of the 1944 Education Act, it was the duty of the local education authorities to provide an education suited to the age, ability and aptitude of the pupil. The LEAs were expected to assign pupils to three separate schools, grammar, modern and technical, by means of a selection test based on intelligence, arithmetic and English, with their school records taken into account. Selection was not new in the English education system; it had been conducted since the beginning of the 20th century by various local education authorities for free places in grammar schools, based on examination papers. This process of selection aimed to classify the capabilities and achievements of young candidates for free places in secondary schools at the age of 11 (Consultative Committee, 1924).[66] From the early 1920s, intelligence tests that included standardised attainments tests in English and arithmetic began to appear in some counties as part of the selection procedure (Vernon, 1957). This development in testing by local authorities was supported by the Hadow Report (1926) and the Norwood Report (1943) and finally adopted by the ministry in 1944.[67]

The trend to diagnose, categorise, frame and predict children's attainment at this early stage of their lives raised natural resistance among local authorities when they were asked, according to the 1944 Education Act, to provide an education suited to age, ability and aptitude. LEAs had difficulty making irrevocable decisions that would affect the future course of a child's life by directing him to a particular school, and some of them resisted and ignored the ministry's direction. Leicestershire could be held up as a typical example of the LEAs' response on this matter:

> No reliable test has yet been invented which can discover at the age of eleven specific technical aptitudes as distinct from general intelligence and capacity for learning.[68]

Other LEAs such as Middlesex, London, Hampshire, Kent, Birmingham, Cheshire and Barrow-in-Furness, raised arguments of the same kind, which were not based on scientific evidence so much as on feelings, intuition, attitudes and values.[69] But the controversy over whether the result of a single examination could provide a satisfactory basis for making decisions about a child's educational future did not die down, and in 1952, the National Foundation for Educational Research in England and Wales presented a report on the subject. The report concluded that there were two main weaknesses to the selection system:
(1) difficulties with the borderline pupils;
(2) testing of arithmetic, English and Intelligence was likely to be affected by different types of preparation, coaching, school and curriculum.

The researchers found that coaching raised the average scores of children in intelligence tests by 5 to 9 points above the standardised score, that teachers varied in the effectiveness of their coaching, and that practising on the same type of selection tests was as effective as an equivalent amount of coaching (Watts et al., 1952).

A confidential report submitted to the ministry in 1954 by the National Foundation for Educational Research further illuminated the problem of placing borderline pupils. The report revealed that "approximately 10 per cent of children in all the age-groups appear to have been wrongly allocated"[70] in both schools – grammar and modern. This meant that 78,000 children were sent to the wrong type of school in England and Wales (Yates & Pidgeon, 1957).[71]

The publication of Professor Vernon's works on the selection problem, in the mid-1950s,[72] amplified the confusion within the Ministry of Education. Vernon's main conclusions were: (a) there was a very close link between socio-economic class and allocation of places in grammar schools; (b) the rigid streaming had harmful educational and social consequences because children's abilities are more variable than was supposed; (c) success in GCE could well occur among pupils who had not been in the top 30% at age 11 as a result of having attended different schools, with different teaching efficiency, school interests and parental backing; (d) even with a validity coefficient of 0.90, roughly one quarter of those who did badly were in the grammar school: (e) IQ fluctuates more widely during development than was supposed, because innate and hereditary factors are largely built up or acquired during childhood and adolescence by environmental stimulation; and (f) marking of English essays shows great variations between markers. Vernon came to the conclusion that there was "insufficient scope for self-determination, irregularities of development, and the virtues of persistence and fortitude in the face of set-backs which are much commended in British education."[73]

The research works of the sociologists Floud, Halsey and Martin in the mid-1950s reinforced these findings, particularly in respect of the influence of the home on children's educational prospects. Family size and parental ambition emerged as the most evident and influential factors in the examination performance of children.[74]

Basil Bernstein contributed to the controversy and broadened it by emphasising the problem of semi-skilled and unskilled strata of linguistic expression, which were powerful conditioners of future learning, for children. Bernstein's studies, carried out since the end of the 1950s, produced strong evidence of the disadvantage of intelligence tests for lower class pupils; working-class pupils had very high non-verbal scores but the gap between verbal scores and non-verbal scores was in the order of 20+ IQ points. Bernstein's argument was that this gap was to be expected in terms of the "linguistic deprivation experienced in their social background."[75] He argued that one should not under-value the lower working class and not measure human worth on a scale of verbal language.

The findings of these studies and the criticism they contained, along with LEAs' attempts to abandon the selection system, provoked a public debate on this matter that the Ministry of Education could not ignore. Discussion within the ministry after 1955 raised five main questions:

(a) What is the validity of the standardised testing in assessing future performance?
(b) What is the influence of home background?
(c) What is the influence of school environment on objective tests?
(d) How should the borderline group be treated?
(e) How does over-age transfer to grammar schools contribute to weak performance?

Internal discussions and correspondence on these questions within the ministry revealed a general tendency to justify and vindicate the existing selection arrangements. Thus, the answer to the first question about the validity of the tests reflected a general satisfaction among ministry officials, who argued that tests were "remarkably accurate" and held that "although this number of misplacements is not negligible, it is of the order to be expected with the best type of allocation examination."[76]

The issue of the influence of home background raised a mixed response. Some argued that if family background affected the child's future success, an assessment of the family background should be included in the tests in order to achieve a better prediction:

> The child is part of a family, and . . . assessing children without assessing their families is like selecting a cricket team entirely on batting averages.[77]

But the crux of the problem, according to the writer of the document just quoted, was the contradiction between the right thing to do concerning the accuracy of the tests on the one hand, and what the public response would be to this proposal on the other:

> Since assessing the families would strike most people as unfair, and since not assessing them is bound to increase the overlap in any selection procedure.[78]

The idea of family assessment occupied officials in the Ministry of Education who went on to blame the LEAs for the inaccuracy of the tests:

> LEAs have not included in their 11+ tests a method of forecasting whether children will stay the whole Grammar School course, mainly, of course, because they do not take into account the major factor, i.e. the home background of the child . . . results ought to be the criterion on which the accuracy of the 11+ forecast is judged.[79]

Responses concentrated heavily on grammar school progress, looking for statistical improvements in order to counter incorrect allocation of pupils in lower standards. The question of the borderline group raised the issue of how to decrease the number of pupils in this group by a "statistically reliable method, and not by arbitrary choice."[80] But the statistical question necessitated a human decision, to be taken by the ministry on the sensitive question of home background:

> *The question is whether it is right to deny the opportunity of a grammar school course to a child of moderate ability who has such a favourable home background* that he will undoubtedly make full use of his talents and the opportunity provided, *in order to give the place to the child of better ability who is unlikely to be able to*

> *make the most of his chance because he lacks the positive support and encouragement of his parents* [original emphasis].⁸¹

The ministry's dilemma on the issue of family background highlighted the fact that any future decision concerning the prediction of children's attainments would lead to a politically complicated choice between allocating grammar school places for able children from weak backgrounds or less able children from better homes.⁸²

And so, unsurprisingly, Eccles was compelled to respond to public pressure and dissatisfaction on the selection issue. He decided not to make a decision, which could be highly risky politically, but to leave the complex issue totally in the hands of the local authorities. In reply to a letter from a parent, the Minister of Education himself said:

> The duty of a local education authority is to provide an education suited to the age, ability and aptitude of the pupil. The pattern of education in this country is highly flexible, and, as you say, the percentage of pupils in grammar schools varies from one area to another. I do not think however that the idea of fixing a "national standard" for grammar school admissions – even if it were possible – is the right way to deal with this.⁸³

The minister's reply denoted a withdrawal from any central interference in local arrangements regarding selection as well as in the proportion between the different types of schools: the same proportion that the ministry had struggled so hard to maintain and which was at the core of disputes between central government and the LEAs during the late 1940s and early 1950s. From now on local authorities would be free of central guidelines dictating proportions between numbers of pupils in types of schools (Circular 73, 1945) and free to decide on further development of secondary education according to local circumstances, needs and traditions.

6.4: THE NEW STRUCTURAL ORDER: THE COMPREHENSIVE SCHOOL

Gradual pressure from educational factors within the local authorities, such as modern schools' demands for access to external examinations, and criticism of the selection system were joined by other administrative factors such as internal emigration, the increasing school population, financial difficulties in maintaining or building three different types of schools and, finally, the collapse of the consensus among the two main political parties on the issue of the tripartite system. All these factors combined contributed to a pragmatic solution that was led by the LEAs. This tendency was accelerated after the ministry decided to let the local authorities make their own decisions on the substantial questions of selection and proportions between schools, according to local circumstances. In this manner the LEAs sought ways to overcome the disadvantages and the criticism of the tripartite system which eventually led towards a new structural order based on the comprehensive school.

The rise in the birth rate presented the education service with problems related to the supply of teachers and accommodation. In 1947 the number of pupils in senior schools was 1,600,000; this figure rose gradually to the peak point of 2,844,000 in 1961 (see Appendix 2).

Population migration was the greatest factor in the need for new schools. Between the years 1946 and 1964 over 5 million homes were built in new suburbs. Population figures in the centres of many large cities remained static or declined, while the suburbs grew. The London region, for example, increased by half a million in population and extended up to 40-50 miles from the centre (Kelsall, 1975; Lowe, 1988).[84] The massive migration from inner towns and villages to the new suburbs raised planning problems. For example, in the year 1960-61 the migration balance in the Midlands Region was +1.1%, in the Eastern Region +2%, in the London Region +2.3%, and in the Southern Region +2.1% (Kelsall, 1975).

These rapid population changes, unforeseen and hardly planned, had to be followed by changes in education services and accommodation. Local authorities like London, the West Riding, Birmingham, Staffordshire, Swansea, Coventry, West Yorkshire and Manchester responded with plans for comprehensive schools and applied for ministry approval (Lowe, 1988; Rubinstein & Simon, 1973). Lowe claims that these plans were marked not so much by ideological commitment as simply by the fact that "they had all identified quickly growing new suburbs in need of some secondary provision."[85] But in practice the development of comprehensive schools in urban areas could only occur on new housing estates (Rubinstein & Simon, 1973). Despite the social changes, the Ministry of Education rejected speedy growth of comprehensive schools and allowed the establishment of these institutions only as an "experiment" or in new suburbs that were homogeneous and had mainly middle class populations. Nevertheless, although the ministry still supported the tripartite system the number of comprehensive schools increased gradually but steadily during the late 1950s and the early 1960s, as shown in the following table:

Table 6.3: The number of comprehensive schools

Year	No	%
1955	16	0.3
1956	31	0.6
1957	43	0.8
1958	86	1.6
1959	111	1.9
1960	130	2.2
1961	138	2.3
1962	152	2.6
1963	175	3.0
1964	195	3.4

Source: *Statistics of Education* 1955-64.

The table clearly shows the development of the comprehensive school and the fact that in 1964, 71% of the local authorities had either established this type of institution or intended to do so, and 25% of local education authorities had already changed the selective system (Rubinstein & Simon, 1969). This trend was finally reinforced by a political shift. The Conservative Party, which won the elections and formed governments in the years 1951 to 1964, adopted a pragmatic approach and from 1955 approved comprehensive schools which had not been justified as "experimental" (see

Table 6.3). In practice, after a decade of rejecting the comprehensive idea and voicing government disapproval of the LEAs' plans, the Ministers of Education, David Eccles, Edward Boyle and Geoffrey Lloyd, approved comprehensive plans more openly. Eccles' words on this issue in the House of Commons express this change in atmosphere with regard to the comprehensive issue:

> The comprehensive school is having a good run. Some of these schools are doing well but we have enough experience now to know that the large comprehensive school puts an exceptional strain on the teachers.[86]

Despite resistance from Conservative backbenchers to any departure from selection policy, Conservative Ministers Geoffrey Lloyd and Edward Boyle withstood the critics and the accusations of a "soft" or "liberal" approach. Boyle made a clear statement on the heart of the controversial issue in the 1950s:

> None of us believe in pre-war terms that children can be sharply differentiated into various types or labels of ability; and I certainly would not wish to advance the view that the tripartite system, as it is often called, should be regarded as the right and normal way of organising secondary education.[87]

These words clearly show that in practical terms the Conservative ministers had fallen in with the LEAs' policy of abandoning the selective system and accepted the idea of comprehensive schools.

This change in atmosphere influenced and accelerated the authorities' plans for comprehensives. London, for example, announced in 1962 that the 20 remaining grammar schools would merge with other schools and become comprehensive;[88] Sheffield, Leeds, Hull, Manchester and Liverpool applied for reorganisation just before the Conservative government was replaced by Labour in the 1964 general election, and Bradford's proposal to depart from the selective system was approved by Edward Boyle in 1964 (Lowe, 1988).

Within the Labour Party the tripartite system had been well supported since the 1944 Education Act was passed by Parliament and there had been full consensus on educational issues between the two major parties. When the Labour Party won the 1945 election and formed a government, their commitment to the tripartite policy remained unchanged and the Labour Ministers of Education Ellen Wilkinson and George Tomlinson were quick to reject local proposals for comprehensive schools, except in extreme cases that justified the definition of an "experimental" comprehensive school. Indeed, only 13 such schools had been approved by the Labour ministers during the five years of their government, and 1951 was the first time that this type of school appeared in the official statistics of the ministry. However, soon after the Conservative party regained power in 1951 there was a shift in opinion, sparking off a long controversy. In the same year the publication *Secondary Education For All* committed the Labour Party to a comprehensive school policy (Parkinson, 1970). A further development of the comprehensive policy was led by Alice Bacon, spokesperson for the National Executive Committee of the Labour Party, proposing a split system of junior and senior comprehensive schools. The suggestion caused a dispute with the National Association of Labour Teachers, who argued:

> They would lessen the number of working-class children staying on at school beyond the statutory leaving age since parental, social and economic pressures would prevent many from making the transfer to senior school at fifteen.[89]

Labour's defeat in the 1955 election resulted in a move towards a soft line in propaganda for comprehensive reorganisation. This shift was reinforced by the results of a public opinion poll carried out by the Party in 1957 which showed that the vast majority of the public did not support the idea of the comprehensive school (Parkinson, 1970).[90] The poll's clear evidence that parents wanted to keep and defend the traditional grammar school caused uncertainty in the Labour Party as to what would be the most beneficial line for it to take in the next election, and particularly what would be the result of abolishing the grammar schools. As a result of this dilemma Labour preferred to keep its options open and adopt an ambivalent view on the secondary reorganisation issue. This ambivalence is explained by Parkinson as follows:

> The 1958 policy statement tried to reconcile two points of view by arguing that, although the comprehensive principle would mean the demise of the grammar school as a separate institution, the important elements of it would be retained in a different form. They offered, in Gaitskell's phrase, "grammar-school education for all."[91]

The Labour Party considered the extent of disagreement on the defects and advantages of the segregated tripartite system and the comprehensive system and wished to avoid arousing further public concern and tension about their education policy; it hence announced that any future Labour government would not compel the LEAs to reorganise secondary education on comprehensive lines. Labour thus committed itself to following the reality of what was happening on the ground in the local authorities. Harold Wilson's announcement that the grammar schools would be abolished "over [his] dead body"[92] was aimed at reducing public anxiety and reassuring people that no radical changes would be made.

When Labour won the 1964 general election, they indeed avoided a radical policy towards a full comprehensive system. Instead they preferred to follow the process already under way in the local authorities, which was shifting away from the tripartite towards the comprehensive system, by giving central recognition and encouragement to this process and by removing all the obstacles on the part of those authorities that had wished to move towards the comprehensive system in the past and had not been encouraged by the ministry. Michael Stewart, the Labour Secretary of State for Education and Science, speaking in the Commons in November 1964, maintained that the steady trend towards comprehensive schools was less a present Labour policy than the result of some factors that had existed before Labour came to power:

> The chance of a grammar school education can be three, four or five times as great for a child living in one county as for a child within another. Within the same area a boy may have a better chance of a grammar school education than his twin sister . . . .

> Secondly, the errors made at 11 cannot adequately be remedied by subsequent transfer.... That brings me to my third objection, the difficulty of finding an appropriate place for the secondary modern in this tripartite.... Another cause for dissatisfaction with the tripartite system ... is that it tends to distort the teaching in the primary school away from its proper purpose to coaching for the 11-plus ... *for all those reasons, that there has been a steady move – away from the separatist pattern to the comprehensive one* [present writer's emphasis].[93]

The Secretary of State argued that these factors had already led to 68 authorities, responsible for 63% of the secondary school population, either implementing or examining concrete proposals for reorganisation on comprehensive lines, and 21 other authorities contemplating such reorganisation.

When Circular 10/65 was published, eight months after the Labour victory, each local authority was left to decide whether it wanted to reorganise secondary education in its area on comprehensive lines. The forms of such reorganisation defined by the Labour government included six different options, and left enough room for local authorities to decide which of them would suit their needs and circumstances.

Furthermore, the six different comprehensive forms allowed for greater variety on top of the variety already existing within the system – and not only between counties, but within the same county and even within the same local authority. From now on, local needs, circumstances, traditions, perception and expectations – which had been a source of ignorance, resistance, confusion and dispute over central policy – were given a more prominent role in determining the most suitable pattern of secondary education for each authority. There would no longer be a framework of three or even four main schools (including the comprehensive), but six different comprehensive options in addition to or instead of the other types of school that already existed in the local authority. This approach recognised the importance of community involvement and the special needs, circumstances, traditions, interests, expectations and perceptions impinging on each authority and community; this approach had in actuality been behind the development of secondary education since 1944 and was the underlying reason for the conflicts and disputes that arose between LEAs and ministry policy.

The decision not to compel the authorities to reorganise secondary education on comprehensive lines was soon revealed as "double talk" though, for Circular 10/65 had stated that "the Secretary of State will not approve any new secondary project . . . which would be incompatible with the introduction of a non-selective system of secondary education."[94]

Labour policy encouraged LEAs to submit reorganisation plans, and in 1969 schemes had been approved in 129 out of 163 local education authorities; 108 of these covered the greater part of the authority (Maclure, 1986). But these figures are more a reflection of LEAs' initiatives or intentions before 1965 and of actual trends and the evolution of secondary education on the ground before this date, than of any new move or direction.[95] Nevertheless, the Labour initiative gave legitimacy and recognition to the desires of many LEAs to abandon the selective system and move towards a common school.

In 1968 the Labour government, with Alice Bacon as Minister of Education and Science, announced its intention to introduce a new Bill that would compel those LEAs still left out of the comprehensive organisation to reorganise their education system on this basis. However, the resignation of the government in 1969 and the defeat of Labour in the general election of 1970 brought this idea to an end.

Margaret Thatcher became Secretary of State for Education when the Conservatives regained power in 1970, and her first action was to cancel Circular 10/65 which had instructed the LEAs to submit a reorganisation scheme on the lines of comprehensive schools to the ministry. Circular 10/70 aimed to stop the trend toward comprehensive schools by returning to tripartite terms:

> All pupils shall have full opportunities for secondary education suitable to their needs and abilities. The Government, however, believes it is wrong to impose a uniform pattern of secondary organisation on local education authorities by legislation or other means.... . Authorities will now be freer to determine the shape of secondary provision in their areas.[96]

Despite the government's intention, however, the trend towards comprehensive reorganisation continued during Mrs Thatcher's five years in office (1970-74); and the number of comprehensive schools doubled, from 1,145 in 1970 to 2,273 in 1974. These figures highlight the limit of the power of even a determined government or Secretary of State for Education to cause or to prevent implementation of a policy that contradicts the needs of pupils, teachers, parents, communities, local authorities and society as a whole, or in Mrs Thatcher's words:

> When I was Minister for Education in the Heath government . . . this great rollercoaster of an idea was moving, and I found it difficult, if not impossible, to stop.[97]

The 1970 government was aware of its powerlessness not only to reverse the comprehensive trend but even to avoid its further development. Therefore the terms of Circular 10/70 were more in the nature of suggestions than of compulsory instructions; instead of prohibiting the local authorities from following the comprehensive trend, the Circular aimed to encourage them to withdraw their previous plans for comprehensive reorganisation and plan an alternative pattern of secondary organisation. But this attempt at central intervention could not change the fact that the tripartite system with its attempt at the rigid classification of pupils was not in the interests of the LEAs, and had in fact collapsed. The government had succeeded fully in achieving secondary education for all but had failed to implement the tripartite system, which was based on inflexible psychological assumptions. The following table shows not only the results of this failure but also the gradual and steady changes that emerged as a new order and a new system structure (for full details see Appendix 3).

Table 6.4: Secondary schools distribution: 1948-1988 (in %)

Year	Modern	Grammar	Technical	Bilateral+ Multilateral	Comp.	Total
1948	66.6	26.3	6.9	-	-	99.8
1953	68.8	23.8	5.9	1.3	0.2	100
1958	69	23.3	5.2	1	1.6	100[98]
1963	69.2	22.9	3.6	1.2	3.1	100
1968	61.3	22.1	2.3	-	14.3	100
1973	41.5	17.8	0.9	-	39.8	100
1978	15.4	7.5	0.5	-	76.8	100
1983	8.2	4.4	0.4	-	87.1	100
1988	5.9	4.1	0.2	-	89.7	100

Source: *Education Statistics. DES, 1949-1989*

6.5: CONCLUSIONS

When the government initiated the tiny change in input – the changing of the status of the modern school to secondary and not elementary – the result was an overwhelming change in output, which subverted the official policy of the tripartite system and established a new structure.

This failure resulted mainly from the need for such things as concrete aims, significant and meaningful studies and prospects for advancement, which would lead to strong motivation and forceful and determined pressure to fulfil these needs. Consequently, the central policy – a policy that ignored and disregarded the needs of the majority of pupils and of the related needs of pupils, parents and teachers – was disrupted, undermined and subverted. Eventually, the government policy of a tripartite system collapsed and was gradually replaced by a system in which such needs could be fulfilled.

When the modern schools became part of the pattern of secondary education – separate from the elementary schools out of which they grew – in terms of higher leaving age, smaller forms and adequate accommodation, expectations were raised far beyond the intention of the planners of the 1944 Education Act. Pupils, parents and teachers ignored the stated purpose of these schools as "free from pressures of any external examination"[99] because although there was merit to the modern school's intended concentration on the "enjoyment of life," its demerit was that it deprived pupils of the advantage of public recognition in the form of a formal attainment certificate. Teachers, parents and pupils wanted to jettison the low expectations that were closely connected with the schools' low status, and demanded access to external examinations which had until then been the exclusive privilege of the grammar school pupils. There were many reasons behind the demand for this certification, but all shared a preference for undertaking dedicated study and making a greater effort over "free[dom] from examinations," provided that they would get some kind of public recognition. The pupils and parents wanted a certificate that would lead them to further achievement in terms of jobs and access to other institutions; the teachers wanted acknowledgement and recognition of their ability and their pupils' ability. The government resisted letting the modern schools have access to examinations of any kind out of anxiety over lower standards. The result of this resistance was that agents other than the ministry took the initiative in establishing examining bodies to supply this need and demand.

Finally, when practical solutions were fostered by the ministry in response to the modern schools' demand, the fact that in the course of a gradual process 21,680 pupils entered for external examinations, was confirmation of the teachers' claims that low expectations and diffuse definition of the modern school were wasting a tremendous amount of ability. This strengthened Vernon's argument that there are some unpredictable factors, such as self-determination and the irregularities of child development, in progress in education. The range of ability that was discovered among modern school pupils and the criticism of selection raised doubt and uncertainty within the Ministry of Education about the desirability of selection between schools, and indeed the ministry did not defend selection when local authorities brought the system to an end.

The modern school issue raised two main findings and conclusions. The first is that those who were less regarded, less respected, and slated to be under-achievers in comparison with pupils at other schools, demonstrated that when provided with a concrete, significant and rewarding purpose, they showed dedication and higher motivation in achieving the target: the certificate. Higher standards could be achieved not by limiting the number of those with access to examinations, but by challenging even less able pupils; this is because unpredictable human factors are involved in passing examinations successfully. Undoubtedly, not every modern school pupil was able to cope with this challenge, but if standards are defined in terms of the number of pupils passing the examinations successfully, as they were at that time, the entrance of modern schools to the examinations did not confirm the fears voiced by Eccles that such egalitarian ideas would "lower the standards." Flexibility of administrative arrangements and the determination of teachers and pupils were among the reasons for this achievement. The surprising results, and the fact that more than 1,000 schools entered pupils for the examinations, were commented on by one of the ministry's officials: "When imagination is caught, ambition is fired and self-confidence is gained, even the dullest child will surprise his teacher by his progress."[100]

The teachers played a dual role in this development, directing pressure and encouragement in two directions: on the one hand at the policy makers – to give public recognition to their schools' success by way of a certificate – and on the other hand on pupils and parents, urging a higher investment of effort in order to enter and pass the examinations. Teachers were ready to take on much more responsibility and accountability and to invest more effort in order to "supply a sense of purpose"[101] and to bring their pupils to a level where they would be able to cope with external examinations. They resisted the early categorisation, labelling, and fixed image of their pupils, and argued that low expectations and administrative restrictions were the real reasons for the waste of talents in their schools. The teachers' ambitions in this respect were motivated not only by pure desire to promote the future and equal opportunity of their pupils but also from the need for a concrete purpose and significance to their curriculum; for them as well as for the pupils, access to the external examinations was a significant aim.

The powerful determination of pupils as well as teachers to obtain significant and meaningful certification is well supported by Handy's (1988) theoretical model, which claims that individuals calculate how much effort they must expend in order to achieve a desired result. In the case of the modern schools, the significance of the certificate was so powerful that even the "dullest child," to use the ministry's official term, surprised his teachers. This proved that the early psychological calculations and assumptions of the tripartite system were defeated by the self-determination and ambition behind pupils' and teachers' goals.

The second conclusion is that when the government finally opened the route to external examinations and when the first aim was achieved and modern pupils were allowed to take the "O" level, gradually the number of pupils seeking to enter for "A" level increased.

The technical schools, for several reasons, were not part of the authorities' main efforts and consequently they decreased to a third of the government's target and had almost totally vanished as a separate and independent institution at the beginning of the 1980s. The reasons for this development are first, that authorities had seen the technical subjects as a means to enrich the curriculum of the grammar and the modern schools and not as a matter for a separate school type; secondly, local considerations dominated the type and volume of technical education needed according to regional tradition, type of industry, prediction of future industrial area needs in terms of professionals; and thirdly, there was a naive expectation that local authorities would be able to reorganise, implement radical changes and increase the volume of the technical schools up to 10 or 15 percent, even when technical schools did not exist at all in 40% of the authorities.[102] Furthermore, this was expected when enormous effort was needed to implement the secondary reform, leaving no energy or resources to cope with the mission of the technical school, which by itself was a radical change.

The criticism of the selection policy and the question of assessing pupils' family background in order to achieve more accurate prediction of pupils' attainment brought the whole issue of selection and classification to breaking point. The cynical and the paradoxical question of whether it is right "to deny the opportunity of a grammar school course to a child of moderate ability who has such a favourable home background" or "to give the place to the child of better ability who is unlikely to be able to make the most of his chance because he lacked the positive support and encouragement of his parents,"[103] brought the issue to the point where the minister could no longer ignore it. For the minister there were two options; to support the continuation of selection and to give central backing to the local authorities, or to depart from this policy and to let the authorities conduct the issue without any central instructions. Inevitably the minister chose the second option in practice without mentioning publicly the change in policy. Instead he expressed it thus: "The pattern of education in this country is highly flexible ... the percentage of pupils in grammar schools varies from one area to another."[104] This letter was one of the central admissions, in the middle of the 1950s, that the psychological assumptions on intelligence underlying selection and rigid classification as laid down by Hadow, Norwood and Spence could not be given central backing as rational policy any more. There was a growing awareness that certain other factors such as determination, ambition, irregularities of development and persistence could confuse any preliminary prediction of performance, and this undermined the ministry's ability to defend the psychological assumptions that had dictated central policy on secondary reorganisation. Unsurprisingly, Eccles and his successors were attacked by members of their own party for abandoning the selection policy; but they could no longer defend Butler's system and the assumptions of the 1944 Education Act.

Thus, the government initiative of the 1944 Education Act, and the initial encouragement of modern school pupils to study up to the age of 15, were quickly matched by pupils' and teachers' aspirations and motivations that the government could no longer control. This development, along with a multiplicity of other factors based on local circumstances and social factors which were more powerful than the government anticipated, led to the establishment of a new structural order in which government had only a marginal influence. The move towards a new structure was gradual – slow but steady. Each division and community came to its own conclusion, according to internal pressures and circumstances, as to what was the desirable shape of secondary education and when and where to reorganise it. And so, finally, the combined factors described above are those that resulted in the 1944 policy being, in McCulloch's word, "exploited, neglected, rigidified and abused [...] a classic example of the gap between policy and practice, between the aspirations and ideals of the elite and the realities of everyday negotiation in the schools."[105]

Notes:

1. Education in 1949: *Report of The Ministry of Education and the Statistics of Public Education for England and Wales*, London.
2. To meet the universities' entrance requirements, the Committee proposed that at the age of 18+ pupils should take a school leaving examination in the subjects that would be required for their particular purpose. The Committee's main idea was to enable schools and teachers to dedicate their efforts to general education without the pressure of external examinations.
3. Denis Lawton (1980). *The Politics of the School Curriculum*. London: Routledge & Kegan Paul, 94.
4. Roy Lowe (1988). *Education in the Post War Years: A Social History*. London: Routledge, 186.
5. PRO ed. 147/303 Document sent by MPR to Mr. Part on 1 December 1954.
6. Ibid. Quoted from The Schoolmaster, 7 January 1955.
7. PRO ed. 147/303. Document of 26 January 1955 entitled: "External Examinations in Secondary Schools Below the Standard of GCE."
8. Ministry of Education (1945). *The Nation's Schools: Their Plan and Purpose*. Pamphlet No.1, London, 21.
9. PRO ed. 147/303.
10. Ibid. Document of 19 January 1955 entitled: "Examinations in Secondary Schools."
11. Ibid., 4.
12. PRO ed. 147/303. Draft speech of the Minister: "Examinations in Secondary Schools."
13. PRO ed. 147/303. This number was quoted by the College of Preceptors.
14. Schools in the Harrow district and in South-West Hertfordshire had organised their own leaving certificate examinations. Manchester had asked the Union of Lancashire and Cheshire Institute to devise an external examination (PRO ed. 147/303).
15. PRO ed. 147/303. Letter of 7 February 1955.
16. Ibid.
17. PRO ed. 147/303. A Draft Speech of the Minister (undated, probably June 1955).
18. Ibid.
19. Ibid.
20. Ministry of Education (July 1955), Circular 289, 1.
21. Ibid.
22. Ibid., 5.
23. The way was blocked by means of two main administrative decisions. First, modern schools were not allowed to extend their studies for able pupils to the age of 16, while compulsory education at that time was only up to age 15. Secondly, the Ministry did not agree to finance the cost of modern school examinations within the schools themselves unless individuals were transferred to a grammar school or technical college.
24. PRO ed. 147/303. Letter from L. Davies of 15 September 1955.
25. Ibid.
26. Ibid., 2.
27. PRO ed. 147/303. Letter to T.C. Pannell, MP of 3 January 1956.

28. Ibid. A letter to Mr Part from Lancashire's Chief Education Officer of 7 December 1955.
29. PRO ed. 147/303. Letter of 18 November 1955.
30. Ibid. Letter of 6 January 1956.
31. Ibid. Letter of 22 December 1955.
32. PRO ed. 147/303. Letter of 12 January 1956.
33. Ibid. Document of 22 December 1955.
34. Education in 1957: *Report of the Ministry of Education and the Statistics of Public Education for England and Wales.* London (HMSO), 16.
35. PRO ed. 147/303. Letter by David Eccles to the Secretary.
36. Education in 1958: *Report of the Ministry of Education and the Statistics of Public Education for England and Wales.* London (HMSO), 29. The reclassification included comprehensive, multilateral and three kinds of bilateral schools. Lowe (1988) explains this redefinition concerning the comprehensive schools in the "inner city" as an "alternative secondary modern for the working classes," which confirmed the stratification of English society (Lowe, 1988, 149).
37. PRO ed. 147/206. Document of 16 November 1954 entitled: "The Pattern of Secondary Education."
38. PRO ed. 147/206. Letter of 22 February 1955.
39. The question of the modern school could not be separated from LEAs' demands for comprehensive schools, the selective problem, secondary education in rural areas and places in the grammar schools, but the fundamental issue remained the future of the modern schools.
40. PRO ed. 147/206. Document of 16 November 1954 entitled: "The Pattern of Secondary Education."
41. Ibid.
42. Ibid.
43. Ministry of Education (1959). 15 to 18, *Report of the Central Advisory Council for Education (England).* London: HMSO, 23.
44. Ibid., 21.
45. Ministry of Education (1945). *The Nation's Schools*, 15.
46. Ibid.
47. Ibid., 17.
48. The normal age of recruitment in technical schools was 13.
49. Education in 1949, 111. By 1948, the population of the technical schools was 71,700 pupils, which was about 4.5% of all the secondary school pupils.
50. PRO ed. 152/119: Northamptonshire. DP, 9.
51. Ibid.
52. Ibid.
53. PRO ed. 152/13: Cheshire. DP, 3.
54. PRO ed. 152/13. Interview memorandum of 8 April 1948.
55. PRO ed. 152/147. Letter from the Minister of 17 December 1948.
56. PRO ed. 152/328: Manchester. Note: Secondary School requirements, paragraph 5.

57. PRO ed. 152/21: Cumberland. DP, 2.
58. PRO ed. 152/208: Barrow-in-Furness. DP, 22.
59. PRO ed. 147/206. Document of 16 November 1954 entitled: "The Pattern of Secondary Education."
60. PRO ed. 147/207. Letter of 20 December 1954 from the minister to the secretary.
61. Ministry of Education (1945). *The Nation's Schools*, 15.
62. A letter of 20 December 1954 from the minister to the secretary.
63. The letter went on to describe the result and the failure of the government to improve technical schools since 1930 and the fact that despite ministry efforts nothing had been changed in terms of pupils and length of studies, which remained two or three years in 1955.
64. Ministry of Education (1959), 21.
65. Ibid., p.22.
66. Board of Education: *Report of the Consultative Committee on Psychological Tests of Educable Capacity and their Possible Use in the Public System of Education*, London, 1924.
67. The origin of testing and classifications lies in the work of the English scientist Sir Francis Galton, who in 1883 announced the possibility of measuring intellectual ability. The first half of the 20th century was characterised by extensive developments in methods of judgement of personal qualities, problems of human nature and the desire for testing movements for human betterment (Vernon, 1956).
68. PRO ed. 152/91: Leicestershire. DP, 3-4.
69. For more details about the LEAs' response in this matter see Chapter 4.2.
70. PRO ed. 147/205.
71. Alfred, Yates & D.A. Pidgeon (1957). *Admission to Grammar Schools*. London: Newnes, 1957.
72. P.E. Vernon (1956). *The Measurement of Abilities*. London: University of London Press; (1957). *Secondary School Selection*. London: Methuen; (1979). *Intelligence: Heredity and Environment*. San Francisco: Freeman.
73. Vernon (1957), 9.
74. J.E. Floud et al. (1953). "*Education Opportunity and Social Selection in England.*" In *Transactions of Second World Conference of Sociology*, Vol.II; (1956) *Social Class and Educational Opportunity*, London: Heinemann.
75. Basil Bernstein (1961). "Social Structure, Language and Learning." *Educational Research* Vol.3 No.3, 164.
76. PRO ed. 147/205. Document of November 1954 addressed to Mr Maxwell Hyslop and Mr Part.
77. PRO ed. 147/205. Document of 16 December 1954, written by G.F. Peaker.
78. Ibid.
79. PRO ed. 147/205. Letter of 10 February 1955 addressed to Mr Maxwell Hyslop and Mr Part.
80. PRO ed. 147/205. Document of November 1954 addressed to Mr Maxwell Hyslop and Mr Part.
81. Ibid.

82. The issues of the influence of school environment on pupils' attainments and over-age transfer to grammar schools were less discussed in the ministry at that stage. The only evidence found was an analysis of a report written by Dr Bartlett, the Essex psychologist, who had done work on the causes of misfit in grammar schools and found that the failure of the grammar school to take full account was the main cause of the break in the transfer at the age of 11. The issue of over-age transfer to grammar school was a result of the fact that local education authorities gave standardised tests as a second chance to children at the age of twelve after the same test had been given in the primary school at the age of eleven. The ministry blamed the authorities for this problem.
83. PRO ed. 147/205. Letter of 16 April 1955 from David Eccles.
84. R.K. Kelsall (1975). *Population*. London: Longman.
85. Lowe (1988), 135.
86. Quoted by I.G.K. Fenwick (1976), *The Comprehensive School 1944-1970: The Politics of Secondary School Reorganisation*. London: Methuen, 118, from Hansard, 17 July 1961.
87. Ibid., 118, quoted from the Conservative Research Department Library, Leaflets and Pamphlets, January-December 1963, Vol.II.
88. In that year 53.4% of the age group in London studied in 58 comprehensive schools (Rubinstein & Simon, 1973).
89. Michael Parkinson (1970). *The Labour Party and the Organisation of Secondary Education 1918-65*. London: Routledge & Kegan Paul, 73.
90. Two main themes could explain the public ignorance of the comprehensive school since the end of the 1940s: first, the illusory wish to gain a place in the traditional and highly respected grammar school; this illusion was apparent among working-class parents as well as the middle-class, despite the fact that only a minority of pupils could gain places in these schools. Secondly, the public had no knowledge of the merits of the comprehensive school and how children could benefit from this type of school.
91. Parkinson (1970), 86.
92. Ibid., 140.
93. Hansard Vol. 702, 27 November 1964, 1779-81.
94. Department of Education and Science, Circular 10/66 (10 March 1966), 2.
95. The figures given by Michael Stewart in the House of Commons before the publication of Circular 10/65 showed that 68 authorities, representing 63% of the secondary school population were at that time implementing or intended to implement reorganisation on comprehensive lines and that another 21 authorities were contemplating this reorganisation. Rubinstein and Simon (1970) mention that in 1959 71% of the LEAs submitted or were intending to submit full or part comprehensive reform. The meaning of 'part' in this sense could be the planning of even one comprehensive school in the authority.
96. Department of Education and Science (30 June 1970), Circular 10/70.
97. *The Daily Mail*, 13.8.87, quoted in Clyde Chitty, 1989, 54-5.
98. In this year the ministry figures for the grammar school included the bilateral schools of grammar/technical type.

99. Ministry of Education (1945). *The Nation's Schools*, 21.
100. PRO ed. 147/206. Document of 16 November 1954 entitled "The Pattern of Secondary Education."
101. PRO ed. 147/303, document sent by MPR to Mr Part on 1 December 1954.
102. We learn to what extent this type of school was not on the agenda of the local authorities from the fact that in the case studies described in Chapter 5, most of the authors did not give any attention to the technical schools in their writings.
103. PRO ed. 147/205. Document of November 1954 addressed to Mr Maxwell Hyslop and Mr Part.
104. PRO ed. 147/205. Letter from the Ministry of Education dated 16 April 1955.
105. Gray McCulloch (1989). *The Secondary Technical School: A Usable Past?* London: Falmer, 74.

PHASE THREE: RESTORING ORDER: TOWARDS A NEW SYSTEM STRUCTURE

INTRODUCTION

A counter-movement calling for a new structure in order to restore the standards and the "glory of the good old days" was stimulated largely by the abolition of selection, the gradual move towards a single type of school – the comprehensive school – the new social composition within this type of school, and the rapid expansion of education. These factors were followed by the drastic contraction of the prestigious grammar schools that served the "elite," from 25% in 1950 to 4.9% in 1981.

The practice of streaming within the comprehensive schools, which aimed to divide pupils into classes according to their academic potential and scholastic attainments, caused difficulties in pupil discipline, a strain on teachers and selection problems. For these reasons streaming was replaced gradually during the 1970s by mixed ability classes and less formal teaching methods. This move was another stimulus for the counter-movement campaign led by the Black Papers and the media, and for allegations that standards had fallen, despite inconclusive research evidence to this effect.

The main call of the campaign was for greater government intervention and control over educational matters. The level of criticism and controversy over the question of standards could not be ignored at the political level, and in 1976 the Prime Minister, James Callaghan, launched a public debate that would become a milestone in the course towards a national core curriculum.

The emergence of the "New Right" and the British economic decline during the 1970s engendered criticism of the welfare state policy and high investment in public services, which were regarded as the source of most of the difficulties and weaknesses of the British economy. The "New Right" movement, which was composed of "neo-liberals" who called for the introduction of the market principle in public services, and the "new-conservatives," called for the restoration of order and greater central intervention. The "New Right" addressed efforts on the macro level and had a direct effect on thinking about education in new terms and consequently on restructuring the education system along the lines of its critique when the Conservatives came to power in 1979.

The penetration of market principles into the education system first took the form of the encouragement of entrepreneurship in schools in order to raise private funds and the view that schools should be regarded as *cost centres*. The 1988 Education Reform Act and the policies that followed during the 1990s strengthened this trend by creating a new order based on competition between schools, which was regarded as the main tool for restoring high standards. Delegation of power over financial and administrative aspects to schools, creation of new types of schools and the introduction of national assessment, which aimed to place schools in a ranking order of achievement, were all steps along the path towards a market system in education and towards offering the customers (parents) a choice between diverse schools as a commodity. This new approach was the basis for the reconstruction of the school system and for the move towards a new structural order.

• CHAPTER 7

FROM CRITICISM OF STANDARDS TO THE CORE CURRICULUM

A powerful movement led to the abolition of selection and the accessibility of external examinations to all pupils. This was accomplished by means of a uniform type of school – the comprehensive school – and led to a drastic reduction in the number of grammar schools catering to the elite. This movement gave rise to a counter-movement calling for restructuring of the secondary education system and a return to the glorious past when grammar schools were dedicated to the production of excellence. This counter-movement was based on an elitist philosophy and a meritocratic approach, but it chose to wage its struggle on the grounds of an alleged decline in standards, despite the lack of empirical evidence to this effect. This chapter describes the abolishment of selection, not across all schools but at the micro level *within schools*. The labelling process – streaming – that resulted led to disciplinary, delinquency and violence problems and subsequently to attempts by schools to reduce the strain of working and teaching under such conditions. These attempts sought to abolish streaming, replace it with mixed ability classes and foster progressive methods. Both of these decreased formality in the classroom and increased the creativity of work, introducing a "discovery learning" approach and greater flexibility. This trend triggered attacks on comprehensive secondary education and led to the crystallisation of an opposition movement that demanded government intervention and restriction of teachers' freedom. Beginning with the Black Papers and reinforced by the media campaign, Labour Prime Minister James Callaghan opened a public debate on standards in response to demands for tighter control over education and greater centralisation by means of a "national core curriculum."

7.1: STREAMING, MIXED ABILITY AND PROGRESSIVE METHODS

The decision taken by an overwhelming majority of local education authorities to abolish the 11+ examinations and establish comprehensive schools, complicated the process by which individual schools divided pupils into classes: on the basis of academic potential or by mixing abilities. The chosen method was influenced by three main factors: (a) the composition of school types within the comprehensive school; (b) teachers' experience; and (c) the perceptions and experience of department heads.

Streaming was the dominant mode employed during the 1960s, whereas mixed-ability classes did not proliferate until the mid-1970s (Davis, 1977; Kelly, 1978; Reid, 1981). The prevalence of streaming in comprehensive schools resulted from the merging of former grammar schools with other types of secondary schools. In many cases the establishment of a comprehensive school was accompanied by a promise made by the local authority to parents that the new type of school would not abolish the grammar stream. This was a particular concern of parents whose children were successful in the 11+ examinations (see Chapter 6). Furthermore, grammar school teachers were accustomed to teaching more able and highly motivated pupils; Kelly (1978) argues that the extent of streaming was in many cases affected by the appointment of department heads from former grammar schools, who were accustomed to streaming.[1]

The increased advent of mixed ability classes leads us to consider the nature, disadvantages and criticisms of streaming in the comprehensive school, particularly during the 1960s. Streaming has been defined as "the division of pupils into classes in which the average general attainment of pupils in a class is assumed to be higher than that in the class next below it in the list."[2] Classes were organised according to the *homogeneous ability* of four selected groups, and each was labelled as A, B, C, or D, with the A stream being superior in intellectual ability and the D inferior. Organisation along these lines raised three principal types of difficulties: pupil discipline, teacher strain and the accuracy of grouping.

Dividing pupils into groups according to their abilities gave rise to self-fulfilling prophecies in terms of the children's behaviour and achievements. A.G. Young, Headmaster of Northcliffe Community High School in Yorkshire, described the consequence of streaming as follows:[3] "The 'C' and 'D' streamers knew they were regarded as the 'thickies' and, expected to behave badly, they played their roles with reactive stupidity, fooling themselves as well as their teachers."

Reid *et al.* (1981) came to a similar conclusion in a comprehensive research project on mixed ability teaching. They identify "self-fulfilling prophecies" and "self-perpetuating labelling" among the problems that led to the initiative that proposed abandoning selective grouping, fostering of the "concept of a 'fresh start' and the avoidance of labelling at the outset of a child's secondary school career."[4]

A study of twelve comprehensive schools carried out by the NFER in 1967-8 found that most streamed groups featured the "existence of a delinquent group of boys, notorious throughout the school for their anti-authoritarian attitude and their aggression towards younger pupils."[5] The discipline problem in schools was first mentioned in the annual Report of the Department of Education for 1966:[6]

> Teachers often found themselves doing what might appropriately be called welfare work and could not in fact divest themselves of a welfare function if they were to do an adequate teaching job.

The implications of this report were discussed at a conference convened by the Department in 1966 on the subject "Education Under Social Handicap." Head teachers, social workers, and lecturers from colleges of education predominantly described the stress and strain placed on teachers in coping with a relatively new type of pupil in secondary education. These pupils come from broken homes or unstable families, which can generate "poor attendance and poor performance" and often lead to "truancy and delinquency, certainly to stress behaviour."[7]

The conference found that schools were unable to separate their education and welfare roles. For example, once urban girls' schools had "become the healing agent, [it was] accepted also that the teacher, unskilled as she is as a welfare officer and psychiatrist, must nevertheless do social work 'as a real part of her job'."[8] The conference emphasised the essential duality in the roles of both the school and any individual teacher in adjusting to the secondary expansion.[9] This expansion raised the need for teachers to review the curriculum and teaching methods in order to meet the needs of the deprived children, reduce the level of strain and tension in the classroom, foster stable behaviour in the pupils and deal with adult members of "problem families."[10]

The expansion of secondary education, streaming and selective grouping placed teachers at the centre of tension and stress. The problem of streaming was further exacerbated by the fact that teachers as well as pupils were 'streamed'. According to Kelly, this "had the same implication for the morale of teachers as . . . for that of pupils."[11] Kelly also argues that "labels such as 'A', 'B', 'C' , 'D', grammar, technical, or modern" applied to teachers would inevitably dictate performance.[12] Young describes the difficulties of managing school staff as follows:[13]

> The matching disciplinary patterns were also self-fulfilling prophecies. 'A' to 'D' in ability synchronised almost exactly with 'A' to 'D' in behaviour. Like most Headmasters, I also found it necessary to match staff to these requirements. The most imaginative and sensitive teachers for the 'A's, almost anyone would be able to manage the 'B's', the toughest and the most insensitive for the 'C's' and thank God for volunteers – very often indeed the most dedicated ones – for the 'D's'.

One consequence of the strain on teachers was a high staff turnover, alongside often contentious "egalitarian" ideas and the difficulty of allocating pupils to streamed groups with an acceptable degree of accuracy (particularly the borderline pupil[14]), in the developing trend towards mixed ability classes

(Davies 1975; Kelly 1978; Newbold 1977; Reid 1981; Young 1975). Kelly claims that "it has become quite clear that wherever selective procedures are used they result in many mistakes being made."[15]

The arguments for abandoning selection at the school level were similar to those promoted nationally (see Chapter 6). Davies explains the move towards a common curriculum in class, or what came to be called "mixed-ability" teaching, as: "rejected selection at the 'macro' or school level; it has been denounced for the same reason at the 'micro'".[16] The "mixed ability class," or the heterogeneous and unselected class, was defined such that "each class in the year group is assumed to have an equal *range of ability*"[17] [original emphasis]. The move from streaming to mixed ability classes was not an overnight transformation, and schools combined many forms of both; but the most common type of organisation adopted was mixed-ability classes in the first and second years, with streaming from the third year onwards.[18]

The move towards mixed ability teaching however, further strained teachers, and resulted in resistance to the trend. Newbold (1977) found in the case of Banbury school that:

> Mixed ability teaching imposes an extra strain on teachers accustomed to largely homogeneous groups . . . the physical and emotional effects of different forms of grouping on teachers and particularly on their morale must not be discounted – it may be that job-satisfaction is less easily achieved in situations where the objectives are less easily defined or recognised.[19]

Reid similarly concludes that the most immediate effect was felt by former grammar school teachers who were asked to teach a new "kind of child."[20] Teachers' fears of new classroom conditions, new methods, and the extra effort required in order to cope with the new situation, were among the reasons for resistance to the move towards heterogeneous ability grouping. Those inexperienced in mixed ability teaching and lacking the confidence to teach the "new kind of pupils" were at the forefront of attachment to the *status quo* (Davies, 1977; Newbold, 1977).[21]

But the opponents of mixed ability classes voiced a much more powerful criticism – that heterogeneous grouping would lead to declining standards and have a direct detrimental effect on the academic process.[22] In support of this argument, teachers claimed that mixed ability classes would not meet the needs of all types of children. Slower children might feel inferior in the same class as bright children, and the more able pupils would develop reduced levels of motivation, producing lower academic results (Kelly, 1975; Newbold, 1977; Reid, 1981). The assumption that mixed ability organisation would harm the achievement of high standards by bright pupils sparked many research projects. But evidence that heterogeneous grouping leads to lower overall levels of attainment remained inconclusive; generally, streaming is no more effective than mixed ability grouping. Moreover, evidence showed the beneficial effects of heterogeneous grouping on the school's social climate and the emotional development of pupils, particularly those with lower ability. There was also evidence of academic benefit from avoiding the negative labelling associated with selection and grouping and the level of expectation that teachers set with respect to their pupils' performance (Kelly, 1978; Newbold, 1977; Reid, 1981; Yates, 1971). HM Inspectorate's Report on the effects and implications of mixed-ability grouping concluded that:

> Generally, mixed ability grouping was associated with good relationships between pupils and between teachers and pupils, and with co-operative attitudes on the part of the pupils.... Often a high level of motivation was engendered among pupils of below average ability.... Standards of courtesy were above those commonly encountered...and it was understood that, where pupils of lower ability had formerly been grouped together in Years 4 and 5, the incidence of disruptive behaviour in this age group had been reduced following the adoption of mixed ability grouping.[23]

Nevertheless, the trend towards mixed ability teaching did not offer an automatic solution to the problems of ensuring appropriate achievements for the different groups within the class, and job satisfaction for teachers. Teachers were placed under stress by having to conduct lessons for pupils of different motivation and abilities. Several trials were held in pursuit of optimum standards and an appropriate system for the majority of the pupils.

A new classroom strategy was fostered by many schools, aimed at "individualised" and "independent" learning, or as Reid put it: a "separate stream for every single child."[24] This approach moved towards greater flexibility and a combination of groups of various sizes; mixed-ability for the first years, streaming within mixed ability classes, some setting of subjects,[25] remedial teaching and team teaching. All this was in order to achieve better standards and reduce the stress that managing and teaching a class of varying motivation and abilities places on the teacher. Kelly described this development and the new features of the class as follows:

> In fact, flexibility has been the theme throughout, the key to all issues and problems...organising individual and group assignments, grouping within the class, dealing with those pupils who are experiencing learning difficulties.[26]

In conclusion, disobedience and delinquent behaviour resulting from the negative labelling of pupils led to a situation fraught with stresses and strains. Teachers and schools, seeking ways to reduce this stress, improve the school climate and the atmosphere in the classroom, looked to the abolition of streaming and a move towards mixed-ability teaching in order to accomplish this. This indeed improved the climate within schools, but it placed a new strain on teachers: how to cope with the mixed motivations of pupils and a variety of abilities in the same class. Consequently, the notion of "a curriculum for each child" and the move towards "sets," "progressive methods" and "child-centred" learning became successively dominant as means of reducing the new kind of stress. This trend towards mixed methods antagonised those teachers and educators who supported selection and the retention of streaming in order to restore standards.[27] This antagonism, based on the claim that mixed ability teaching and "progressive methods" lowered standards, soon spread outside the school system, leading to a movement against this trend.

7.2: THE BLACK PAPERS

The years 1969-77 saw the publication of a series of articles known as the "Black Papers," edited by C.B. Cox, professor of English at the University of Manchester, and A. Dyson, senior lecturer at the University of East Anglia.[28] They aimed to draw the attention of the public and Members of Parliament to the decline of standards at all levels of the education system – primary schools, secondary schools and universities – and the urgent need for government intervention and control in order to restore them.

The introduction to the first Black Paper, a letter to Members of Parliament, opened with the contention that "many people have become increasingly unhappy about certain aspects of the general trend. Anarchy is becoming fashionable."[29] The editors explain this "anarchy" as follows:

> The teacher is no longer regarded as the exponent of the great achievements of past civilisation... the traditional high standards of English education are being overthrown.... At the post-eleven stage there is a strong impetus to abolish streaming... there is a feeling that excellence in education is snobbish or undemocratic.[30]

These publications asserted that standards were declining drastically – indeed, that the education service was collapsing – as a result of egalitarian ideas, the comprehensive trend, the abolition of selection between and within schools and "progressive methods" of teaching.[31] Two main threads run through many of the arguments on falling standards: first, a romanticised emphasis on the glorious past when selection of an elite and formal teaching methods were the main features of the education system;[32] and second, how these days of excellence might be regained. Some articles drew on comparisons with countries that had abolished selection, citing evidence that educational attainments in these countries were among the lowest.[33]

The attack was marshalled under the heading "Comprehensive Disaster," which encapsulated the thesis and attitude of the Black Papers towards the consequences of egalitarian ideas and comprehensive schools. In the first Black Paper, published in 1969, MP Angus Maude raised the contradiction between "equality" and "standards." In an article entitled "The Egalitarian Threat" he argued: "In the name of 'equality of opportunity' the egalitarian seeks to destroy or transmogrify those schools which make special efforts to bring out the best in talented children . . . . [T]he egalitarian takes the alternative course of levelling down the higher standards towards uniform mediocrity."[34] The author claimed that the egalitarian trend in the education system inhibited effort and excellence, making it difficult for an elite to emerge. He posited central intervention and control over education as the only ways to avoid mediocrity and anarchy.

R.R. Pedley, the headmaster of St. Dunstan's College, also attacked egalitarian trends, speaking of the detrimental affect of mixed ability groups on the able pupil:

> The able child in company of his peers finds an atmosphere, an ethos, specially relevant to him and therefore receives a stimulus and an incentive fully to stretch his abilities.[35]

Pedley not only raised the problem of the able child within a single school, but made the following argument against the abolition of selection between schools:

> The move to the establishment of total comprehensiveness seems to be a part of the sinister attack on excellence.[36]

The first Black Paper set an "agenda for educational debate,"[37] opening a forum for educators, university lecturers, psychologists, economists, and Members of Parliament who did not accept the comprehensive scheme and the mixed-ability trend and instead glorified the recent past, when intelligence tests, selection, streaming, grammar school and the elite were key terms of the education system. They also called for a return to the high performance and high standards deemed to be the hallmarks of the education system of England and Wales.

Thus, in the second Black Paper, Richard Lynn, a Professor of Psychology in Dublin, called on cultural factors, comparative data, innate intelligence and home conditions to explain the need to reinstate selection and grammar schools. The article claimed that: "British education has been designed primarily to produce an intellectual elite,"[38] and charged that the 1944 Education Act was a "dreadful mistake." It concluded as follows:

> Britain has a great cultural tradition of intellectual achievement. Even in the post war period, Britain has won more Nobel prizes for science and literature per head of population than any other major country. Britain has been enabled to do this partly because of her outstanding education system which has been so efficiently geared to producing an intellectual elite. This is the system the progressives are now demolishing on the basis of false premises which seriously underestimate genetic class differences . . . The British grammar and independent schools have been extraordinarily successful in the purpose for which they were designed, the training of an intellectual elite for the maintenance of a cultural tradition. The progressives are destroying this system in a hopeless quest for a degree of equality which can never be attained . . The preservation of quality in a democratic age may well be impossible and we should perhaps resign ourselves to the imminence of a new dark age in which the envy, malice and philistinism of the masses, and the intellectuals who identify with them, lead to the destruction of a culture that can never be enjoyed by the majority.[39]

Professor Lynn proposed practical suggestions for preserving the quality of education in Britain. For example, he encouraged grammar schools threatened with the prospect of becoming comprehensive to become direct grant schools, and advocated tax allowances for parents educating their children privately, thus giving parents the choice of school and encouraging individual competition. Likewise Cyril Burt, Professor of Psychology, calling for recognition of the advantages of streaming, advocated an increase in the number of independent or direct grant schools and wider freedom of choice for parents.[40] He argued that standards were lower in the 1960s than they were before the First World War.[41] Arthur Pollard, a Professor of English in Hull, followed Lynn by saying that "the grammar schools of this country have been and remain the glory of British education and their sixth-forms the brightest jewel in their crown."[42] He called on the next Conservative government to fight for the retention and restoration of the grammar schools in order to maintain standards and prevent any new and inferior alternative, such as comprehensive schools, from spoiling this achievement.

The Black Papers became an outlet for attacks on the Labour Party, accusing it of harming education standards by so-called "progressive education." They also echoed calls for greater government intervention in order to allow more freedom of choice and reduce the perceived "totalitarian" coercion of the comprehensive school. The leading article of the third Black Paper, which was addressed to Members of Parliament, attacked Edward Short, the Labour Secretary of State for Education and Science,[43] and welcomed Margaret Thatcher as the new Secretary of State, in the hope that: "in the next few years . . . the consensus of moderates may once more gain control of decision-making."[44] Pedley concluded his article by saying: "Let us hope that the trend *has* been reversed and the destructive element avoided"[45] [original emphasis].

The Black Papers also raised several ideas concerning secondary education. These included freedom of choice via the educational voucher, streaming, competition between schools, the closing of weak schools, special academic schools for 20-40 percent of children, the breaking-up of large schools, and direct grant schools as "super-selective academic schools to keep scholarship alive and show the standards possible with bright children."[46]

Criticism of higher education focused mainly on the expansion of the universities in accordance with the Robbins Report of 1963, and on student unrest during the 1960s.[47] The argument was that the new function of the university – to answer social, technological and economic needs – created a new climate affecting standards and independent thought. "B," the author of an article entitled "The Decline and Fall of the University Idea," claimed that: "If, as I believe, the essential function of the university is to maintain, perpetuate and inculcate those standards, then their assertion is nowadays remarkably rare."[48] William Walsh, Professor of Education at Leeds University, came to a similar conclusion concerning the Robbins Report, namely that the modern preoccupation with equality and efficiency in the universities would "bring them almost to the point of dissolution."[49]

John Sparrow, at that time the Warden of All Souls College, Oxford, dealt with the slowing down of the education machine in order to achieve gains in social justice and the consequent lowering of academic standards. He came to the conclusion that

> Universities and schools that cast away their inheritance not because they have ceased to believe in its value but out of deference to egalitarian pressure are betraying an intellectual trust and becoming parties to the most recent manifestation of *la trahison des clercs*.[50]

The editors of the Black Papers called on the government to stop expanding the universities, and to introduce a system of student loans rather than grants. The underlying theme supported an increase in government intervention in and control over the universities.

These publications propounded an elitist philosophy, emphasising the disadvantages of egalitarian ideas by over-simplifying the complex development of the education system, at the expense of social cohesiveness.[51] The critics of the Black Papers pointed out that their authors had ignored research data (Griggs, 1989; Musgrove, 1987; Wright, 1977) that would have undermined their arguments: in Griggs' words, "with a few notable exceptions … most of the articles are short pieces of a subjective nature lacking in academic rigour."[52] Similarly, averred Wright "not one of the ninety articles in the four Black Papers is devoted to a full and systematic review of the evidence on any topic."[53]

Wright (1977) explains that the Black Papers intended "to make a stand on behalf of the traditional standards of academic and intellectual excellence."[54] However, he argues that these "traditional standards" were achieved through a highly selective system when education was the privilege of only a few. Therefore the argument against "falling standards" resulting from "progressive teaching methods" was a cover for the real argument in favour of the restoration of selection, with grammar schools, and an elite and rigid stratification of the education system of England and Wales. Musgrove explains the Black Paper movement in macro-sociological terms of confrontation between two movements:

> The Black Paper movement occurred not because progressivism was rampant and there was strong evidence for the collapse of

standards: it occurred at the point of intersection between the powerful Arnold-Sidgwick tradition of highly moralised literary studies and a belated wave of post-war modernisation.⁵⁵

But the assimilation and transformation of elitist arguments into political terms needed a stronger and wider movement; according to Chitty, the role of the Black Papers was to launch a movement that was finally converted into political terms:⁵⁶

> The Right was preparing itself to go on to the offensive with the floating of radical ideas . . . . It would be another ten years before a Conservative government felt strong enough to put the new ideas into practice, but the process of making them respectable began with the Black Papers of 1975 and 1977.⁵⁷

In Griggs' view (1989) the main influence of the Black Papers lay in the questions they raised, which could then no longer be ignored by the political parties.

7.3: THE MEDIA CAMPAIGN

The ideas of the Black Papers were highlighted by "the manner in which they were taken up by the press at the time."⁵⁸ The abolition of the grammar schools and the grammar stream in the comprehensive schools, and the emergence of mixed-ability classes and "progressive methods," stimulated media criticism of the new nature and direction of the education system.

The early 1970s were characterised by: (a) declining standards; (b) disciplinary problems, classroom violence and the school climate; and (c) political indoctrination. According to Ball, "fuelled by press and television 'horror stories', the level of 'public concern' about the state of the nation's schooling had reached the level of a moral panic."⁵⁹ Research undertaken by the Centre for Contemporary Cultural Studies (CCCS, 1981) concluded similarly that the main message conveyed by the *Daily Mail* and the *Daily Mirror* in the years 1975-77 was concern over failing standards, and that the "weight of negative reporting is impressive."⁶⁰ Clive Griggs concurred, arguing that the major newspapers at that time were crucial in "helping to undermine public confidence in the local authority."[61]

The media's criticism was articulated, reinforced, and stimulated first by the Black Papers and later by government publications and research reports which together crystallised into a negative impression of school order and standards of attainment. This climate finally led to the "Great Debate" announced by Prime Minister James Callaghan, which centred on the fundamental question of educational standards in the system that had evolved.

A *Daily Telegraph* article headlined "The Growing Threat to Education," argued that standards had declined because "so many influential 'progressives' in educational theory have turned out to be enemies of academic work."[62] Therefore, only the restoration of selection could raise the standards again: "selection is not a dirty word … the egalitarian seem prepared like Samson to pull down the temple on all of us. They must not be allowed to wreak their destruction and to put the clock back 200 years."[63]

The Times raised the disciplinary problems of the comprehensive school, particularly the problem of the able child who "may suffer from the lower standards."[64]

The *Sunday Times* discussed the monolithic nature of the education system, citing that almost 90% of secondary schools were now comprehensive schools; it posed fundamental questions under dramatic titles such as "The truth about the comprehensive,"[65] "Classroom confrontation,"[66] and "Crisis in the classroom."[67] According to the CCCS analysis, "images of incompetence, slovenly, subversive or just trendy teachers who had failed to teach or control the undisciplined pupils" were central to the reporting of the *Daily Mail* and the *Daily Mirror*.[68] This atmosphere cultivated the idea that without government control and structural transformation, standards would continue to deteriorate.

In 1972 the NFER published a national survey of reading. The results of the survey emphasised that reading standards in the early 1970s were "not better than they were a decade ago."[69] The NFER Report prompted Margaret Thatcher as Secretary of State for Education to set up a commission of inquiry into the teaching of language. The report submitted by the commission indicated that there was a "slight decline in the scores of 11 year olds … [and] some evidence that children of seven are not as advanced as formerly

... in reading ability."[70] The issue provoked a series of articles about the state of reading and illiteracy among the nation's children (Chitty, 1989; CCCS, 1981).

The 1976 publication of the William Tenderly Report on a controversial junior and infant school focused on the disorder, lack of discipline and damage wrought by "progressive" teaching methods: "Staff sympathising with their approach, failed in general to strike the right balance between direction by the teacher and freedom of choice by the child."[71] That same year, Neville Bennett published a similar conclusion in his *Teaching Styles and Pupil Progress*. The research report found that children taught by "formal methods" were, on average, four months ahead of those taught by "informal methods."[72] Both Reports confirmed the media images of contemporary schools and strengthened the claim that "progressive teaching methods" were the direct cause of declining standards (CCCS, 1981; Chitty, 1989).

The media used these major publications not only to attack current standards and discipline in schools, but also to stimulate ideas and proposals as to what steps the education system should take to remedy these weaknesses. Analysis of press reports during 1975-77 reveals emphasis on the need for increased government intervention and greater control over education.

In a series of articles, The *Economist* contended that the decline of reading standards, the William Tenderly school situation (1976) and Bennett's survey of "progressive methods" resulted from a lack of control by the government. Only a nationally dictated "core curriculum," new examinations to monitor school performance, and "more central and local control,"[73] were capable of restoring higher standards. The *Economist* saw the first priority as setting examinations to invade the "secret garden" – the curriculum – and to shift control over the curriculum from the teachers to the government.[74] The *New Statesman* also spoke out for a national core curriculum that could remedy low performance and standards,[75] and urged the government to take the lead in this direction. The *Observer* argued that there was consensus with regard to the curriculum and that the government should impose one that included technical and scientific subjects that had been ignored by schools as a result of "progressive," "informal," "child-centred," and "discovery" methods: "They all mean much the same thing, the breaking down of traditional classroom teaching."[76] The *Daily Mail* and the *Daily Mirror* were united in proposing "greater control of schooling by non-teachers and a return to the traditional competitive education system."[77]

This level of criticism and controversy[78] could not be ignored at the political level. Finally Labour Prime Minister James Callaghan responded in a speech given in October 1976 at Ruskin College, Oxford, thus opening a public debate on the standards of the education system. The Green Paper of July 1977, presented by the Secretary of State for Education, Shirley Williams, evaluated the role of the media in bringing about James Callaghan's speech:

> The speech was made against a background of strongly critical comment in the Press and elsewhere on education and educational standards. Children's standards of performance in their school work were said to have declined. The curriculum, it was argued, paid too little attention to the basic skills of reading, writing, and arithmetic, and was overloaded with fringe subjects.

Chitty (1989), in an interview with Bernard Donoughue, the Head of the Downing Street Policy Unit, confirmed that Callaghan's speech was mainly motivated by the media campaign against progressive developments in education. He explained this extraordinary intervention of a Prime Minister in education matters in terms of Callaghan's fear that "unless something could be done very quickly, the failing of the system would work to the Conservative Party's electoral advantage."[79] *The Times* saw the speech as a "milestone": "The recent speech by the Prime Minister supporting the case for a basic or core curriculum, the need for enforcement of national minimum standards, and for education to be brought into some relationship with industry, could be another milestone."[80] The *Spectator* did not see Callaghan as starting the debate: "It is curious that Mr Callaghan if he really thought he was *starting* a debate, should have apparently referred slightly to the Black Papers, which have for some time been making the same points."[81] Nevertheless, the Prime Minister's speech bore clear traces of the Black Papers and the media campaign. It marked the beginning of a political trend favouring more and tighter government control over education.

7.4: TOWARDS A NATIONAL CORE CURRICULUM

The Prime Minister's speech constituted a new step towards a national core curriculum. In his speech James Callaghan mentioned three main factors that had prompted him to speak out on the controversial education issues: (a) criticism of educational standards by employers; (b) the informal methods in use; and (c) the Black Papers:

> I am concerned on my journeys to find complaints from industry that new recruits from the schools sometimes do not have the basic tools to do the job that is required .... There seems to be a need for a more technological bias in science teaching that will lead towards practical applications in industry rather than towards academic studies ... there is concern about the standards of numeracy of school-leavers ... . On another aspect there is the unease felt by parents and others about the new informal methods of teaching which seem to produce excellent results when they are in well-qualified hands but are much more dubious when they are not ... . My remarks are not a clarion call to Black Paper prejudices. We all know those who claim to defend standards but who in reality are simply seeking to defend old privileges and inequalities.[82]

Despite the Prime Minister's view on the Black Papers' prejudices, he came to a similar conclusion on the role of the government in preserving national standards and the importance of a core curriculum:

> Let me repeat some of the fields that need study because they cause concern. There are the methods and aims of informal instruction; the strong case for the so-called "core curriculum" of basic knowledge; next, what is the proper national standard of performance; then there is the role of the inspectorate in relation to national standards; and there is the need to improve relations between industry and education.[83]

The speech was a milestone in the trend towards a national core curriculum and assessment. It was a turning point at which the comprehensive system, the abolition of selection between and within schools, mixed ability instruction and informal methods were together identified as having led to the deterioration in standards. A core curriculum supported by examinations would counter such a decline, and its proponents claimed that this was the only way to return to the good old days of the education system.

A new aspect of the debate was the government's declared wish to end teacher freedom in the setting of the curriculum, what Lawton describes as *laissez faire* and a "golden age" for teachers (Lawton, 1980). Since the Butler Act, the government had been concerned with maintaining consensus and partnership with the teachers by avoiding any major changes in the curriculum or restrictions on teachers' freedom. It had striven to effect every change on the basis of dialogue rather than confrontation. This policy had given rise to some frustration among ministers. Thus, for example, in a letter to the Parliamentary Secretary and other officials within the Ministry of Education, Eccles asked to what extent he could use his power as a minister to insist on particular aspects of teaching: "Mr Butler insisted on religious teaching in all schools: could I now insist, had I a mind so to do, on greater emphasis on English?"[84]

In 1956 Eccles had asked Sir Geoffrey Crowther, the Chairman of the Central Advisory Council for Education, to consider the balance of general and specialised studies in relation to the changing social and industrial needs. The committee recommended a revision of the sixth form syllabuses and Eccles revealed his deep frustration when he said that the Report was an "irresistible invitation to a sally into the secret garden of the curriculum."[85] In a 1962 parliamentary discussion on foreign language studies, Eccles admitted that: "in general I agree I have no control over the curriculum."[86] Soon after that, the Ministry of Education established a new unit called the Curriculum Study Group, with the aim of adapting syllabus content and teaching methods "to meet the demands of our changing society and our developing knowledge."[87] However, the minister immediately went on to emphasise that there was no change in the policy of partnership:

> No one in the Ministry has the slightest intention of forcing anything down the throats of any teachers or authorities, we are going to offer a new service . . . which the teachers and the local education authorities can use or not as they wish.[88]

The Russian achievement of putting a satellite in orbit in 1957 generated deep frustration in the ministers of education Lord Hailsham and Sir Geoffrey Lloyd, both of whom referred to the satellite as a triumph of technical education.[89] The ministry responded to this event by encouraging grammar schools to include more science studies, and Lloyd informed Parliament in March 1958 that "there was a swing to science."[90] But responding to a suggestion in Parliament that this constituted ministerial intervention in the curriculum, Lloyd referred to the importance of maintaining the partnership tradition, saying: "it would not be a departure from long established practice."[91]

The maintenance of harmony and consensus within the education system had been fundamental to the ministry's policy since the War. According to Lawton however, the intensification of criticism during the 1960s and 1970s over "various aspects of progressive and comprehensive school policy" and "concern about the question of standards"[92] were among the reasons for a swing to central control. Consensus was based on satisfaction with the curriculum and achievements of grammar schools, but when standards came under criticism, methods changed in order to meet the needs of pupils other than the traditional grammar types. Informal teaching thus became more dominant and the ministry's commitment to the partnership weakened. This weakness had a direct effect on the government's commitment to maintaining the old structure and was a legitimate ground for new ideas to reconstruct secondary education. Furthermore, there were growing doubts over the government's obligation to allow teachers full freedom over the curriculum, particularly under the new circumstances where standards were being criticised. Consequently, when the equilibrium of the system was shaken in terms of the type of pupils, the curriculum, and access to external examinations for pupils outside the grammar schools, the secondary structure order was also shaken, including the equilibrium of the long tradition of partnership.

In 1974, two years before Callaghan's speech, Reg Prentice, the Labour Secretary of State for Education, established the Assessment of Performance Unit (APU) which aimed "to promote the development of methods of assessing and monitoring achievement."[93] According to Lawton the DES realised that this step would be "strongly resisted by the teaching profession."[94] The debate launched by the Prime Minister in October 1976 was followed by regional conferences that were convened and controlled by the DES in order to discuss four main issues: curriculum, monitoring/assessment, teacher training, and school and working life (Chitty, 1989). The Green Paper of July 1977, published by the Secretary of State for Education at the time, Shirley Williams, aimed to draw these discussions together, emphasising the importance of harmony and partnership with government's main partners, the teachers and the LEAs. But it also stated the need for a "protected" or "core" curriculum common to all secondary schools, for three main reasons:

(a) Curricula were said to be overcrowded and overloaded;
(b) Variations in the curriculum between different schools were giving rise to inequality of opportunity and penalising pupils who moved from one area to another;
(c) A need to provide education in tune with the life of industrial society.

The Green Paper went on to stress the importance of achieving standards and assessing pupil performance through diagnostic tests and assessment of individual schools, taking account of "examination and test results, reports by inspectors and advisers, and self-assessment by the schools."[95] Local education authorities were asked to report on their existing means of recording pupils' progress, but warned against using the assessment as a "league table" that could be "seriously misleading."[96]

In 1977 the Inspectorate called for a common curriculum. In a document entitled *Curriculum 11-16*, the need for a core curriculum was explained in terms of recent developments in secondary education:

> Most secondary teachers now find themselves working in fairly recently constituted schools, generally larger than those they were used to before; many are dealing with an unaccustomed ability range among the pupils; the pupils themselves are, since 1973, at school for a year longer.... More and more responsibilities have been accepted by schools, particularly in matters of the personal and social welfare of pupils. During these years a host of projects, schemes, proposals and suggestions about the curriculum has appeared.[97]

These developments in secondary schools, according to the HMI, raised a number of difficulties that justified a common curriculum:
(a) Schools were changing their curricula often but many teachers had little experience and were not prepared for such developments;
(b) Schools operated in comparative isolation, developing their own curriculum and learning from their own mistakes;
(c) The system was inefficient, wasting efforts through experimentation and unnecessary repetition;
(d) There was a lack of agreement on fundamental objectives.

A subsequent series of official publications consolidated the trend towards a "core curriculum" and gave rise to consensus. The DES published *A Framework for the School Curriculum* in 1980 and *The School Curriculum in 1981*; in 1983 *The Curriculum 11-16* was reissued as a reappraisal of progress towards a common curriculum. At the same time HM Inspectorate published *A View of the Curriculum*, and in 1981 a joint study by HMI and five LEAs on the progress towards a common curriculum in a range of subjects entitled: *Curriculum 11-16; A Review of Progress* was issued. These publications, although they recognised the professional autonomy of teachers, created the atmosphere and consensus that were needed before more substantial steps could be taken towards the national curriculum that would become part of 1988 Education Act (see Chapter 9).

7.5: CONCLUSIONS

The move towards a mixed-ability system was less a deliberate policy than a response to the strain placed on teachers as a result of the expansion of education, the comprehensive trend and the new social composition of schools. Teaching classes of mixed ability, in an effort to relieve strain rather than to realise an egalitarian ideology, was soon criticised at the school level by those who assumed that this trend would harm the more able pupils. The concern of teachers and schools that mixed ability classes failed to provide appropriate work programmes and "were at greatest disadvantage"[98] led to more particular methods aimed at accommodating the range of abilities within the class by fostering greater flexibility and more individualised methods of independent learning, along with methods like setting and streaming within mixed ability classes. Thus, schools were not apathetic to the social dilemma, and they gradually developed internal means to accomplish both their duties: social cohesiveness and expected standards.

Despite the lack of conclusive evidence that mixed ability classes harmed attainment and standards, neo-conservative forces claimed that only centralisation of the curriculum supported by achievement tests would remedy low standards in the education system. Such forces protested against the "totalitarianism" of the comprehensive school and the disappearance of the traditional grammar school, which was a source of pride and glory. The abolition of streaming and the merging of brighter pupils with the less able also stimulated protest. There was a strong emotional reaction against the loss of the symbols of excellence and the dissolution of institutions for intellectual elites. Phrases like "the jewel in the crown," the loss of a "great cultural tradition," "subversive of intellectual elite" and "destruction of culture" confirm the argument (see Chapter 1) that slogans harked "back to the days of glory," appealing to the desire for the old education order. This response to the loss of part of the British tradition strongly stimulated arguments that a national core curriculum would re-establish some of the brilliance of England's formerly prestigious education system.

The partnership between teachers and government had been secured only by the grammar schools or at least their streaming methods. When this equilibrium and the whole secondary structure system was shaken, streaming was abandoned. Only 7 percent of grammar schools remained, shaking the government's commitment to this partnership. This broke the long tradition of teacher freedom over curriculum and was the initial step towards ideas on how to restore standards, and the structural implications of such restoration. Some of these ideas gathered political momentum in both parties, and ten years later tighter control was realised. The breakdown of the traditional grammar school thus created a chain reaction that led to the breakdown of the partnership tradition and a restriction of teacher control over the curriculum by means of a national core curriculum.

Notes:

1. Mixed ability classes were more common in schools which had been modern schools before becoming comprehensive, in which teachers were accustomed to teaching mixed abilities (except in those cases where modern schools were streamed for a limited number of pupils who were being prepared for external examinations).
2. ILEA (1976). *Mixed Ability Grouping. Report of an ILEA Inspectorate survey*. London, quoted by M. Reid et al. (1981), 4-5.
3. A.G. Young (1975). Northcliffe Community High School, in A.V. Kelly (ed.) (1975). *Case Studies in Mixed Ability Teaching*, London: Harper & Row, 31.
4. Reid (1981), 25.
5. R. Peter Davies (1975). *Mixed-Ability Grouping*. London: Temple Smith, 35.
6. Department of Education and Science: *Education in 1966*. London, 18.
7. Department of Education and Science (July 1966), *Trends in Education*. London, 4. A description given by the Superintendent of the Education Welfare Service in Sheffield.
8. Ibid., 10.
9. The behaviour problem was accentuated by the fact that an increasing number of children stayed at school beyond the compulsory age of 15, and by the raising of the earliest school leaving age to 16, in 1972.
10. The education of 13-16 year-old pupils with lower abilities became a prominent issue in the education system and four books were published aiming to raise ideas and suggestions for school policy on this matter were published between 1966 and 1977. (Edmund King (1966). *Education and Social Change*. Oxford: Pergamon; F.H Pedley (ed.) (1967). *Education and Social Work*. Oxford: Pergamon; John Barron Mays (1967). *The School in its Social Setting*. London: Longman; Maurice Craft et al. (eds.) (1967). *Linking Home and School*. London: Longman.)
11. A.V. Kelly (1978). *Mixed-Ability Grouping: Theory and Practice*. London: Harper & Row, 12.
12. Ibid.
13. Young (1975), 31-2.
14. Reid (1981), 25. He claims that a "substantial number of pupils at the top of the second band...did better than pupils in the first band."
15. Kelly (1978), 11-12.
16. Davies (1975), 36.
17. ILEA (1981), 3.
18. A survey of over a thousand comprehensive schools carried out by NFER in 1974-5 revealed that half of the first year were taught in mixed ability classes, 37% in the second year and 25% in the third (Reid, 1981, 7).
19. David Newbold (1977). *Ability Grouping: The Banbury Enquiry*. Windsor (NFER), 115.
20. Reid (1981), 32. The main problem areas were mathematics and modern languages, and after a short time groups of equal ability were usually formed in these subjects (by banding or setting).
21. Davies argued that self-interest, laziness and commitment to existing values were among the reasons for resistance to the change.

22. This claim, which originated with educators inside the school system, later spread and stimulated criticism by several other outside organisations.
23. Department of Education and Science (1978), *Mixed-Ability Work in Comprehensive Schools*. London: HMSO, 57.
24. Reid (1981), 26.
25. Particularly in mathematics and foreign languages.
26. Kelly (1978), 198.
27. Reid (1981) notes that several years after the introduction of mixed-ability groups "many staff still retained their antagonism" (33).
28. For the fourth Black Paper in 1975, Dyson was replaced as co-editor by Rhodes Boyson, a comprehensive school headmaster and later a Tory MP.
29. C.B. Cox & R. Boyson (eds.) (1969). *Black Paper: Fight for Education*. London: Critical Quarterly, 1.
30. Ibid.
31. The term progressive methods includes pedagogical terms such as "discovery methods," "creativity," "self expression" and "child-centred" learning.
32. Formal education refers to an emphasis on such matters as oral teaching, order, structure, hierarchy and formality.
33. The main attack was directed at the secondary and higher levels of education. Attention was focused on the primary level more particularly after the publication of the William Tenderly Report in 1976, with articles pointing out the centrality of reading and mathematics and the importance of "being literate."
34. Ibid., 7.
35. R.R. Pedley (1969(a)). *Comprehensive Disaster*. Black Paper, 45.
36. Ibid., 47.
37. Stephen J. Ball (1984). "Comprehensive in Crisis?" In Stephen J. Ball (ed.), *Comprehensive Schooling: A Reader*. London: Falmer, 5.
38. Richard Lynn (1969). *Comprehensives and Equality: The Quest for the Unattainable*. Black Paper Two, London: Critical Quarterly, 26.
39. Ibid., 31.
40. The author argues that a number of research projects that tested children from streamed and unstreamed schools indicated that, at every age, the performance of the pupils from the streamed schools proved to be slightly superior. These findings contradict other studies quoted earlier in this chapter, which claim that there is no proof of the superiority of performance of either streamed or unstreamed pupils.
41. Leon Kamin, who has examined Professor Burt's work, says that the statistical evidence is "simply not worthy of our current scientific attention." Quoted in Griggs (1989), 110.
42. Arthur Pollard (1969). *O and A Level: Keeping Up the Standards*. Black Paper Two, London: Critical Quarterly, 72.
43. For the period between 1968 and 1970, the years during which the first three Black Papers were published.

44. C.B. Cox & R. Boyson (eds.) (1969). "Letter to Member of Parliament." *In Black Paper Three*. London:Critical Quarterly, 1.
45. Ibid., 62.
46. C.B. Cox & R. Boyson (eds.) (1977). *Black Paper 1977*. London: Temple Smith, 9.
47. Frank Musgrove (1987). "The Black Paper Movement." In: Roy Lowe (ed.), *The Changing Primary School*, London: Falmer. Musgrove argues that the university expansion was the real occasion for the first Black Paper, which devoted half of its articles to universities.
48. 'B' (1969). "The Decline and Fall of the University Idea." *Black Paper: Fight for Education*. London: Critical Quarterly, 60. The changing climate was a result of independent lobbies within the university students, junior faculty, senior faculty, professors and other pressure groups.
49. William Walsh (1969). "Dialogue and the Idea." *In Black Paper: Fight for Education*, London: Critical Quarterly, 67.
50. John Sparrow (1969). "Egalitarianism and an Academic Elite." *Black Paper: Fight for Education*. London: Critical Quarterly, 64.
51. Not surprisingly, Mr Short, the Secretary of State for Education said in April 1969 that the publication of the Black Papers was "one of the blackest days for education for 100 years." Quoted in Cox & Boyson (1977), 5.
52. Clive Griggs (1989). "The New Right and English Secondary Education." In: Roy Lowe (ed.), *The Changing Secondary School*, London: Falmer.
53. Nigel Wright (1977). Progress in Education. London: Croom Helm, 140.
54. Ibid.
55. F. Musgrove (1987). "The Black Paper Movment." In Roy Lowe (ed.), *The Changing Primary School*. London: Falmer, 123.
56. Clyde Chitty (1989). *Towards a New Education System: The Victory of the New Right?* London: Falmer, 52.
57. Chitty distinguishes between the role of the Black Papers published during 1969-70 and those that were published in the years 1975 and 1977. The former were seen as wanting to "put the clock back" and expressive of reactionary ideas, whereas the latter introduced more constructive ideas.
58. Ibid.
59. Stephen J. Ball (ed.) (1984). *Comprehensive Schooling: A Reader*. London: Falmer, 6.
60. Centre for Contemporary Cultural Studies (1981). *Unpopular Education*, London: Hutchinson, 211.
61. Griggs, 1989, 110.
62. Daily Telegraph, 18.12.70.
63. Ibid., 21.1.71.
64. *The Times*, 23.11.72, 18.
65. Ibid., 26.1.75.
66. Ibid., 2.2.75.
67. Ibid., 25.1.75.
68. Centre for Contemporary Cultural Studies (1981), 211.

69. K.B. Start & B.K. Wells (1972). *The Trend of Reading Standards*. Windsor: NFER, 72.
70. Department of Education and Science (1975). *A Language for Life*, Report of the Committee of Inquiry (The Bullock Report). London: HMSO, 517.
71. Robin Auld (1976). *The William Tyndale Junior and Infant Schools: Report of the Public Inquiry. A Report to the Inner London Education Authority*. London: Inner London Education Authority, 275.
72. Despite criticism of the research method, the media made extensive use of this finding.
73. *The Economist*, 10.7.76, 13-14.
74. This view was expressed in the articles and their titles, such as "Into the Secret Garden" (16.10.76) and "Testing Times" (10.12.77).
75. *New Statesman*, 18.2.77.
76. *The Observer*, 17.10.76.
77. Centre for Contemporary Cultural Studies (1981), 212.
78. The hostility and criticism were not confined to the national press; a series of television reports criticised the comprehensive schools and progressive teaching methods (Chitty, 1989).
79. Chitty (1989), 67.
80. *The Times*, 30.12.76.
81. *Spectator*, 23.10.76.
82. James Callaghan: "Toward a National Debate." In *Education*, 22.10.1976, 333.
83. Ibid.
84. PRO ed. 147/207. Letter of 3 January 1955.
85. *The Times*, 2.3.60.
86. Ibid., 23.2.62.
87. Ibid., 13.3.62.
88. Ibid.
89. Among the reasons for this frustration was the fact that one of the chief Russian scientists received his technical education at Cambridge University.
90. *The Times*, 23.3.58.
91. Ibid., 26.6.59. The minister's response was to a question by Mr Blenkisop, MP, who asked that the book entitled *Race Prejudice and Education* be brought to the attention of all schools.
92. Lawton (1980), 23.
93. Department of Education and Science: *Educational Disadvantage and the Educational Needs of Immigrants*. London (HMSO) 1974, p.16. The foundation of the Unit was one of the steps taken by the government in response to the Report on Education by the Select Committee on Race Relations and Immigration.
94. Denis Lawton (1980). *The Politics of the School Curriculum*. London: Routledge & Kegan Paul, 51.
95. Ibid., 42.
96. Ibid.
97. Department of Education and Science (1977). Curriculum 11-16, London: HMSO, 3.
98. Department of Education and Science (1978), 50.

• CHAPTER   8

FROM HUMAN CAPITAL TO MARKET ECONOMY VALUES IN EDUCATION

The two decades that followed the 1944 Education Act were years of commitment to expansion of the education system, as a part of the government's policy of public welfare and investment in public services. The demand for education and for general access to external examinations backed up the assumptions of three different committees – on secondary education (Crowther, 1959; Newsom, 1963) and higher education (Robbins, 1963) – which regarded investment in education as a condition for economic growth. These decades demonstrated the value that was placed on the development of human capital through government intervention and on the maximisation of the ability of every individual through capitalising on their opportunities and talents. This period came to an end with the emergence of a counter-movement, the so-called New Right, comprising both neo-liberals, who called for decentralisation, and neo-conservatives, who called for tough steps towards centralisation in order to bring recovery to the British economy. Both streams shared the view that government intervention and investment in education as well as in other public services should come to an end, calling for abolition of the welfare state and adoption of the market economy system in all public services. This voice had a direct effect on restructuring of the education system. The Thatcher administration, from 1979 onwards, adopted an explicit policy of fostering market conditions in education, encouraging entrepreneurship in schools in order to raise private funds, and the view that schools should be regarded as *cost centres*.

Whereas the previous chapter (7) aimed to concentrate on the internal factors within the school system, which stimulated criticism and the campaign for government intervention to restore order and standards in education, the goal of the present chapter is to describe the factors and ideology of the campaign at the macro level against the entire collective approach to social problems, and the consequences of the new movements and ideas that finally brought an end to the human capital approach and formed the basis for reconstruction of the education system.

8.1: THE HUMAN CAPITAL APPROACH

Post-war welfare policy in public services, including the rapid expansion of and investment in education, were among the reasons for inflationary pressures. In order to reduce these pressures, three waves of attempts were made to change the post-war policy and to reduce the heavy investment in education: all proved successful.

The first wave was initiated by the Attlee government in 1949, when the Economic Policy Committee proposed reducing by 30% that part of the 1950 investment programme dedicated to education. The proposal provoked a sharp response from the Labour Minister of Education, George Tomlinson, who wrote of the cuts in a top secret letter to the Prime Minister: "They would make it quite impossible to maintain that there is to be no major change in the present education policy of the Government."[1] The Prime Minister, in response to this, rejected any idea of major changes in post-war education policy but asked the Minister of Education to secure more economising in administration in order to join with the public corporations in reducing the inflationary pressure.[2]

The second attempt to reduce government expenditure on education was made by Butler himself, who became Chancellor of the Exchequer in the second Churchill Government in 1951. As Chancellor – and we must remember that as the minister who led the 1944 Education Act during the war he was the real architect of the post-war policy of education (see Chapter 3) – Butler raised ideas that clearly contradicted his own policy of expansion of education. In a letter to Frances Horsburgh at the Ministry of Education, Butler explained the new measures that were needed by the Government in order to maintain a healthy economy which could restore the British position in the world market: "We must think in terms of *changes in policy*" [present writer's emphasis].[3] Among the several options for changes in policy were lowering the school leaving age to 14 and raising the age of entry to 6; the opposite of what was recommended by Parliament in 1944. In a confidential letter to the Ministry of Education Butler says: "What troubles me quite frankly is whether the size of our educational apparatus is not in excess of our resources and whether we are not attempting to do much more than we can in the long run afford."[4] In response to Butler's proposals Horsburgh asked whether Butler was proposing a shift from the party policy of commitment to educational expansion:

> This means that the only major change of policy which would give a major economy would be one which reduced the number of children in the schools, and that means a change in the law of school attendance either at one end or the other. I am sure that you will not expect me to suggest that either of these alternatives is politically or educationally practicable.[5]

Despite the Chancellor's attempt, education policy remained unchanged, and expansion continued to be the Ministry of Education's central aim as part of the government's overall welfare policy.

The third attempt to reduce government expenditure on education was made in 1957 by another Chancellor of the Exchequer, Peter Thorneycroft. In response to this proposal to cut the education budget, the Minister of Education, George Lloyd, wrote to the Conservative Prime Minister Harold Macmillan in 1958:

> I agree with you in thinking that Education is probably the right card to play at the present time. Informed opinion currently believes that a highly educated nation is the key to our national future in trade and nearly all else.[6]

Macmillan's refusal to cut the education budget as well as other family services led to Thorneycroft's resignation as Chancellor in January 1958. The Prime Minister, in response to the resignation, accused the Chancellor of misunderstanding the recent developments in education:

> Many of these increases were unavoidable, partly because of the larger number of children at school, the expansion of secondary and university education.[7]

The "informed opinion" that the Minister of Education mentioned in his letter to the Prime Minister had by this time generally adopted the concept of human capital theory, a theory which assumes that there is a relation of principle between investment in schooling and economic growth.

This theory was first propounded in the USA around 1960 by Theodore Schultz as a branch of the economics of education.[8] It was triggered by the rapid rise in the amount of schooling received after the War, which Schultz analysed in order to establish "what effect it is having on productivity of human effort."[9] The theory proposed that investment in education be looked on as a major form of investment in human capital, analogous to investment in physical capital, which would make an economic return as well as a return on physical investment. It was assumed, in other words, that a greater input into cognitive learning in schools increased the financial benefits and earning power of an individual,[10] as well as national human capital stock, which is a source of economic growth. The new element introduced by human capital theory was the weight given to education as a major and significant variable that could explain differences in earning power and therefore in economic growth, as opposed to the traditional pre-1960 economic view which argued that *ability* or *social class* were the main factors behind these differences (Blaug, 1976; Woodhall, 1972).[11]

The Central Advisory Council for England submitted a report on the education of boys and girls between the ages of 15 and 18 in 1959 (the Crowther Report), that bore explicit markers of human capital theory. The main recommendations of the report were: raising the leaving age to 16; keeping a larger number of pupils in full-time education to 18 or beyond; allowing all pupils to take the GCE Ordinary level;[12] and revising syllabuses and practices in order to give easier access to the Sixth Form. Among the reasons advanced by the council for its recommendation was the right of every boy and girl to be educated for the benefit of his or her own future:

> Two of the enquiries made for us have shown, as have many other pieces of evidence, that *the boy who has stayed on at school catches up on earning capacity to the boy who left at 15* . . . if a boy stayed at school to increase his intellectual attainments, that he would be able to find a job, either at once or for many years, that would match up to the additional qualifications he would obtain [present writer's emphasis].[13]

But the Crowther Report went on to explain the benefit of additional education and national investment in education not only from the point of view of the individual but also from that of the national economy and national efficiency. The report's main assumption was that investment in education was "in the national interest, to avoid any preventable waste of talent"[14] and hence directed at increasing the national income. The report calculated the cost benefit ratio of investment in education:

> What we are suggesting is that, in addition, a volume of resources equal to less than one-twentieth of the national increase should, by that time be devoted to improving and extending education between 15 and 18…particularly since it will help to bring about the increase in productive capacity on which the whole calculation depends.[15]

Two years after the publication of the Crowther Report, which addressed the 15 - 18 age group, Eccles asked the Central Advisory Council for Education in 1961 to advise him on the education of pupils aged 13 to 16 of average and less than average ability. The resulting report, which was entitled *Half Our Future* (the Newsom Report), reaffirmed the conclusions reached by the Crowther Report about raising the school-leaving age to 16, and added recommendations such as: extension of the hours spent in educational activities; provision of a choice of programme including a range of courses related to occupational interests; and development of teaching techniques in order to help pupils whose ability is suppressed by environmental factors. These were all aimed at meeting the needs of pupils with abilities below average. The council claimed that there was unrealised talent among boys and girls "whose potential is masked by inadequate powers of speech and limitation of home background";[16] and that these pupils would become "half the citizens of this country, half the workers, half the mothers and half the fathers and half the consumers."[17] The report placed much emphasis on social weaknesses in explaining the wasting of talent, stressing the consequences of these weaknesses in terms of economic results rather than social issues. According to the report, it was in the nation's interests to "require a much larger pool of talent"[18] because of the future pattern of employment:

> The need is not only for more skilled workers to fill existing jobs, but also for a generally better educated and intelligently adaptable labour force to meet new demands.[19]

Therefore, according to the Newsom Report, it is essential to invest in pupils, for example by giving them a longer school life, thus generating more educated employees in the interests of a healthy national economy.

These two reports on secondary education were followed by the Robbins Report on higher education, published in 1963.[20] The Robbins Committee, nominated by the Prime Minister in 1960, recommended major changes in the provision of higher education. At the heart of these changes was a proposal to increase the number of students in the relevant age group from 8% to 17% – from 216,000 students in 1962 to 560,000 in 1980. In order to achieve the expansion target the committee proposed the growth and development of existing universities, the foundation of six new universities, the foundation of a new special institution for scientific and technological education and research, and the promotion to university status of ten regional colleges and colleges of education.

The main arguments behind the committee's recommendations were, on the one hand, the social demand for places in higher education as a result of the rapid development of secondary education and the growing number of pupils with GCE at Advanced level, and on the other the benefit of developing such a pool of ability for the country. Expanding on the latter point, the committee argued:

> While the reserve of untapped ability may be in the poorer sections of the community, this is not the whole of the story. It is sometimes imagined that the great increase in recent years in the numbers achieving good school-leaving qualifications has occurred almost entirely among the children of manual workers. This is not so. The increase has been almost as great among the children of professional parents, where the pool of ability might have been thought more nearly exhausted. In these groups the performance of children of a given measured ability has in fact continually improved. The desire for education, leading to better performance at school, appears to be affecting children of all classes and all abilities alike, and it is reasonable to suppose that this trend will continue.[21]

In the report's view, the growing number of schools offering academic courses leading to GCE, growing parental expectations of academic achievement, reduction in the size of classes and longer periods of higher education for teachers were all affecting the proportion of children capable of entering higher education. The committee considered the implications and advantages of this development for the economy clear:

> We wish to state unequivocally that... there is a broad connection between the size of the stock of trained manpower in a community and its level of productivity per head. Doubtless there is some ambiguity here. For it is certainly true that the richer a community the more education it wants and can afford. But if productivity is to advance at anything like the rate deemed desirable there is a strong presumption that a substantial increase in the proportion of the population that is both skilled and versatile will be necessary. And in modern societies the skill and the versatilities required are increasingly those conferred by higher education.[22]

The Robbins Report did not pursue the contemporary economic approach to education with respect to measuring the rate of return on investment in education or demonstrating the relation between productivity and national income by statistical means because of the existence of unquantifiable variables, identified by the report, such as the capacity for systematic invention, the capacity to apply the results of scientific progress, and the capacity of leadership. But the report came to the conclusion that "the communities that have paid most attention to higher studies have in general been the most obviously progressive in respect of income and wealth."[23]

The Robbins Report was immediately accepted by the government; within twenty-four hours it had allocated £650 million for capital expenditure. The approval of the report was the climax of development of the education system since the War, the culmination of a chain reaction that had started with the struggle for opportunities and for access to GCE at Ordinary level and spread to the increased demand for Advanced level and then for higher education. The government's higher education policy amounted to a vindication of the modern schools' claim that talent and ability were being wasted in their schools. The schools' demand for wider access to external examinations and the results of such access when it was eventually given, proved their point; these results in turn raised parents' and teachers' expectations and led to a further demand for higher education. Not surprisingly the 1960s were called the "golden years" and "the time of optimism" when education planning revolved around the merits of the "'social demand approach', the 'manpower requirements approach', and 'rate of return analysis'."[24]

A few years later however, other economic views "contrasted with the first" began to emerge.[25] The earlier optimism of the expansion policy gave way to a new pessimism and growing criticism, particularly from employers, of the quality of school leavers (Chitty, 1989; Denison in McNay et al., 1985) and the possibilities of "altering the distribution of income by educational means."[26] The emergence of a screening approach "devoted to qualitative reform rather than quantitative expansion,"[27] contrasted with the expansion policy and echoed the employers' criticisms. Stiglitz (1975) explains the screening mechanism in education as aiming to "place individuals into the right 'slots'"[28] according to the following principles: classification of information "about the individual,"[29] performance tests, and a hierarchy of schools, ranging "from those for the most able to those for the least able."[30] Such economic hypotheses emerged alongside the new ideas, and a new vocabulary sprang up that included terms such as market system, competition, choice, privatisation and entrepreneurship. These ideas all contradicted the human capital approach, according to which education was a sound economic investment.

8.2: THE RISE OF THE 'NEW RIGHT': TOWARDS CENTRALISATION AND DECENTRALISATION UNDER THE SAME UMBRELLA

From the 1970s onwards pressure groups emerged that were collectively dubbed the "New Right." The New Right involved two different philosophies on how to treat social problems: on the one hand the neo-liberals argued for complete decentralisation leading to a pure market economy system, and on the other the neo-conservatives argued for greater government control by means of greater centralisation. Despite the fundamental differences of principle between the two philosophies, they had one aim in common – the wish to bring the welfare state and the collective approach to social problems to an end.

The collective approach to social problems emerged in Britain towards the end of the Victorian period as a result of social reforms that had been inspired by egalitarian movements such as the Fabian Society. These reforms, which developed gradually over more than a century, gradually added to the responsibilities of the state and became directly state-operated after the Second World War (Fogarty, 1961).[31] This state responsibility covered social security matters such as health insurance, industrial injuries compensation, unemployment benefits and old age pensions, and other services such as medical health, education, nationalised industries, and housing.

Disappointment with the result of the collective approach to social problems was the main inspiration of a highly influential book published in 1960, *The Constitution of Liberty*, which was authored by Professor Hayek, a Nobel prize-winner in economics. For Hayek, the increasing recognition that the production of a socialist organisation is much less than that of a private enterprise, and that the outcome of this arrangement is not social justice and greater freedom but greater arbitrary power, led to the conclusion that the only viable course was to move away from the welfare state policy:

> If government wants not merely to facilitate the attainment of certain standards by the individuals but to make certain that everybody attains them it can do so only by depriving individuals of any choice in the matter. Thus the welfare state becomes a household state in which a paternalistic power controls most of the income of the community and allocates it to the forms and quantities which it thinks they need or deserve.[32]

The central results and chief dangers of the welfare state, in Hayek's view, are inflation, paralysing taxation, coercive labour unions and increased government dominance and bureaucracy. He argued that only the replacement of government control by the free market mechanism and competing agencies could safeguard respect for human desires and individual liberty and save the state from the danger of paralysis. His view was that the decentralisation of national services by the introduction of a free market and competition would not necessarily create social disturbance or disadvantages but on the contrary would be more efficient, appear more just and create greater satisfaction among individuals. Above all, it was vital to human development and liberty.

Hayek's book was a "powerful restatement of the liberal principles of free moral choice, voluntary and maximum individual liberty in a society,"[33] that took an "anti-totalitarian stance."[34] It became one of the main sources of inspiration for the neo-liberal pressure groups, particularly for the Institute of Economic Affairs (IEA) which was formed in 1957 as a research and educational trust and would become the most prominent and influential such group.[35] The IEA's main emphasis was on the theory of the market economy, to which end it published several works by distinguished and influential academics and economists.[36]

The IEA took the classical liberal line on the need to limit the role of the government in order to advance economic freedom and achieve prosperity by the "interplay of competitive enterprise with consumer choice."[37] It argued that the collectivist conception, believing that greater and indeed almost unlimited scope for government power was the way to improve social welfare and therefore the best way to pursue the public interest, had failed, as evidenced by unemployment, inflation, the balance of trade figures and the dissatisfaction of both suppliers and customers. The IEA view was founded on the liberal conception that the individual is motivated solely by self-interest and the desire to improve his own conditions of existence. The behaviour of the individual motivated by self-interest was spontaneous and could not be predicted – it could hence not be controlled by the government. The only system compatible with spontaneous behaviour was a system that was not defined by rigid rules, one in which the interest, the motivation, the ambitions and the freedom of the individual could be expressed; and this system was "nothing more nor less than a competitive market."[38]

The neo-liberal assumed that the market economy system would not only serve the interests of the free individual but also advance the economic situation and lead to economic growth. According to this view, the need to abandon the welfare state – a policy that led to high government expenditure, high taxation and powerful bureaucracy and ranked high among the reasons for unemployment, inflation and economic stagnation – was a first priority. With the move to a market system, services formerly provided by government, such as health, social security education and nationalised industries, would instead be supplied by a competitive market of suppliers; the consumer, not the government, would be supreme, and this would lead to a more efficient market, reduction of government spending,[39] low inflation,[40] a reduction in the "natural rate" of unemployment[41] and eventually to economic growth. Gamble explains the market view concerning the public services as follows:

> Welfare spending comes under such attack because it is argued, most of the services, including health, education and housing, could be provided almost entirely through the market. Individuals would have to pay for all the services they used.[42]

According to this view, cutting back public expenditure, including education, was the prime aim "for reversing decline"[43] in order "to inject greater dynamism and incentives into the economy by making market forces harsher and taxation lower."[44]

The economic crisis of the 1970s intensified the controversy over what direction the government should take. Despite the assumption that investment in education, and particularly in higher education would lead to economic growth, Britain had suffered a decline, albeit a measured one, in economic growth. From 1974-78 the UK's economic growth was below zero; even before this crisis the annual rates of growth had been between 2 and 3 percent, below those of the other major capitalist countries. In 1977 unemployment reached 6.3% of the labour force and inflation was above 15%, having peaked at 24.2% in 1975 (Gamble, 1985; Hough, 1987).[45]

The fact that British performance was so inferior to that of most other industrial countries led many to offer diagnoses of the source of the problems in British society. What Olson called the "British disease" was blamed on the nature of British society as a whole:

> Many commentators, British as well as foreign, claim that the slow growth of the British economy is due to some endemic trait of the British people or to one or another of its social classes. Britain, they allege, has been growing slowly because the British are inherently inclined to take it easy, or because the British working class is naturally unruly, or because the primordially class-conscious middle and upper classes are prejudiced against business careers and lacking in entrepreneurial drive.[46]

A similar diagnosis is made by Gamble: "The British become lazy, eager to consume, reluctant to work, and resistant to innovation."[47] Geiger goes on to explain the source of the problem as a result of the size of the welfare system and tax policy which has led to the development of a dependency culture and weak motivation to work:

> The growing size of and the methods of financing the welfare system produced a variety of adverse and sometimes contradictory effects. On the one hand, the heavy burden of taxation has impelled blue- and white-collar workers to press for continually rising money wages so as to increase their after tax incomes. On the other hand, the steeply mounting marginal tax rates have deterred many workers from qualifying for higher-paid skilled

jobs, leading to shortages in these categories despite a comparatively high rate of general unemployment. Combined with the loss of certain income-related welfare benefits (e.g., child benefits and rent subsidies), high personal income tax may make it more advantageous for the head of a family to live on tax-free unemployment payments than to accept a nominally higher-paying job.[48]

Eatwell shares the same argument and says that "the state provision of private benefits may create a dependency culture, rather than civic sentiment."[49]

The attribution of Britain's economic decline to either the welfare system or the nature of the "British people," gave rise to a view among neo-conservative groups that contrasted with the one held by the neo-liberals. The main claim of the neo-conservatives was that further decline could be avoided by restoration of past conditions under which Britain had been among the leading economic nations. They contended that only a strong central government would be able to achieve this and so avoid chaos and disorder in British society; therefore strong centralisation was the only solution to economic decline. Roger Scruton, a leading member of the neo-conservative Salisbury group, established in 1977, summarised this philosophy as follows:

2. Conservatism places duty before right.... Right must be paid for by reciprocal duties.
3. The duty of obedience arises most naturally in a society ordered according to three principles: tradition, consensus and rule of law...
5. Conservatives oppose the attempt by the state to take control of those aspects of social life in which it has neither the competence nor the right to deal. In particular they oppose state interference in the market.
6. The emphasis on authority and obedience, rather than contract, as the foundation of consensual order.
7. Conservatives place politics, culture and morality before economic order and distribution of power. These, they argue, are the true foundations of political order and the driving forces of social continuity.[50]

The neo-conservatives stressed the need for a strong state in order to guide people's behaviour, to protect the superior personal, cultural and intellectual elites whose inherited values and standards have great and beneficial influence on public order, and prevent authority and law being undermined. They drew particular attention to some areas in which the state was seen to have lost authority and standards were deemed to have declined, posing real threats to public order.

The conservatives did not ignore the principle of market freedom, but they argued that only a strong state would be able to control and police that market order, to make the economy more productive and to uphold social and political authority (Gamble, 1988). Their conclusion was that only centralisation could provide an antidote to the anomie of contemporary life, and re-establish the social continuity, tradition and national identity "upon which durable political order depends."[51]

The neo-conservative aim of a strong and centralised state with a high level of government intervention was in direct contradiction to the neo-liberal view that the nation's recovery could be achieved by a decentralised system which would foster competition and free choice. The core of the difference between the neo-conservatives and the neo-liberals lies in what was defined by Hayek as spontaneous forces "on which the policy of freedom relies."[52] While the neo-liberals believed that these forces should not be bound by rigid rules but should be given a high degree of freedom, the neo-conservatives argued for coercive control of the same forces. This difference between the two explains their respective advocacy of decentralisation and centralisation; in Hayek's words: "it has always been characteristic of those favouring an increase in governmental powers to support maximum concentration of these powers, those mainly concerned with individual liberty have generally advocated decentralisation."[53] The slogan adopted by the New Right, "free economy – strong state" (Gamble, 1988), does not explain the roots of the inherent differences concerning individual behaviour between the two wings of the movement. Gamble admits that this slogan contains a paradox: "the state is to be simultaneously rolled back and rolled forward. Non-interventionist and decentralised in some areas, the state is to be highly interventionist and centralised in others."[54] Allison raises the complexity of combining marketism and conservatism in the context of English society

"There are important beliefs which are, in England, recognisably conservative, which are in logical opposition to the main tenets of marketism."[55]

In 1979 the Conservatives won the general election. Griggs mentions that "Mrs Thatcher's personal political success has been achieved by her ability to harness the energy of all these [pressure] groups, whether they contradicted each other or not."[56] Soon after the general election the new market ideas penetrated the education system, raising the fundamental questions: Which direction was the government going to choose in relation to education? Were centralisation and decentralisation compatible? If so how? Was the paradox real, or could the logics of liberalism and control co-exist under the same umbrella? Could the paradox be resolved in practice? What was the meaning of the policy steps taken by the government in this area? An attempt will be made to evaluate the policy concerns raised by these questions, later in this chapter and in the next.

Meanwhile some other developments in education were taking place in the direction of market values such as competition, choice and privatisation of education, which deserve further attention.

8.3: MARKET VALUES PENETRATE THE EDUCATION SYSTEM

Two main market ideas have penetrated the education system since the end of the 1970s: first, competition and choice; and second, privatisation. The idea that schools would achieve better standards and greater efficiency for the same resources if they were driven by consumers (parents) rather than producers (politicians, officials, teachers), was first put forward in 1962 by Professor Milton Friedman.[57] The idea was to establish a direct link between choice of education and taxation by giving all parents allowances to be spent on education, not in cash but in the form of a voucher. The value of the voucher would be the same for each child and "parents would then be free to spend this sum and any additional sum they themselves provided on purchasing educational services from an "approved" institution of their own choice"[58] and to move their children from an unsatisfactory school to a preferred one. Schools would be allowed to charge additional fees. The whole point of the voucher scheme was that parents would seek to enrol their children in better schools. This would stimulate competition between schools, in the form of new courses, new methods and new forms of teaching. It would also ensure a greater investment of effort by staff in order to attract more parents, who would hold the capital (the voucher) in their hands. This would constitute incentive to keep the school lively, entrepreneurial and attractive (Seldon, 1986).[59]

The first lobby group to promote the voucher scheme in Britain was the Conference of the National Council of Women in 1974. That same year support for the idea led to the establishment of Friends of the Education Voucher Experiment in Representative Regions, or FEVER (Seldon, 1986).

In 1975 the Institute of Economic Affairs published a booklet outlining eight alternative voucher schemes. The publication called for a pilot study of one (or more) of these schemes, claiming that this type of system would increase the resources available to finance other education programmes and to raise standards because:

> The producers of education (teachers and academics) [would be] more responsive to pupil-student preferences. These pressures could push the industry along the road to technological change more rapidly.[60]

FEVER and the IEA campaign persuaded Kent County Council to adopt an experimental voucher system in 1978. The initiative was, however, abandoned after it was found that the administrative cost of running it would be enormous (Griggs, 1989).

Two years after the election of the first Thatcher administration in 1979, Sir Keith Joseph, Secretary of State for Education, responded to the campaign of two pressure groups, the National Council for Education Standards and FEVER:

> This government is committed to the extension of parental choice and involvement in education. The Education Act 1980 takes us a long way in the right direction, giving primacy to parental preferences; requiring the publication of detailed information, including examination results, about individual schools.... I am intellectually attracted to the idea of education vouchers as a

means of eventually extending parental choice and influence yet furthering and improving educational standards.[61]

In 1982 Sir Keith explained to the Conservative Party Conference what it was that so attracted him to the voucher idea:

> I believe that if vouchers were combined with open enrolment, some of the least good state schools would disappear, and increased competition might galvanise the less good state schools to achieve better results. These are the prospects that attract me to a combination of the voucher idea and open enrolment.[62]

The voucher scheme, while attractive to the Education Secretary, faced a variety of objections from its opponents on legal, economic, egalitarian and administrative grounds. This resistance became an obstacle to the implementation of a full market system which would give ultimate power to the consumer. The legal argument was that the government has a statutory obligation to provide free education without any additional charge and that the voucher system contravenes this (Seldon, 1986). The second objection was that vouchers would not achieve the government's aim of reducing the education budget; Professor Blaug, in raising this argument, says:

> Even if the full value of the vouchers were added to taxable income, the additional cost to the Exchequer of a national voucher scheme might be as much as half a billion pounds . . . this clearly took the steam out of the voucher movement in Britain.[63]

The third point advanced was that the voucher scheme would deepen existing inequality in education:

> According to the market principle, all the schools in the area would be in a league table of desirability, graded, just like the housing in the town, according to purchasing power. The appeal to parental choice in theory will be a reality only for those with the necessary income to make their choice an effective one.[64]

The fourth objection was an administrative one: How could schools cope with the logistical problems of fluctuating demand? The voucher scheme was based on the assumption that schools would expand by adding mobile classrooms according to demand. Moreover, some schools would have to employ more teachers at the same time as less attractive schools would have to make their surplus teachers redundant (Chitty, 1989).

These major objections, on top of political resistance within the Conservative Party which regarded the issue as "politically explosive,"[65] made it difficult for the Secretary of State for Education to implement the voucher scheme. On June 1983 in answer to a question from Randall Couchman MP on this matter, Sir Keith declared that the issue was no longer on the Education Department's agenda. He explained his statement in the following terms:

> I was intellectually attracted to the idea of education vouchers because it seemed to offer the possibility of some kind of market mechanism which would increase the choice and diversity of schools in response to the wishes of parents acting as customers ...I concluded that the difficulties which would arise from the many complex changes required to the legal and institutional framework of the education system, and the additional cost of mitigating them, were too great to justify further consideration of the voucher system as a means of increasing parental choice and influence. For these reasons, the idea of vouchers is no longer on the agenda.[66]

The voucher scheme was taken off the public agenda for a short time; but not the ideas of competition, freedom of choice and diversity. In 1987 the third Thatcher administration submitted an Education Bill which accommodated the idea of greater choice by devolution of power from suppliers to consumers. The government needed time to assess the difficulties involved in the voucher system and to find a new vehicle to achieve the same end. Chitty concludes his chapter on this issue with the words: "The Baker Education Bill would appear to fit this strategy perfectly"[67] (see next chapter).

The second element of the market approach that penetrated the education system was privatisation. This took the form of a two-stage process. The first, the devolution of power from LEAs to schools, was recommended by the Taylor Report of 1977. This report responded to a growing interest in "lay participation in education as part of a wider consumer movement"[68] by advocating that the community take a greater part in and responsibility for school life by means of greater parental representation on the governing body of each school. The Committee's assumption was that parents are a major source of support for the school and that in co-operation with teachers they could increase the school's effectiveness (Owen, 1978).[69] But this effectiveness would depend on each individual school if power were devolved from LEAs to create autonomous schools:

> We consider, however, that every local education authority should keep to the minimum necessary the restrictions which, for financial reasons, they impose on freedom of action at the school level. Indeed, we believe that authorities should encourage initiative and independent action to the utmost extent that is compatible with their own education responsibilities. We RECOMMEND *that they study the possibilities of making financial arrangements to facilitate this.*
> ...We hope, however, that authorities will find it possible to go further in many respects, that their general approach will be positive rather than negative and their guiding principle will be to encourage independence of thought and action wherever there is no need for restriction [original emphasis].[70]

During the first stage of privatisation the Taylor Report's message concerning schools' independence of thought and action was limited to the use of public resources. It was assumed that such decisions taken at the school level would be more sensitised to the needs of the parents and the community. This initial approach was a precondition for transferring greater responsibility first from the centre (The Department of Education and Science or LEAs) to schools and later to the parents and the community, by creating conditions for the raising of private funds for enriching school curricula and activities.

In 1980 an Education Act aimed at implementing the recommendations of the Taylor Report by requiring the election of parent and teacher governors was approved by Parliament.[71] Two years later, in 1982, Cambridgeshire set up a pilot scheme in six secondary schools and one primary school, devolving financial management by giving the head teachers and governors of each school power over 75% of the budget, up to £1.5 million, and over decisions on spending priorities. Five years later the pilot scheme was extended to 47 secondary schools and ten primary schools.[72] The view of the school as a *cost centre or accountability centre*, was applied more widely in 1987 when an arrangement was made to set training budgets not in accordance with DES consideration but in respect of individual institutions according to schools' priorities: "Thus a relatively large comprehensive school received about £15,000 to spend on in-service in whatever way it wanted."[73]

The initial process was to regard the school as a *cost centre*, devolving decision-making power regarding the use of public money from the centre to schools; the second phase was to view schools in a more active way as *entrepreneurial cost centres* by setting out the conditions for the raising of private funds for education. The aim of the government was to encourage better quality by enabling schools to practise entrepreneurship, innovation and enterprise in order to attract consumers (parents).

This view and the corresponding trend in the education system were closely matched and considerably influenced by a parallel process taking place in private industry. During the 1960s and 1970s, large enterprises in the private industrial sector suffered, losing their market position and market share to small and medium-sized newcomers and to innovative companies that emerged: "Small businesses have done far better than the giants."[74] In many cases the new successful enterprises were founded by entrepreneurs who had left their previous employers to set up in competition with them. The result was a shrinkage and erosion of big companies to the benefit of smaller companies. The US National Science Foundation found that small firms "produced about four times as many innovations per research and development dollar as medium-sized firms and about twenty-four times as many as large firms."[75]

A consequence of this process was economic organisations concluding that enterprises needed a much greater degree of autonomy, innovation and entrepreneurship. The resulting slogan was *small is beautiful*, meaning a firm could still be big and yet "act small" by means of radical decentralisation, revitalisation of the entrepreneurial spirit even at the cost of overlapping, lack of co-ordination, and internal competition.

The new approach would lead to the establishment of a new relationship between the centre and the wider organisation, through the firm's value system.[76] The main assumption was that the centre would gain authority and effectiveness "if the freedom and responsibility of the lower formations are carefully preserved . . . each of them will have a large amount of freedom, to give the greatest possible chance to creativity and entrepreneurship."[77] Therefore it was assumed that by being tough regarding the main aims and values yet giving maximum freedom in their execution, the organisation would achieve both its ends: autonomy and innovation for the individual on the one hand, and fulfilment of company goals on the other.

This management approach, initially developed by private industry and giving rise to an enormous number of management books in support of its ideas, eventually penetrated the public sector, which suffered from problems similar to those of large firms: management and conducting of the welfare services, which had developed very rapidly and become large and clumsy, was increasingly difficult.[78]

The idea of a greater degree of freedom and autonomy in the education system in England had attracted support since the end of the 1970s,[79] and conditions were created to decentralise power in order to create an innovative environment at the school level and conditions for schools to become "entrepreneurial cost centres."[80] This approach was in tune with Conservative policy, which was to create the potential for schools to become entrepreneurs. Measures were taken to encourage both maintained schools and private schools to look for private finance, in line with the campaign of the New Right. These steps, according to Pring (1987) and Walford (1990) should be seen as part of the overall privatisation process.

The measures taken after 1979 included encouraging covenants and charities to attract donors by tax relief of up to £3000 per year, increased to £10,000 in 1985. Raising the maximum amount of relief on high tax rates enabled high-earning individuals to donate money to fee-paying schools. Tax exemption included relief for employers on that part of their salary that was donated to charities, tax exemption for gifts (inheritance tax), tax relief for dividends that were contributed by companies and companies' donations for shares (Griggs, 1985; Pring, 1986, 1987; Walford, 1990).

More specific measures were taken on behalf of private schools "as part of the policy of making them more accessible to people who otherwise would use the maintained sector."[81] These included the Assisted Places Scheme (APS), introduced in 1979, which aimed to transfer high-ability pupils from maintained to private schools and in 1985/6 covered 21,400 pupils by the financial allocation to private schools of £34 million.[82] Heavy government subsidies for private education included fees for government personnel, the children of those in the armed services; direct grant payments, youth training and LEAs' purchased places. Pring estimates that the cost of these subsidies to the taxpayer reached at least £200 million per year (see Appendix 4).[83] The concept of regarding schools as *entrepreneurial cost centres* led to greater differentiation, widening both the diversity within the maintained system and the gap between the maintained and the private system.[84]

Eric Bolton, HM Chief Inspector, reported in evidence to the Select Committee on Education in 1985, that there was an "enormous increase" in cash contributions from parents to schools through the covenant schemes, particularly in primary schools where sums could be "as large or larger than the total capitation."[85] In March 1986 the BBC TV programme *Panorama* showed the disturbing gap in facilities as a result of schools' attempts to rely on private funding, and their initiatives to raise private money. One comprehensive school in a well-heeled Cheshire suburb raised £12,000 from parents to help supplement the school's books and other facilities while the comprehensive school in a deprived urban area in Bankfield could not raise money from parents and had to survive on its capitation allowance alone.[86] A report published by HMI in 1986 said on this matter: "There are sharp polarisations in provision between schools in different part of the country and within the same LEA."[87] This trend, and the widening gaps between schools, caused concern; the National Confederation of Parent Teacher Associations warned that "it will increase the differences that already exist between schools where parents can afford to contribute, and schools where they can't."[88]

Sponsorship became another source of funding for school curricula and activities, and also for contributing to the staff above what was provided by the LEA. Pring draws attention to the dangers of private sponsorship by highlighting the results of such funding, giving as an example of the extent of a sponsor's intervention in a comprehensive school in a town in the South-West where the sponsorship aimed to attract potential employees who lived outside the town by providing extra teachers of mathematics and languages in order "to meet the need of their [potential employees] gifted offspring."[89] He raises the danger that sponsors would intervene in the curriculum in order to get value for their money; the result of this development, according to Pring, is that "schools have become, as they never were before, business and entrepreneur centres, seeking the best value for the money [...] which they increasing[ly] control, and as such are entering into different kinds of relationship with the private sector."[90]

Moreover, public spending on education had fallen (Pring, 1987) and in March 1986 Chris Patten, Minister of State at the Department of Education and Science, admitted as much.[91] In other words, the development of schools as centres of business entrepreneurship reflected a new economic and social outlook that mirrored the aims of the neo-liberals in replacing the welfare system with market rules, public money with private.

8.4: CONCLUSIONS

The policy of educational expansion which in the late 1950s and 1960s was regarded as an investment in human capital and therefore as a contribution to economic growth, came to an end with the emergence of the New Right. This new movement expressed disappointment with the failure of the collective approach to social problems on the macro level, and called for a radical change of the old economic policy and order. Subsequently, the new ideas became the basis of fundamental changes in educational values which inevitably affected the structure of education. The first Thatcher administration, which came to power in 1979, fostered the neo-liberal and the neo-conservative policy of coexistence between centralisation and decentralisation. Decentralisation based on market forces was a means of creating diversity and differentiation between schools, while centralisation measures were used by the government to ensure that this differentiation developed in the right direction.

The decentralisation process developed gradually in two main phases:

first by devolution of the power over public money according to schools' priorities (the schools as cost centre) and secondly, by generating the conditions for raising private money (the schools as entrepreneurial cost centre). This process was based on market rules and the assumption that better quality would be achieved through freedom, autonomy and entrepreneurship, and that schools should no longer expect to have to rely solely on public funds, but instead on their ability to raise private money.

This course became a deliberate policy at the expense of social cohesiveness, creating "winners" and "losers," and causing wide gaps between those institutions able to compete and those unable to do so. The application of market rules created new values and priorities in education: head teachers came to be valued for the ability to raise money and to compete in cash terms rather than in educational terms such as engagement with academic, social or disciplinary problems. Pring responds to the penetration of market values into the education system by saying: "The inappropriateness of the market metaphor needs to be exposed. It is a dangerously misleading analogy for understanding educational processes and for directing educational policies ... the improvement of schools requires long-term planning – not the quick alteration of the commodity to meet changing fashions."[92] The creation of gaps between schools in terms of resources was a policy geared towards the elimination of what Sir Keith Joseph called the "least good state schools,"[93] a statement that underscores the replacement of traditional education values by market values and the expectation that every individual head would become an entrepreneur and would compete in economic rather than educational terms.[94]

The government controlled conditions for these developments, regarding decentralisation as a means to achieve the desired aim by creating diversity and differentiation both within the maintained system and between the maintained and the private systems.[95] The means that it used in pursuit of its aims, such as charities regulations, tax exemptions and public subsidies to private institutions, all deployed and manipulated to have particular required effects, could be regarded as a means of centralisation. Thus, both directions took place in the process: decentralisation in order to create distinction and differentiation between schools, and centralisation in order to control the direction of this differentiation.

The exact direction of government policy aims needs to be clarified. Pring argues that the government's aim was the "impoverishment of the maintained sector" such that parents would be driven into choosing "heavily subsidised private education."[96] Walford takes a similar view, claiming that the government's "general policy of favouring private provision should be seen as part of the overall privatisation process."[97] Blaug, in analysing the general direction of the economics of education, argues that the screening approach, which took account of qualitative rather than quantitative factors, became a general trend in the education system (Blaug, 1987; see next chapter).

Turning to the theoretical terms (Chapter 1), the meaning of a policy that increases "exchange of energy with the community" (in this case, money) is, according to the General System Theory a means of avoiding extinction and increasing probabilities, or, in educational terms, a means of enabling the enrichment of school activities and curriculum. But Dissipative Structure Theory argues that exchange of energy with the environment is a source of increasing disorder (entropy production), forcing the system towards instability and the formation of a new structural order; in our case deepening the gap within the maintained school (state school) sector by widening the discrepancy between the resources available to some and to others, thus setting off a chain reaction: disorder results from differentiation between school resources, instability follows, and consequently a new structure emerges within the public sector of schools ranked by their level of activities and variety of curriculum.

The criticisms that were voiced about the nature of inequality and the ideas raised on how to bridge the gap between schools by positive discrimination using government resources, particularly within the maintained system, failed to realise that the human capital policy, which was reflected in the development of the education system from the end of the 1950s to the 1970s and which regarded investment in education for all as an economic benefit, had been replaced by other economic views and by a new construct of education.

The government's intention in inculcating market values in the education system is still not clear enough, and yet more information is needed to understand fully the meaning of this trend. The 1988 Education Act and the policies of the 1990s, examined in the next chapter, will throw more light on this question.

Notes:

1. PRO ed. 136/891. Letter of 18 October 1949.
2. Ibid. Letter by the Prime Minister to the Minister of Education, October 1949. Actually, the total reduction for education was £5 million, which was far less than the initial proposal and could not affect post-war policy.
3. PRO ed. 136/890. Letter of 7 October 1953.
4. Ibid. Letter of 3 December 1953. Butler's statement in this letter touches the heart of the issue central to this chapter. The human capital approach regarded education as an economic investment and was therefore a positive view for expansion and investment in education, while those who criticised the welfare state and government investment in public services, including education, argued that a remedy for the weaknesses of the British economy would be achieved by cutting government investment. During the war priority was given to investment and educational expansion, while Butler as Chancellor represented another view of cutting and shrinking the size of the education system.
5. Ibid. Letter of 27 October 1953.
6. PRO ed. 136/889. Letter of 1 January 1958.
7. PRO ed. 136/889. The correspondence was published by *The Times*.
8. Earlier papers by Jacob Mincer in 1958 and Milton Friedman in 1945 provided some elements of the theory (Blaug 1976; Woodhall, 1972).
9. Theodore W. Schultz (1963). *The Economic Value of Education*. New York: Columbia University Press, 42.
10. The assumption of the theory is that higher earnings result because additional schooling of individuals raises their relative productivity.
11. Maureen Woodhall (1972). *Economic Aspects of Education*. Windsor: NFER. Mark Blaug (1976). "The Empirical Status of Human Capital Theory." In *Journal of Economic Literature*, September, Vol. XIV No. 3. Schultz, Dennison and Woodhall argue that two-thirds of the extra earning could be explained by the education variable.
12. The assumption was that all the pupils were able to take the Ordinary level unless there were exceptional circumstances.
13. Ministry of Education (1959). *15 to 18*. A report of the Central Advisory Council For Education (England). London: HMSO, 47.
14. Ibid., 57.
15. Ibid., 59.
16. Ministry of Education (1963). *Half Our Future*. A report of the Central Advisory Council for Education (England). London: HMSO, 3.
17. Ibid., XIII.
18. Ibid., 5.
19. Ibid.
20. The Robbins Report was published in the same year as the Newsom Report.
21. Committee on Higher Education (1963). *Higher Education Report*. London: HMSO. 53.
22. Ibid., 73. The Committee compared the numbers of students in higher education in several countries; it took particular note of what the Soviet Union had achieved in developing schools "to the limit of their potential" (74).

23. Ibid., 206.
24. Mark Blaug (1987). "Where Are We Now in the Economics of Education?" In M. Blaug, *The Economics of Education and the Education of an Economist*, London: Edward Elgar, 129.
25. Ibid., 130.
26. Ibid., 129.
27. Ibid.
28. Joseph E. Stiglitz (1975). "The Theory of "Screening," Education, and the Distribution of Income." In *The American Economic Review*, Vol. 65, No.3, 294.
29. Ibid., 293.
30. Ibid., 294.
31. Michael Fogarty (1961). "Social Welfare." In Seldon, Arthur (ed.): *Agenda for A Free Society: Essays on Hayek's The Constitution of Liberty*, London: IEA.
32. F.A. Hayek (1960). *The Constitution of Liberty*. London: Routledge & Kegan Paul, 260-1.
33. Ian Bradley (1985). *The Strange Rebirth of Liberal Britain*. London: Chatto & Windus, 148.
34. Charles Covell (1986). *The Redefinition of Conservatism*. London: Macmillan, 162.
35. Seldon (1961) mentions that this wave included opponents as well as admirers.
36. The IEA, according to Griggs (1989), deserves "the greatest credit for moving the political debate to the right" and Colin Clark regarded the IEA as "the antithetical counterpart of the Fabian Society" (Colin Clark (1981)."The IEA and Fabians: Comparison and Contrast." In Arthur Seldon (ed.): *The Emerging Consensus*, London: IEA, 191).
37. Ralph Harris & Arthur Seldon (1977). *Not from Benevolence: 20 Years of Economic Dissent*. London: IEA, 1.
38. Ibid., 3.
39. As a result of abandoning the subsidisation of welfare services and other national services and reducing the size of bureaucracies.
40. Low inflation would be achieved, according to this view, by ending the monetary policy of price and income control and by raising the rate of unemployment.
41. Based on the assumption that low inflation would be one of the main measures to restore the confidence of the business community, thereby creating a higher rate of employment. Andrew Gamble (1988). *The Free Economy and the Strong State*. London: Macmillan Education.
42. Ibid., 159.
43. Ibid., 158.
44. Ibid.
45. G.R. Hough (1987). *Education and the National Economy*. London: Croom Helm.
46. Mancur Olson (1989). "How Ideas Affect Societies: Is Britain the Wave of the Future?" In *Ideas, Interests and Consequences*, London: IEA, 27.
47. Andrew Gamble (1985). *Britain in Decline*. London: Macmillan, 11.
48. Theodore Geiger (1987). *Welfare and Efficiency*. London: Macmillan, 77.

49. Roger Eatwell & Noel O'Sullivan (1989). *The Nature of the Right: European and American Politics and Political Thought Since 1789*. London: Pinter, 189.
50. Roger Scruton (ed.) (1988). *Conservative Thinkers: Essays from the Salisbury Review*. London: Claridge, 9-11.
51. Scruton, 1988, 10.
52. Hayek, 1960, 401.
53. Ibid., 263.
54. Gamble, 1988, 28.
55. Lincoln Allison (1984). *Right Principles*. Oxford: Blackwell, 15.
56. Griggs (1989). 105.
57. An earlier version of Milton Friedman's idea of purchasing places in schools was expressed by Thomas Paine in the eighteenth century (Blaug, 1987) and Cardinal Bourne in 1926, who campaigned on behalf of parents who wanted their children to attend Roman Catholic schools. The first two British economists who examined and supported the idea were Professors Alan Peacock and Jack Wiesman (Seldon, 1986).
58. Milton Friedman (1962). *Capitalism and Freedom*. Chicago: UCP, 89.
59. According to Professor Friedman's argument the total costs of education would be covered by the voucher system (Seldon, 1986, 20).
60. Alan Maynard (1975). *Experiment with Choice in Education*. London: IEA, 65.
61. The full letter is published in Seldon (1986), 36.
62. Quoted by Chitty (1989), 184-5.
63. Mark Blaug (1987). "Education Vouchers – It All Depends on What You Mean." In Mark Blaug. *The Economics of Education and the Education of an Economist*, London: Edward Elgar, 259-60.
64. Griggs (1989), 112. According to Griggs this was the main reason why Sir Keith Joseph was deterred from introducing the voucher scheme.
65. Blaug (1987), 245. According to Blaug the main reason for the Tory government's abandonment of the voucher idea was the huge cost of subsidising the children who were already going to independent schools or the additional cost for children switching from maintained to independent schools.
66. Hansard: Vol.62, Col.290, 22 June 1984.
67. Chitty (1989), 188.
68. Stuart J. Maclure (1968). *Educational Documents*. London: Methuen, 387.
69. Joslyn Owen (1978). "A New Partnership for Our Schools: The Taylor Report." *Oxford Review of Education*, Vol.4, No.1.
70. Department of Education and Science (1977). *A New Partnership for Our Schools*. London: HMSO, 67.
71. Education Act 1980, Section 2 (5).
72. *Times Educational Supplement*, 17.1.86.
73. Richard Pring (1987). "Privatisation in Education." *Education Policy*. Vol. 2, No.4, 290.
74. Peter Drucker (1977). *People and Performance: The Best of Peter Drucker on Management*. London: Heinemann, 148.

75. Quoted by Thomas Peters & Robert Waterman: *In Search of Excellence* (1982). New York: Harper & Row, 200.
76. The term "value system" became a key element in understanding the development of the phrase "small is beautiful." The main assumption is that the only way to control a complex company with thousands of workers is by creating and instilling a few basic values that would be shared by all workers at all levels. *These shared values or overriding values* are the basic beliefs which create the commitment of each individual, even at the very bottom of the organisation, to the aims of the company and allow the company to create autonomy and freedom within the organisation without losing sight of its basic aim.
77. E.F. Schumacher (1973). *Small is Beautiful.* London: Blond Briggs, 228-9.
78. Rodney Lord (1984). *Value for Money in Education.* London: Public Money.
79. Neglecting the slogan *small is beautiful* in its title, the booklet *Big and Beautiful* was published in 1979 by the Secondary Heads Association (TOPICS) claiming to justify the size of the comprehensive schools. Secondary Heads Association (1979). *Big and Beautiful.* Brackley: SHA.
80. Pring (1987), 297. The implication of the term "cost centre," according to Pring, is responsibility for marketing, budgeting and financial arrangements.
81. Richard Pring (1986). "Privatisation of Education." In Rick Rogers (ed.), *Education and Social Class*, London: Falmer, 65-6.
82. The source is Tapper and Salter (1986), quoted by Geoffrey Walford (1990). *Privatisation and Privilege in Education*, London: Routledge.
83. Pring (1986), 81.
84. The creation of an innovative environment in the school as a "cost centre" was promoted by publications on how to raise school funds through various activities such as fetes and bazaars, sponsored events, tee-shirts and uniforms, Christmas cards, concerts and plays, jumble sales, films and even a special post for co-ordinator or bursar. See: Oliver Hamilton (1986). *Your School Fund.* London: NEPO.
85. *Times Educational Supplement*, 25.5.85.
86. Ibid., 21.3.86.
87. Department of Education and Science: Report of *Her Majesty's Inspectors on the Effects of Local Authority Expenditure Policies on Education Provision in England - 1985* (1986). London: DES, 16.
88. Ibid.
89. Pring (1987), 292.
90. Ibid., 293.
91. *Times Educational Supplement*, 21.3.86.
92. Pring (1987), 299.
93. Quoted by Chitty (1989), 184 in connection with the voucher debate. But the substance of the voucher debate relies on the attraction to the customers basically in terms of enriching the curriculum by raising private money as well as becoming more efficient, assuming that parents eventually would choose the richest schools by abandoning the

less attractive in terms of resources up to point of their vanishing.
94. The assumption was that a school with better economic resources would probably be better in educational terms.
95. Private institutions benefit more as a result of the class composition of these institutions which enable them to receive much more generous donations than the maintained schools.
96. Pring (1986), 66.
97. Walford (1990), 72.

• CHAPTER 9

OLD VALUES, NEW STRUCTURE: FROM THE EDUCATION REFORM ACT 1988 TO THE POLICIES OF THE 1990s

Twenty years of criticism levelled by pressure groups at low standards in the education system gathered momentum in the direction of fundamental reform at the end of the 1980s. In December 1987 the Education Reform Bill was introduced before Parliament by Kenneth Baker, the Secretary of State for Education. Baker argued that the first and foremost aim of the new bill was to raise the quality and standards of schooling.

The 1988 Education Act was a radical reform that created a new order by shifting power between the four main partners in the education system – teachers, parents, local education authorities and government – and establishing a new relationship between them. The fundamental changes it introduced included the establishment of a national core curriculum supported by assessment of attainment targets at ages 7, 11, 14 and 16; parental choice; the possibility of schools "opting out" of LEAs and becoming "independent" grant maintained schools; the establishment of city technology schools and the delegation of power from the LEAs to local management of schools (LMS).

The birth of the 1988 Education Reform Act brought to an end almost two decades of attempts to correct the education system's "deviation" from the "good old days" of high education standards, by swinging the "pendulum" towards a new order that would facilitate the restoration of old standards. This chapter concentrates on the main elements of the Reform in the policies of the 1990s, observing and analysing a further shift of the pendulum. In this sense the chapter not only describes the end of an era but also the start of a new one. Analysis of both the raising of standards and the ingredients for the next move of the pendulum will make reference to the "effective school" movement and present some case studies for explanatory purposes.

Criticism of standards and dissatisfaction with school attainment was not confined to England alone; the expansion of education after the Second World War generated a wave of criticism of low standards in other industrialised countries. Several research projects carried out during the 1960s concluded that the "student's progress at school, his or her success in academic study, is overwhelmingly more dependent on home background than on what the school does for the student."[1] The most striking of these was the Coleman Report in the USA, which stated that "schools bring little influence to bear on a child's achievement that is independent of his background and general social context."[2] Jencks et al. (1973), in another prominent study, reached the same conclusion about the weight of home environment factors in the variance in pupils' achievement: "Family background explains nearly half the variation in education attainment."[3]

This conclusion – that the school has minimal influence on individual achievement and unwittingly "reaffirms an unjust social order,"[4] – motivated educators to seek and identify factors within schools that did actually affect outcomes and could diminish the family's influence, so that external forces could not be blamed for poor outcomes within schools (Reynolds, 1985). During the 1970s and 1980s, several research projects were carried out with the aim of discovering and characterising the virtues of exceptional schools that were regarded as "effective," "high achieving," "good" or "excellent" (Beare et al., 1989; Reynolds, 1985; Rutter, 1979).

The result of this research drive was the development of a movement in support of *effective schools*. The main thesis of this movement was based on research findings which strongly indicated that under particular functional and management conditions schools could significantly raise their standards, achieve better results, and be more efficient. The research studies identified several features of the effective school; the three most common and prominent of which were: clear and realistic objectives, assessment of whether these objectives had been achieved, and high expectations held by teachers and pupils. But the value of these three factors depended on their being defined and applied according to each school's particular context; therefore, the locus of control needed to be internal to the school if progress in standards was to be achieved (Bashi et al., 1990; Beare et al., 1989; Caldwell and Spinks, 1998; Cheng 1996; Cuttance, 1985; Dalin and Rust, 1983; Dimmock 1993; Goodlad, 1984; Hopkins, 1985, 1987; Reynolds, 1985).[5] The implication of "school context" and "school circumstances" was that attainment targets, assessment, and the definition of expectations were regarded as relative rather than absolute terms. Therefore, only the school itself, by virtue of its knowledge of its pupils' capabilities and their internal diversity, could define and assess proper learning aims and raise real expectations according to the pupils' needs and capabilities. Thus, Cuttance's main finding was that the effectiveness of schools will be associated with variations in pupil performance; an effective school is not "constant for all subgroups within it. The term *effectiveness* may thus be used with reference to particular subgroups within schools" [original emphasis].[6] David Hopkins argues that quality schooling occurs when agreement on goals, high expectations and the teaching/learning process "[is] embedded within the fabric of the school."[7] Another report by Hopkins, based on school improvement in OECD countries, concluded that the ability to "review, evaluate and monitor performance"[8] is central to schools' improvement and that such improvement does not occur unless the "particulars of a school and its context are taken into account."[9] Bashi et al. came to a similar conclusion, arguing that "the various elements of school culture are interrelated. We cannot expect any lasting change without being aware of these interrelations."[10]

Consequent to the development of the *effective school* movement, the idea that the locus of control needs to remain close to the school in order to serve the real needs of pupils and raise standards was crystallised. Decision making would have to be delegated to the schools, and the degree of central control and intervention in school life accordingly limited (Goodlad, 1984; Hopkins, 1985). Moreover, because attainment targets need to be flexible and subject to continuous change, schools should be regarded as, and expected to be, self-correcting and self-renewing institutions. Thus, more weight was given to schools' need for greater freedom with respect to several aspects of decision making.

The "effective school" concept bears some similarity – in terms and philosophy – to another trend in education, the "accountability movement." This movement gathered momentum in Britain during the 1970s in response to growing public dissatisfaction with the quality of education, the abolition of the 11+ examinations and the allegation that pupils were entering secondary school with poorer levels of attainment (Becher and Maclure, 1978; Clift, in Hopkins, 1987). The movement called for teachers to be more accountable for their pupils' performance. This was translated into the ministerial demand "for standards to be monitored at the level of each individual school, and even, each individual classroom."[11] The phrase "performance accounting" was translated into management accounting, and has been seen as a means whereby schools can make various efforts to improve standards and quality of education. It allows schools to define their "goals, the content of the school curriculum, the organisation of the teaching-learning process and teaching styles."[12] Moreover, there was a growing recognition that schools should be more accountable to the public interest, less "isolated from the communities they were built to serve."[13] Schools were therefore expected to account for themselves to the community and to parents, and to "declare their educational goals, programmes and their success in achieving objectives."[14]

The findings of the "effective school" studies regarding the conditions for achieving higher standards; recent developments in other countries in the quest for better scholastic attainment; DES criticisms and the "accountability movement," together constitute a frame of reference for analysis of the British government's attempt to raise educational standards via the various steps of the Education Reform Act of 1988 and other policies that followed during the 1990s.

9.1: THE NATIONAL CURRICULUM

The publication of the White Paper entitled *Better Schools,* in 1985, was another step in the gradual process leading towards a National Curriculum.

The document followed DES Circular 6/81, which asked schools to set out their curricular aims, and Circular 8/83, which asked the LEAs to draw up a policy for the curriculum at primary and secondary levels. These two circulars were aimed at encouraging schools to clarify and sharpen their own definitions of the curricula. The interaction between the DES – which later became the DfEE – the schools, and the LEAs over the nature of the curriculum gave the ministry a better and more informed view of the state of schools' curricula and made it possible to assess the system's weaknesses. The most prominent weakness, in the government's view, was low standards. It was attributed to two main causes. The first was the labelling of pupils, which often resulted in self-fulfilling prophecies:

> Many teachers' judgements of pupils' potential and their learning needs tend to reflect preconceptions about the capabilities of different categories of pupils. These preconceptions are often shared by parents and by the pupils themselves.[15]

The second weakness was the lack of challenging goals rooted in high expectations: "guidelines exist for English and mathematics in about three-quarters of the schools but they frequently do not extend to other important elements of the curriculum."[16] The government identified two main steps that were to be taken towards remedying these weaknesses: first, "to secure greater clarity about the objectives and content of the curriculum"[17] and second, to reform the examination system in order to assess the "objectives of the curriculum, the achievements of pupils and the recording of those achievements" more effectively.[18] The logic behind this thought inevitably led to the conclusion that only a National Curriculum would create clear objectives and challenging goals for subjects other than English and mathematics.

When Kenneth Baker introduced the Education Reform Bill in December 1987 he argued that raising standards would be the outcome of "a broad-based and relevant curriculum"[19] in which the "Technical and Vocational Education Initiative created a block of time for cross-curricular activity"[20] on the one hand, complemented by necessary diversity in the curriculum on the other.[21] A document entitled *The National Curriculum 5-16*, published by the DES in the same year, further illuminates government expectations of the National Curriculum. It formulated the primary task thus: "we must raise standards consistently, and at least as quickly as they are rising in competitor countries."[22] Another aim was "to secure for all pupils in maintained schools a curriculum which equips them with the knowledge, skills and understanding that they need for adult life and employment."[23]

In other words, the government's aim in raising standards was to "equip" different types of pupils with the knowledge that the national workforce needed to compete with other countries. This aim on the part of the government raises fundamental questions about the nature of the National Curriculum that was eventually devised in order to meet this challenge. Just how flexible is the National Curriculum? Is it adaptable enough to encompass all types of pupils' abilities and aptitudes within schools? To what extent is school decision-making on curriculum matters flexible enough to meet pupils' realistic objectives? Answers to such questions require close analysis of the nature of the National Curriculum and of the steps taken by the government in the 1988 Education Reform Act.

The National Curriculum established a framework of three core subjects for the period of compulsory education – mathematics, English and science – and six foundation subjects – history, geography, technology, music, art and physical education – with a modern foreign language at the third stage. The Act went on to specify that the programme of study in each subject should be linked to attainment targets which would be subject to assessment. For each subject the Secretary of State appointed a working group to advise on appropriate attainment targets.[24] The working groups became the machinery by means of which central targets were set for all the nation's pupils over the full age range of 5-16.

Thus, for example, Professor Brian Cox, the head of the English working group and the editor of the Black Papers during the 1970s, explained the need for broad attainment targets in order to "enable children to develop confidence and competence as speakers and listeners in a wide variety of situations."[25] On the basis of this rationale, requirements for different kinds of skills at ten levels between the ages of 5 and 16 were identified, and attainment targets were defined for each skill at each level. 39 attainment targets were defined for speaking, 52 for reading, 42 for writing, 12 for spelling, 4 for description and 10 for presentation – altogether 169 attainment targets for English, 427 for science, 319 for mathematics, and so on. Desmond Nuttall commented that the targets "multiply like mice."[26] Nuttall illustrates the mechanism of attainment targets by quoting Maurice Holt's view:

> The entire document is steeped in the mechanistic assumption that schools can be run like biscuit factories. Providing the skills and technology are there, backed by clear objectives and precise assessment, the right product will roll off the assembly line.[27]

Nuttall argued against the pre-ordained nature of the attainment targets, saying that targets should instead be negotiated between the teachers and the pupils and defined in a manner more responsive to the pupils' progress rather than one remote from the real site of learning – the classroom.

Moreover, Clause 19 of the Act introduced a mechanism which not only shifted power from the teachers to the Secretary of State but revoked schools' discretionary power to modify or adapt the National Curriculum by giving head teachers a strict prescription as to the cases in which temporary modification would be allowed for exceptional individual pupils. This utterly contradicted the idea that schools know best regarding realistic objectives in their particular context. Central control over the curriculum determined not only the objectives and the content but even the speed of learning and the level of attainment that a child should reach at each particular stage of his or her school life. In Professor Tomlinson's words, the Act "apparently forbids all innovation without the express approval of the Secretary of State, and that by a cumbersome procedure."[28]

Despite the fact that the Act revoked schools' discretionary powers and imposed such a heavy burden of multiple attainment targets on them that it became difficult to see "how so much material can practically be fitted into the school year,"[29] the National Curriculum did not become a matter of public controversy (Golby, 1989). Teachers felt competent to teach the National Curriculum, particularly in English, mathematics and history, though less so in the new subjects of science and technology (Coulby and Ward, 1990). Coulby's view on the teachers' response to the National Curriculum is as follows:

> Passing an Act at Westminster and giving teachers a collection of loose-leaf binders does not automatically change what they teach on Monday mornings. Teachers are appropriately regardful of national legislation in that what they teach will change as they develop the appropriate skills and collect current information and materials: but it will change slowly and not necessarily in the predicted or desired direction.[30]

A series of interviews conducted in 1991 with fourteen teachers in primary and middle schools in Oxfordshire, with the aim of ascertaining the teachers' view of the National Curriculum, showed that the teachers emphasised two aspects. On the one hand, the teachers regarded the National Curriculum as a general framework for their work in the classroom, one that gives clearer direction and is more task-oriented than the previous system. On the other hand, the teachers regarded the National Curriculum and the associated attainment targets as a broad field of options within which they made *their own decisions* as to which attainment targets would be taught, when and how. The overall feeling was that the National Curriculum did not radically change their degree of discretion or flexibility in these matters. In practice, they did not regard themselves as strictly bound to the linear development of the attainment targets and felt free to make decisions regarding their pupils' needs, suitable objectives for them, and to teach according to various combinations of attainment targets rather than follow the National Curriculum in the manner laid out by the government.[31] This view accords well with Coulby's statement that the new Act does not "automatically change what they teach on Monday morning."

The government's stated aim of developing technological skills – "advanced knowledge, to improve technological capability, and to produce qualified manpower"[32] – in order to meet the challenge of competing with other industrial countries, should be assessed in the light of a close analysis of two main developments: the Technical and Vocational Education Initiative (TVEI) within secondary schools, and the plan to establish City Technology Colleges (CTCs).

TVEI was launched by Prime Minister Margaret Thatcher in 1982 as a result of "growing concern about existing arrangements for technical and vocational education provision for young people,"³³ and "to improve the staying-on rates."³⁴ It aimed to develop the curriculum within secondary education in such a way as to tackle massive unemployment among school leavers at the age of 16. The organisation that was made responsible for this programme was the Manpower Services Commission (MSC) with David Young as Chairman, in co-operation with the Secretary of State for Education and Science. The principles of the programme, which was introduced in secondary schools in 1983, were very flexible; the aim was to cater to a wide range of abilities, for the ages 14 to 18, in full-time technical, vocational, and general education. The scheme was to be developed according to "local circumstances": the "precise curriculum should be a matter for local determination within certain general criteria/guidelines applying nationally."³⁵ Lord Young, who initiated the programme, explained his inspiration and the reasons for the TVEI:

> I had been the Chairman of British Ort³⁶ and I had spent quite a bit of time in Israel, and in France, looking at Ort schools in the 1970s and I had become very convinced by the value of vocational and technical education for two reasons; one is work I saw in Israel which I think had a big effect on motivating young children, and secondly by the standards of technical skills which they actually got, which certainly meant when they left school they were more employable. The United Kingdom, on the other hand, had been going entirely in the wrong direction…the great mistake I thought that they made then…was that they were modelling all the schools on academic institutions. There was a great big plot really; all the members of the parliament, politicians, by and large, 95 percent had come from an academic background. All the civil servants had come from Oxbridge, universities or an academic background and they naturally thought that the only good education is an academic education…. I thought three out of four young people actually were switched off by academic [education] by abstract concepts…. I knew that this was actually wrong.³⁷

The TVEI principles, quickly welcomed with enthusiasm by local education authorities and secondary schools, echoed the guiding principles of "child-centred" and "progressive" methods that underlay the development of the comprehensive schools, underlining that the curriculum should be based on the needs, progress and ability of the child rather than laid down by external definition of those unfamiliar with the school context. The TVEI development, which was in complete contradiction to the movement towards an academic National Curriculum, emerged to reinforce the teaching methods that were regarded by the neo-conservatives[38] of the New Right as the "evil" that was to blame for the low standards of the English education system and that had stimulated pressure for a National Curriculum.

The TVEI programme was based on a "student-centred approach"[39] and a modular curriculum committed to "mixed ability, experiential learning, equal opportunities, special needs and so forth," that "complements rather than contradicts comprehensive principles."[40] Therefore, in Gleeson's view, the programme met a universal need and was accommodated "within the demands of the existing school organisation and curriculum."[41] Rapid expansion of the programme in order to enable TVEI to catch up with the rest of the curriculum was acknowledged to be essential by the DES:

> £900m has been made available over the ten year period from September 1987 to support the extension of TVEI to all maintained secondary schools and colleges. The government is committed to the continuity and expansion as a national scheme available to 14-18 year olds... . Thus TVEI will provide substantial help to LEAs and secondary schools in developing their curricula to meet the aims of the Education Reform Act.[42]

The National Curriculum, in the form it was published, posed two major difficulties for the future development of the TVEI in terms of the philosophy of "student-centred" education and schools' decision making in curricular matters. The first is that the National Curriculum tied the TVEI curriculum to the seven foundation subjects. This development embodied not only a shift of power from teachers and schools to the government, but a change in the philosophy that the curriculum – with regard to TVEI – would be based on the identification of students' needs by the school and developed on a modular basis, rather than confined to subject matter dictated centrally for all schools. When the National Curriculum Council (NCC) published curriculum guidance on linking education and industry they did not ignore the importance of TVEI, but made it clear that the continuation of the programme would take place within the National Curriculum of seven foundation subjects.[43] The second difficulty for the future development of TVEI was the assessment system, which followed the attainment targets of the National Curriculum (see later in this chapter). Dale et al. (1990), who evaluated the TVEI program in fourteen local education authorities, mention that "whenever there appeared to be a clash of priorities between the requirement of TVEI and the requirements of obtaining exam passes, TVEI lost out."[44]

The authors explain TVEI's disadvantaged position in terms of the new spirit of competition between schools:

> Competition between them [schools] had been further sharpened by the very real threat that one of them would be closed. This competition had been based on a "league table" of exam results. Maintaining their position in the league table was each head teacher's main priority. Though TVEI was an unknown quantity, all of the head teachers considered it too risky to invest a great deal of effort in it, because it might detract from the main objective of their schools.[45]

Peter Senker voiced a similar argument on the contradiction between the TVEI policy as practised since 1983 and the advent of the National Curriculum and GCSE, saying that "TVEI efforts to bridge traditional subject boundaries are in danger of being undermined by the proposed National Curriculum which involves individual subject testing."[46] Finegold and Soskice (1990) explain the failure of training in Britain by arguing that the government has neither the infrastructure nor the intention to develop education and training (ET). Thus, the funding for TVEI "appears inadequate to sustain its early successes" and its "decline in importance"[47] is reflected in the fact that about 55 percent of young British people leave school by 16, while in competing countries like Japan, Germany and Sweden, "90 per cent of young people are in full-time highly structured education and training until 19 or 20."[48]

The CTCs, another wing of a non-traditional academic curriculum, emerged as part of the 1988 Education Act and were aimed at "provid[ing] education for pupils of different abilities who have attained the age of eleven years . . . in science and technology."[49] ORT, the world-wide technological education organisation, which has headquarters in London, could be regarded as one of the main sources of inspiration for this type of school.[50] Prominent among ORT schools all over the world are highly equipped, well-designed colleges aimed at attracting the most able students with technical and scientific aptitude. The link between ORT and the British education system led some DES officials and HMI to visit such schools. Eventually, in 1986, the Prime Minister visited one of Israel's technical colleges. As a result of this visit Thatcher wrote to Joseph Harmatz, the Director General of World ORT:

> I should like you to know how very much I enjoyed my visit to the ORT School in Jerusalem and how grateful I was for your illuminating remarks on the part played by ORT International. I very much welcome the close ties which you have with Britain and hope that these will flourish.[51]

The flourishing of ties mentioned by Margaret Thatcher in her letter took the form of co-operation between the DES and ORT over the CTC project when Kenneth Baker, as Secretary of State for Education and Science, commissioned ORT to provide advice on the implementation of the science and technology curriculum for twenty new City Technology Colleges.[52] The establishment of these colleges was announced at the Conservative conference six months after Thatcher's visit to Jerusalem.

The curriculum recommended by ORT was based on two main assumptions. The first was that modern technology is essentially a "multi-disciplinary subject, in that it incorporates and links a wide variety of apparently disparate topics."[53] The implication of this assumption was that technological knowledge needs to be presented as an integrated "package" in terms of the cognitive tools for "thinking and problem solving."[54] Pupils should learn a range of disciplines related to design, manufacture, testing of industrial and consumer goods, as well as financial and marketing aspects.

The design of the curriculum reflected this assumption and proposed that instead of isolated pockets of knowledge of single subjects, pupils would study various disciplines through "educational events" relevant "to carrying out the project or solving the original problem . . . to develop in him or her both an interest in the subjects themselves and a wider perspective, and a capacity for independent thought and creativity."[55] This, in the view of those designing the curriculum, is an essential approach to training pupils for the modern technological environment and the kind of problems that a scientist, engineer or technician has to solve in industry and commerce – problems of an integrated nature whose solution is based on practical and technological knowledge.

The second assumption was linked to the first, namely that problem-solving in the modern technological environment should be learnt by the principle of:

> "Research and discovery," where the teacher acts as a facilitator to the learning process rather than the source of all knowledge. Students are taught to use problem-solving methods to develop and improve their creative abilities and thereby to find solutions to the problems they encounter, whilst carrying out their project work.[56]

In fact, the proposed curriculum for the CTCs was in line with the "progressive" and "self-discovery" methods that had been employed by the comprehensive schools since the 1960s. This was the very same approach to teaching that had been the central target of New Right criticism, which had forced a trend towards more formal and academic learning in the opposite direction to that of ORT's curriculum proposals. In this sense, what the designers of the CTC curriculum failed to grasp was not the needs of the education system, which was actually accustomed to such methods, nor the needs of industry, but the political climate and the government's desire for radical change in the teaching methods hitherto practised by teachers (see Chapter 7).

Thus, the idea proposed to the DES that technical subjects would dominate the CTCs' curriculum failed, against the background of the new national academic curriculum. The second draft of the CTC Trust's document on the curriculum dealt with the difficulties that had emerged for the CTC idea. It referred to "the three core subjects of Mathematics, English and Science, and other Foundation Subjects which, all told, absorb 80-90% of school time."[57] Any expectation that the DES would take into consideration the specific virtues and characteristics of the new institutions was dashed by a sharp response from the Secretary of State, who "made it a condition of grant to CTCs that they adhere to the eventual statutory requirements of the National Curriculum."[58] Section 105 of the Act took into consideration the CTCs' need for a broad curriculum, not in terms of the core and foundation subjects, but a "broad curriculum with an emphasis . . . on science and technology."[59] This policy overloaded the CTCs' curriculum to the point of disadvantaging them in competition with other narrow curriculum schools in the matter of achieving GCSE and A level results.[60] The full scale of the new policy's effect on the CTCs was made evident by various statistical publications. For example, the results published in the year 2000 show that the CTC schools achieved 52.2% on the GCE A Level in comparison with the secondary schools' 75.3% and the independent schools' 86.8%.[61]

Thus, the inflexibility of the National Curriculum had severe drawbacks in two areas. First, it presented an obstacle to achievement of the government's own goal of competing with other countries in terms of developing technical knowledge and skills on the one hand, and of supplying industry's needs for qualified youngsters on the other. Even the single foundation subject in technology in the new National Curriculum cannot be considered a sufficient response to the problem. Secondly, while the academic curriculum suits part of the students, 55% of school leavers in 1988 still had no proper and meaningful curriculum option to meet their needs and abilities. The inflexibility of the National Curriculum, as demonstrated by the cases of TVEI and the CTCs, exposed as lip service the government's stated wish and intention to develop advanced technological knowledge in schools in order to compete with other industrial countries. The desire to perpetuate an academic curriculum, of the same sort as in the grammar schools with A levels dominating the academic route, albeit with a gradual move towards incorporating science and technology as foundation subjects, still left technology with the status of a second-class option in the government's view and failed to offer a proper education to school leavers towards the end of the 1980s.[62]

Soon after the 1988 Education Act was approved by the Parliament it became clear that a gradual move towards greater flexibility of the National Curriculum would provide meaningful study for the full range of post-16 pupils, particularly the less able ones, and constitute a further attempt to meet their needs. Decreasing the rigidity of the curriculum became a clear direction, with two main stages aimed at meeting two different needs.

The first stage was implemented in the 1990s, with the National Vocational Qualification (NVQ) having been designed in 1986 in order to bridge the divide between vocational and academic studies and offer more meaningful studies to those who had attended the much more vocational and training-oriented TVEI courses. The range of studies varied from engineering to envelope-manufacturing and from hairdressing to museums (Stanton, 1997).

In 1991 the National Council for Vocational Qualifications (NCVQ) submitted a White Paper entitled *Education and Training for the Twenty-First Century,* which aimed to establish General National Vocational Qualifications (GNVQ) as a halfway house between academic and vocational studies. The White Paper clearly stated that these studies could lead to acquisition of basic skills in literacy and numeracy, and access to further education as well as higher education. In the 1990s the GNVQ was developed in what would ultimately be 15 vocational areas of study, on three levels. The aim was to achieve equivalent status with the GCSE-A Level.[63]

Another attempt to move away from the rigidity of the National Curriculum and bridge the divide between the three routes – GCSE-A Levels; NVQ; and GNVQ – occurred in 1996 when Ron Dearing submitted a report proposing a coherent national framework of study that covered the three main qualifications and the attainments of young people between the ages of 16 and 19 at every level of ability. The declared aim of Dearing's report was to "identif[y] barriers to achievement and ways to deal with them (1.11)." It proposed that the Advanced GNVQ be renamed the "Applied A Level (1.12)."[64]

The "Applied A Level" suggestion was rapidly rejected by the government.

The main qualifications of the three-track post-16 system remain, according to Tomlinson, as follows:[65]
- The craft or occupational – NVQ
- The "vocational" – a midway path between academic and vocational, leading to GNVQ
- The "academic" route leading to A and A/S levels

The main criticism levelled against the government policy was that without adopting the GCSE-A level courses as study modules – with accumulation of credits towards a common General Certificate – the divide could not be bridged (Stanton, 1997; Tomlinson, 1997). Tomlinson claims there was no real attempt to bridge between the routes and that a Left to Right political consensus that sought to protect the A level qualification as a major conduit to higher education was still prevalent throughout the system:[66]

> It will require a seismic shift in the thinking of politicians, employers, many educators and the general public, to change the culture which has become accustomed to thinking that the majority of young people should be encouraged on to vocational or occupational routes at 16, or even 14, while an expanded elite take a narrow specialist subject-centred route....This scenario suggest a 40/30/30 in which a contented majority (with A-Levels and higher education) enjoy secure jobs and a comfortable lifestyle, a middle group (the GNVQ group?), even with their "applied education" to high levels, undertake contract work and insecure employment, and the bottom group, despite NVQs, are fortunate to find any kind of employment or niche in the economy.

Geoff Stanton, who served on the working group of NCVQ and the National Curriculum Council, and who was involved in many steps taken with regard to post-16 studies, raised a similar argument. In a critical article he claims: "When the Secretary of State asks that 'A-Levels standards should be maintained' she does not mean that for instance, the learning outcomes of A-Level Physics should be the same now as they were in 1945, or as they should become by the year 2005. She means that – whatever the development in the subject over time – its level of intellectual demand remains equivalent."[67]

The nature of the new hierarchy and the new boundaries of the three curriculum and qualification routes are also addressed and explained by Macrae, Maguire and Ball (1997) as an "intensification of polarisation in the post-16 sector which signals the increasing division between the well-behaved middle class who proceed through a high-status route and the 'disaffected' or 'less able' working class students who are steered firmly towards the vocational or work-based tracks."[68] Thus, the structure became a reinstitution of explicit barriers to access and participation in the more prestigious study route.

The second stage, working in another direction towards reducing the restrictive inflexibility of the National Curriculum, was first initiated in 1992 in order to meet the needs of Key Stage 4 and transfer more discretionary power to schools. The general purpose of the circular was to provide "more choice in the study of history and geography."[69] The New Labour government took further steps in the same direction in 1998, when it announced that pupils under the age of 11 would no longer be required to stick to the "detailed national syllabuses in history, geography, design and technology, art, music and physical education."[70] This modest change had much in common with the idea that decision-making should be carried out by those close to the customers and to the characteristics of local management of schools and hence school empowerment. The move was explained by the QCA as a kind of autonomy, enabling schools to "make their own judgements about how far individual pupils might benefit from work-related learning." Schools therefore "do not need to seek formal approval but should inform the QCA of their plans."[71]

Easing the aforementioned overload of the National Curriculum, and hence the pre-ordained nature of the attainment targets, can be seen as a small scale departure from the mechanistic assumption about the nature of teaching and learning and a slight swing of the pendulum towards decentralisation and greater school autonomy.

9.2: NATIONAL ASSESSMENT

The National Curriculum and the setting of attainment targets was followed, according to the 1988 Education Reform Act, by national assessment of pupils' achievements. Among the duties of a new body that was established, the School Examination and Assessment Council, was to arrange school assessments and "to furnish the Secretary of State with such reports and other information with respect to the exercise of its functions" as he requires.[72] This regulation transforms assessment from a means by which teachers can improve the learning/teaching process to a central mechanism for monitoring and controlling standards.

A circular published in February 1989 described assessment in terms of a means for providing the public with information on the quality of schools in order to enable parents to choose between schools. This approach was part of the market philosophy that aimed to provide the customers (parents) with information about the qualities of the commodity (schools); the assessment results would "offer parents, schools, LEAs and the Government clear and comparable information about the achievements of pupils and schools."[73] Therefore, from 1989 onwards teachers were expected to record and monitor pupils' progress in relation to attainment targets which would "lead to formal assessment under national arrangements."[74]

The structure of national assessment was based on the report submitted to Kenneth Baker in 1987 by Professor Black, Chairman of the Task Group on Assessment and Testing (TGAT). The TGAT proposals for national assessment were based on four criteria: the information assessment results provided about children's achievements should be *criterion referenced*; this information should form the basis "for decisions about pupils' further learning needs"[75] (i.e., be formative); teachers' assessments should be calibrated and moderated; and assessment should relate to the progression through different ages, on the assumption that there is an "expected route of development."[76] Among other proposed purposes was that information derived from assessment should be diagnostic, in order to enable the provision of remedial help to individuals and schools.

According to the TGAT proposal, each child would be assessed against attainment targets at the ages of 7, 11, 14 and 16 along sub-divisions of subjects into so-called "profile components" at 10 levels. At the age of 7 a child is expected to achieve a level of attainment between 1 and 3, at the age of 11 between 3 and 6, at the age of 14 between 4 and 8, and at the age of 16 between 4 and 10[77] (see Appendix 5).

The first published expression of concern at possible misuse or abuse of national assessment on these lines, and at the possibility of resultant disorder, was the TGAT Report itself. Its first reservation addressed the government's intention to publish the assessment results as a "league table," stating that such publication should take place:

> If, and only if, this is done in context of reports about that school as a whole, so that it can be fair to that school's work and take account as far as possible of socio-economic and other influences.[78]

Secondly, it identified the risk of national assessment losing its reliability, validity and credibility because of the nature of the National Curriculum which "involves a chain with five links: each carries the possibility of error."[79] The report went on to analyse the potential for error, arguing that the reliability of national assessment depended on clear definition of attainment targets, and therefore that the prime task was to achieve "agreement about what has to be learned."[80] The proviso was that this agreement should not be one of principle but of *reality*, within and between schools; otherwise, comparison between schools would not be reliable – which explains the need for a rigid curriculum in view of the validity of the assessment machinery. Another requirement in order to avoid the "chain of errors" is the use of a combination of assessment instruments, including internal assessment, in order to avoid "teaching to the tests." A variety of assessment instruments would be needed not only in order to cover the full range of the curriculum, but to achieve reliable overall results: "individually the instruments are open to misinterpretation but in combination they minimise the risks."[81]

The conditions set out in the TGAT Report for conducting national assessment in such a way as to ensure that the system remains valid and reliable, require a high level of government intervention in order to maintain reliability through several combinations of assessment instruments, including a complex system of moderation, and to finance such a complicated assessment system. Other points raised by the TGAT Report relate to the need for a high degree of commitment along the chain: the attainment targets would need to be implemented fully within each class in order to facilitate a reliable moderation system, and a heavy investment of teachers' time would be required in order to assess the various attainment targets.

These complications, which were discussed by the members of TGAT, raised several questions: Could such a complicated system survive in the long run? Could government intervention be effective in implementing such a system in the day-to-day life of the education system? What would be the social and the educational costs of such a system as was eventually devised? What are the centrifugal factors which would act against such a central apparatus? Some of these factors and their complications were raised by the TGAT Report itself; others call for further analysis of two areas: the fate of national assessment in other countries; and the effect of the national assessment on standards and schools' expectations.

The relationship between assessment practices and communities – pupils, teachers and parents – is a very under-researched area. Special attention should be paid to the effect of such practice on motivation, identities and pupils' achievements. Ann Filler (2000) argues that controversy has surrounded the lack of privacy in relation to test results in the US. According to her, "scores can be used, or misused, by anyone with access to student records." Further opposition has come from cultural minorities who are "resentful of having their histories and cultural meaning represented in curricula by white governing elites of European descent."[82] Harold Berlak (in Ann Filer, 2000) argues that during Clinton's term of office efforts were made to bring about a higher degree of centralisation and institute standardised tests, but these were successfully resisted and defeated. He claims, moreover, that African-American and Latino students' achievement tests scores showed little change, "drop-out rates are about the same and the inequalities between rich and poor schools have widened."[83] Paul Black (in Chitty and Simon, 1993) argues that during the 1980s many states in the US abandoned the assessment system because "it is evident that they have done almost nothing to improve education."[84] Colin Power (1984) came to similar conclusions in reviewing the development of national assessment in three countries – the US, Australia and the UK – up to 1984. In the US, national assessment[85] has been used to assess and monitor the achievements of 9-13 and 17 year-old pupils in ten subjects, with the aim of establishing a "new accountability mechanism and information system."[86] Despite the fact that neither teachers and schools nor states had been evaluated, it took seven years for the programme "to get off the ground."[87] The long tradition of local control over the curriculum eventually caused the pilot programme to become:

> general and bland – reduced, some would assert, to the lowest common denominator.... While at times it was hinted that the NAEP could serve an accountability function, it was designed in such a way that there is no possibility of calling any particular state, district, school or program to account for its performance.[88]

Furthermore, Colin Power found that far from being useful to decision makers and practitioners, the national data gathered as a result of this effort "have proved more confusing than enlightening."[89] The most significant evidence is that the data which were collected nationally were ignored by those expected to make most use of them – the schools.

In Australia, concern over low standards led to the establishment of "Australian Studies in Student Performance" (ASSP) in 1979, with the aim of providing a national database on performance in basic skills. This assessment system ran into two main difficulties: first, it became a "political time bomb"[90] when the atmosphere that was supportive of national assessment in the 1970s dissipated and opposition arose during the early 1980s; secondly, criticism was levelled at the validity of the assessment programmes. Schools' ignorance of the testing programmes became clear:

> Less than 2 percent of schools made changes in lesson-time allocation, curriculum, remedial activities, teaching, or testing practice as a consequence of the testing program. In most schools, staff did not even discuss the results. Half of the parent organisations contacted knew nothing of the project.[91]

Despite the initial vision and the intention of making information available to the public, the ASSP had not measured up in reality. The Australian government decided "to continue to support the Australian Co-operative Assessment Program but not national survey testing."[92]

Power's conclusion is that the assessment system was revealed as a government-devised central mechanism for monitoring standards and a decision making tool. Teachers' view of this mechanism as a governmental "weapon rather than a tool" and their fear "of its effect on schools"[93] partly explains the lack of co-operation it encountered and the eventual shift of assessment from central control to local and school level.

Patricia Broadfoot describes the shift from central examination to profile assessment at the school level in France. The nature and the tradition of French education had been highly centralised since Napoleonic days. The curriculum was controlled, and selection and competition were dominant factors in a system based on "examinations for selection for various kinds of secondary schooling, and a range of formal, exam-based qualifications."[94] From the early 1960s onwards, pressure to provide greater opportunities in education eventually led to a "radical restructuring of the traditionally highly selective and elitist education system."[95] The main form taken by this change was the abolition of formal pass/fail tests at the age of 16+ in favour of assessment and judgement by teachers, based on "the average of class marks."[96] Selection at secondary level was replaced by observation for the first two years and orientation for the last two years,[97] based on the philosophy that "What must be avoided, above all, is 'orientation' by failure.... No career should be seen as a failure."[98] This meant less government intervention and bureaucratisation on behalf of the traditionally academic curriculum, more teacher responsibility for assessment, and a move towards school records rather than external and public examinations.

The abolition of attainment tests in most of the Scottish authorities reflects, according to W.B. Dockrell, dissatisfaction with information that was "partial and might therefore be misleading."[99] The early national surveys, dating back to 1932, aimed to measure ability by intelligence tests; later, they were aimed at measuring achievement, particularly in arithmetic and English. The results of these surveys were of "negative value";[100] they were revealed as invalid in the identification of specific and local needs. Also "there were no differences among pupils in different types of areas,"[101] and therefore no argument for "more schools, more teachers, or more instructional materials in one part of the country rather than in another."[102] National policy could hence not be determined on the basis of these surveys. Moreover, Dockrell argues that teachers' experience, rather than any external recommendation, was the main factor in decision making. How "teachers will take account of [such a recommendation] will depend very much on their own values and their own perceptions of their current practice."[103] Dockrell came to the conclusion that if any research were to have an impact on classroom practice it "must be teacher tested"[104] rather than externally assessed; this conclusion corresponds to developments in France, the US and Australia.

Thus far the analysis has concentrated on the complicating factors that led to the distortion, neglect and eventual amendment of government plans to develop an external monitoring system that would serve as a feedback mechanism in the countries described. The change there was from an external mechanism, as the government had initially intended, to an internal assessment based on teachers' judgement and aimed in the main at improving the learning/teaching process, rather than functioning as a government mechanism for monitoring school performance.

As to the second question raised regarding the effect of national assessment on standards and schools' expectations in England, the government's main aims in devising the assessment system were to improve standards and provide parents with information to enable them to make choices between schools. The market approach according to which schools were regarded as a commodity produced an internal paradox for the TGAT group. The Report was against publishing the results of assessments unless such publication took account of the social context of each particular school, while in the government's view the prime aim was the public ranking of the commodity – the schools – in order of quality, without taking the schools' contexts into consideration. Fulfilling TGAT's conditions would mean complicating the information to the point where parents, as customers, would not be able to make a simple judgement regarding the school's attainment and thus defeat the objective of enabling them to make their own informed choice. In order to be able to rank schools according to a clear and simple order of attainment, the TGAT Report solved the paradox by minimising their own stipulation, recommending that "results should not be adjusted for socio-economic background, but the report should include a general statement, prepared by the Local Authority for the area, of the nature and possible size of socio-economic and other influences which could affect schools in the area."[105]

This brings up another aspect of the role of *expectations* in the raising of standards.[106] The "effective school" movement regarded high expectations, on the part of both pupils and teachers, as one of the prime features of high-achieving schools. This approach is not new; numerous studies have shown that a "person's expectation of another's behaviour could come to serve as a self-fulfilling prophecy."[107] In research on teachers' expectations and pupils' development, Rosenthal and Jacobson (1968) argue that when teachers "know" that their pupils are capable of high achievements and express this expectation, this has "helped the child learn by changing his self concept, his expectations of his own behaviour, and his motivation, as well as his cognitive style and skills."[108] This philosophy and associated approach (the so-called "Pygmalion effect") are based on the assumption, supported by research data, that children can achieve and learn more when higher expectations are created. According to Pidgeon, children "will have no incentive to perform at higher levels"[109] if the teacher expresses low expectations.

The government's insistence on publishing "league tables" of achievement as an incentive for teachers and children to achieve better standards, not only ignores the TGAT recommendation but moreover takes the opposite line to what it acknowledged in the document *Better Schools* (1985) as a key approach to higher standards. This was an approach strongly endorsed by the research findings regarding the "effective school" movement and the "Pygmalion effect," preferring a policy by which those who were disappointed with the rank allotted to their school would probably fall into their role of under-achiever in a self-fulfilling prophecy rather than regard that rank as an incentive for greater effort towards achieving higher standards. The policy chosen by the governments of both main parties, either in the form of the Education Reform Act 1988 or further policies instituted by the New Labour Party from 1997 onward, was explained thus in the White Paper entitled *Excellence in Schools*:[110]

> One of the most powerful underlying reasons for low performance in our schools has been low expectations which have allowed poor-quality teaching to continue unchallenged.... In some cases the excuse has been that "you cannot expect high achievement from children [in] a run-down area like this."

The White Paper asserts that one of the main remedies likely to challenge pupils, parents and teachers, is the publication of much more performance data than ever before. The government, it says, intends to "speed up the publication of information on primary schools' performance by requiring 11 year-olds' assessment results to be prepared and published locally, but in a form that continues to facilitate national comparisons."[111] The extent to which test results were to be published became clear when the Paper addressed not only comparison between schools, and within and between LEAs, but "differences in performance between girls and boys, or between groups from different ethnic minorities."[112]

The results of such policy should be more carefully examined and explored. During the ten years during which the assessment system was implemented, standards rose slowly and gradually in all the key stages. The following data sheds some light on this development:

Table 9.1: Percentage achieving 5 or more GCSE grades of A*-C during the 1990s

1990/1	36.8
1991/2	38.3
1992/3	41.2
1993/4	43.3
1994/5	43.5
1995/6	44.5
1996/7	45.1
1997/8	46.3
1998/9	47.9

Source: Statistics of Education, Public Examinations GCSE/GNVQ and GCE/GNVQ in England 1999, National Statistics, p.9.
(The GCSE grade A* was introduced in 1993/4; Percentages from 1996/7 include GNVQ equivalencies.)

The figures show a steady and gradual rise of about 1.2% per annum – and 11.1% over nine years – in those achieving 5 or more GCSE grades of A*-C. They show a more modest achievement between the years 1992/3 (at which time the assessment system was first implemented) and 1998/9, while the rate of those who achieved 5 or more GCSE grades of A*-C rose 5.5% in nine years.

At the same time, standards also rose at the primary level. The following table gives some indication as to the improvement:

Table 9.2: Percentage of pupils achieving Level 2 and above in 1995-2001 key stage 1 tests

Subject	1995	1996	1997	1999	2000	2001
Reading	78	78	80	82	83	84
Writing	80	79	80	83	84	86
Mathematics	79	82	84	87	90	91

Sources: DfEE, National Curriculum Assessment of 7,11 and 14 Year Olds in England (1997) p.15 and DfEE, National Curriculum Assessment of 7,11 and 14 Year Olds, 2001 (Provisional).

Table 9.2 clearly shows that standards rose in all three subjects and that the most impressive improvement took place in mathematics. If raising of standards is an indication, it might be argued that the new practice and market philosophy is effective. Such a conclusion might require further analysis from three different points of view: To what extent did standards rise before the new policy became valid? What progress was made by ethnic groups? What effect did such policy have on pupils and teacher motivation and expectations?

The first question can only be answered with reference to the secondary level, since primary level data is only available from 1993. The following table provides more details about rising standards during the 1980s, before the new assessment machinery came into effect.

Table 9.3: Percentage achieving 5 or more O-Level/CSE/GCSE grades of A*-C during the 1980s

Year	%
1981/2	26.1
1982/3	26.2
1983/4	26.7
1984/5	26.9
1985/6	26.7
1986/7	26.4
1987/8	29.9
1988/9	32.8
1989/90	34.5

Source: Statistics of Education, 1995

It can thus be argued that between the two decades – the 1980s (8.4%) and the 1990s (11.1) – there was no significant change in schools' progress. In both decades progress was made, demonstrating that a levelling-up motif is built into the system and human nature, and is not merely a function of external assessment machinery. Gillborn and Youdell (2000) shed some light on progress made by ethnic groups. In a more detailed picture of the GCSE test results, these researchers argued that there are growing gaps between groups of different ethnic origin, as the following figure illustrates:

Table 9.4: Percentage of pupils attaining five or more higher-grade GCSE passes, according to social class

Year	1988	1990	1991	1993
Professional	58	58	64	66
Managerial	40	46	47	50
Skilled (non-manual)	26	30	30	33
Skilled (manual)	18	20	21	26
Partly skilled	13	15	18	19
Unskilled	9	11	10	12

Source: Adapted by Gillborn and Youdel (2000) p.40.

The figures clearly show that children who have unskilled and partly-skilled parents were at the bottom of the achievement league table, while those pupils whose parents are professionals are at the top. Gillborn and Youdel further argue that in the two case studies that were closely analysed, teachers predicted that a disproportionate number of white pupils would attain five or more A*- C grades than pupils from other ethnic groups. The researchers attribute this to a stronger trend during the 1990s to triage pupils in the "hidden" tiers of three different levels of the GCSE as part of the assessment system. While prior to the implementation of the new assessment system pupils could confound their teachers' expectations by taking a higher-status exam and passing – despite advice to the contrary – this was no longer possible in the 1990s. Pupils "must accept the grade ceilings imposed by the exam tier that their teacher judges 'appropriate'."[113] Tomlinson came to a similar conclusion regarding how the overall result of such a policy was "cementing [of] a system that cuts off large numbers of young people from education at 16, and perpetuates the notion there are separate types of students suitable for separate tracks."[114]

The following example might clarify the third question concerning the affect of the "league table" policy on pupils' motivation and expectations.

The table clearly shows that some schools, such as London Oratory and Sacred Heart, have made impressive progress, while other schools remain at the bottom of the league despite a slight improvement (Ravenscourt Theatre and Henrry Copton), but Phoenix High even lost ground in Hammersmith's league table.

Chapter 9 - Old Values, New Structure: From the Education Reform Act 1988 to the Policies of the 1990s

Table 9.5: Percentage of age 15 pupils attaining GCSE results of 5+ A*-C grades in Hammersmith

Secondary schools	1996	1999
Burlingtom Danes	24	35
Fulham Cross	26	30
The Godolphin & Latymer	100	100
Henry Compton	11	15
Hurlingham & Chelsea	9	17
Lady Margaret	90	93
Latymer Upper	99	99
The London Oratory	70	93
Phoenix High	14	4
Ravenscourt Theatre	0	8
Sacred Heart High	61	80
St. Paul's Girls	100	99
LEA averages	35.3	48.9
England averages	44.5	47.9

Source: TES, Schools and College Performance Tables 1996 (22.11.1996) p.16.
TES, Schools and College Performance Tables 1999 (26.11.1999) p.13.

The data calls for more careful observation of those schools at the bottom of the league. Given that such a league table is published not only at the school or LEA level, but all over the country, it raises several questions pertaining to the pupils' morale and motivation. The first of these is whether this kind of wide publication increases pupils' individual motivation or depresses such motivation. Another is how such a policy affects teachers' morale and status, and what parents and teachers expect from pupils at Ravenscourt Theatre and Phoenix High. It calls for clarification of the role of teaching and learning in particular in a multicultural society. Assuming that the assessment system is beneficial for the majority of pupils, would it be right to implement such a policy knowing the negative effect on minorities, who are sometimes the weakest link in society?

A great many articles, books and papers have been published on this matter. Many of the articles present the effects of such a system on pupils' aspirations, motivation, ambition and self-image, while most of the papers emphasise the price that pupils in particular, but also teachers and parents, are forced to pay for such policy (Broadfoot, 1996; Broadfoot and Pollard in Filer (ed.), 2000; Broadfoot in Phillips, 2001; Davis, 1998; Gillborn and Youdell, 2000; Lacelle-Peterson in Filer (ed.), 2000; Murphy, 1999; Pryor and Torrance in Filer (ed.), 2000; Tymms and Fitz-Gibbon in Phillips, 2001;). David Gillborn and Deborah Youdell (2000) published their research on the effect of the assessment system on two schools, a GM and a comprehensive school, in a book entitled *Rationing Education*. Among their main findings is that teachers feel trapped between the conflicting demands of their pupils and their particular ideology, educational philosophy and beliefs. One of the teachers put it thus:[115]

> How do the league tables impact on us? It puts permanently more, more, more, more pressure on us. Flog us to death, flog us to death, flog us to death. You do that anyway. But if at the end of the day you're going to be told, "Hang on, we haven't got x per cent of A-to-Cs, so you must be bad teachers" – ah ah, no.

Analysing a school case study from Oxfordshire, Woodings (1997) argues similarly that teachers' ideology of dedication to their pupils and commitment to doing their best by every child has evaporated with the new assessment practices and been replaced by the new "assessment values."[116] Davies (1998) offers the critique that the whole system effectively becomes a means of "teaching to the test" which enforces "proper knowledge" and similarity in pupils' understanding and interpretation. In his opinion this has much in common with the old "payment by results" system which governed teaching methods for three decades of the nineteenth century (see Chapter 2).

The response of the teachers and head teachers was "a deep feeling of injustice,"[117] and Margaret Philpot, the head of St. Richard of Chichester, a secondary school in Camden, responded: "The extent of the coverage surprised me and depressed me a bit because it makes life more difficult and it lowers morale."[118] In a series of interviews with teachers in Oxfordshire, *all* the teachers concerned expressed a sense of injustice and great concern over this policy. Teachers in a middle school raised the fact that there was a

47% turnover of pupils as a result of visiting academics on temporary attachment to Oxford University, many of whom are not native English speakers. This had a double effect on the school: first, such pupils had to be supported with extra lessons, and secondly, they could affect the school's assessment results and its place in the "league table" as it was explained by one of the interviewed, who put it as follows:

> ...if you become so frightened in case you lose one point of your "league table" and you become so restricted in your teaching you lose the enjoyment, you would not get the quality that you expected and then the whole school would suffer.[119]

Ann Filer and Andrew Torrance (2000), who carried out a study of primary school assessment, contribute to our understanding of parents' perspectives on the testing system. According to the research findings, there is evidence that parents began to receive during the 1990s more detailed reports on their children's attainments. The main argument is that an education system that regards parents as customers rather than partners sharing similar targets with the teacher, discriminates between pupils who come from "supportive" and "problem" families. This has a direct affect on children's expectations, motivation and perceptions. Cullingford (1997) raises a similar argument, after having interviewed 200 parents, teachers and pupils, about the effect of the assessment system. The following interview is illustrative of the point:[120]

> Stress starts to build up and I think it's unnecessary, unnecessary stress and I don't think we should be doing it to our children. (A father)
> I think there seems to be a lot of pressure put on testing and assessment.... I think it could make them against school and learning. I think there's too much of it. (A mother)

A further look at the effect of the ceiling policy and preliminary judgement of pupils' ability by teachers demonstrates that the main impact of the policy on pupils' ambition, motivation, expectations and self-image is negative. Cullingford (1997) established this and the attendant sense of failure in the following interview:[121]

> I do feel terrible when I'm not the best at something because I always go last. Terrible, because I would never get any work done. It would take me probably all week. [6-year-old boy]
>
> English sometimes is hard, physics and chemistry I just find hard. I can't do them. Not do well. I don't think so; no. I haven't done that much revising. I thought I did really well in my mock but I didn't....I'll be able to go out and earn money. Get a job. Not having to come back [to school] again. [11-year-old girl]

This was the state of affairs after the assessment system had been implemented for about a decade and the achievements of each school published annually. This publication, reproduced in national and local newspapers, became what Tomlinson calls "an orgy of analysis,"[122] Broadfoot terms "obsessive neurosis that manifests itself in an almost pathological belief in the value of assessment,"[123] and Walford describes as an "annual ritual feast of celebration or condemnation."[124] This raises the question of whether "condemnation," in Walford's words, or "failure policy" in Broadfoot's words, could become a part of a national approach that seeks to reinforce the weak links in a society.

9.3: CHOICE FOR PARENTS: OPEN ENROLMENT

The intention to publish the test results and to "make available information about the results of assessment which can offer parents, schools, LEAs and the Government clear and comparable information about the achievements of pupils and schools,"[125] was aimed at enabling parents to make their own decisions regarding the right and desirable school for their children. This approach was consonant with the market idea of giving consumers – in this case the parents – greater power of choice and was one of the main steps of the Education Reform Act 1988.

The new policy gained momentum and stimulated initiatives from various groups that eventually reduced the quantity of the uniform comprehensive schools. In 1996 there were 1100 grant maintained schools, including 660 schools at the secondary level, 15 city technology colleges and 196 specialist schools and colleges. The number of specialist schools rose to 992 in the year 2002. These can be divided into the following 8 categories:

Table 9.6: Number of maintained secondary schools according to specialist status in 2002

Category of school	Number of schools
Arts	173
Business and Enterprise	18
Engineering	4
Language	157
Mathematics & Computing	12
Science	24
Sports College	161
Technology College	443
Total	992

Source: DfEE, School Statistics for UK. E-mail to the DOES at the University of Oxford, 15.10.2002.

The above table clearly indicates the success of the new policy of choice and diversity. Such diversity, which was the direct result of the 1988 Education Reform Act, was accelerated during the 1990s by further steps carried out by both parties, eventually creating a new education structure at the beginning of the 2000s.

One consequence of this approach is a change in the local standard concerning the number of pupils to be admitted to any particular school. According to the 1980 Education Act, it was within the LEA's power to specify the maximum number of pupils a school should be required to admit (Lawton, 1989; Leonard, 1988).[126] According to the 1988 Education Act, LEAs "shall not fix as the number of pupils in any relevant age group ... less than the relevant standard number."[127]

In 1992, the new Major government published a White Paper called *Choice and Diversity: A New Framework for Schools*. The aim of this White Paper was to form a basis for further legislation in support of diversity. In the foreword to the White Paper the prime minister wrote:

> Our reforms rest on common-sense principles – more parental choice; rigorous testing and external inspection of standards in schools; transfer of responsibility to individual schools and their governors; and above all, an insistence that every pupil everywhere has the same opportunities through a good common grounding in key subjects. Few people would now argue with these principles. They are all helping to shape a more open, a more responsive and a more demanding system of education....It enhances parental choice by simplifying the creation of grant-maintained schools and by opening the way to greater variety in education through the formation of new schools and by encouraging specification....That is why the great themes of quality, diversity, parental choice, school autonomy and accountability run through the White Paper. They are the way to secure what I believe to be essential – to ask the best *for* every child: to ask the best *from* every child. Excellence must be the key word in all our schools; that is what our children deserve. That is what we intend to achieve.[128]

The 1992 White Paper describes the extent of choice that was instituted, particularly at secondary level – namely in comprehensive schools that had developed specialities in particular subjects such as music and technology, grammar schools, bilateral schools, and city technology colleges. At the same time, more and more primary and secondary schools were becoming grant-maintained – all operating at different levels of parental selection. The 1992 White Paper expresses the government's wish to develop schools that "specialis[e] in [a] particular curriculum area, such as science, music, modern languages or technology"[129] in order to facilitate greater diversity while still ensuring that the full National Curriculum is offered to all pupils.

The White Paper tries to bridge between what was referred to as parity of esteem and the policy that affords choice and parental selection. The White Paper argues that a hierarchy of schools is likely to result from such diversity. "The Government is committed to parity of esteem between academic, technological and creative skills, with children – whatever their aptitude and in whatever type of school ....The Government wants to ensure that there are no tiers of school within the maintained system but rather parity of esteem between different schools, in order to offer parents a wealth of choice."[130] The White Paper challenges those who might claim that it represents a return to the selectivity of the tripartite system that was in place during the post-War period (see Chapters 3 and 4) by explaining how the proposed structure differed: [131]

> After wartime deliberations, and the Education Act 1944 which followed, those who argued so vigorously the pros and cons of selection and the 11 Plus examination in the 1950s and 1960s lived in a different educational world, which had no National Curriculum taught in common throughout the tripartite system of secondary schools, ensuring equality of opportunities.

Therefore, it was argued, the present system guaranteed all children an equal chance – which could not be said of the old system.

Despite vigorous debate, a "no confidence" vote, and some amendments, many of the ideas in the White Paper became the 1993 Education Act. According to John Patten, Education Secretary at that time, the new bill "was designed to provide a framework for school[s] for the next 25 years, and to speed [up] the opting-out process among the 25,000 state schools."[132] A new Education Act was approved by Parliament in 1996, which leaned in the same direction by reinforcing the status of the GM schools as one of the main paths to diversity and greater choice. The White Paper entitled *Self-Government for Schools,* which was published in the same year, emphasised the government's wishes concerning choice and diversity in catering to the needs of children with different abilities, aptitudes and interests. Therefore, according to the 1996 White Paper, parents who want to choose from a range of "choice should include schools which select by academic ability, so the most able children have the chance to achieve the best of which they are capable."[133] The White Paper of 1996, probably unconsciously, employed a tone very similar to that of the White Paper of 1943 that had addressed the issue fifty years previously. The earlier document states: "It is just as important to achieve diversity as it is to ensure equality of opportunity."[134]

When the New Labour Party published the White Paper *Excellence in*

Schools in 1997, it made a clear statement that there would be no return to the uniformity of the comprehensive school era. Instead, "as many parents as possible [would] be able to send their children to their preferred school."[135] The Tory agenda of freedom of choice in the 1990s was essentially a continuation of the line espoused by the two main parties in the united government when the 1944 Education Act was approved by Parliament. Now, New Labour explains its departure from the comprehensive schools policy as follows:[136]

> The demand for equality and increased opportunity in the 1950s and 1960s led to introduction of comprehensive schools. All-in secondary schooling rightly became the normal pattern, but the search for equality of opportunity in some cases became a tendency to uniformity. The idea that all children had the same rights to develop their abilities led too easily to the doctrine that all had the same ability. The pursuit of excellence was too often equated with elitism.

The 1997 White Paper was not only a departure from what had been the Labour Party's main policy for almost three decades (1960s to 1980s), but an expression of regret for having supported such uniformity in the comprehensive school idea. Therefore, the new policy was deeply committed to "equal opportunities for all pupils" but no longer through:[137]

> … a single model of schooling. We want to encourage diversity, with schools developing their own distinctive identity; and expertise. Specialist schools – focusing on technology, languages, sports or arts – should be a resource to local people.

When the Strategy Plan to 2006 was published in 2001, the desire for accelerating choice and diversity became even clearer. Estelle Morris, the Secretary of State for Education explained that the Strategy Plan aimed to "build a fair and inclusive society [in which] everyone must have the opportunity to realise their full potential,"[138] by widening the range of choice for all.

The scope of school diversity and choice have been extended since the end of the 1980s. This brings us to the heart of the issue: Who benefits from such a policy? For whom is such an approach meaningful and for whom meaningless? Perusal of some research findings on the open enrolment issue offers some answers to these questions.

Raab and Adler (1988) researched the impact of parental choice on admission to primary schools in Edinburgh and Dundee, further to the Scottish Education Act of 1980, which gave parents greater choice. The research showed that about one in five parents (19% in Edinburgh and 22% in Dundee) requested that their child would go to a new school. The desired movement was two-directional: most requests involved moving to an adjacent school within a socially homogeneous area.[139] These requests, which came from the entire social class spectrum, were influenced by the wish to move "away from schools in areas of economic and social deprivation"[140] and attend schools that "contain fewer socio-economic problems."[141] The move to non-adjacent schools involved "travel over considerable distances"[142] for children coming from families where the parents were able to finance the transportation costs to schools in "middle-class areas and areas where a high proportion of adults ha[d] been through higher education."[143] These results showed, in the researchers' view, that the opportunity to choose did not aid the "'disadvantaged' ones whom the legislation was purportedly intended to help."[144]

In a comprehensive research report Adler et al. shed more light on the social and educational impact of the 1980 and 1981 Scottish Education Acts. This study supported Raab and Adler's finding that for primary schools, the loss of pupils in areas characterised by social problems had a particularly strong effect on the remaining pupils:

> Although children who have opted out of schools serving these communities may have benefited, those who have remained with the district school may have had to pay a heavy price if they and their schools have become even more stigmatised than they were previously. . . . At both primary and secondary level, the loss of some pupils has, in the case of some under-enrolled schools, left other pupils in a very exposed position.[145]

The research did not find any evidence to support the assumption that parental choice by means of open enrolment would force "bad" schools to improve or to be closed: "no school in our three study regions closed as a result of parental choice and there is, as yet, no evidence that the legislation has contributed to an overall improvement in standards."[146] Furthermore, evidence that popular schools which attracted more pupils "were 'more effective' schools"[147] and that pupils "who transferred to them will necessarily do better as a result of doing so," was inconclusive.[148]

David Kirp, in an analysis of American racial issues and school policy, has argued that despite a policy of integration and several initiatives in favour of mixing races in schools, open enrolment has "separated blacks from whites,"[149] – the reverse of promoting desegregation. In Oakland, open enrolment led "to increased segregation because of a sizeable proportion of whites transferring"[150] and the system therefore functioned "to 'maintain faith' among whites."[151] In the inner-city district of Richmond, the blacks who took advantage of the integration policy were "only those students whose families believe that desegregation offers an escape from low expectations and low pupil achievement."[152]

The open enrolment system raises the judicial paradox of simultaneously respecting the civil rights of *individuals* to choose and promoting the interests of the *community* as a collective (Adler, 1989; David, 1982); the contradiction between the right of individuals to have free choice and the right of communities to avoid collective stigmatisation and labelling of schools. The "shift towards an individual client orientation threatens the achievement of too many of the goals associated with collective welfare orientation,"[153] maintaining a constant tension between the two needs – that of the individual and that of the community.

Later studies conducted in the 1990s yielded inconclusive evidence regarding the benefit of market principle enhancement in education. For example, Woods, Bagley and Glatter (1998), gathered a great deal of research data pertaining to three towns in England, which indicates that choice and competition created an "increased sense of accountability about the quality of education to the families who are most immediately concerned with schooling, a greater openness by schools to them and their local communities, and a continuing impetus to raise academic achievement."[154] However, the research data also clearly indicates that choice and competition sharpen the hierarchy of schools and maintain or even exacerbate social divisions; cause difficulties for schools lower down the hierarchy while benefiting popular schools not only in terms of prestige, but also in financial and cultural resources.[155]

Geoffrey Walford argues, in an examination of the concept of choice, that the essential feature of British schooling has been its hierarchical nature in terms of "status, facilities and privileged entry into high-ranking occupations."[156] Walford reaches a similar conclusion to other researchers, i.e., that there is a correlation between the quality of schools and their population. Those who were educationally advantaged from the start multiply their advantages while "those children with most need for high quality education will not receive it."[157] Harry Brighouse agrees that the features of the British system are clearly non-egalitarian. This is the reason he suggests that greater funds for weaker pupils could make them more attractive to schools.

Thus, it transpired that the choice and diversity that were a major policy track during the 1990s extended the polarisation and hierarchical nature of the education system in England and Wales. It has yet to be determined whether Brighouse's idea of using a funding formula to limit the non-egalitarian scope of the system – or as a remedy to reduce polarisation between schools – will be effective.

9.4: EFFICIENCY THROUGH DECENTRALISATION: TOWARDS THE ESTABLISHMENT OF AN "ENTERPRISE CULTURE"

The 1988 Education Reform Act and further policies instituted during the 1990s are indices of both centralisation and decentralisation. While decision making with respect to the curriculum and the monitoring of performance against agreed-upon targets was shifted from teachers to the centre, the decentralisation trend was characterised by maximum freedom and flexibility over management matters.

The new management philosophy was set out in a document entitled *The Next Steps*, which aimed to formulate management reform in the civil service.

This philosophy has had a direct effect on the civil service departments and an indirect effect on attached services, such as the maintained sector defined by the Education Reform Act of 1988.

The government initiative documented in *The Next Steps* was launched by Prime Minister Margaret Thatcher, in February 1988, with the aim of improving the management of the civil service for the "benefit of taxpayers, customers and staff."[158] The main assumption of the reform was inspired by liberal thinkers such as Hayak who maintained that spontaneous behaviour and forces should play a greater role in the market if efficiency and productivity are the primary goals. Accordingly, E.P. Kemp, the head of the Next Steps Project, concluded that the government's policy was to achieve the "release of managerial energy and the inculcation of a greater sense of personal responsibility ,"[159] with the proviso that there be "freedom and flexibility."[160] Thus individual effort, "elements of competition,"[161] abolition of controls, and greater freedom for managers, became key aims so that "people have the maximum incentive to create wealth, and the objective of better services."[162]

But there is a condition for the inculcation of "enterprise culture" – a market spirit or "service-oriented culture."[163] In the words of Norman Lamont, Chancellor of the Exchequer: "The objective, of delegating as much freedom over operational matters as possible, is more likely to be achieved the *more decentralised* an agency is"[164] [present writer's emphasis]. And so the second assumption in the government's drive towards liberalisation of public services – which involved freedom and flexibility in management – is that "the man or woman at head office or Whitehall does not necessarily know what is best for their colleagues at the work place."[165] Therefore, in the government's view, the achievement of any improvement of services – any change towards a service-oriented culture – would depend on decision-making being carried out by those who are close to the customers, who can make the right decisions about the customers' needs, and who have the tools to make flexible decisions to meet these needs. The condition of being "close to the customer" is fulfilled by delegation of power and personal accountability, even at the cost of weakening the central departments' position over decision making. For this reason the organisational implication of such an assumption involved not only the granting of the necessary freedom to implement government policy, but also the provision of "a structure which would promote the efficiency and service-oriented culture which characterises similar activities in the private sector."[166] In accordance with its vision of creating a mechanism similar to that of the private sector, the government proposed that public services should be delivered by "Executive Agencies, which to the greatest extent practicable will carry out the executive functions of government,"[167] with full autonomy over a large range of management matters.

This government policy, based on the assumptions that only the release of human energy through the creation of *flexible organisations* would improve the efficiency and productivity of the public services on behalf of the customers and the taxpayers, raised two main questions. What would be the government's role in a decentralised system? How would ministers remain accountable to Parliament? Norman Lamont explains the government's policy and the management reform philosophy, outlining the government's role in a decentralised system:

> In some departments nearly all activities could eventually be conducted through their Agencies, leaving the centre of the department to concentrate on policy-making, resource allocation, strategic planning, and monitoring performance.[168]

The government would thus retain decision making power over central values and main aims, and monitor the fulfilment of these aims, while the agencies' duty would be to execute government policy.

Decentralisation of government functions raised the second question of how ministers would be kept accountable to Parliament and continue to deal with inquiries about matters of policy, if executive action on operational matters were no longer carried out directly by the government but instead by executive agencies. Such recommended policy gives rise to a paradox, or conflict of values, between the government's accountability to Parliament and its desire to improve the public services, which would rely on power and responsibility being delegated to managers in a decentralised system. In weighing up the two forces, the government gave priority to improving services by giving them a greater degree of freedom:

> We do not regard Parliamentary accountability as a cost which must be weighed in the balance against the benefit of effective management. It is not only important in its own right, it is also an extremely effective pressure for improvement.[169]

In the government's view, ministers would be able to retain their responsibility and to give an account to Parliament within the new framework of responsibility and delegation of freedom over operational matters. Therefore, that framework is not in "conflict with the external accountability of Ministers to Parliament."[170] With respect to this conflict Lamont concluded as follows:

> There is obviously a tension in any organisation between the need to *control* and be *accountable* and the need to *delegate* and be *flexible*. People often see an insoluble conflict here between the interests of the Treasury and those of departments. But the key point as I see it is this. We both have an overriding interest in *value for money*. And the Treasury does recognise that you cannot get the results you want from greater individual responsibility and motivation unless you are prepared to have real delegation to the people who take operational decisions and who in practice determine the quality of service on the ground.... We *are* now moving towards a more hands-off approach, which allows for the maximum degree of delegation consistent with essential central and departmental controls [original emphasis].[171]

The Education Reform Act of 1988 put this private-sector inspired management philosophy, with its emphasis on "small is beautiful" and greater decentralisation, into practice by giving schools the power to release *human energy*, setting up a new category of independent schools – the grant maintained (GM) schools, and delegating control of management and financial matters to schools by means of a system known as local management of schools (LMS).

The establishment of grant-maintained (GM) schools aimed to give schools with over 300 pupils the right to opt out of local education authority control and receive funding directly from the Secretary of State as self-governing schools. The government saw this as another step towards higher standards:

> The Secretary of State believes that the establishment of grant-maintained schools will prove to be a stimulus for higher standards at all schools. Grant-maintained schools will compete on equal terms with LEA-maintained schools.[172]

Thus, the establishment of a network of maintained schools was aimed, according to the Circular, at decreasing the LEAs' power and at introducing competition between GM and LEA-maintained schools. Flude & Hammer argue that this step is part of "enterprise culture,"[173] which places a high value on innovation and enterprise and encourages individual efforts at the expense of the splitting and shrinking of the LEA system. The new machinery of GM schools, a "new category of schools,"[174] embodied the idea that LEA-maintained schools should not, in a market system, be the only choice available to parents if raising of standards is the goal. So, widening the choice through competition, innovation, individual accountability, and freedom to improve the education service, even if this results in further impoverishment of the LEAs as a single machinery of maintained schools, is a desirable course. It creates a range or "hierarchy of schools,"[175] thus facilitating greater parental choice by encouraging the development of a diversity of schools – LEA-maintained schools, GM schools, CTCs and private schools.[176]

Whereas the 1944 Education Act had aimed to empower the LEAs by establishing them as the main administrative machinery and single executive agency for control and implementation of educational policy, the 1988 Education Reform Act took the opposite course, aiming to weaken the LEA machinery on behalf of a market philosophy of competition, liberalism and individual freedom of choice.

The new categories of school called into question what Maclure termed the "hierarchy of schools" and the nature of the new choice available to parents. This challenge should be analysed in three respects: in terms of curriculum, in terms of selection and in terms of finance.

The characteristics of the National Curriculum, and the government's intention of imposing a single strictly defined type of academic curriculum without allowing schools any degree of freedom to offer a variety of options for pupils of different types of ability, removed the leeway for differentiation between schools in terms of curriculum. Regarding selection, the Act determines that a grant maintained school may not change its character for a minimum period: Circular 10/88 gives discretionary powers to the Secretary of State to consider such a change, though he would "not normally approve proposals for a change of character within five years of its acquiring grant-maintained status."[177] Thus, a GM comprehensive, non-selective school would be able to become a selective grammar school after a minimum of five years. Flude & Hammer argue that the opting-out of LEA control was devised by the government as a means of returning to selection: "Thatcher has consistently shown that she is anxious to reinstate selective education and 'believes opting out would open the door to this'."[178] The Centre for Policy Studies also maintains that GM schools "should have flexibility over admission policy. Selection is always required whenever the demand for places exceeds the supply."[179] In Stuart Maclure's view the new machinery would be "of particular interest to surviving grammar schools in areas threatening to go comprehensive."[180] On financial matters, Circular 10/88 is ambiguous. It states that GM schools "will be funded on the same basis as other schools in their neighbourhood,"[181] but Clause 59 suggests the opposite by stating that "in addition to their annual maintenance grant, grant-maintained schools may from time to time be paid a 'special purpose' grant."[182]

This analysis demonstrated the possible development of the "hierarchy of schools" in the direction of financial differentiation, eventual selection and homogeneity in terms of curriculum choice. The number of GM schools rose from 50 in 1990 to about 1100 in 1996. These are mainly secondary schools. But the main test of this machinery probably lies in its subsequent combination with the assessment system and the publication of the "league tables." Parents who were disappointed with the school's results could blame the local authority.[183] In such circumstances a GM school could be considered a better, preferable, choice – an escape from the local authority schools towards an independent school run as a self-governing school. The development of GM schools faced some difficulties at the beginning of the 1990s. Chitty (1999) finds that the "co-existence of grant-maintained and LEA secondary schools made local planning almost impossible, and generated chaos in school admission systems in certain areas."[184] By the end of 1992 it became clear to John Major's government that steps had to be taken with regard to the GM schools. Five years later, after two months in power, Labour made clear its intention that schools with grant maintained status would continue to prosper but have to return to the control of the local education authorities. The reason given was as follows: "The pattern of ownership of school premises is complex....Trying to achieve complete consistency of ownership for aided and foundation schools would create too much turbulence."[185] The GM schools would therefore continue to maintain a higher degree of freedom and autonomy, but be locally incorporated.

The second means towards decentralisation and the development of an "enterprise culture" is local management of schools (LMS). The essence of this step, which Williams defined as a radical change "in the management and culture of schools,"[186] is giving schools full discretionary powers over school management, including the power to "secure the maximum delegation of financial and managerial responsibilities to governing bodies."[187] These powers cover two main areas: full financial control[188] and the appointment and dismissal of staff. The delegation of power is part of the "Government's overall policy to improve the quality of teaching and learning"[189] and will enable governing bodies and head teachers to plan their resources in accordance with "their own needs and priorities, and to make schools more responsive to their clients – parents, pupils, the local community and employers."[190]

The Act set out a new order, with LEAs expected to allocate the salary costs of teaching and non-teaching staff to schools, and a new budgeting system for schools that covered finance *per capita*, day-to-day premises costs, expenditure on books and equipment, examination fees and insurance. In addition, LMS affords the governing body the necessary flexibility to decide a particular school's designation by taking into consideration "the amount of any expenditure of a capital nature initially planned for the purposes of the school."[191] These two elements, finance *per capita* (combined with open enrolment) and individual school power over their own objectives, together with the freedom given to schools as *entrepreneurial cost centres* to raise private funds (see Chapter 8), constitute a radical change towards reform in management of the education system. This was part of the general shift towards decentralisation in government policy and a greater degree of freedom for public services.

Eight years after the 1988 Education Reform Act was approved by Parliament, a further attempt was made to reinforce school empowerment. The White Paper *Self-Government for Schools*, which was published in 1996, expresses the government's wish to extend schools' power in the following words: [192]

> Some LEAs had started developing the principles of LMS before the Education Reform Act 1988 established a national framework. At the time, there were misgivings about making LMS a requirement. But few would now want to go back to pre-LMS arrangements.... LMS has strengthened the incentives for schools to respond to what parents want.

The Government believed in a further push to extend local management of schools with a new LMS framework, and presented its intention to "redefine the Potential Schools Budget (PSB) and raise the proportion of that Budget which LEAs must delegate to schools" to 95%.[193] The following chart explains the plan:

Chart 9.1: Percentage of Potential School Budgets Delegated by LEAs in England 1991- 97.

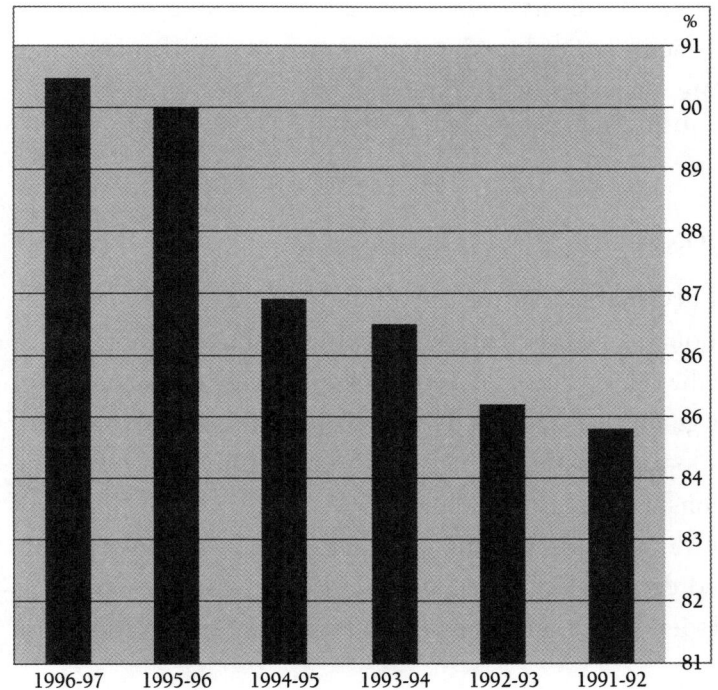

Source: DfEE (1996), *Self-Government for Schools*, 11.

The New Labour Government followed Conservative policy as it was reflected in the core of the Education Reform Act 1988. The White Paper, *Excellence in Schools* (1997), which was published by Labour, followed the local management of schools line by stating that "schools have thrived on the opportunities offered by delegation of budgets and managerial responsibilities....The Government will require LEAs to delegate more of their budgets to heads and governors. LEAs should also minimise the proportion of their budget that is spent on central administration....LMS will be the means through which all schools are funded."[194] The paper went on to emphasise the need for a different arrangement in recognition of "different starting points for different schools. We must avoid unnecessary disruption to the education of pupils."[195]

There is widespread agreement that local management of schools in England was a successfully implemented policy that has been largely favoured by head teachers, as it gives them greater control to secure efficiency in the running of their school. (Bullock and Thomas 1994,1997; Levačić 1995a; 1998; Maychell 1994; Williams 1995, 1998, 2003). But still, the possible consequences of such a policy for education, as part of a market system of education, require analysis in the context of the whole Act and all the measures involved. The following section will provide this analysis.

9.5: CONCLUSIONS

The principal declared aim of the 1988 Education Reform Act was the raising of educational standards. This restructuring of the education system aimed to restore the "glory of the old days" and re-establish the standards of attainment of the grammar school era. The new constitution aimed to achieve such goals by adopting market principles in education. This raises the following questions: Do research findings suggest that such principles will realise this aim? If yes, for whom? At what price? And how do the centralisation and decentralisation elements of the Act come to serve this aim? An overall view of the directions taken by the Act may clarify these questions.

The essence of the government's philosophy of management reform was set down in Norman Lamont's statement that no one in Whitehall[196] knows "what is best for their colleagues at the work place"[197] in order to meet the customers' needs. The idea that "being close to the customer" is a condition for making the right decision based on customer needs, should be observed through the National Curriculum. The shift of power from teachers to the government over curriculum matters could be regarded as an allocation of power by means of which the DfEE determined the main values and targets of the education system, an approach that was welcomed by the teachers and regarded as a framework for their decision making rather than a rigid system imposed upon them. Analysis of the National Curriculum revealed that the academic sort of curriculum that was devised by the government at first met only part of the customers' needs, but was slightly amended in the course of the 1990s in order to meet the needs of the less able pupils, particularly post-16, and facilitate greater curriculum flexibility and choice for teachers at the primary level. The government failed to develop a more flexible curriculum suited to the entire range of pupils – from the less able to the more academic – at the early stage of the implementation of the 1988 Education Act. It was however, forced to do so after the effect the rigid academic curriculum had on a substantial portion of the pupils was realised. Such development raises the question of what kind of reform the government aimed to achieve by taking a tough line over curriculum matters without giving schools any leeway to "meet the needs of the customer" – unless they are the academic type. Moreover, it raises the question whether in the absence of real vocational and technical studies for 55%, at the end of the 1980s, and given the nature of the academic curriculum, there was any real intention on the part of the government to meet industry's needs and to compete with other industrial countries.

In the government's view the assessment system, as another policy mechanism to be run by the LEAs, is essential to the conduct of a market system. The idea of providing customers with information on the quality of the commodity by publishing the test results without taking into account the schools' contexts, takes this mechanism to the extreme by privileging the individual's right to choose at the price of harming and stigmatising particular schools, communities, individual pupils and parents in the bottom of the "league table." The conclusive evidence that a feedback system is essential if "effective schools" are to improve scholastic attainment – provided it serves as an internal school mechanism and a tool for teachers to improve the teaching/learning process rather than an external yardstick – was ignored by the government in favour of market ideas in terms of which monitoring of standards was an essential part of establishing a market system as a means to achieve better standards. The failure of such systems in the US and Australia, and the shift in France and Scotland towards an internal assessment system conducted by teachers for the benefit of their teaching/learning process, might be a reflection of how far the governments went in promoting market principles.

The government policy of publishing test results for the sake of the market idea ignored the essential role of "expectations" or the "Pygmalion effect" in raising standards. The conclusive evidence of research on the importance of high expectations for "effective schools," corresponded to the government's conclusions about the importance of "expectation" as they were explained in two different White Papers by the two main parties. The White Paper *Better Schools,* published by the Tory party in 1985, and the White Paper *Excellence in Schools,* published by Labour in 1997, both followed the same line. Both Papers regarded low expectations as one of the causes of low standards.[198] Both, however, were disregarded and neglected as an inevitable result of the pursuit of the market idea of choice and competition among schools. The new system of displaying publicly schools' test results and of placing schools in a simple ranking order of quality was in direct conflict with the raising of expectations as an educational method. By establishing a market system in education, the government turned a deaf ear to the negative effect of such publications on the expectations of children, parents and teachers. The cases of those schools at the bottom of the league in Hampshire elucidate the entire argument.

By adopting such a policy the government has opted for a "failure policy" just like the one rejected by the French education system after a long experience of "orientation by failure."[199] Moreover, the government has oversimplified the idea of "choice," legitimising the publication of test results without taking school context into consideration, thus failing to understand the meaning of the same idea in the private sector, where "high expectation" is regarded as a necessary element in building success. According to this view, the path to excellence is based on encouraging the *average man* in his ability to achieve an "extraordinary performance"[200] and not on a "handful of brilliant performers."[201] This approach is rooted in the assumption that high expectations and reinforcement for each individual – even in cases of temporary failure – are essential for the achievement of good results and for instilling a sense of commitment, confidence, and the will to persevere in people. The government's 1988 Education Reform Act and the policies which followed, were either unaware of this point or deliberately ignored it, despite relying heavily on private sector management concepts. It hence failed to learn the private sector lesson properly, preferring instead to encourage and support only part of the schools, part of the pupils, and part of the teachers, while repressing, exposing and stigmatising the others.

Choice, diversity and the open enrolment system are the other side of the same coin. On the one hand, as Watford and Brighouse averred, they are part of the nature of the British system. On the other, a large volume of research findings indicates that such diversity contributes to school hierarchy and exacerbates social divisions. Educational advantage is perpetuated while those children most in need of high quality education will not be afforded it through the mechanism of choice. Case studies carried out in England by Glatter in Woods *et. al* (1998) and the Scottish experience (Adler, 1989) clearly support these arguments.

The paradox of combining marketism and conservatism – a non-interventionist policy with a highly interventionist one, freedom for spontaneous forces and control of these forces, centralisation with decentralisation – all under the same umbrella, is seen more clearly in the light of the government's direction in reforming the education system. The shift of power gives the government full control over the content of instruction, the main subjects of the curriculum, and a mechanism to monitor performance against attainment targets, while the delegation of power to schools throws light on the admixture of centralisation and decentralisation. Giving schools discretionary powers over wide management issues is aimed at enabling them to plan their resources in accordance with the needs of "their clients – parents, pupils, the local community and employers."[202] But the clients' need, in educational terms, is for diversity of curriculum, particularly at secondary level. This was eventually acknowledged in the establishment of the GNVQs during the early 1990s and of 992 specialist schools towards the beginning of the 2000s. In this sense decentralisation, embodying the idea of freedom and flexibility, was a machinery tied to a single course – to serve a relatively narrow band of customers who have the aptitude and ability to study according to an academic curriculum.

The real freedom of the private sector, which the government was so eager to imitate in reforming the public services, is based on the philosophy that the provider in the market recognises the value of "being close to the customer" and should identify the *whole range* of customers' needs. The government failed to apply this principle to education customers when it planned the delegation of power – excluding curriculum and assessment matters – to schools. This policy was partially amended when the government became fully aware of the consequences of curricular inflexibility on the aspiration of better standards for all.

The trend towards a centralised academic curriculum and a national assessment system creates a renewed focus on the more able pupils in the education system of England and Wales, a move towards the kind of differentiation that the 1944 government attempted to achieve by devising the tripartite system and by controlling access to external examinations in the 1940s and 1950s. The straitjacket of the curriculum, and the limited choice given to the full range of students, created a decentralised machinery that is severely limited in its *freedom of choice* – a central term in any market system. Whatever freedom was afforded at the initial stage benefited only the more able pupils. Consequently, decentralisation became a means of facilitating competition without giving the less able proper choice. Some corrective measures were taken in the attempt to establish the GNVQs at the post-16 level, but without removing the barriers or creating a proper bridge between academic and vocational studies by means of a modular system. The main feature of the policy therefore remains unchanged.

Each of the Act's measures individually, and all of them together, give us a clear view of the 1988 Education Act's effect on the education system's customers. In educational terms those who will benefit from the Act will be the children who are able to cope with the academic curriculum, achieve better marks and to earn a higher position in the "league table."

In social terms the 1988 Act, and some of the policies of the 1990s, emphasise the price deprived areas have to pay. The choice provided by open enrolment would lead to greater inequality, with some schools in particularly weak neighbourhoods at risk of becoming "ghetto schools." The assumption that such schools would eventually be closed is not borne out by the research findings of either Adler et al. (1989) or Raab and Adler (1988) in the Scottish case. Moreover, the research found that those who remained in the deprived district school paid the price and became more stigmatised than they were previously – a "widening of educational inequalities."[203] In Ranson's view the 1980s aimed to place and to label the individual "in order to socialise different sections of the age group into alternative layers and strata of the social order."[204] Thus, the 1988 Education Reform Act and the policies of the 1990s represent an acceleration of the trend Ranson identified and a further move towards maintaining the social order, and in some cases deepening the gulfs between the strata.

Chapter 9 - Old Values, New Structure: From the Education Reform Act 1988 to the Policies of the 1990s

In economic terms the 1980s, with the 1988 Education Act and further acts of the 1990s as their peak, saw a move towards screening in education. Mark Blaug describes this trend as being "increasingly devoted to quality reform rather than quantitative expansion."[205] This trend, which emerged in the form of performance tests and the hierarchy of schools "from those for the most able to those for the least able,"[206] is in Stiglitz's view (1975) the essence of the screening mechanism in education, which aims to classify and to "place individuals into the right 'slots'."[207] Those who raised the arguments of the "British disease" (see Chapter 8) might find that the screening process functions in the direction of maintaining the "British disease" in a steady state, and towards perpetuation of the lower class as the main class affected by the "disease."

Such a development might contain the potential ingredients of a new movement of the pendulum towards blurring, distorting and deforming the new structural order by those among students, parents and teachers whom the 1980's and 1990s and its structural system is liable to repress, expose and stigmatis

Notes:
1. Beare, Hedley et al. (1989). *Creating an Excellent School*. London: Routledge, 2.
2. Coleman, James et al. (1966). *Equality of Educational Opportunity*. Washington: Government Printing Office, 325.
3. Christopher Jencks et al. (1973). *Inequality: A Reassessment of the Effect of Family and Schooling in America*. London: Allen Lane, 143.
4. Beare et al. (1989), 6.
5. Much of the research based on case studies raises several other factors in school efficiency, such as the importance of the role of leadership, the school climate, homework and the work-oriented atmosphere.
6. Peter Cuttance (1985). "Framework for Research on the Effectiveness of Schooling." In D. Reynolds (ed.), *Studying School Effectiveness*. London: Falmer, 14.
7. David Hopkins (1987). "Implications for School Improvement at the Local Level." In D. Hopkins (ed.), *Improving the Quality of Schooling*. London: Falmer, 193.
8. David Hopkins (1985). *School Based Review for School Improvement*. Leuven: Acco, 12.
9. Quoted by Hopkins (1985), 13, from: J.L. David (1982). *School-Based Strategies: Implications for Government Policy*. Mimeo. Group Palo Alto, California: Bay Area Research Group.
10. Joseph Bashi et al. (1990). *Effective Schools: From Theory to Practice*. Jerusalem: Van Leer, 77.
11. Tony Becher & Stuart Maclure (eds.) (1978). *Accountability in Education*. Windsor: NFER, 17.
12. Hopkins (1987), 5.
13. William Bacon (1978). *Public Accountability and the Schooling System*. London: Harper, 2.
14. Kenneth Brooksbank & Eric Ackstine (eds.) (1984). *Educational Administration*. Harlow: Councils and Education, 14.
15. Department of Education and Science (1985). *Better Schools*. London: HMSO, 6.
16. Ibid., 5.
17. Ibid., 8.
18. Ibid., 8. The two other aspects that were mentioned in the document were the importance of improving teacher and management effectiveness and of harnessing parents and employers to schools.
19. Hansard. 1 December 1987, Col.775.
20. Ibid., col.774.
21. The Secretary of State had to resort to international comparison: "The education systems in France and Germany do not narrow and specialise as does ours. They remain broad, and that is the thrust of the National Curriculum and the General Certificate of Secondary Education examination" (Hansard: 1 December 1987, Col.775).
22. Department of Education and Science (1987). *The National Curriculum 5-16*, 2-3.
23. Ibid., 3.
24. Education Reform Act 1988, Section 4(2).
25. Department of Education and Science (1989). *English for Ages 5 to 16*. Section 15, 17.

26. Desmond Nuttall (1989). "National Assessment: Complacency or Misinterpretation?" In D. Lawton (ed.), *The Education Reform Act: Choice and Control*. London: Hodder & Stoughton, 52.
27. Quoted by Nuttall (1989), 54, from Maurice Holt. "Bureaucratic Benefits." *Times Educational Supplement*, 18.9.87.
28. John Tomlinson (1988). "Curriculum and Market: Are they Compatible?" In J. Haviland (ed.), *Take Care, Mr Baker*. London: Fourth Estate, 11.
29. D. Coulby (1990). "The Construction and Implementation of the Primary Core Curriculum." In D. Coulby & S. Ward (eds.). *The Primary Core National Curriculum*. London: Cassell, 16.
30. Ibid., 19.
31. Teachers' views were given in reference to existing circumstances, where attainment targets are not linked to any external assessment; a different view was forcefully expressed on the intention to link attainment targets with the assessment system (see next section).
32. Department of Education and Science (1989). *Science Policy: The Way Ahead*. Speech by Kenneth Baker, MP, London, 11-12.
33. Hansard: 12 November 1982.
34. David Finegold & David Soskice (1990). "The Failure of Training in Britain: Analysis and Prescription." In D. Gleeson (ed.), *Training and its Alternatives*. Milton Keynes: Open University Press, 35.
35. TVEI Review (1984), 3.
36. Interview with Lord Young, 13.2.91.
37. ORT (Organisation for Rehabilitation through Training) is a world non-governmental organisation for technology and vocational education with headquarters in London, founded in 1880 to train Jewish refugees from Russia for useful vocations; today it runs 800 technical schools in 30 countries.
38. The neo-liberals of the New Right, in opposition to the neo-conservatives, supported the idea of giving complete freedom to schools to develop various dimensions and directions of the curriculum.
39. Denis Gleeson (ed.) (1987). *TVEI and Secondary Education: A Critical Appraisal*. Milton Keynes: Open University Press, 4.
40. Ibid., 5.
41. Ibid.
42. Department of Education and Science: Circular 5/89 (22 February 1989).
43. National Curriculum Council (1990). *Education for Industrial Understanding*. No. 4, York: NCC.
44. Roger Dale et al. (1990). *The TVEI Story: Policy, Practice and Preparation for the Work Force*. Milton Keynes: Open University Press, 109.
45. Ibid.
46. Peter Senker (1990). "TVEI: Evaluation, Economic Policy and Ideology." In D. Hopkins (ed.), *TVEI at the Change of Life*. Clevedon: Multilingual Matters, 126.
47. Finegold & Soskice (1990), 49.

48. Ibid., 38.
49. Education Reform Act 1988, London: HMSO, Section 105.
50. *Education*, 23.9.88, considered ORT influential on the CTCs under the heading "Brainfather of the CTC"; a similar reference was made in *The Times*, 4.6.87.
51. Letter of 30 May 1986.
52. Interview with Joseph Harmatz, ORT General Director, 15 November 1990.
53. ORT (1988). *The ORT Curriculum and Recommendations for the City Technology Colleges*. London: ORT.
54. Ibid.
55. Ibid.
56. Ibid.
57. City Technology Colleges Trust (1987). *The City Technology Colleges: Curriculum Objectives – Formulation and Implementation*. Unpublished document.
58. Ibid.
59. Education Reform Act 1988, Section 105.
60. The prospect of the development of CTCs now faces new obstacles. The existing plan to set up 20 Colleges ran into severe financial difficulties, with cost estimates differing markedly from initial design plans. Although there were available buildings that could be used to accommodate the CTCs, the LEAs were excluded from participation in the new institutions. This throws into question not only the further development of the CTCs but also the government's ability to establish a new network of a new type of schools without either the full amount of money or a partnership with the owners of the overwhelming majority of education property in England. Sir Cyril Taylor, the Chairman of the CTCs Trust Council, admitted the government's difficulties in financing the new colleges and the TES has mentioned that the government has "no longer any date for reaching the target" of setting up the 20 CTCs (*Times Educational Supplement*, 23.11.90).
61. Statistics of Education Schools in England (2000). London: The Stationery Office, 78. In the same year the CTCs not only achieved 52.2% but also another 30% in the GNVQ.
62. In the academic year 1987-8 only 11.3% of school leavers achieved three or more passes in A level, 4.3% two passes and 3.1% one pass. In the same year 29.9% obtained five or more GCSE/O level grades of A-C and/or CSSE grade 1, and 27.5% obtained 1-4 GCSE/O level grades of A-C, (source: DES Statistics of Education: School Leavers GCSE and GCE 1988).
63. The Advanced Level of the GNVQs (Level 3) intended to be on a par with two A levels, and GNVQ (level 2, intermediate), equal to four GCSEs.
64. Ron Dearing (1996). *Review of Qualifications for 16 – 19 Year Olds*. London: SCAA. 3-4.
65. Sally Tomlinson (ed.) (1997). *Education 14-19: Critical Perspectives*. London: Athlone, 5.
66. Ibid., 7.
67. Geoff Stanton (1997). "Patterns in Development." In Sally Tomlinson (ed.), *Education 14-19: Critical Perspectives*, London: Athlone, 50.

68. Sheila Macrae, Meg Maguire and Stephen J. Ball. "Competition, Choice and Hierarchy in a Post-16 Market." In Sally Tomlinson (ed.), *Education 14-19: Critical Perspectives*. London: Athlone, 99.
69. DES, Circular No 1/92, 1992.
70. Clyde Chitty (1999). *The Education System Transformed*. Great Yarmouth: Baseline, 104.
71. QCA (1999). Wider Opportunities for Work-Related Learning at Key Stage 4, 1.
72. Education Reform Act 1988, Section 14 (6).
73. Department of Education and Science (1988). *The Education Reform Act 1988: The School Curriculum and Assessment*. Circular 5/89 (22 February 1989), 14.
74. Ibid.
75. Ibid., Paragraph 5.
76. Department of Education and Science (1987). *National Curriculum: Task Group on Assessment and Testing* – A Report. Paragraph 91.
77. Levels 6 to 10 are regarded as GCSE grades of A to F.
78. Department of Education and Science (1987). *National Curriculum: Task Group on Assessment and Testing*. Paragraph 18.
79. Ibid., Paragraph 55.
80. Ibid., Paragraph 56.
81. Ibid., Paragraph 63.
82. Ann Filer (2000). "Assessment as Loved Experience Beyond the Classroom." In Ann Filer (ed.), *Assessment: Social Practice and Social Product*. Routledge: London, 130-1.
83. Harold Berlak (2000). "Cultural Politics, the Science of Assessment and Democratic Renewal of Public Education." In Ann Filer (ed.), *Assessment: Social Practice and Social Product*. Routledge: London, 201.
84. Paul J. Black, "The Shifting Scenery of the National Curriculum." In Clyde Chitty & Brian Simon (eds.), *Education Answers Back: Critical Responses to Government Policy*. London: Lawrence, 54.
85. Supported by the federal government.
86. Colin Power (1984). "National Assessment: A Review of Programs in Australia, the United Kingdom, and the United States." *Comparative Education Review*, 28(3), 356.
87. Ibid., 362.
88. Ibid.
89. Ibid., 370.
90. Ibid., 363.
91. Ibid., 375.
92. Ibid.
93. Ibid.
94. Patricia Broadfoot (1984). "From Public Examinations to Profile Assessment: The French Experience." In P. Broadfoot (ed.), *Selection Certification and Control*. London: Falmer, 203.
95. Ibid.
96. Ibid., 204.

97. In the last two years pupils have been directed to one of three types of streams: classical, modern and technical.
98. Quoted by Broadfoot (1984), p.204, from an interview with the Education Minister.
99. W.B. Dockrell (1988). "The Impact of Scottish National Surveys of Achievement on Policy and Practice." In H.D. Black & W.B. Dockrell (eds.), *New Developments in Educational Assessment*. British Journal of Educational Psychology, Monograph Series No. 3, Edinburgh: Scottish Academic Press, 181.
100. Ibid., 180.
101. Ibid.
102. Ibid.
103. Ibid., 183.
104. Ibid., 186.
105. TGAT Report, Paragraph 134.
106. The White Paper, Better Schools, published in 1985, raised the problem of teachers' judgement of pupils' potential and the reflection of such judgement on parents and pupils' expectations (see footnote 11 in this chapter).
107. Robert Rosenthal & Lenore Jacobson (1968). *Pygmalion in the Classroom*. New York: Holt, 174.
108. Ibid., 180.
109. Douglas A. Pidgeon (1970). *Expectation and Pupil Performance*. London: NFER, 122.
110. DfEE (1997). *Excellence in Schools*, 25.
111. Ibid.
112. Ibid., 26
113. Ibid.
114. S. Tomlinson (1997), 16.
115. David Gillborn and Deborah Youdell (2000). *Rationing Education: Policy, Practice, Reform and Equity*. Open University: Buckingham, 197.
116. Val Woodings (1997). "How Primary Schools Deal with Assessment in the National Curriculum." In Cedric Cullingford (ed.), *Assessment Versus Evaluation*. Cassel: London, 139.
117. *Times Educational Supplement*, 11.5.89.
118. Ibid.
119. Interview conducted on 16 November 1990.
120. Cullingford (1997), 268.
121. Cullingford (1997). 270-1, 274.
122. S. Tomlinson (1997), 9.
123. Patricia Broadfoot (2001). "Empowerment or Performativity? Assessment Policy in the Late Twentieth Century." In Robert Phillips and John Furling (eds.). *Education, Reform and the State – Twenty-five Years of Politics, Policy and Practice*. London; Routledge, 137.
124. Geoffrey Walford (2002). "Redefining School Effectiveness." Westminster Studies in Education, 25(1).

125. Circular 5/89 (22 February 1989), 14.
126. Denis Lawton (ed.) (1989). *The Education Reform Act: Choice and Control*. London: Hodder & Stoughton; Martin Leonard (1988). *The 1988 Education Act*. Oxford: Blackwell.
127. Education Reform Act 1988, Section 26.
128. DFE (1992): *Choice and Diversity – A New Framework for Schools*, iii.
129. Ibid., 43.
130. Ibid., 10.
131. Ibid.
132. Clyde Chitty (1999), 87.
133. DfEE (1996). *Self-Government for Schools*, 2.
134. Board of Education (1943). Education Reconstruction, 3.
135. DfEE (1997), 71.
136. Ibid., 11.
137. Ibid., 40.
138. DfEE (2001). *Education and Skills: Delivering Results – A Strategy to 2006*.
139. 83% in Edinburgh and 85% in Dundee.
140. Gillian Raab & Michael Adler (1988). "A Tale of Two Cities: The Impact of Parental Choice on Admissions to Primary Schools in Edinburgh and Dundee." In: L. Bondi & M.H. Matthews (eds.). *Education and Society: Studies in the Politics, Sociology and Geography of Education*, London: Routledge, 114.
141. Ibid., 145.
142. Ibid., 144.
143. Ibid., 114.
144. Ibid., 145.
145. Michael Adler et al. (1989). *Parental Choice and Educational Policy*. Edinburgh: EUP, 215.
146. Ibid., 218.
147. Ibid., 219.
148. Ibid.
149. David Kirp (1982). *Just Schools*. Berkeley: University of California Press, 288.
150. Ibid., 230.
151. Ibid.
152. Ibid., 143.
153. Adler (1989), 226.
154. Philip A. Woods, Carl Bagley and Ron Glatter (1998). *School Choice and Competition: Markets in the Public Interest?* London: Routledge, 200.
155. Ibid., 208.
156. Geoffrey Walford (1994). *Choice and Equity in Education*. Cassel: London, 161.
157. Ibid., 123.
158. HM Treasury (1989). *The Financing and Accountability of Next Steps Agencies*. London: HMSO, 6.

159. House of Commons (1988). "Treasury and Civil Service Committee. Eighth Report." *Civil Service Management Reform: The Next Steps* Vol.2. London: HMSO, 6.
160. Ibid.
161. House of Commons (1988), 8.
162. Speech of 9 May 1990 by Norman Lamont, MP, at that time the Chief Secretary to the Treasury. Unpublished document, 2.
163. Ibid., 7.
164. House of Commons (1988), 6.
165. Norman Lamont's speech, 9 May 1990, 20.
166. Ibid., 7.
167. House of Commons (1988), 3.
168. Norman Lamont's speech, 9 May 1990, 7.
169. Ibid.
170. Ibid., 9.
171. Norman Lamont's speech, 9 May 1990, 12.
172. Department of Education and Science: Circular 10/88, 1
173. Michael Flude & Merril Hammer (1990). "Opting for an Uncertain Future: Grant-Maintained Schools." In M. Flude & M. Hammer (eds.). *The Education Reform Act 1988*. London: Falmer, 51.
174. Flude & Hammer (1990), 54.
175. Ibid., 66.
176. According to Maclure (in Lawton, 1989), LEA-maintained schools would shrink to 65-70% out of over 90%.
177. Department of Education and Science: Circular 10/88.
178. *The Observer* (20.11.1987) in Flude & Hammer (1990), 64.
179. Julian Havilland (1988). *Take Care, Mr Baker*. London: Fourth Estate, 107.
180. Stuart J. Maclure (1989). *Education Reform Act*. London: Hodder & Stoughton, 67-8.
181. Circular 10/88, p.1.
182. Ibid., 14. The Circular clarified the intention behind special purpose grants "to ensure fair treatment of grant-maintained schools in comparison with LEA-maintained schools" but the interpretation of the term "fair" was left to the Secretary of State's discretion.
183. Such disappointment could affect the whole range of schools in the "league table," not only those at the bottom, for all basically depend on parents' expectations of their school's place in the rank order.
184. Clyde Chitty (1999), 56.
185. DfEE (1997), 70.
186. Vivian Williams (1988). *Education Reform Act [ERA]*. Unpublished document.
187. Department of Education and Science: Circular 7/88, 3.
188. The delegation applies to all secondary and primary schools with 200 pupils and over.
189. Circular 7/88, 3.
190. Ibid.

Chapter 9 - Old Values, New Structure: From the Education Reform Act 1988 to the Policies of the 1990s

191. Education Reform Act 1988, Section 50.
192. DfEE (1996), 9.
193. Ibid.
194. DfEE (1997), 70.
195. Ibid.
196. Headquarters Office.
197. Norman Lamont's speech, 9 May 1990, 20.
198. Teachers were blamed for preconceptions about pupils' capabilities, as a result of which "expectations of pupils are insufficiently demanding," affecting school standards at all levels (see footnote 11).
199. Broadfoot (1984), 204.
200. Peters Thomas & Robert Waterman (1982). *In Search of Excellence*. New York: Harper & Row, xxii.
201. Ibid.
202. Ibid.
203. Adler (1989), 219.
204. Stewart Ranson (1984). "Towards a Tertiary Tripartism: New Codes of Social Control and the 17+." In Patricia Broadfoot (ed.), *Selection, Certification and Control*. London: Falmer, 242.
205. Mark Blaug (1987). "Where Are We Now in the Economics of Education?" In Mark Blaug, *The Economics of Education and the Education of an Economist*. London: Edward Elgar, 129.
206. Ibid., 294.
207. Joseph E. Stiglitz (1975). "The Theory of 'Screening', Education, and the Distribution of Income." *The American Economic Review*, 65(3), 294.

• CHAPTER 10

CONCLUSIONS

The main aim of this research has been to describe and explain the "pendulum syndrome" of the movement along the centralisation-decentralisation axis in the education system of England and Wales. In order to formulate such an explanation it was necessary to analyse the factors that affected structural transformation. The analysis is primarily a descriptive synthesis of the dialectical interplay between the interests, needs and perceptions of subordinate systems (individuals, groups or communities) and the interests of the central authority – namely, the government. The continual presence of abuse, neglect and distortion of the central order, on the one hand and government attempts to curb freedom on the other, is central to understanding two key terms in this study: order and disorder. Below we focus on this dialectic – the interplay between the centre and the periphery, between the government and other educational subsystems in England and Wales.

10.1: THE INITIAL POSITION OF THE PENDULUM

The so-called "centralisation process" in the education system of England and Wales can be divided into two main periods, in each of which an attempt was made to construct a new order through radical government intervention.[1]

The two periods differ in the routes taken, the factors involved, the evolution of events and the sequence of actions and reactions, as well as in the outcomes in terms of structural principles and system construction. Both periods however, were characterised by a common aim: to create differentiation between schools – a hierarchy of schools. This section aims to summarise the factors involved in government intervention in creating the 1944 structure.

The 1944 education system was focused on a framework of educational and organisational principles, the two primary struts of which were secondary education for all and a uniform administrative system. The first principle – secondary education for all – arose out of three main developments. The first was a rise in general levels of attainment and an improvement in the quality of primary education following the establishment of entitlement to basic education for all at the end of the nineteenth century (1870 Elementary Education Act). This improvement in standards raised expectations and led to pressure on elementary school boards to improve the range and the quality of instruction by creating higher grades. Such grades were attached to the elementary schools but amounted to "secondary [schools] in their character,"[2] constituting the embryo of popular secondary education. The second factor was a sense of injustice and inequality reinforced by two main processes: the emergence of left-wing groups such as the Fabian Society, with their calls for a "new liberalism" – the just distribution of national resources and equality of opportunity – and an associated trend rooted in the spirit of national solidarity that resulted from the huge sacrifice of lives during the First and Second World Wars. These events stimulated a highly emotional consensus and prompted calls to abolish social deprivation and break down social and educational privilege. This mood was expressed in 1917 by Fisher, the President of the Board of Education, in the context of an attempt to raise the school leaving age. He argued that "the poor are asked to pour out their blood"[3] without having full citizens' rights to education. Butler asserted in 1944 that "the 'two nations' still existed in England a century after Disraeli had used the phrase."[4] Both processes had a major effect on the government's commitment to undertaking the central intervention considered necessary in order to establish secondary education for all.

The second principle – the conviction that a single type of administration should be created – also had its origins in the early years of the century. The attempt to establish connections between the different educational agencies and their component parts had been on the Board of Education's agenda for several decades. Terms such as "isolated," "independence," "unconnected," "overlapping competition" (the Bryce Report), "omissions" (the Balfour period), "lack of control," "dangerous and muddled state," "dissatisfaction" (the Butler period) all reflected the perception of disorder in three main areas of the education system: the dual system, with the independent church schools; the incoherence of administration, particularly in the links between primary and secondary education;[5] and the proliferation of authorities, leading to wide discrepancies between education services in different areas. The expressions quoted above represented the view that under a single administrative order, controlled by the LEAs, these organisational disadvantages would disappear.

The government's approach was that the abolition of competition and overlapping between isolated and unconnected educational agencies, and a shift towards a single administrative order under full control of the LEAs, would create a powerful machinery for the exercise of government policy. The expression "central system locally administered" emerged to encapsulate the government's view that its main aims for education could be implemented and monitored if the hitherto unconnected elements of the education system were administered by local education authorities. According to this vision the local authorities, as tools for the implementation of government policy, would be closely controlled and inspected, and their plans subject to approval by the ministry, thus ensuring consistency with central policy.

A key place in the new order was occupied by an educational axiom that had direct implications for the proposed structure, viz. the psychologists' claim that it is possible to predict the ultimate level of individual intellectual characteristics at a very early age. Therefore the new structure should be based on the rough grouping and classification of pupils for schools suitable to their age, ability and aptitude, and on the selection of children for three different types of school: grammar, technical and modern, which were designed to fulfil the different needs of different groups of pupils.

Despite government attempts to encourage LEAs to take the needs of their local communities into consideration, in practice the government took a highly interventionist approach in order to implement the tripartite policy, controlling the proportions of pupils allocated to each of the three different types of school by means of the requirement that all local authorities' Development Plans receive ministerial approval. Such central intervention was an attempt to specify in definite terms the proportion of the nation's children in each type of school, with allocations set out not just as general guidelines but in terms of definite numbers of entry places, even down to the level of the individual school.

For the government, the main aim that justified this highly interventionist policy and the use of its powers to approve or reject local plans was the maintenance of the structural order and of the differences between individuals, and particularly the preservation of the respected tradition of the grammar school in fulfilling a national need by educating the country's most intellectually able children. According to this view, which was shared from the 1940s to the late 1950s by ministers from both the Conservative and Labour parties, the grammar school was a symbol of success and high standards, and was essential for supplying the state with high quality professionals. Thus, in the government's view, if high standards should be the main priority of the nation's education system, only central control over the LEAs' implementation of the educational structure could secure the realisation of that aim. It was therefore in the government's interest to vet the allocation of children to the three different types of school and to foster a tough policy in securing the exclusiveness of the grammar school.

The following comments by the ministry in the case of Gloucestershire's development plan typify its interventionist policy: "The figure of 12.5% is too high if the quality of Grammar School academic training is to show any marked improvement under the new conditions of the 1944 Act."[6] Again, in the case of Oxfordshire: "It is suggested that there could with advantage be some reduction in the amount of the provision for education of grammar school kind, estimated by the Authority as 18%."[7] Thus, a single system with a connected and coherent structure controlled by the local authorities enabled the government to monitor the numbers of grammar school places, making them available for the brightest and most able children only. For this reason the ministry's intervention went as far as dealing with details of every single school in those cases where the grammar schools' quality was seen to be in danger and the number of places exceeded what was regarded by the ministry as desirable. Inevitably, such intervention demanded ministerial involvement in an enormous number of tiny details in order to curb any deviation of the LEAs from the uniform national policy. Deviations from what was regarded as the desired proportions risked levelling down of standards and departure from the desired national structural order of secondary education.

10.2: THE SWING OF THE PENDULUM: THE DECENTRALISATION PROCESS

The government policy of restricting LEAs' freedom by taking a highly interventionist line encountered spontaneous factors leading to abuse, neglect and distortion of the uniform order that the ministry was attempting to dictate. The so-called decentralisation process was not so much a discretionary process of distributing power between the centre and the periphery on the basis of a mutual understanding regarding the role of each part of the system, as a continuous process of blurring and subverting centralised power at the periphery. In practice, this process created a new structural order, swinging the pendulum from a uniform and national order towards a structure based on local needs, local perceptions, local circumstances and local tradition. This process was characterised by the dialectic and interplay between centre and periphery, between government and other subsystems of the education system in England and Wales. Three main counter-forces or groups of factors were involved in the subversion and undermining of the government attempt to devise a national and uniform system; these factors are the main subject of the following discussion.

The generation of a new national uniform order inevitably involved attempting to obliterate the previously existing local order, an order which had been gradually and steadily self-organised, self-conducted and self-renewed by each local authority according to local circumstances, needs, and interests. This leads us to the first factor conducive to decentralisation: local traditions and local perceptions of the 1944 Education Act. The government attempted to impose or to decree a uniform or nearly uniform proportion of admissions to grammar schools of about 15% of all pupils, despite the fact that the proportion of the age-group who went to grammar schools at that time varied among the authorities from "under 10 percent to over 40 percent."[8] In the case of grammar schools, local authorities argued that their own traditions, experience and commitment to local people prevented their implementing the reorganisation in accordance with the government figure of 15 percent. Eccles' 1955 letter which said, "the pattern of education in this country is highly flexible . . . the percentage of pupils in grammar schools varies from one area to another,"[9] confirmed the role of local tradition and the obstacles to the imposition of a uniform structure by central government. The importance of self-reference and local tradition was also reflected in the attempt to implement central policy concerning the third leg of the tripartite system, the technical schools. Local types of industry, local demand for male labour, the circumstances of rural areas, local views on technical subjects as a means for enriching the curriculum of either grammar or modern schools, were all powerful factors in claims made by the LEAs that their perceptions of reality, local needs, traditions and practice, were in many cases opposed to the official policy and were the foundation for their proposal of alternative plans to those laid down by the Ministry of Education. Thus, a multiplicity of factors – the circumstances of rural areas, industrial or non-industrial cities and counties, the state of school buildings, attitudes towards selection, previous arrangements for selection, the status of modern schools, sixth forms in technical schools, previous allocations of pupils among the three types of school – were all powerful influences that played major and sometimes dominant roles in shaping the education structure, with corresponding neglect and rejection of the ministry's central policy and rigid instructions.

The second factor that undermined the 1944 order was the increased involvement of subsystems, either in the initial stage of preparation of the Development Plan or at the implementation stage, after the minister's approval had been given. With each additional subsystem involved, the implementation of the tripartite system advocated by government policy became more complicated. The involvement of divisional executives in order to protect local interests was enshrined in the 1944 Education Act in the form of joint education boards set up to protect the rights of the divisions vis-à-vis the interests of the local education authority. The Act required each

LEA to submit a Development Plan, taking into consideration community interests and the wide differences in their circumstances and requirements. In practice, LEAs did not use their power to impose a central LEA policy or to implement the tripartite policy as expected by the Ministry of Education. Huntingdonshire explained its approach thus: "every effort has been made to ensure by such consultation that the provision proposed . . . is soundly based on the needs of the districts, so that the Plan will need a minimum of adjustment."[10] London's view was that "it is impossible to generalise with accuracy about it as a whole";[11] therefore, it argued, it was in the interests of the city that each of the divisions should decide on the best shape for its secondary education. Thus, the involvement of divisions, the LEAs' tendency not to impose uniform order but give priority to the community's needs, traditions and practices, and the fragmentation of decision-making at the design stage of the Development Plan, together formed the initial stage in carrying education policy far away from the original intention of the planners of the Act and from the central tenets of government's planned secondary reform.

The LEAs and the Ministry of Education attempted to set the reorganisation in motion rapidly. However, when it came to implementation, the teachers, who did not have a significant role in decision-making, nevertheless had the power to resist, ignore and avoid the changes for many years. The reform was regarded by the teachers as a threat to every aspect of their status: salary, recognition, qualifications and prestige. The fact that the teachers as a group were not regarded as a significant party to the discussions, and were not consulted at the first stage, was among the reasons for their resistance, suspicion and alienation with respect to the LEAs' proposals. When teachers were eventually invited to take part in the discussion as partners, other factors that had not been taken into consideration at the initial stage delayed and paralysed execution of the reform. Amalgamation of schools and concern over the loss of posts, particularly those of heads and deputies, and of special benefits for those who taught in the sixth form, was one such factor. Another was the fact that local education authorities could not guarantee that each teacher would continue to teach the same type of pupils the same curriculum in the same school, thus making teachers fear losing what they knew best: their teaching expertise. This was another source of anxiety and consequently of resistance to change. The fight to defend the status and prestige, particularly of the grammar school teachers, as a result of the changes, and the general feeling of teachers that they were going to lose their school heritage and status, was another factor in the resistance to change and to further complication of the reform.

Similarly, although parents did not play a major part in consultation about the reform, they too had the power to ignore and resist any suggestion that in their view harmed their status and threatened to reduce their prestige. The 1944 Education Act required that pupils "be educated in accordance with the wishes of their parents."[12] This section gave parents of grammar school pupils the power to resist local plans not to send their children to a grammar school, while parents of modern school pupils wanted to get away from the low status of the modern school and to send their children to more prestigious facilities. Both groups of parents resisted and delayed local plans. The common feature of the two was not only the pursuit of status and esteem, but also their effect in disrupting and delaying LEAs' attempts to lead the reform.

Local politicians' support for or disregard of the secondary reform proposals proved to be a further factor that disrupted and confused LEA plans. The complexity of administrative and selection problems, the commitment to local interests irrespective of local or national party policy, and the attitudes and perceptions of individual local politicians, all contributed to the complexity of executing the secondary reform. From this point of view it may be concluded that each level of involvement in the attempt to implement the secondary reform increased the complexity of the process and exacerbated the deviation from the government's vision and intention.

The second factor has been characterised mainly in terms of a delaying mechanism, bringing increased disorder and complexity to the reform of secondary education; the third emphasises the dimensions and direction of the deviation and the emergence of a new order from apparent disorder. The government's change of the status of modern schools led to a major change in their output. When the modern schools became part of the pattern of secondary education, separate from the elementary schools out of which they had grown, corresponding expectations were raised far beyond the intentions of the planners of the 1944 Education Act. The tripartite system was based on a fundamental principle of selection for three different types of school, with a curriculum for the modern school that granted no certification. The idea of a secondary modern school with diffuse aims just for the "enjoyment of life," with no sense of purpose and excluding the majority of the nation's children from the pressures of any external examination, and therefore from any qualifications, had been revealed to be based on a false assumption.

The growing demand by modern schools for examination qualifications and an external certificate, encountered ministry resistance both to allowing pupils to take O level examinations at the existing standards and to introducing a new and separate inferior examination, and developed in two different directions. The first took the form of initiatives by LEAs to organise their own leaving certificate examinations,[13] and by head teachers entering their pupils for qualification certificates through private organisations.[14] Even when these initiatives were blocked by the government and LEAs were asked to forbid their teachers to run courses and make use of school facilities in ways that were incommensurate with the minister's policy, the modern schools' ambitions and search for significance in their studies did not abate. Teachers', pupils' and parents' desire for some kind of certificate led to other practical solutions: selected children were allowed to take a five-year course in the modern school; marginal pupils who attained the necessary standards were transferred to grammar schools; and entry to external examinations was opened up through the gradual establishment of comprehensive, multilateral and bilateral schools. The results achieved by modern school pupils in the external examinations gave rise to doubt about the validity of the ministry's policy and of the educational canon of the 1940s regarding the early prediction of individual achievement. Internal discussions conducted among officials within the Ministry of Education revealed factors other than those that corroborated the psychological assumption that academic ability could be predicted early and that selection should therefore take place at the age of 11. Ministry officials now faced real evidence to the contrary, not only from those such as Vernon, who claimed that children's abilities are more variable than was supposed, and that there are elements of self-determination, irregularities of development and virtues of persistence which cannot be predicted, but also from the conclusive figures of the increased numbers of modern school pupils who had done well in the external examinations. Ministry officials concluded that the new evidence revealed factors of ambition and self-confidence which explained how "Geese can never become swans but a surprising number of them can take the GCE."[15]

This fact, which struck at the heart of the previous educational orthodoxy and eroded officials' faith in the rationale of the tripartite system, generated a new and more flexible line of thought, with the ministry ceasing to insist on selection, rigid numbers of grammar-school places and approval of comprehensive schools only for "experimental purposes." From this point onwards the ministry ceased to erect administrative barriers and allowed more pupils access to external examinations by granting local authorities greater flexibility, freedom and discretion over the allocation of pupils to schools and therefore over the whole structure of secondary education. Thus, the determination and ambitions of head teachers, parents and pupils, their willingness to invest effort in order to achieve a desired result, was revealed not only as an influential factor which affected the structural order, but as a demonstration of the inferiority of the policy of selection, screening and exclusion *vis-à-vis* the powerful factor of individual determination. This factor gave rise to a significant educational principle: when administrative barriers were lifted, educational achievements were raised by a growing number of determined pupils who passed the external examinations.[16]

When other factors came to be included in submissions for ministerial approval for comprehensive schools, such as internal migration, increasing school population, financial difficulties in maintaining or in building three different types of school, these combined to reinforce the pressure from the modern schools. Now that the tripartite system had been recognised by ministry officials as an "unrealistic" and "utopian" policy, they were considered more openly within the ministry.

The main conclusion concerning the decentralisation process, the deviation from the initial order of the tripartite system and the swinging of the pendulum to a new position that differed from the one the government had attempted to impose from the mid-1940s to mid-1950s, is that it was not so much a failure of the tripartite system as a failure of a policy of exclusion. This is not to argue against the need for differences between schools or for different curricula; on the contrary, any attempt to abolish differences between schools in terms of scholastic attainment would fail, for the nature of the system, teachers' qualifications, parents' and pupils' motivation, determination and expectations, create these differences without any external intervention or administrative mechanism. But central administrative barriers blocking teachers' determination, students' ambitions and parents' expectations failed as a policy. Individual determination and expectations, whether of teachers or students, proved that such factors were more powerful in structuring and establishing an educational order than any central attempt to block such ambitions and motivations. So, the individual factors gathered momentum and were revealed as more dominant than any ministerial determination, however strong, or parliamentary legislation. Once a particular threshold of modern school pressure had been crossed, ministry policy was adjusted to accept reality rather than continue to impose the educational canon and policy of the 1940s. The policy of rigid classification and categorisation of pupils, the policy of excluding modern school pupils and privileging the minority of grammar school students collapsed once the basic individual need for success had been recognised.

10.3: RESTORING ORDER: CORRECTING THE SWING OF THE PENDULUM

When the policy of differentiating between schools through the central authority had failed, and structural changes had diminished the distinctions, another structure was devised in order to achieve the desired differentiation. The new policy was based on market principles and the assumption that less control in a system based on competition, choice, freedom of management and enterprise would achieve the differentiation that the highly controlled system of the 1940s and 1950s had failed to achieve. This was the policy that characterised the second period of centralisation dealt with in this study. The new policy involved a shift in the relative power of the main elements of the education system in the opposite direction to that of the 1944 Education Act, in order to create the desired structural transformation.

Two main factors influenced the formation of the new policy and the degree of government intervention in its implementation. The first was the vanishing of the traditional grammar school. The collapse of the tripartite system, the exposed weakness of predictive selection tests with respect to pupils' scholastic attainments and the subsequent departure from selection policy, all provoked a strong emotional reaction against the loss of symbols of excellence and the dissolution of the institutions for intellectual elites. Terms like "jewel in the crown," the loss of a "great cultural tradition," "subversion of intellectual elite" and "destruction of culture" exemplified the deep feeling of loss. This response to the loss of part of the English educational heritage was a strong stimulus for the elitist tradition in British culture, provoking and propelling a counter-process that called for a return to the "days of glory" and appealed to the memory of the old educational order in seeking to re-establish something of the brilliance of England's formerly prestigious education system. The abolition of streaming and the merging of bright pupils with the less able in mixed ability classes, which in practice entrenched the departure from selection policy not only between schools but within schools, strengthened the protests and the demands for government intervention over falling standards and for central steps to restore the high standards of the past. Despite the lack of conclusive evidence for falling standards, the gradual and steady contraction of the grammar schools (from 25% in 1950 to 4.9% in 1981) and the abolition of selection within schools shook the long tradition of freedom given to teachers over the curriculum, and was the initial stimulus for a flow of ideas on how to restore standards and what the structural implications of such restoration would be.

The second factor preparing the way for government intervention, which consequently affected the restructuring of the education system, was the emergence of neo-liberal and neo-conservative groups (the "New Right"). The groups had one shared aim – the wish to bring to an end the welfare state and the collective approach to social problems. The earlier optimism of the belief that government power and state responsibility for social security matters was the way to improve social welfare, and therefore the best way to pursue the public interest, gave way to a new pessimism arguing that such policies did more harm than good to the public interest, as demonstrated by unemployment, inflation, balance of trade figures, high taxation and the increased dominance of government bureaucracy. According to this view, greater freedom to market forces and competing agencies on the one hand,[17] in tandem with a strong state to control the market system on the other, could bring recovery to the British economy and remedy social weaknesses.[18]

On the macro level the "New Right" movement expressed disappointment with the failure of the collective approach to social problems and called for a radical change in the old economic policy and order. With respect to education, disappointment was expressed with the policy of educational expansion, which had been regarded in the 1950s and 1960s as an investment in human capital and therefore as a contribution to economic growth. The British economic decline in the 1970s did not bear out that assumption. Subsequently, the new ideas became the basis of fundamental changes in educational values, based on the encouragement of quality rather than quantity, which inevitably affected the structure of education. After the Conservative victory in the general election of 1979, new market ideas penetrated into the education system and were adopted to the full extent in the 1988 Education Reform Act.

The main assumption of the 1988 Education Reform Act was that restoration of the high standards of the grammar school era would be achieved by adopting the market principles of competition and choice. For this reason the government fostered an administrative approach directly in contrast with that of the 1944 Education Act, but which shared with it a common educational target: to create a hierarchy of differentiated schools. This aim would be achieved, in the government's view, by maximising freedom and flexibility over management matters. Such maximisation would entail: formulating the constitutional conditions according to which schools could raise private money (schools as entrepreneurial cost centres); fostering a "failure policy" – by displaying publicly schools' test results on the assumption that publication of such a "league table" would provide a challenge and an incentive for the "less good" schools in the ranking order; introducing an open enrolment system – assuming that some schools would be more effective and attractive, others less so (and more stigmatised than they were previously); establishing a new category of grant maintained schools embodying the idea that the splitting and shrinking of the LEA system would create choice for parents encouraging competition with LEA-maintained schools and more incentives for higher standards; and imposing a rigid

National Curriculum, initially geared particularly towards the more academic sort of pupil rather than the whole range of pupils.

The new structure aimed to address and correct the perceived failure of the 1944 Education Act to create a hierarchy of schools. The new machinery afforded freedom in some areas and increased centralisation in others, assuming that competition, choice and changes in the direction of an "enterprise culture" would propel schools' initiatives, and consequently structural changes that would result in the desired qualitative differentiation between schools. The highly interventionist policy of the 1940s, the inflexible and rigid instructions aimed at constraining structural elaboration, were replaced by full flexibility in order to allow market forces to create a new education structure. Choice, competition, grant maintained schools and open enrolment are all elements of a powerful machinery designed to bring about the desired hierarchy. Moreover, while the 1944 Education Act aimed to create a single administrative machinery, connecting the previously unconnected elements of the education system, abolishing competition and overlapping and creating a uniform tripartite system, the 1988 Education Act took the opposite direction. Now, market principles encourage the diminution of the single, clumsy organisational machinery, reducing the LEAs' power in favour of competition and choice at the price of the splitting and shrinking of the LEA system, and of encouraging single schools to become independent, separate from the LEA administration and outside the local authority's control.

In the 1940s, dissatisfaction and criticism on the part of parents was one of the main stimuli for the creation of a single administrative system in order to build a more coherent school system,[19] correct the inequality of resources, and achieve a uniform standard of educational service. The 1988 Education Reform Act, taking the opposite direction, created the conditions for abandoning the policy of encouraging parent and community responsibility for and participation in school life and school achievement. The outcome of encouraging the customers (parents) to choose the desired commodity (school), abandon the less highly regarded ones and express satisfaction or dissatisfaction by wielding customer power, created a "passive relation" between parents and schools, bringing the long tradition of "partnership" between schools and parents to an end. This ran counter to attempts made since the 1970s to effect greater parental involvement in school life. The shift in parents' position, from partners in responsibility to customers, could in some cases (i.e; in the less good schools) take the form of a shift towards the "customer behaviour" of expressing demands and dissatisfaction and leaving the school staff to run the school and undertake the complicated task of improving standards and school life alone, without parents as partners.

The extent to which market principles in education, fostered as a policy in the 1988 Education Reform Act and during the 1990s, have been allowed free play is limited. The trend towards a centralised academic curriculum and a national assessment system makes for a renewed focus on the more able pupils. Such a curriculum is a move towards the kind of differentiation that the government attempted to achieve in 1944 by devising the tripartite system and by controlling access to external examinations during the 1940s and 1950s. The straitjacket of the curriculum, and the limited choice offered to the full range of students, particularly at the secondary stage, has created a decentralised machinery that is fully controlled by the nature of the curriculum and by the limits on freedom of choice. In terms of the curriculum, the neo-conservative view, which opposed interference in the market but argued that the market system should be controlled by a strong state, has been fully reflected. A market system on the one hand, and central control over the curriculum on the other, is powerful machinery for controlling the direction and the development of the education structure. The academic nature of the curriculum left the less academic type of students with no real alternative qualification nor real possibility of bridging between academic and vocational studies. This could be regarded as a recreation of the tripartite system, although this time it was differently named – GCSEs A-Level; GNVQ; NVQ – as opposed to the old grammar; technical and modern schools. Inevitably, in combination with open enrolment and national assessment, this situation led to deepening differences between schools, increased inequality and deprivation of less able pupils and the fostering of a screening policy. Such a structure is similar in nature to the policy of exclusion followed in the 1940s and the 1950s, which privileged the grammar schools and deprived the modern schools. Thus the market idea ended up serving the old values of the 1940s, when the government aimed to devise a similar policy through different machinery.

Most of the structural principles that guided thinking in the 1940s were replaced by new principles aimed at achieving the same type of structural order that the 1944 Education Act and later government circulars failed to construct. "Independence," "unconnected," "isolated," "overlapping," "dissatisfaction," "lack of control" and "competition," terms that had been used to express government omissions during the first half of the twentieth century, became positive terms in constructing the new structural order of the 1980s and 1990s. Thus, the administrative pendulum moved, from the 1980s onwards, to the polar opposite of its position in the 1940s, in pursuit of the same educational and structural goals that had eluded the government forty years previously. The failure of strong central intervention to maintain a ranking order of schools within the tripartite system has been remedied by allowing a greater degree of freedom and enterprise towards creating a structure of the same type as was sought after in the 1940s. The 1944 Education Act, which aimed to connect the fragments of the system, was replaced once again by an "unconnected" and competitive system as of the late 1980s. The elements that were centralised in the 1940s (admission policy and administrative control through the LEAs) were decentralised in the 1980s, while those elements that were decentralised in the earlier period (curriculum and assessment) were later centralised. But when it became clear that grant maintained competition with other maintained schools created some sort of disorder, the former returned to the control of the LEAs and the pendulum corrected itself, beginning to swing the other way.

By generating both centralisation and decentralisation, and by limiting the scope of choice through government control over the curriculum, the government in the 1980s aimed to achieve the goal that the 1944 Education Act had failed to realise: differentiation between schools and a hierarchy of schools in terms of quality. The common ground for the forces of centralisation in the 1940s and in the 1980s was the view that high standards should be the crux of any structural transformation; whereas the 1944 Education Act aimed to achieve this target through tight control, the 1988 Education Reform Act gave scope to competitive elements in order to secure high standards. Both acts were directed at the same target but they employed opposite means to achieve it.

For additional explanatory insight into the whole process, theoretical perspectives can be usefully compared with the practical reality. The following discussion highlights the complexity of the structural transformation and the issues at stake.

10.4: BETWEEN THEORY AND PRACTICAL REALITY

The systems theories reviewed here emphasise two main propositions: (1) the permanent trend towards disorder and the mechanism that perpetuates that disorder; and (2) the correction mechanism towards order and renewed stability. These two propositions are the focus of the present analysis.

Two of the main instances of government intervention towards structural change in education, the 1944 Education Act and the 1988 Education Reform Act, both aimed to create a similar structural order. The first aimed to connect the education subsystems and to achieve control by means of a uniform and unified administrative structure that covered the entire education system, assuming that a highly interventionist policy and tight ministerial control would protect the prestigious grammar schools and the policy of screening and exclusion, and therefore secure high standards. The second aimed to correct the downward trend towards the loss of the traditional source of pride, the grammar schools, along market principles. By devising a market system, the government aimed to restore high standards, which were regarded as having faltered between the 1960s and the 1980s, re-establish hierarchical differentiation between schools and reconstruct some schools as symbols of excellence.

The correction process in the structural transformation confirms the existence of factors within the system working to maintain balance and stability and correct deviations and states of disorder. But what is the nature of this correction process? Is it a return to a "previous level," as in Kurt Lewin's view? Is it a "control mechanism," as Parsons holds? Is it to "damp smaller and medium fluctuations," as in the non-equilibrium paradigm of the Dissipative Structure view? The answer lies in analysis from the perspective of space and time. At the local level, when new plans were devised and change introduced into the local structure, "non-change" forces emerged that delayed or paralysed the decision-making process and therefore also structural change. Such delay apparently confirms Lewin's (1947) and

Parsons' (1962) views on quasi or moving equilibrium, which imply a "reversible" view of structural change and a more static model of system development.

But the same analysis of space and time with respect to the entire system produces a different finding. Over twenty to thirty years, the initial structure changed dramatically. The forces opposing deviation from the tripartite system of the 1940s and its philosophy as expressed in forms such as the Black Papers, the media campaign and the "New Right," resisted the changes of the 1960s and the 1970s, referring back to the "days of glory" of the grammar school era and the elitist tradition. The essential element of this resistance was a cultural trend to classify and categorise schools and their students. In this sense we might explain the emergence of such counter-forces in terms of forces aiming to maintain the metastable (fundamental) cultural state. This would actually confirm Prigogine's (1976) and Jantsch's (1980) arguments in favour of a system directed at maintaining a metastable state.[20] Thus, the late emergence of the counter-forces, in the 1970s, did not represent a call for returning to a "previous level." It was not a response to each particular development in each LEA, nor an attempt to reverse the schools' development or structural change (in schools), but an attempt to devise a machinery to maintain the traditional heritage of distinctions between schools. In this sense the correction process was not a move towards equilibrium but a process of preserving stability in a system characterised by non-equilibrium.

The contradictory interests and forces within a system form the essence of the interplay between the larger whole and its parts. Thus, the interests of LEAs, the divisions, the modern schools and the various forces that abused, neglected and distorted the 1944 order, faced counter-forces which tried to curb their attempt to depart from the government order of the 1940s. Prigogine's view that such an interplay takes the form of a continuous process between subsystems is supported by Buckley's "collective behaviour" approach, according to which from the system's view, elements containing both negative (stabilising or rigidifying) and positive (structure-elaboration, increasingly disorganising) features "help to create and recreate themselves in an ongoing development process."[21] Thus, the conjunction of the theories and the practical reality between the 1940s and the 1980s confirms the existence of an interplay between forces which act to preserve the old order and forces which act to depart from that order. Such theories posit a continuous process and a continuing interplay within the system; if this is so, can we observe a new dimension and development of the process, a departure from the 1988 Education Reform Act structure? Can we identify the emergence of new forces which move the pendulum towards another position on the axis of centralisation (as a rigid element) and decentralisation (as a disorganised element)?

The swing of the pendulum in two main respects reflects the emergence of new forces. The first occurred when the volume and the nature of the academic national curriculum was changed to a more flexible one with the attempt to establish a more flexible diploma, and to bridge between an academic sort of curriculum and vocational and training studies for the less able pupils (the NVQ and the GNVQ studies). Further change in the nature of the curriculum was carried out on a greater scale in 1998 when the government announced that pupils at age 11 would no linger be required to stick to a "detailed syllabus" in foundation subjects and greater discretionary power was granted to schools.

The second swing of the pendulum took place when grant maintained schools returned to the initial order and became part of the LEAs system and under their control.

These recent developments support the main arguments here, that the pendulum syndrome of centralisation and decentralisation is a continuous process of interplay between forces attempting to restore a rigid order and forces undermining such rigidity and tending towards increased particularisation.

The second proposition of systems theory is the permanent trend towards disorder and the mechanism that fosters disorder. The trend towards disorder in the case of England and Wales has widely been described as propelled by three main factors: first, the dominance of local tradition, local perceptions, local needs and local circumstances in shaping and elaborating the education structure, with a corresponding neglect and rejection of the central policy; second, the participation of several subsystems which increased the level of complexity with each additional level of involvement: thus, the divisions' discretion at the first stage and teachers' parents' and local politicians' involvement at the second contributed to a wide gap between the vision of the government and the practical reality; third, the ministry's confusion over the difficulties in implementing the educational principles of the 1940s based on the psychological assumption of early established differences between pupils, led to a more flexible policy. The confusion resulting from modern schools' achievements in external examinations, which was unexpected on the part of the government, opened the way for a departure from the rigidity of the 1944 education order.

Bertalanffy (1968) in *General Systems Theory* characterised an open system as one which increased involvement with the environment in order to increase stability and decrease disorder. Such involvement in our case, which was regarded as essential in the 1940s – by both the government, in the 1944 Education Act, and the LEAs, in giving discretionary power to divisions and by taking into consideration local circumstances – has been revealed as a source of stability at the local level but of instability and criticism at the national level. Implementation of the secondary reform in accordance with local needs and circumstances as a result of community involvement produced in the long run a complete departure from the initial structure devised by the 1940s government, which stimulated counter-forces. This type of development fits well with the Dissipative Structure Theory, which argues that with an increased level of involvement with the environment (in our case, with the several subsystems), the disorder level increases, forcing the system through instability to a new qualitative structure formation (see Appendix 6). Community involvement at different stages and in different subsystems, and the multiplicity of factors involved in the reform process, all contributed to the creation of a new structural system. The following figure represents this process:

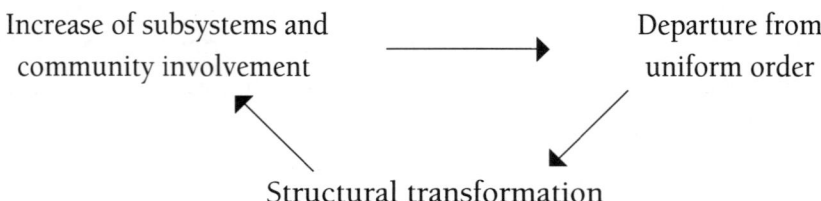

Figure 10.1: Structural transformation as a result of increasing community involvement.

Thus, each level of involvement in the process contributed new and unpredicted factors which forced deviation from the 1944 order, and eventually the emergence of a new structure different from that devised and planned by the government.[22]

The departure from the initial order and the permanent trend towards disorder which resulted in the evolution of a new structure raise the question: What were the human factors which affected such change? Two main types of theories – theories of *avoidance* of participation in activity on the one hand and theories of *seeking participation* and involvement on the other – deserve close analysis in the light of the actual reality of the structural changes.

After the 1944 Act, division executives, teachers, parents and local politicians all struggled keenly to protect their own interests, and this became a delaying mechanism against the execution of the secondary reform. Parents had some power to resist and ignore any attempt to compel them to send their children to an undesired school. The teachers regarded the changes as harmful to all aspects of their status and therefore resisted them. Even when a route for solving these problems was opened, once it became clear that the reform could not be implemented without teachers' commitment to the reorganisation, suspicions of and alienation from the reform remained strong. For local politicians, whenever the party interest of an elected member did not fit in with his or her own beliefs, perceptions or interests, the vote was given without any commitment to the local or national party.

Despite the limited power of teachers, parents and individual politicians, their conflicting interests, the attempts of each group to secure its own status and interests neutralised one another, causing confusion and paralysis.

Such factors of delay and resistance confirm the main elements in those theories which deal with the avoidance of participation in action. In Argyris' (1982) view mistrust, uncertainty, inter-group rivalry and parochial interests result from miscommunication and misinformation, elements which were the main ingredients in teachers' suspicion and alienation, when they were last to be informed of the changes. The fact that teachers as a group were disregarded as a significant party to the discussion and were not consulted was a cause of their resistance at the preliminary stage. In Meyer and Zucker's view (1989), those who seek change, despite having the formal authority, are confronted by those with interests that 'sometimes correspond but sometimes conflict'. Thus, parents, teachers and politicians were divided between supporters of change and opponents to change; this confirms Meyer and Zucker's view as well as Kurt Lewin's (1947) quasi-equilibrium model, which argues that the process of change involves groups which seek change and those which resist it, and leads to a return towards the previous level. In the case studies reviewed, any decision made raised resistance from a counter-group that regarded the decision as damaging their interests; consequently, the decision making process was paralysed.

But in reality, despite the *delaying mechanism* and factors causing paralysis of decision making, structural elaboration did progress; which raises the question: What were the forces that, despite the delaying mechanism, were powerful enough to effect structural change and bring about a new order? This brings us to the second group of motivation theories and to those elements of human behaviour which are conducive to participation in activity and which affect structural change.

The essence of the structural change of the 1950s and 1960s and the decentralisation process in these years was the internal efforts made by modern schools to *level up*: they showed unexpected motivation and determination to invest the effort required to prove their potential and capability for success in the external examinations. This motif, despite the policy of exclusion, and despite the accusation that their demands would lead to a *levelling down* of educational standards, has been amply demonstrated through different aspects of the discussion of the modern schools. The first type of evidence in support of the *levelling up* motif is the enormous pressure exerted by modern schools' head-teachers, parents, students and local authorities for access to external examinations and for some kind of public recognition through a formal attainment certificate. Teachers, parents and pupils wanted to jettison the low expectations, which were strongly linked to the schools' low status. Those who were predicted to be under-achievers demonstrated that when provided with a concrete, significant and rewarding purpose, they showed dedication and higher motivation in achieving the target: the certificate. The second aspect of the evidence was the ministry's deliberations on how to manage not only with the demand for access to external examinations, but with the real success of modern school pupils in those external examinations. The fact that over

Chapter 10 - Conclusions

1000 schools asking for suitable external examinations and 21,680 pupils entered for such examinations in 1960 was confirmation of the teachers' claim that the low expectations and diffuse definition of the modern school were wasting a tremendous amount of ability. The changing of attitudes within the ministry and the various expressions by ministry officials of the striking extent of the pupils' success, proved the strong impact of the modern schools' determination over decision making.

The range of ability that had been discovered among modern school pupils proved Vernon's argument against selection: that there are some unpredictable factors, such as self-determination and the irregularities of development of children, which cannot be predicted. Turning to the theoretical perspective, the case of the modern schools matched two main aspects of the theory. The first is the argument that the outcome of a change initiated at a high level in the hierarchy (in our case by the 1944 government), is a radical change of output (Watzlawick, 1974 – "a second order change"). When the modern schools became part of the secondary education system they were not included in the plan for access to external examinations, but teachers', parents' and students' expectations were raised and a corresponding pressure grew for meaningful certification and access to external examinations. Such changes confirm Knight's arguments (1967) that the outcome of organisational change is thousands of innovations which produced "dramatic improvements."

The local authorities' and head-teachers' initiatives, either to introduce an LEA leaving certificate or to make use of private organisations in seeking a formal certificate, confirm the theoretical arguments that even a tiny change in the input can produce a major change in the output. The modern school development also confirms Handy's (1988) model, which claims that the individual calculates how much effort he must expend in order to achieve a desired result, and McGregor's view (1985) that an individual commits himself to objectives in order to gain a reward, in the modern school case, the certificate.

In an attempt to summarise the "pendulum syndrome" and the continuous process of the interplay of spontaneous factors to undermine any given order, and counter-forces to restore order, the following paradigm might be useful.

Simplification of the interplay between the centre and the periphery:

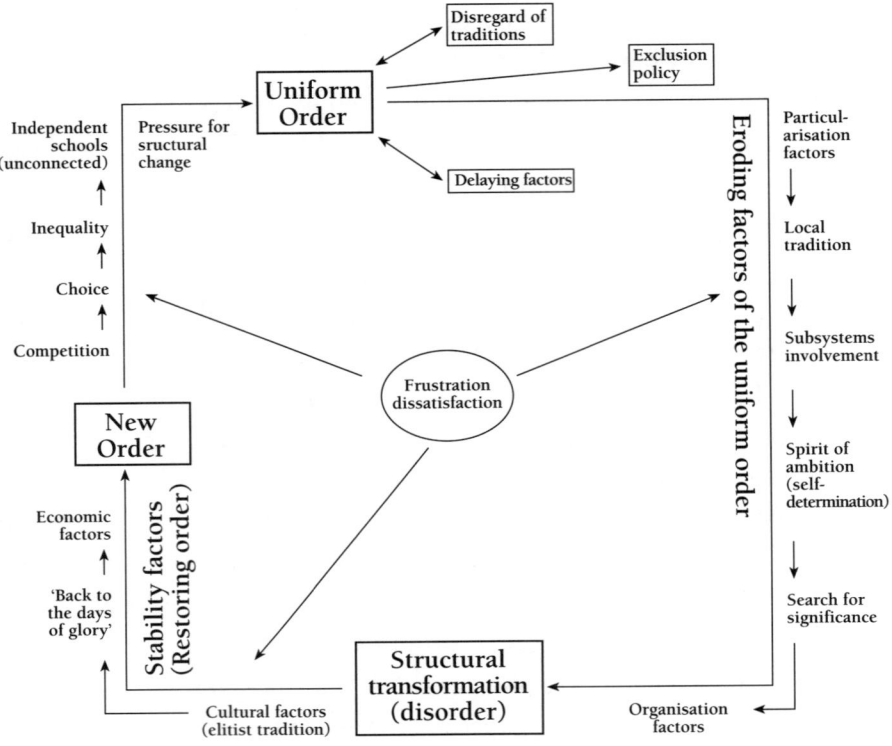

Figure 10.2: Simplification of the interplay between the centre and the periphery

The paradigm throws light on the main argument of the research, namely the existence of interplay between government intervention (centralisation) on the one hand, and spontaneous factors involved in the process on the other, undermining the central structure in order to meet different needs. The uniform order of the 1940s, led by the philosophy of the tripartite system, comprised two elements which relied on one another: a uniform policy of exclusion and, therefore, disregard of local tradition. This policy was designed by connecting the isolated, overlapping and competitive elements of the system, to reduce inequality and move towards a uniform order. Restrictions on LEAs' freedom raised spontaneous and multiple factors which abused, neglected, distorted and blurred the uniform order. Such factors were characterised by: a move towards a growing particularisation of local interests, implementing the secondary reform on the basis of local needs, local circumstances and local tradition; increased involvement of subsystems which increased complexity; levelling up elements as a result of self-determination and searching for significant certification by modern schools' teachers and students; organisational factors such as internal migration and increasing school populations; increased central flexibility after the ministry had recognised the falsity of the 1940s principles. All these led to structural transformation. The new structure, characterised by diminished distinctions between schools, stimulated forces aiming to restore the elitist tradition, calling for a return to the "good old days" and the high standards of the grammar school era. The economic decline of the 1970s accelerated the devising of a new order as a mechanism to achieve high standards and a hierarchy of schools, by fostering administrative conditions which have some similarities with the pre-1940s period based on competition, choice and inequality of school resources, aimed at creating hierachy and distinctions between schools.

Matching the theory with the practical reality leads our discussion to the conclusion that each of the theories concerning the interplay between the centre and the periphery contributed in some part to understanding the reality. Buckley, indeed, provides the stimulus for the paradigm (see Appendix 1), in particular the concept of the continuous and dynamic nature of the system. There is strong evidence for the theoretical claim that much of the structural change occurred as a result of internal or intrinsic development in the periphery and not as a result of a centrally planned vision. Moreover, major developments which became national policy were a result of local initiatives and local organisation. Such developments include the "agreed syllabus" which was first used by over 100 local education authorities before being adopted at the national level; the local management of schools (LMS); modern school entry for external examinations, which brought about a more flexible policy; and the development of the comprehensive schools. All these developments support the contention that many of the major developments and structural changes were self-conducted and self-organised up to the point that they were recognised and actually adopted as a national policy. This confirms the Dissipative Structure view that structural transformation is a result of forcing a system over the threshold of small changes to a formation of a new structure and a new order.

The powerful factors at the local level which affected structural change raise some practical and theoretical questions. On the practical level, evidence of the strong internal and intrinsic factors at school and local level which affected structural change prompts the question of the locus of decision making. Which sort of decisions should be made at the centre and which at the periphery? Which sort of decisions might be more effective made centrally, and which sort might be subverted? Furthermore, the conclusion respecting the eroding effect of subsystems' involvement in undermining central policy strengthens these questions and raises some others. Could this *eroding effect* be minimised by "closing" the system to external effect? Could direct links between schools and the government, which would exclude some subsystems' involvement, therefore minimise such effects? Is it desirable to isolate schools from environmental and community influences? Is it a real policy option in democratic states and democratic cultures? In many respects these questions are practical as well as philosophical.

Some recent publications consider these questions. Caldwell (1988; 1998; 2003), Cheng (1996; 2003), Sungaila (1990) and Williams (1998; 2003) call for a new science of leadership in education and management of schools as a direct result of the research findings on the self-renewing and self-conducting element in organisations (the intrinsic elements which dominate structural elaboration). The research findings on the nature of "effective schools" support the line of giving much discretionary power to schools over various aspects of school life and school goals (see Chapter 9). Numerous publications of the last decade on the development of the private sector support the move towards diminishing the central power and increasing the freedom of subsystems and subordinate elements, as a direct result of difficulties caused by the weakness of decision making originating in the centre and being undermined and subverted by a multiplicity of factors in the environment (see Chapter 8).

At the theoretical level, the next cycle of structural change and the continuing process of the interplay between the periphery and the centre stimulate certain other types of research questions. Thus, in the English case, the introduction of the 1988 Education Reform Act machinery, with competition between schools as the crux of the government's policy, raises questions related to the *eroding elements* which might emerge as an outcome of this educational strategy. The differentiation between schools' resources, as a result either of open enrolment or of schools as *entrepreneurial cost centres*, and therefore towards greater inequality, the stigmatisation of students, parents, teachers and schools by the assessment policy – all these factors have a strong theoretical basis in the argument for the continuity of the interplay between the centre and the periphery. In Prigogine's words, "we can no longer speak of the end of history, only of the end of stories."[23]

Notes:
1. The periods covered by the 1944 Education Act and the 1988 Education Reform Act.
2. House of Commons: (1895). *Secondary Education, Report of the Commission on Secondary Education*. (Vol.XLIII) 9.
3. Hansard: (1917). Vol.XCVII, 1917, 800.
4. R.A. Butler (1971). *The Art of the Possible*. London: Hamish Hamilton, 92.
5. As a result of the existence of separate types of local education authorities for elementary and higher (secondary) education.
6. PRO ed. 152/47: Gloucestershire.
7. PRO ed. 152/130: Oxfordshire.
8. PRO ed. 147/206: Secondary Education.
9. PRO ed. 147/205: Secondary Education, as well as other documents which prove this argument.
10. PRO ed. 152/61: Huntingdonshire. DP, 2.
11. PRO ed. 152/107: London. DP.
12. Education Act 1944, Section 76.
13. For example, South-West Hertfordshire, Manchester, Sheffield.
14. Such as the School Commercial Certificate, Pitman, RSA examinations, College of Preceptors School Certificate Examination.
15. PRO ed. 147/206, Secondary Education.
16. A similar development was mentioned in the Bryce Report (1895) which argued that the influential factor for the rise of secondary education was recurrent expectation and pressure within the elementary schools to improve the range and the quality of instruction.
17. The neo-liberal view.
18. The neo-conservative view.
19. Particularly because of the poor state of the church schools.
20. Actually the system is not in an non-equilibrium state.
21. Walter Buckley (1967). *Sociology and Modern Systems Theory*. New Jersey: Prentice Hall, 137.
22. Concerning this aspect, the 1988 Education Reform Act created some conditions which reduced the potential of multilevel involvement by creating the GM school and a direct link between school and government without LEAs involvement, and some conditions which increased the level of community involvement (the LMS mechanism) aimed to create different qualities of schools in terms of financial resources.
23. Quoted by Jantsch (1980), 255.

• BIBLIOGRAPHY

Adler, Michael et al. (1989). *Parental Choice and Educational Policy*. Edinburgh: EUP.

Allison, Lincoln (1984). *Right Principles*. Oxford: Blackwell.

Archer, Margaret S. (1979). *Social Origins of Educational Systems*. London: Sage.

────────────── (1984). *Social Origins of Educational Systems*. London: Sage, 2nd ed.

Argyris, Chris (1982). *Reasoning, Learning, and Action – Individual and Organisational*. London: Jossey-Bass.

Auld, Robin (1976). *The William Tyndale Junior and Infant Schools: Report of the Public Inquiry. A Report to the Inner London Education Authority*. London: Inner London Education Authority.

'B' (1969). "Decline and Fall of the University Idea." In C.B. Cox & R. Boyson (eds.), *Black Paper: Fight for Education*. London: Critical Quarterly Society.

Bacon, William (1978). *Public Accountability and the Schooling System*. London: Harper.

Ball, Stephen J. (ed.) (1984). *Comprehensive Schooling: A Reader*. London: Falmer.

────────────── (1984). "Comprehensive in Crisis?" In Stephen J. Ball (ed.), *Comprehensive Schooling: A Reader*. London: Falmer.

Bashi, Joseph et al. (1990). *Effective Schools: From Theory to Practice*. Jerusalem: Van Leer.

Batley, Richard et al. (1970). *Going Comprehensive*. London: Routledge & Kegan Paul.

Beare, Hedley et al. (1989). *Creating an Excellent School*. London: Routledge.

Becher, Tony & Maclure, Stuart (eds.) (1978). *Accountability in Education*. Windsor: NFER.

Bell, Moberly E. (1958). *A History of the Church Schools Company 1883-1958*. London: SPCK.

Bendix, Reinhard (1960). *Max Weber*. London: Heinemann.

Berlak, Harold (2000). "Cultural Politics, the Science of Assessment and Democratic Renewal of Public Education." In Ann Filer (ed.), *Assessment, Social Practice and Social Product*. London: Routledge.

Bernstein, Basil (1961). "Social Structure, Language and Learning." *Educational Research*, 3(3), June.

Bertalanffy, L. Von (1968). *General Systems Theory*. New York: Braziller.

Black, Paul J. (1993). "The Shifting Scenery of the National Curriculum." In Clyde Chitty & Brian Simon (eds.), *Education Answers Back: Critical Responses to Government Policy*. Lawrence: London.

Blaug, Mark (1976). "The Empirical Status of Human Capital Theory." *Journal of Economic Literature*, XIV(3), September.

———————— (1987). "Education Vouchers – It All Depends on What You Mean." In Mark Blaug, *The Economics of Education and the Education of an Economist*. London: Edward Elgar.

———————— (1987). "Where Are We Now in the Economics of Education?" In Mark Blaug, *The Economics of Education and the Education of an Economist*. London: Edward Elgar.

Board of Education (1924). *Report of the Consultative Committee on Psychological Tests of Educable Capacity and their Possible Use in the Public System of Education*. London.

———————— (1926). *The Education of the Adolescent*. Consultative Report. London: HMSO.

———————— (1941). *Education After the War*.

———————— (1943) *Educational Reconstruction*.

Bradley, Ian (1985). *The Strange Rebirth of Liberal Britain*. London: Chatto & Windus.

Brennan, E.J.T. (1975). *Education for National Efficiency: The Contribution of Sidney and Beatrice Webb*. London: Athlone.

Brighouse, Harry (2000). *School Choice and Social Justice*. Oxford: OUP.

Broadfoot, Patricia (1984). "From Public Examinations to Profile Assessment: The French Experience." In Patricia Broadfoot (ed.), *Selection, Certification and Control*. London: Falmer.

———————— (1985). "Towards Conformity: Educational Control and the Growth of Corporate Management in England and France." In Jon Lauglo & Martin McLean (eds.), *The Control of Education*. London: Heinemann.

———————— (1988). "Research and Policy-making in Assessment: Some Unanswered Questions." In H.D. Black & W.B. Dockrell (eds.), *New Developments in Educational Assessment*. British Journal of Educational Psychology Monograph Series No.3. Edinburgh: Scottish Academic Press.

———————— (1996). *Education, Assessment and Society*. Open University Press: Buckingham.

———————— (2001). "Empowerment or Performativity? Assessment Policy in the Late Twentieth Century." In Robert Phillips and John Furling (eds.), *Education, Reform and the State – Twenty-five years of Politics, Policy and Practice*. Routledge: London.

Broadfoot, Patricia and Pollard, Andrew (2000). "The Changing Discourse of Assessment Policy: The Case of English Primary Education." In Ann Filer (ed.), *Assessment: Social Practice and Social Product*. Routledge: London.

Brooksbank, Kenneth & Ackstine, Eric (eds.) (1984). *Educational Administration*. Harlow: Councils and Education.

Brown, R.J. (1978). "Systems Analysis and Decision-making in the Local Government of Further Education." *Educational Administration*, 6(2).

Buckley, Walter (1967). *Sociology and Modern Systems Theory*. New Jersey: Prentice Hall.

Bullock, A. & Thomas, H. (1994). *The Impact of Local Management on Schools*. Birmingham: National Association of Head Teachers and the University of Birmingham.

Bullock, A. and Thomas, H. (1997). *Schools at the Center*. London: Routledge.

Butler, R.A. (1971). *The Art of the Possible*. London: Hamish Hamilton.

—————————— (1982). *The Art of Memory*. London: Hodder & Stoughton.

Caldwell, Brian J. & Spinks, J.M. (1988). *The Self-Managing Schools*. London: Falmer.

—————————— (1998). *Beyond the Self-Managing School (Student Outcomes and the Reform of Education)*. London: Falmer.

Caldwell, Brian J. (2003). "A Theory of Learning in the Self-Managing School." In A. Volansky and I. Friedman (eds.), *School Based Management – An International Perspective*. Jerusalem: Ministry of Education.

Callaghan, James (1976). "Toward a National Debate." *Education*, 22.10.1976.

Centre for Contemporary Cultural Studies (1981). *Unpopular Education*. London: Hutchinson.

Cheng, Yin Cheong (2003). "School Effectiveness: An International Persepctive." In Ami Volansky and Isaac A. Friedman (eds.), *School Based Management – An International Perspective*. Jerusalem: Ministry of Education.

Chitty, Clyde (1989). *Towards a New Education System: The Victory of the New Right?* London: Falmer.

—————————— (1999). *The Education System Transformed*. Great Yarmouth: Baseline.

City Technology Colleges Trust (1987). *The City Technology Colleges: Curriculum Objectives: Formulation and Implementation*. Unpublished document.

Civil Service Management Reform (1988). *The Next Steps*. London: HMSO.

Clark, Colin (1981). "The IEA and Fabians: Comparison and Contrast." In Arthur Seldon (ed.), *The Emerging Consensus*. London: IEA.

Coleman, James et al.(1966). *Equality of Educational Opportunity*. Washington: Government Printing Office.

Committee on Higher Education (1963). *Higher Education Report*. London: HMSO.

Coulby, D. (1990). "The Construction and Implementation of the Primary Core Curriculum." In D. Coulby & S. Ward (eds.), *The Primary Core National Curriculum*. London: Cassell.

Coulby, D. & Ward, S. (eds.) (1990). *The Primary Core National Curriculum*. London: Cassell.

Covell, Charles (1986). *The Redefinition of Conservatism*. London: Macmillan.

Cox, C.B. & Boyson, R.(eds.) (1969). *Black Paper: Fight for Education*. London: Critical Quarterly Society.

Cox, C.B. & Boyson, R.(eds.) (1977). *Black Paper 1977*. London: Temple Smith.

Craft, Maurice et al. (eds.) (1967). *Linking Home and School*. London: Longman.

Cruickshank, Marjorie (1963). *Church and State in English Education: 1870 to the Present Time*. London: Macmillan.

Cullingford, Cedric (1997). "Conclusion: The Personal Effects of Assessment." In Cedric Cullingford (ed.), *Assessment Versus Evaluation*, Cassel: London.

Cuttance, Peter (1985). "Framework for Research on the Effectiveness of Schooling." In D. Reynolds, (ed.), *Studying School Effectiveness*. London: Falmer.

Dale, Roger et al. (1990). *The TVEI Story: Policy, Practice and Preparation for the Work Force*. Milton Keynes: Open University Press.

Dalin, P. & Rust, V.D. (1996). *Towards Schooling for the Twenty-first Century*. London: Cassell.

David, Miriam E. (1977). *Reform, Reaction and Resources: The 3 Rs of Educational Planning*. Windsor: NFER.

David, J.L. (1982). *School-Based Strategies: Implications for Government Policy*. Palo Alto: Bay Area Research Group.

Davies, Andrew (1998). *The Limits of Educational Assessment*. Blackwell: Oxford.

Davies, R. Peter (1975). *Mixed Ability Grouping*. London: Temple Smith.

Dearing, Ron (1996). *Review of Qualifications for 16-19 Year Olds*. London: SCAA.

Dent, H.C. (1947). *The Education Act*. London: University of London Press.

————— (1949). *Secondary Education for All*. London: Routledge & Kegan Paul.

Dennison, W.F. (1983). *Doing Better for Fewer: Education and Falling Rolls*. London: Longman.

————— (1985)." Education and the Economy: Changing Circumstances." In I. McNay et al. (eds.), *Policy-Making in Education: The Breakdown of Consensus*. Oxford: Pergamon.

Department of Education and Science: Circular 10/65.

————— : Circular 10/66.

————— : Circular 10/70.

————— : Circular No. 7/88.

————— : Circular No. 10/88.

————— (1966). *Education* in 1966.

————— (1966). *Trends in Education*.

————— (1974). *Educational Disadvantage and the Educational Needs of Immigrants*. London: HMSO.

————— (1975). *A Language for Life*. Report of the Committee of Inquiry (the Bullock Report). London: HMSO.

——————— (1977). *Curriculum 11-16*. London: HMSO.

——————— (1977). *A New Partnership for Our Schools*. London: HMSO.

——————— (1978). *Mixed Ability Work in Comprehensive Schools*. London: HMSO.

——————— (1985). *Better Schools*. London: HMSO.

——————— : *Education Statistics. 1965-88*.

——————— (1986). *Report of Her Majesty's Inspectors on the Effects of Local Authority Expenditure Policies on Education Provision in England – 1985*. London: DES.

——————— (1987). *National Curriculum: Task Group on Assessment and Testing – A Report*.

——————— (1987). *The National Curriculum 5-16*.

——————— (1988). *Statistics of Education: School Leavers' GCSE and GCE*.

——————— : (1988). *The Education Reform Act 1988: The School Curriculum and Assessment*, Circular No. 5/89.

——————— (1989). *Science Policy: The Way Ahead*. Speech by Kenneth Baker, MP, London.

——————— (1989). *English for Ages 5 to 16*.

Dimmock, C. (ed.) (1993). School-based Management and School Effectiveness. London: Routledge.

DfEE, School Statistics for the UK. E-mail to the DOES at the University of Oxford, 15.10.2002

DfEE (1992). *Choice and Diversity – A New Framework for Schools*, p. iii.

DfEE (1996). *Self-Government for Schools*, II.

DfEE (1997). *Excellence in Schools*, 25.

Dockrell, W.B. (1988). "The Impact of Scottish National Surveys of Achievement on Policy and Practice." In H.D. Black & W.B. Dockrell (eds.), *New Developments In Educational Assessment. British Journal of Educational Psychology*, Monograph Series No. 3. Edinburgh: Scottish Academic Press.

Drucker, Peter (1977). *People and Performance: The Best of Peter Drucker on Management*. London: Heinemann.

Eatwell, Roger & O'Sullivan, Noel (1989). *The Nature of the Right: European and American Politics and Political Thought Since 1789*. London: Pinter.

Education Act 1944, London: HMSO.

Education Act 1980, London: HMSO.

Education Reform Act 1988, London: HMSO.

Education in 1949: *Report of The Ministry of Education and the Statistics of Public Education for England and Wales*. London.

Education in 1957: *Report of the Ministry of Education and the Statistics of Public Education for England and Wales*. London: HMSO.

Education in 1958: *Report of the Ministry of Education and the Statistics of Public Education for England and Wales*. London: HMSO.

Fenwick, I.G.K. (1967). *Organised Opinion and the Comprehensive School, 1944-64: A Study of Some Educational Groups and the Policy-making Process for Education in England*. Unpublished thesis. University of Manchester.

—————————— (1976). *The Comprehensive School 1944-1970: The Politics of Secondary School Reorganisation*. London: Methuen.

Filer, Ann (2000). "Assessment as Loved Experience Beyond the Classroom." In Ann Filer (ed.), *Assessment, Social Practice and Social Product*. London: Routledge.

Filer, Ann and Torrance, Andrew (2000). "Assessment and Parents' Strategic Action." In Ann Filer (ed.), *Assessment, Social Practice and Social Product*. London: Routledge.

Finegold, David & Soskice, David (1990). "The Failure of Training in Britain: Analysis and Prescription." In D. Gleeson (ed.), *Training and its Alternatives*. Milton Keynes: Open University Press.

Finn, Chester E. Jr. & Rebarber, Theodor (1992). "The Changing Politics of Education Reform." In Chester E. Finn & Theodor Rebarber (eds.), *Education Reform in the 1990s*. New York: Macmillan.

Floud, J.E. et al. (1953). "Education Opportunity and Social Selection in England." In *Transactions of Second World Conference of Sociology*, Vol.II.

—————————— (1956). *Social Class and Educational Opportunity*. London: Heinemann.

Flude, Michael & Hammer, Merril (1990). "Opting for an Uncertain Future: Grant-Maintained Schools." In M. Flude & M. Hammer (eds.), *The Education Reform Act 1988*. London: Falmer.

Fogarty, Michael (1961). "Social Welfare." In Arthur Seldon (ed.), *Agenda for A Free Society: Essays on Hayek's The Constitution of Liberty*. London: IEA.

Friedman, Milton (1962). *Capitalism and Freedom*. Chicago: University of Chicago Press.

Gamble, Andrew (1985) *Britain in Decline*. London: Macmillan.

—————————— (1988). *The Free Economy and the Strong State*. London: Macmillan Education.

Geiger, Theodore (1978). *Welfare and Efficiency*. London: Macmillan.

Gillborn, David & Youdell, Deborah (2000). *Rationing Education – Policy, Practice, Reform and Equity*. Buckingham: Open University.

Gleeson, Denis (ed.) (1987). *TVEI and Secondary Education: A Critical Appraisal*. Milton Keynes: Open University Press.

Gleeson, Denis (ed.) (1990). *Training and its Alternatives*. Milton Keynes: Open University Press.

Gleick, James (1988). *Chaos*. London: Cardinal.

Golby, Michael et al. (1989). *Parents As School Governors*. Tiverton: Fair Way Publications.

Goodlad, John I. (1984). *A Place Called School*. New York: McGraw-Hill.

Gosden, P.H.J.H. & Sharp P.R. (1978). *The Development of an Education Service: The West Riding 1889-1974*. Oxford: Martin Robertson.

Griggs, Clive (1989). "The New Right and English Secondary Education." In: Roy Lowe (ed.), *The Changing Secondary School*. London: Falmer.

Halsall, Elizabeth (ed.) (1970). *Becoming Comprehensive: Case Histories*. Oxford: Pergamon.

Halsey, A. H. et al. (1980). *Origins of Destinations*. Oxford: Clarendon.

Hamilton, Oliver (1986). *Your School Fund*. London: NEPO.

Handy, Charles B. (1988). *Understanding Organisations*. London: Penguin.

Hansard: Hansard's Parliamentary Debates, Third Series, Vol. CXCIX, 17 February 1870.

────────────── : Vol. CV, 24 March 1902.

────────────── : Vol. XCVII, 1917.

────────────── : Vol. 396, 8 February 1944.

────────────── : Vol. 396, 9 February 1944.

────────────── : Vol. 702, 27 November 1964.

────────────── : Vol. 31, 12 November 1982.

────────────── : Vol. 62, 22 June 1984.

────────────── : Vol. 123, 1 December 1987.

Harris, Ralph & Seldon, Arthur (1977). *Not from Benevolence: 20 Years of Economic Dissent*. London: IEA.

Havilland, Julian (1988). *Take Care, Mr. Baker*. London: Fourth Estate.

Hayek, F.A. (1960). *The Constitution of Liberty*. London: Routledge & Kegan Paul.

Hee-Chun, Kang (1982). *Education Policy and the Concept of Equality of Opportunity in England*. Unpublished thesis.

Hewitson, J.N. (1969). *The Grammar School Tradition in a Comprehensive World*. London: Routledge.

HM Treasury (1989). *The Financing and Accountability of Next Steps Agencies*. London: HMSO.

Hopkins, David (1985). *School Based Review for School Improvement*. Leuven: Acre.

────────────── (1987). "Implications for School Improvement at the Local Level." In D. Hopkins (ed.), *Improving the Quality of Schooling*. London: Falmer.

Hough, G.R. (1987). *Education and the National Economy*. London: Croom Helm.

House of Commons: *Estimates and Accounts*, Vol. XLII, 1834.

———————— : *Schools of Design, Accounts and Papers*, Vol.XXIX, 1840.

———————— : *Bills*, Vol.II, 1840.

———————— : *Accounts and Papers*, Vol.XX, 1841.

———————— : *Bills*, Vol.II, 1844.

———————— : *First Report of the Department of Science and Art*, Reports of the Commissioners, Vol. XXVIII, 1854.

———————— : *Schools Inquiry Commission on Technical Education*, Reports of the Commissioners, Vol.XXVI, 1867.

———————— : *Bills*, Vol.I, 1870.

———————— : *Bills: Elementary Education* (Continuation Schools) Vol.I, 1888.

———————— : *A Bill to Provide Technical Education in England and Wales*, 1889.

———————— : *Secondary Education, Report of the Commission on Secondary Education*, Vol.XLIII, 1895.

———————— : *Education Bill*, Vol.I, 1902.

———————— (1988). "Treasury and Civil Service Committee: Eighth Report." *Civil Service Management Reform: The Next Steps*. Vol.2. London: HMSO.

Howard, Anthony (1986). *RAB – The Life of R.A. Butler*. London: Jonathan Cape.

ILEA (1976). *Mixed-Ability Grouping*. Report of an ILEA Inspectorate Survey. London.

Jantsch, Erich (1980). *The Self-Organising Universe*. Oxford: Pergamon.

Jencks, Christopher et al. (1973). *Inequality: A Reassessment of the Effect of Family and Schooling in America*. London: Allen Lane.

Jennings, Robert (1977) *Education and Politics: Policy-making in Local Education Authorities*. London: Batsford.

Kelly, A.V. (1978). *Mixed-Ability Grouping: Theory and Practice*. London: Harper & Row.

———————— (1975). *Case Studies in Mixed Ability Teaching*. London: Harper & Row.

Kelsall, R.K. (1975). *Population*. London: Longman.

Kenway, Jane (ed.) (1995). *Marketing Education: Some Critical Issues*. Deakin University Press.

Kesternard, Isaac-Henry (1970). *The Politics of Comprehensive Education in Birmingham 1957-67*. Unpublished thesis: University of Birmingham.

King, Edmund J. (1966). *Education and Social Change*. Oxford: Pergamon.

———————— (1968). *Comparative Studies and Educational Decision*. London: Methuen.

Kirp, David (1982). *Just Schools*. Berkeley: University of California Press.

Kirst, Michael W. (2003). "School-Based Management: The United States's Experience." In A. Volansky and I. Friedman (eds.), *School-Based Management – An International Perspective*. Jerusalem: Ministry of Education.

Knight, Kenneth E.(1967). "A Descriptive Model of the Intrafirm Innovation Process." *Journal of Business*, Vol.40.

Kogan, Maurice (1978). *The Politics of Educational Change*. Manchester: Manchester University Press.

Lacelle-Peterson Mark (2000). "Choosing Not to Know: How Assessment Policies and Practices Obscure the Education of Language Minority Students." In Ann Filer (ed.), *Assessment: Social Practice and Social Product*. Routledge: London.

Lamont, Norman (1990). *Making Government Services: The Taxpayer and the Customer*. Unpublished document.

Langerman, Shoshana & Bar Siman-Tov, Ronit (1989). *Additional Studies Programme Financed by Parents in Primary School*. Jerusalem: Szold Institute (Hebrew).

Lauglo, Jon & McLean, Martin (eds.) (1985). *The Control of Education*. London: Heinemann.

Lawton, Denis (1980). *The Politics of the School Curriculum*. London: Routledge & Kegan Paul.

────────── (ed.) (1989). *The Education Reform Act: Choice and Control*. London: Hodder & Stoughton.

Leonard, Martin (1988). *The 1988 Education Act*. Oxford: Blackwell.

Levačić, Rosalind (1995). *Local Management of Schools: Analysis and Practice*. Buckingham: Open University Press.

────────── (1998). *Journal of Educational Policy*, 13(3), 331-350.

Lewin, Kurt (1947). "Frontiers in Group Dynamics." *Human Relations*, Vol.1.

Liell, Peter & Saunders, John B. (eds.) (1989). *The Law of Education*. London: Butterworth.

Lord, Rodney (1984). *Value for Money in Education*. London: Public Money.

Lowe, Roy (ed.) (1987). *The Changing Primary School*. London: Falmer.

Lowe, Roy (1988). *Education in the Post-War Years: A Social History*. London: Routledge.

Lowe, Roy (ed.) (1989). *The Changing Secondary School*. London: Falmer.

Lynn, Richard (1969). *Comprehensives and Equality: The Quest for the Unattainable, Black Paper Two*. London: Critical Quarterly Society.

Maclure, Stuart J. (1986). *Educational Documents*. London: Methuen.

────────── (1989). "Parents and Schools – Opting In and Opting Out." In Denis Lawton (ed.), *The Education Reform Act: Choice and Control*. London: Hodder & Stoughton.

────────── (1989). *Education Reform Act*. London: Hodder & Stoughton.

Macrae, S., Maguire, M. and Ball, S.J. (1997). "Competition, 'Choice' and Hierarchy in a Post-16 Education and Training Market." In Tomlinson, S. (ed.), *Education 14-19: Critical Perspectives*, London: Athlone.

Maslow, Abraham H. (1987). *Motivation and Personality*. New York: Harper.

Maychell, K. (1994). *Counting the Cost: The Impact of LMS on Schools' Patterns of Spending*. Slough: NFER.

Maynard, Alan (1975). *Experiment with Choice in Education*. London: IEA.

Mays, John Barron (1967). *The School in its Social Setting*. London: Longman.

McCulloch, Gray (1989). *The Secondary Technical School: A Usable Past?* London: Falmer.

McGinn, Noel & Street, Susan (1986). "Educational Decentralisation: Weak State or Strong State?" *Comparative Education Review*, 30(4).

McGregor, Douglas (1985). *The Human Side of Enterprise*. New York: McGraw-Hill.

Meyer, Marshall W. & Zucker, Lynne G.(1989). *Permanently Failing Organisations*. London: Sage.

Ministry of Education: Circular 5, 1944.

———————————— : *Draft Building Regulations*, Circular 10, 1944.

———————————— : Circular 73, 1945.

———————————— (1945). *The Nation's Schools: Their Plan and Purpose*. Pamphlet No.1, London.

———————————— (1946). *Report of the Committee on School Sites and Building Procedures*. London.

———————————— : Circular 144, 1947.

———————————— (1949). *Education Statistics in 1949*. London.

———————————— : Circular 289, 1955.

———————————— : *Statistics of Education*. London, 1955-64.

———————————— (1959). *15 to 18. A Report of the Central Advisory Council for Education* (England). London: HMSO. ("Crowther Report").

———————————— (1963). *Half Our Future. A Report of the Central Advisory Council for Education* (England). London: HMSO. ("Newsom Report").

———————————— (1963). *Report of the Committee on Higher Education appointed by the Prime Minister* ("Robbins Report").

Ministry of Education and Culture (Israel) (1977). *The General Director's Circular, A.* (Hebrew).

———————————— (1988). *Facts and Figures on the Education and Culture System in Israel*. Jerusalem.

———————————— (1991). *The General Director's Circular, I*. (Hebrew).

Murphy Patricia (ed.) (1999). *Learners, Learning & Assessment*. Open University: London.

Musgrove, Frank (1987). "The Black Paper Movement." In Roy Lowe (ed.), *The Changing Primary School*. London: Falmer.

NCC (National Curriculum Council) (1990). *Education for Industrial Understanding*, No. 4. York: NCC.

Newbold, David (1977). *Ability Grouping: The Banbury Enquiry*. Windsor: NFER.

NUT (National Union of Teachers) (1987). *National Curriculum and National Testing*, London: NUT.

Nuttall, Desmond (1989). "National Assessment: Complacency or Misinterpretation?" In Denis Lawton, (ed.), *The Education Reform Act: Choice and Control*. London: Hodder & Stoughton.

OECD (Organisation for Economic Co-operation and Development) (1989). *Decentralisation and School Improvement: New Perspectives and Conditions for Change*. Paris: OECD.

ORT (Organisation for Rehabilitation Through Training) (1988).*The ORT Curriculum and Recommendations for the City Technology Colleges*. London: ORT.

Olson, Mancur (1989). "How Ideas Affect Societies: Is Britain the Wave of the Future?" In *Ideas, Interests and Consequences*. London: IEA.

Owen, Joslyn (1978). "A New Partnership for Our Schools: The Taylor Report." *Oxford Review of Education*, 4(1).

Parkinson, M.H. (1973). *Politics of Urban Education*. University of Liverpool.

Parkinson, Michael (1970). *The Labour Party and the Organisation of Secondary Education 1918-65*. London: Routledge & Kegan Paul.

Parsons, Talcott (1977). *Social System and Evolution of Action Theory*. New York: Macmillan.

Parsons, Talcott & Shils, Edward A. (eds.) (1962). *Towards a General Theory of Action*. New York: Harper.

Pedley, F.H. (ed.) (1967). *Education and Social Work*. Oxford: Pergamon.

Pedley, R.R. (1969a). *Comprehensive Disaster*. Black Paper.

Peters, Thomas & Waterman, Robert (1982). *In Search of Excellence*. New York: Harper & Row.

Philip, James H. (1980).*The Reorganisation of Secondary Education*. Windsor: NFER.

Phillips, Robert and Furlong, John (eds.) (2001). *Education, Reform and the State – Twenty Years of Politics, Policy and Practice*. London: Routledge.

Pidgeon, Douglas A. (1970). *Expectation and Pupil Performance*, London: NFER.

Pollard, Arthur (1969). *O and A Level: Keeping Up the Standards, Black Paper Two*, London: Critical Quarterly Society.

Power, Colin (1984). "National Assessment: A Review of Programs in Australia, the United

Kingdom, and the United States." *Comparative Education Review*, 28(3).

Prigogine, Ilya (1976). "Order through Fluctuation: Self-Organisation and Social System." In Erich Jantsch & Conrad Waddington (eds.), *Evolution and Consciousness: Human Systems in Transition*. London: Addison-Wesley.

Pring, Richard (1986). "Privatisation of Education." In Rick Rogers (ed.), *Education and Social Class*. London: Falmer.

——————— (1987). "Privatisation in Education." *Education Policy*, 2(4).

Pryor, John and Torrance, Harry (2000). "Questioning the Three Bears: The Social Construction of Classroom Assessment." In Ann Filer (ed.), *Assessment: Social Practice and Social Product*. Routledge: London.

Pugh, Patricia (1984). *Educate, Agitate, Organise: 100 years of Fabian Socialism*. London: Methuen.

QCA (1999). *Wider Opportunities for Work Related Learning at Key Stage 4*, 1.

Raab, Gillian & Adler, Michael (1988). "A Tale of Two Cities: the Impact of Parental Choice on Admissions to Primary Schools in Edinburgh and Dundee." In L. Bondi & M.H. Matthews (eds.), *Education and Society: Studies in the Politics, Sociology and Geography of Education*. London: Routledge.

Ranson, Stewart (1984). "Towards a Tertiary Tripartism: New Codes of Social Control and the 17+." In Patricia Broadfoot (ed.), *Selection, Certification and Control*. London: Falmer.

Ranson, Stewart et al. (1985). *Between Centre and Locality*. London: George Allen & Unwin.

Ranson, Stewart & Tomlinson, John (eds.). *The Changing Government of Education*. London: Allen & Unwin.

Reid, M. et al. (1981). *Mixed Ability Teaching*. Windsor: NFER-Nelson.

Report of the Commissioners (1861). *The State of Popular Education in England*. Vol.I.

Reports from Commissioners, Inspectors, and Others. (1885). *Secondary Education*. Report of the Commissioners on Secondary Education. Vol.I.

Report of the Consultative Committee of the Board of Education (1926). *The Education of the Adolescent*. (The Hadow Report).

Report of the Consultative Committee of the Board of Education on Secondary Education with special reference to Grammar Schools and Technical High Schools (The Spens Report), 1938.

Report of the Committee of the Secondary Schools Examination Council on Curriculum and Examinations in Secondary Schools (The Norwood Report), 1943.

Reynolds, David (ed.) (1985). *Studying School Effectiveness*. London: Falmer.

Reynolds, David & Sullivan, Michael (1987). *The Comprehensive Experiment*. London: Falmer.

Ribbins, P.M. & Brown, R.J. (1979). "Policy Making in English Local Government: The

Case of Secondary School Reorganisation. In *Public Administration*, Vol.57.

Ribbins, Peter (1985). "Comprehensive Secondary Reorganisation: A Case of Local Authority Policy-making?" In M. Hughes et al. (eds.), *Managing Education: The System and the Institution*. London: Holt.

Rosenthal, Robert & Jacobson, Lenore (1968). *Pygmalion in the Classroom*. New York: Holt.

Rubinstein, David & Simon, Brian (1969). *The Evolution of the Comprehensive School, 1926-1966*. London: Routledge & Kegan Paul.

────────── (1973). *The Evolution of the Comprehensive School, 1926-1927, 2*. London: Routledge & Kegan Paul.

Rutter, M. et al. (1979). *Fifteen Thousand Hours*. London: Open Books.

Saran, Rene (1973). *Policy-Making in Secondary Education: A Case Study*. Oxford: Clarendon.

Schiff, Martin (1976). "The Educational Failure of Community Control on Inner-City New York." *Phi Delta Kappa*, February.

Schultz, Theodore W. (1963). *The Economic Value of Education*. New York: Columbia University Press.

Schumacher, E.F. (1973). *Small is Beautiful*, London: Blond Briggs.

Scruton, Roger (ed.) (1988). *Conservative Thinkers: Essays from the Salisbury Review*. London: Claridge.

Secondary Heads Association (1979). *Big and Beautiful*. Brackley: SHA.

Seldon, Arthur (ed.) (1961). *Agenda for a Free Society: Essays on Hayek's The Constitution of Liberty*. London: IEA.

────────── (1986). *The Riddle of Voucher: An Inquiry Into the Obstacles to Introducing Choice and Competition in State Schools*. London: Holbert.

Senker, Peter (1990). "TVEI: Evaluation, Economic Policy and Ideology." In D. Hopkins (ed.), *TVEI at the Change of Life*. Clevedon: Multilingual Matters.

Slavin, Robert E. (1999). "The Pendulum Revisited: Faddism in Education and its Alternatives." In Gregory J. Cizek (ed.), *Handbook of Educational Policy* (Educational Psychology Series). New York: Academic Press.

Sparrow, John (1969). "Egalitarianism and an Academic Elite." In *Black Paper: Fight for Education*. London: Critical Quarterly.

Srivastva, Suresh & Barrett, Frank J. (1988). "Foundations for Executive Integrity: Dialogue, Diversity, Development." In S. Srivastva, *Executive Integrity*. London: Jossey Bass.

Stanton, Geoff (1997). "Patterns in Development." In Sally Tomlinson (ed.), *Education 14-19: Critical Perspectives*. London: Athlone.

Start, K.B. & Wells, B.K. (1972). *The Trend of Reading Standards*. Windsor: NFER.

Stiglitz, Joseph E. (1975). "The Theory of "Screening," Education, and the Distribution of Income." *The American Economic Review*, 65(3).

In Sungaila, Helen (1990). "The New Science of Chaos: Making a New Science of Leadership?" In *Journal of Educational Administration*, 28(2).

Swanson, Austin D. (1988). *The Bureaucratisation of Education: A Comparative Perspective*. Unpublished document. Buffalo: State University of New York.

Swedish National Board of Education. (1989). *Effects of Decentralisation in the School Sector*. Lund: University of Lund.

Tawney, H.R. (1964). *Equality*. London: George Allen.

Thompson, Joan (1947). *Secondary Education for All*. London: Fabian Publications.

Tomlinson, John (1988). "Curriculum and Market: Are they Compatible?" In J. Havilland (ed.), *Take Care, Mr. Baker*. London: Fourth Estate.

Tomlinson, Sally (ed.) (1997). *Education 14-19: Critical Perspectives*. London: Athlone.

TVEI Review, 1984.

Tymms, Peter and Fitz-Gibbon Carol (2001). "Standards, Achievement and Educational Performance: A Cause for Celebration?" In Robert Phillips and John Furling (eds.), *Education, Reform and the State – Twenty-five years of Politics, Policy and Practice*. London: Routledge.

Vernon, P.E. (1956). *The Measurement of Abilities*. London: University of London Press.

———————— (1957). *Secondary School Selection*. London: Methuen.

———————— (1979). *Intelligence: Heredity and Environment*. San Francisco: Freeman.

Volansky, A. (1995). *Trends and Reforms of the U.S. Education System, 1983-1995*. Jerusalem: Ministry of Education and Culture, (Hebrew).

Volansky, A. and Friedman I. (2003). *School Based Management – An International Perspective*. Jerusalem: Ministry of Education.

Walford, Geoffrey (1990). *Privatisation and Privilege in Education*. London: Routledge.

Walford, Geoffrey (1994). *Choice and Equity in Education*. London: Cassel.

Walford, Geoffrey (2002). "Redefining School Effectiveness." In *Westminister Studies in Education*, 25 (1).

Walsh, William (1969). "Dialogue and the Idea." In *Black Paper: Fight for Education*. London: Critical Quarterly Society.

Watts, A.E. et al. (1952). *Secondary School Entrance Examinations*. Publication No.6. Windsor: NFER.

Watzlawick, Paul et al. (1974). *Change*. New York: Norton.

Wells, M.M. & Taylor, P.S. (1949). *The New Law of Education*. London: Butterworths.

Whitty, Geoff, Power, Sally and Halpin, David (1998). *Devolution & Choice in Education – The School, the State and the Market*. Buckingham: Open University.

Williams, Vivian (1988). *Education Reform Act [ERA] 1988*. Unpublished document.

———————— (ed.) (1995). *Towards Self-Managing Schools*. London: Cassell.

――――――― (ed.) (1998). *Conceptual and Practical Issues in School Leadership – Insights and Innovations from the U.S. and Abroad.* San Francisco: Jossey-Bass.

――――――― (2003). "Innovative Concepts For Effective School Cultures: Earned Leadership and Elective Contributorship." In Ami Volansky and Isaac Friedman (eds.), *School Based Management – An International Perspective.* Jerusalem: Ministry of Education.

Woodhall, Maureen (1972). *Economic Aspects of Education.* Windsor: NFER.

Woodings, Val (1997). "How Primary Schools Deal with Assessment in the National Curriculum." In Cedric Cullingford (ed.), *Assessment Versus Evaluation.* London: Cassell.

Woods, Philip A., Bagley, Carl and Glatter, Ron (1998). *School Choice and Competition: Markets in the Public Interest?* London: Routledge.

Woodward, R.J. (1970). "Sir William Romney's School, Tetbury, Gloucestershire." In Elizabeth Halsall (ed.), *Becoming Comprehensive: Case Histories.* Oxford: Pergamon.

Wright, Nigel (1977). *Progress in Education.* London: Croom Helm.

Yates, Alfred & Pidgeon, D.A. (1957). *Admission to Grammar Schools.* London: Newnes.

Young, A.G. (1975). "Northcliffe Community High School." In A.V. Kelly (ed.), *Case Studies in Mixed-Ability Teaching.* London: Harper & Row.

Public Record Office Papers:

PRO ed. 136/224: Discussion and correspondence with Association of Governing Bodies of Public Headmasters Conference and Joint Committee of the Four Secondary Associations.

PRO ed. 136/228: Discussion and correspondence on the Archbishop's Five Points and the Dual System.

PRO ed. 136/229: Discussions with the Archbishop of Canterbury and National Society.

PRO ed. 136/235: Discussions with the National Union of Teachers.

PRO ed. 136/354: Revision of the existing system of local educational administration. Consideration of Sir William Jowitt's report.

PRO ed. 136/358: Official Committee on Post-war Economic Problems. Board's reply to questionnaire on post-war local government.

PRO ed. 136/377: Miscellaneous correspondence. President's minutes to Prime Minister reporting progress.

PRO ed. 136/382: Preparation of a note on educational reform for Lord President's Committee.

PRO ed. 136/889: Letter from Treasury with note sent to Chancellor of Exchequer on lowering of school leaving age to 14 on a voluntary basis.

PRO ed. 136/890: Estimates 1954/1955: Chancellor of the Exchequer's letter of 7 October 1953.

PRO ed. 136/891: Economy cuts in educational programme from October 1949.

PRO ed. 147/205: Selection arrangements.

PRO ed. 147/206: Secondary education.

PRO ed. 147/207: Secondary technical schools.

PRO ed. 147/303: Examinations in secondary schools other than the GCE.

PRO ed. 152/1: Bedfordshire.

PRO ed. 152/4: Berkshire.

PRO ed. 152/7: Buckinghamshire.

PRO ed. 152/8: Buckinghamshire.

PRO ed. 152/10: Cambridgeshire.

PRO ed. 152/13: Cheshire.

PRO ed. 152/21: Cumberland.

PRO ed. 152/24: Derbyshire.

PRO ed. 152/28: Devon.

PRO ed. 152/36: Durham.

PRO ed. 152/45: Essex.

PRO ed. 152/47: Gloucestershire.

PRO ed. 152/50: Hampshire.

PRO ed. 152/53: Hertfordshire.

PRO ed. 152/60: Huntingdonshire.

PRO ed. 152/61: Huntingdonshire.

PRO ed. 152/64: Isle of Ely.

PRO ed. 152/74: Kent.

PRO ed. 152/91: Leicestershire.

PRO ed. 152/102: Lincolnshire: Lindsey.

PRO ed. 152/105: London.

PRO ed. 152/107: London.

PRO ed. 152/110: Middlesex.

PRO ed. 152/119: Northamptonshire.

PRO ed. 152/121: Northamptonshire.

PRO ed. 152/130: Oxfordshire.

PRO ed. 152/147: Staffordshire.

PRO ed. 152/173: Westmorland.

Pro ed. 152/204: Barnsley.

PRO ed. 152/205: Barnsley.

PRO ed. 152/207: Barrow-in-Furness.

PRO ed. 152/208: Barrow-in-Furness.

PRO ed. 152/213: Birkenhead.

PRO ed. 152/216: Birmingham.

PRO ed. 152/223: Blackburn.

PRO ed. 152/229: Bolton.

PRO ed. 152/235: Bradford.

PRO ed. 152/238: Brighton.

PRO ed. 152/239: Brighton.

Pro ed. 152/245: Burnley.

Pro ed. 152/246: Burnley.

PRO ed. 152/260: Coventry.

PRO ed. 152/325: Liverpool.

PRO ed. 152/327: Liverpool.

PRO ed. 152/328: Manchester.

Newspapers and Journals

Daily Mail

Daily Telegraph

Education

New Statesman

Spectator

The Economist

The Observer

The Times Educational Supplement

The Times

Appendix

APPENDIX 1

Simplified Systemic View of the "Collective Behaviour" Approach to a Theory of Institutionalisation

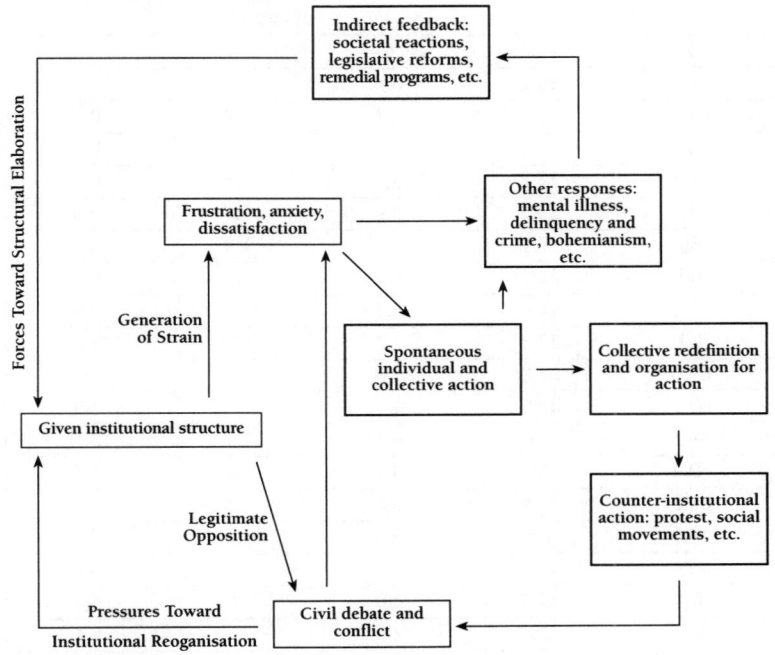

Source: Buckley, 1967, p.138.

APPENDIX 2

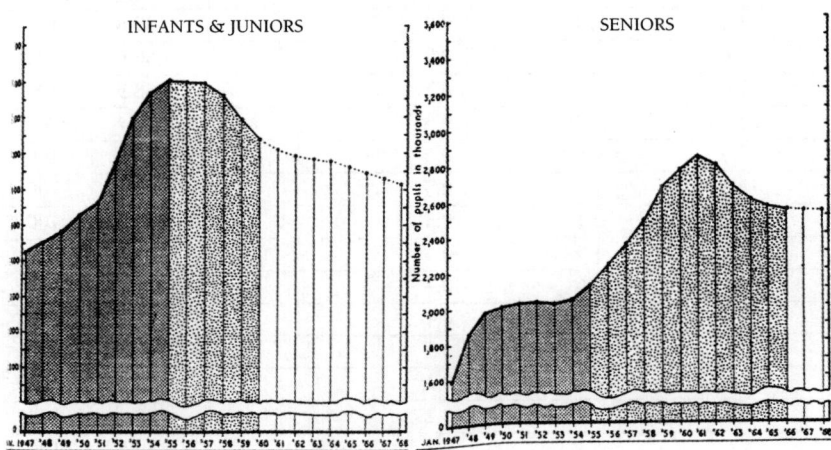

Source: Education in 1955, London (HMSO), July 1956.

359

APPENDIX 3

Secondary School Distribution: 1948-1988 (in %)

Year	Modern	Grammar	Technical	Bilateral + Comprehensive	Comprehensive	Total
1948	66.6	26.3	6	-	-	99.8
1949	67.1	26.2	6.6	-	-	99.9
1950	67.7	25	6.3	0.7	0.2	99.9
1951	68.1	24.6	6.1	1	0.3	100
1953	68.8	23.8	5.9	1.3	0.2	100
1954	68.9	23.4	5.9	1.6	0.3	100
1955	69	22.9	5.9	1.9	0.3	100
1956	69	22.7	5.7	2	0.6	100
1957	69.1	22.4	5.4	2.3	0.8	100
1958	69	23.3	5.2	1	1.6	100
1959	69.3	22.8	4.8	1.1	2	100
1960	69.2	22.9	4.5	1	2.3	100
1961	69.3	23	4.1	1.1	2.5	100
1962	69.4	22.9	3.9	1.1	2.7	100
1963	69.2	22.9	3.6	1.2	3.1	100
1964	69.1	2.3	3.3	1.2	3.4	100
1965	68.4	23.6	3.2	-	4.8	100
1966	66	23.3	2.8	-	7.1	100
1967	65	23	2.6	-	9.4	100
1968	61.3	22.1	2.3	-	14.3	100
1969	57.7	21.	2.1	-	18.8	100
1970	54.3	20.9	1.7	-	23.1	100
1971	52.6	19.9	1.4	-	28.2	100
1972	46.6	18.8	1.9	-	33.4	100
1973	41.5	17.8	0.9	-	39.8	100
1974	33.6	15	0.8	-	50.6	100
1975	27.6	12.8	0.7	-	58.9	100
1976	22.9	10.9	0.5	-	65.7	100
1977	19.3	9.4	0.5	-	70.9	100
1978	15.4	7.5	0.5	-	76.8	100
1979	12.9	6.1	0.5	-	80.5	100
1981	9.3	4.9	0.4	-	85.4	100
1982	8.8	4.6	0.4	-	86.2	100
1983	8.2	4.4	0.4	-	87.1	100
1984	7.2	4.5	0.1	-	88.2	100
1985	7.1	4.3	0.2	-	87.2	100
1986	6.4	4.1	0.2	-	89.4	100
1987	6.2	4.1	0.2	-	89.6	100
1988	5.9	4.1	0.2	-	89.7	100

Source: Statistics of Education 1948-1988.

APPENDIX 4

Esimation of the Cost to the Taxpayer of Private Education

	£ m
Assisted places	15
Government personnel	70
Direct grant	10
LEA purchase of places	30
Youth training	25
Charity status	50
	£ 200m

Source: Richard Pring (1986). "Privatisation of Education." In Roger Rick (ed.), *Education and Social Class*. London: Falmer, 81.

APPENDIX 5

Sequence of Pupils' Achievement of Levels Between Ages 7 and 16

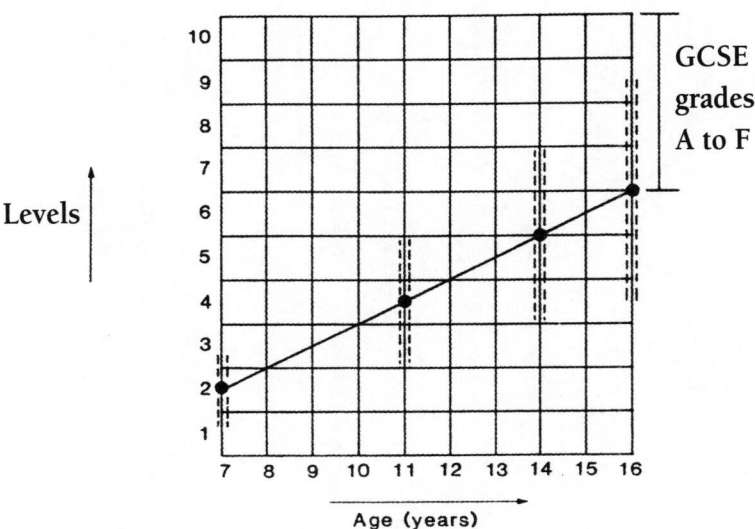

Source: Department of Education and Science (1987). *Task Group on Assessment and Testing*, section 104.

APPENDIX 6

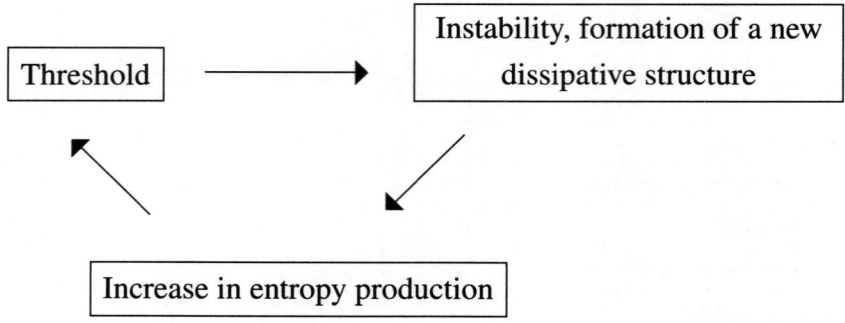

Source: Jantsch, 1980, p.43.

INDEX

A
abused 31, 187, 330, 336
accountability 15, 185, 240, 254, 271, 284, 288, 290, 291, 292, 293, 304, 309, 341, 347
accountable 46, 254, 291, 292
accounting 254
advanced level 153, 227, 228, 306
agreed syllabus 55, 64, 66, 67, 80, 82, 337
ambition 34, 121, 162, 171, 185, 186, 187, 280, 281, 322
Anglican and Free Church 58
Anglican church 53, 58, 61, 83
Archbishop of Canterbury 58, 62, 65, 80, 82, 355
assessment 7, 11, 14, 15, 16, 18, 22, 25, 29, 32, 172, 173, 194, 211, 213, 214, 251, 253, 256, 257, 261, 268, 269, 270, 271, 272, 273, 275, 276, 277, 278, 279, 280, 281, 282, 294, 299, 301, 302, 305, 307, 308, 327, 328, 339, 341, 342, 344, 345, 346, 349, 351, 352, 355, 360
attainment targets 251, 253, 256, 257, 258, 261, 267, 268, 269, 270, 301, 305
attendance rates 50
Australia 18, 27, 32, 271, 273, 299, 307, 351
autonomy 18, 20, 21, 24, 66, 91, 99, 215, 240, 241, 244, 249, 267, 284, 291, 295

B
Barrow-in-furness 103, 124, 166, 170, 190, 357
Better Schools 235, 254, 274, 300, 304, 308, 345
bilateral schools 99, 100, 110, 112, 113, 114, 115, 117, 161, 189, 191, 284, 321
Birkenhead 96, 102, 124, 130, 141, 147, 357
Birkenhead's 115
Birmingham 113, 126, 131, 132, 138, 147, 170, 175, 343, 348, 357
Black papers 6, 193, 196, 202, 205, 206, 207, 208, 210, 211, 218, 219, 256, 330
Blackpool 98, 165
Board of education 32, 33, 38, 46, 47, 49, 51, 55, 57, 58, 61, 62, 63, 68, 71, 72, 74, 75, 82, 84, 85, 123, 190, 309, 314, 342, 352, 354
Bolton's 97
Brighton 111, 115, 125, 126, 357
Britain 38, 44, 45, 204, 229, 232, 233, 236, 237, 247, 254, 261, 262, 305, 342, 346, 351
British disease 232, 303
Bryce report 46, 315, 340
Buckinghamshire 165, 356
bureaucratic control 16, 58, 63

C
Cambridgeshire 55, 80, 82, 240, 356
centralisation 1, 7, 8, 9, 13, 14, 15, 16, 18, 19, 20, 21, 23, 27, 28, 29, 30, 31, 52, 196, 216, 221, 229, 233, 234, 235, 243, 244, 270, 289, 303, 313, 323, 326, 328, 331, 336
central control 8, 16, 17, 21, 22, 26, 91, 94, 213, 253, 257, 272, 316, 327
Charles panel 158, 159
Cheshire 103, 113, 117, 124, 165, 170, 188, 189, 242, 356

child-centred 201, 209, 218, 260
choice 7, 9, 61, 71, 76, 79, 80, 85, 108, 112, 129, 130, 132, 138, 144, 164, 173, 174, 194, 204, 205, 209, 225, 229, 230, 234, 235, 236, 237, 238, 248, 251, 267, 273, 282, 283, 284, 285, 286, 287, 288, 289, 293, 294, 298, 300, 301, 302, 305, 307, 309, 323, 325, 326, 327, 328, 337, 341, 342, 345, 349, 350, 351, 352, 353, 354, 355
Christian education 58
Church organisations 37
Church schools 36, 41, 47, 48, 52, 53, 60, 61, 64, 79, 82, 83, 315, 340, 341
Church system 41
competition 9, 43, 44, 46, 51, 72, 194, 204, 205, 229, 230, 234, 235, 237, 238, 240, 241, 261, 264, 272, 288, 289, 290, 293, 300, 302, 307, 309, 315, 323, 325, 326, 328, 337, 338, 350, 353, 355
comprehensive schools 6, 85, 88, 96, 101, 108, 113, 126, 128, 129, 130, 132, 134, 135, 136, 137, 138, 140, 141, 142, 144, 147, 148, 156, 161, 175, 176, 177, 178, 179, 181, 182, 189, 191, 193, 195, 196, 197, 202, 205, 207, 208, 213, 216, 217, 218, 220, 240, 242, 243, 249, 260, 263, 280, 282, 284, 286, 322, 337, 345, 346, 353
compulsory school age 71, 90, 91
compulsory school attendance 40, 50
conservative 25, 43, 60, 140, 141, 142, 155, 176, 177, 178, 191, 204, 207, 210, 216, 223, 233, 234, 235, 237, 238, 241, 243, 248, 262, 297, 316, 324, 325, 327, 340, 353
Conservative Party 43, 60, 141, 142, 176, 178, 237, 238
cost centres 194, 222, 240, 241, 242, 244, 249, 295, 325, 339
counter-forces 8, 9, 21, 28, 317, 330, 332, 335
Coventry 101, 113, 124, 175, 357
creativity 97, 195, 218, 241, 263
criterion referenced 268
Crowther report 163, 168, 224, 225, 350
CTCs 11, 251, 258, 262, 263, 264, 293, 306
Cumberland 101, 111, 115, 124, 166, 190, 356
curriculum 6, 7, 11, 14, 15, 16, 17, 18, 23, 24, 27, 41, 44, 50, 51, 52, 58, 70, 77, 83, 92, 109, 110, 113, 123, 130, 134, 153, 156, 163, 167, 170, 185, 186, 188, 194, 195, 196, 198, 199, 201, 209, 210, 211, 212, 213, 214, 215, 216, 220, 243, 245, 249, 251, 254, 255, 256, 257, 258, 259, 260, 261, 262, 263, 264, 265, 266, 267, 268, 269, 271, 276, 272, 284, 285, 289, 293, 294, 298, 299, 301, 302, 304, 305, 306, 307, 308, 318, 319, 321, 324, 326, 327, 328, 331, 341, 343, 345, 349, 351, 352, 354, 355
curriculum guidelines 41, 52

D
Darlington 137, 140, 141, 147
decentralisation 1, 7, 8, 9, 13, 14, 15, 16, 17, 18, 19, 20, 21, 22, 23, 27, 28, 29, 30, 31, 32, 33, 52, 221, 229, 230, 234, 235, 240, 243, 244, 267, 289, 298, 300, 301, 303, 313, 317, 322, 328, 331, 334, 350, 351, 354
decision-making 13, 14, 20, 29, 85, 205, 240, 256, 267, 290, 319, 329, 338, 342
delaying mechanism 320, 333, 334
delegation of power 194, 251, 290, 295, 301
denominational schools 47, 48, 55
Department of Education and Science 11, 38, 191, 217, 218, 220, 239, 243, 248, 249, 304, 305, 307, 310, 344, 360
Derbyshire 111, 119, 125, 356
Derbyshire's 105, 111, 113
DES 11, 30, 183, 206, 213, 214, 215, 240, 249, 254, 255, 256, 260, 262, 263, 264, 306, 307, 345
desegregation 288
determination 8, 88, 100, 131, 171, 184, 185, 186, 187, 259, 321, 322, 323, 334, 335, 337

devolution 13, 19, 52, 76, 78, 238, 239, 244, 354
devolving 240
Devon 105, 125, 356
DfEE 345, 11, 30, 255, 276, 283, 297, 298, 308, 309, 310, 311
discovery learning 195
disequilibrium 20, 21
disorder 121, 146, 209, 233, 245, 269, 313, 315, 320, 328, 329, 331, 332, 333
disorganisation 28
disorganising 330
disrupted 140, 143, 183, 320
Dissipative Structure Paradigm 23, 24
Dissipative Structure Theory 33, 146, 245, 332
districts 15, 37, 40, 53, 54, 94, 101, 105, 108, 319
diversity 33, 50, 70, 76, 107, 238, 242, 243, 244, 253, 255, 283, 284, 285, 286, 287, 289, 293, 300, 301, 309, 345, 353
dullest child 162, 185

E
Education Act 1870 – 1889
Education act 1870 39, 40, 41, 42, 46, 77, 84
Education act 1888 45
Education act 1889 45
Education act 1899 46, 53
Education act 1902 48, 58, 72, 77, 82
Education act 1918 43, 49, 50, 77
Education act 1921 68
Education act 1944, 104, 124, 285, 340, 345
Education act 1944 36, 41, 51, 76, 77, 78, 79, 96, 103, 116, 118, 316, 333
Education act 1944 5, 8, 30, 31, 52, 57, 77, 85, 87, 89, 92, 95, 96, 121, 124, 133, 143, 152, 163, 164, 167, 169, 170, 178, 183, 187, 203, 221, 222, 286, 293, 317, 318, 320, 321, 323, 325, 326, 328, 329, 332, 340
Education act 1988 31, 194, 215, 245, 251, 256, 262, 265, 268, 283, 289, 296, 298, 299, 302, 303, 309, 325, 326, 327, 328, 329, 331, 338, 340, 349
education for all 8, 31, 36, 49, 50, 51, 52, 57, 68, 71, 72, 73, 77, 100, 107, 125, 151, 178, 179, 182, 245, 314, 344, 354
Education of the poor 38, 53
educational inequalities 302
effective schools 33, 252, 299, 338, 304, 341
Effectiveness 19, 171, 239, 241, 253, 304, 308, 343, 344, 345, 352, 354
egalitarian 156, 158, 185, 198, 202, 203, 206, 208, 215, 229, 237, 289
Egalitarianism 18, 219, 353
elementary education for all 51
elementary schools 35, 38, 40, 42, 49, 68, 93, 98, 101, 109, 123, 183, 314, 320, 340
England 1, 8, 18, 20, 27, 29, 31, 32, 39, 44, 48, 49, 53, 54, 57, 64, 66, 69, 82, 83, 84, 85, 147, 151, 170, 171, 188, 189, 190, 203, 206, 224, 235, 241, 246, 249, 252, 273, 275, 276, 279, 288, 289, 297, 301, 302, 306, 313, 314, 317, 331, 342, 345, 346, 347, 348, 350, 352
enterprise 7, 29, 34, 65, 97, 229, 230, 240, 283, 289, 290, 293, 295, 323, 326, 328, 350
entrepreneurial cost centres 240, 241, 242, 295, 325, 339
entrepreneurship 194, 222, 229, 240, 241, 243, 244
equal opportunities 5, 52, 68, 69, 77, 260, 286
equality of opportunity 42, 59, 60, 63, 68, 69, 70, 77, 78, 79, 285, 286, 314, 347
equilibrium 27, 34, 146, 213, 216, 329, 330, 334, 340
eroding 146, 169, 338

Essex 76, 191, 356
ethnic groups 276, 277, 278
ethnic origin 277
Examinations 11+ 11- 84, 129, 137, 138, 180, 196, 254
Excellence in schools 274, 285, 297, 300, 308, 345
expectations 15, 93, 97, 139, 145, 154, 180, 183, 184, 185, 227, 228, 253, 255, 256, 270, 273, 274, 275, 276, 278, 281, 288, 299, 300, 308, 310, 311, 314, 320, 323, 334, 335
external examination 93, 109, 155, 157, 160, 161, 183, 188, 321

F
Fabian society 43, 229, 314
failure policy 282, 300, 325
foster 9, 39, 40, 88, 195, 198, 234, 316
France 18, 32, 44, 259, 272, 273, 299, 304, 342
Frances horsburgh 223
Free churches 58
free moral choice 230
freedom 8, 21, 24, 26, 27, 66, 77, 79, 83, 91, 100, 101, 102, 103, 105, 106, 110, 153, 161, 196, 204, 205, 209, 212, 213, 216, 229, 230, 231, 234, 238, 239, 241, 244, 248, 249, 254, 286, 289, 290, 291, 292, 293, 294, 295, 296, 301, 302, 305, 313, 317, 322, 323, 324, 325, 326, 327, 328, 336, 338, 346
French 16, 22, 26, 32, 54, 272, 300, 307, 342
further education 30, 42, 69, 70, 71, 72, 76, 84, 85, 91, 155, 265, 342

G
GCE 11, 153, 154, 156, 157, 158, 159, 160, 161, 163, 168, 171, 188, 224, 227, 228, 264, 275, 306, 322, 345, 356
GCSE 11, 261, 264, 265, 266, 275, 276, 277, 278, 279, 306, 307, 345, 360, 11, 261, 264, 265, 266, 275, 276, 277, 278, 279, 306, 307, 345, 360
Geese 136, 163, 322
GNVQ 11, 265, 266, 275, 306, 327, 331
General system theory 23, 28, 33, 245
Germany 44, 261, 304
Gloucestershire 112, 116, 125, 136, 147, 316, 340, 355, 356
goals 8, 17, 20, 21, 22, 24, 25, 26, 31, 36, 52, 57, 77, 80, 186, 241, 253, 254, 255, 288, 290, 298, 328, 338
golden years 228
good old days 9, 193, 212, 252, 337
grammar school era 9, 298, 325, 330, 337
grammar schools 6, 44, 69, 71, 84, 93, 94, 102, 108, 109, 110, 111, 112, 113, 114, 115, 116, 117, 118, 126, 130, 131, 134, 135, 137, 138, 141, 145, 153, 154, 158, 161, 164, 166, 167, 169, 170, 171, 172, 174, 177, 178, 179, 187, 189, 190, 191, 193, 195, 196, 203, 204, 205, 206, 207, 213, 216, 264, 284, 294, 317, 318, 321, 324, 327, 329, 352, 355
grant maintained schools 251, 282, 325, 326, 331
Great debate 208

H
Hadow 50, 69, 72, 87, 92, 93, 96, 103, 109, 153, 170, 187, 352
Hampshire 96, 100, 103, 125, 170, 300, 356
health services 69, 84
heterogeneous 199, 200
hierarchy of schools 228, 284, 289, 293, 294, 303, 314, 326, 328, 337
hierarchical nature 289

higher education 30, 38, 39, 68, 72, 73, 84, 85, 110, 205, 221, 226, 227, 228, 232, 246, 265, 266, 287, 343, 350
HM Inspectors 11, 38, 39, 53, 59, 82, 113, 119, 200, 215, 242, 262
HM Treasury 347, 309
home background 172, 173, 186, 226, 252
human capital 7, 221, 222, 224, 229, 243, 245, 246, 325, 341
Huntingdonshire 100, 104, 112, 124, 319, 340, 356

I
individual liberty 230, 234
inequality 9, 50, 80, 214, 237, 245, 302, 304, 314, 326, 327, 336, 337, 339, 348
inflation 121, 230, 231, 232, 247, 324
injustice 35, 42, 49, 69, 80, 280, 314
innovation 95, 97, 232, 240, 241, 257, 293, 349
inspectors 113, 119
instability 21, 22, 23, 24, 245, 332, 362
intellectual elites 216, 234, 324
Israeli 10, 16, 22, 23, 24, 27

J
Japan 18, 32, 261

K
Kent 101, 112, 124, 170, 236, 356
Kent's 101
Kidlington 115, 120

L
Labour 46, 80, 83, 84, 86, 140, 141, 142, 148, 153, 166, 177, 178, 179, 180, 181, 191, 196, 205, 210, 213, 222, 226, 230, 232, 267, 274, 285, 286, 295, 297, 300, 316, 318, 351
Lancashire 74, 76, 126, 138, 142, 147, 158, 160, 188
Lawton 153, 154, 188, 212, 213, 220, 283, 305, 309, 310, 349, 351
LEAs 6, 8, 11, 23, 28, 31, 36, 43, 47, 48, 50, 51, 52, 54, 57, 58, 60, 61, 62, 64, 67, 71, 72, 73, 74, 75, 76, 77, 78, 79, 80, 82, 85, 87, 88, 89, 90, 91, 92, 95, 96, 97, 98, 102, 103, 105, 106, 107, 108, 110, 113, 114, 117, 118, 120, 121, 123, 124, 126, 127, 129, 132, 133, 139, 140, 142, 143, 144, 146, 148, 154, 157, 160, 163, 169, 170, 173, 174, 175, 176, 177, 179, 181, 182, 191, 196, 212, 214,league table 214, 237, 261, 269, 278, 279, 281, 299, 302, 310, 325, 214, 237, 261, 269, 278, 279, 281, 299, 302, 310, 325
leaving age 35, 36, 49, 50, 55, 63, 64, 68, 76, 77, 80, 84, 151, 158, 161, 167, 178, 183, 217, 223, 224, 225, 314, 355
Leicestershire 103, 112, 116, 124, 142, 147, 170, 190, 356
levell up 277, 334, 337
levelling down 203, 317, 334
Liberal 43, 177, 230, 231, 234, 243, 247, 290, 324, 340, 342
Lincolnshire 118, 126, 356
Liverpool 40, 133, 142, 147, 155, 177, 351, 357
LMS 11, 251, 267, 292, 295, 296, 297, 337, 340, 349, 350
local control 15, 209, 271
local needs 8, 17, 20, 89, 94, 95, 96, 98, 106, 108, 120, 122, 143, 145, 180, 72, 317, 318, 331, 332, 336
local tradition 8, 74, 95, 110, 118, 121, 317, 318, 331, 336, 337
London county 78, 96, 124, 160

M

Manchester 55, 84, 119, 126, 147, 165, 175, 177, 188, 189, 202, 340, 346, 349, 357
market freedom 234
market principles 9, 194, 298, 299, 323, 325, 326, 327, 329
market system 194, 229, 231, 237, 293, 298, 299, 300, 302, 325, 327, 329
Middlesex 99, 100, 101, 102, 124, 128, 129, 130, 132, 134, 138, 147, 160, 170, 356
Ministry of education 16, 18, 32, 38, 88, 92, 94, 95, 102, 106, 114, 118, 119, 120, 121, 123, 125, 126, 127, 137, 139, 144, 148, 154, 155, 162, 164, 165, 166, 171, 172, 173, 176, 184, 188, 189, 190, 192, 212, 223, 246, 318, 319, 321, 343, 346, 349, 350, 354, 355
minority 153, 157, 191, 323, 349
mixed ability classes 193, 195, 196, 198, 199, 200, 201, 215, 216, 217, 324
Modern schools 34, 107, 111, 113, 115, 116, 129, 136, 139, 152, 153, 156, 158, 161, 162, 165, 168, 183, 340, 343, 360
modern 6, 8, 17, 21, 23, 39, 72, 73, 87, 88, 89, 92, 93, 94, 99, 103, 107, 108, 109, 110, 112, 113, 115, 116, 117, 124, 125, 128, 129, 130, 131, 134, 135, 136, 137, 138, 139, 144, 145, 148, 152, 153, 154, 155, 156, 157, 158, 159, 160, 161, 162, 163, 165, 166, 167, 169, 171, 175, 180, 183, 184, 185, 186, 187, 188, 189, 198, 205, 217, 227, 228, 256, 262, 263, 284, 308, 315, 318, 320, 321, 322, 323, 327, 330, 332, 334, 335, 337
modular curriculum 260
motivation theory 146
Multilateral school 94, 95, 100, 102, 103, 105, 107, 110, 112, 113, 114, 117, 118, 119, 123, 124, 126, 135, 136, 161, 189, 321

N

national assessment 7, 14, 15, 22, 32, 194, 268, 269, 270, 271, 273, 301, 305, 307, 327, 351
National Curriculum 7, 14, 16, 17, 215, 254, 255, 256, 257, 258, 260, 261, 264, 265, 266, 267, 268, 269, 276, 284, 285, 293, 298, 304, 305, 307, 308, 326, 331, 341, 343, 345, 351, 355
national core curriculum 7, 194, 196, 209, 211, 216, 251
national minimum 43, 210
national society 37, 53, 63, 64, 83, 355
national solidarity 69, 314
NUT 11, 66, 78, 148, 154, 155, 156, 161, 351, 355
NVQ 11, 265, 266, 327, 331
neglected 31, 81, 167, 187, 300, 330, 336
neo-conservatives 216, 221, 229, 233, 234, 243, 305, 324, 327, 340
neo-liberal 230, 231, 234, 243, 324, 340
new liberalism 42, 314
New right 7, 194, 219, 221, 229, 234, 241, 243, 260, 263, 305, 324, 325, 330, 343, 347
New york 246, 249, 308, 311, 341, 346, 347, 350, 351, 353, 354
new-conservatives 194
Newcastle report 39
Newsom report 225, 226, 246, 350
Norman lamont 290, 291, 310
Norwood 69, 87, 92, 123, 143, 153, 170, 187, 352

O

objectives 22, 26, 28, 128, 199, 215, 253, 254, 255, 256, 257, 258, 295, 306, 335, 343
OECD 351, 11, 14, 16, 17, 32, 253
opting out 251, 294, 349
order 5, 6, 7, 8, 9, 13, 17, 20, 21, 23, 24, 26, 27, 28, 29, 30, 31, 33, 34, 35, 36, 38, 41, 44, 45, 46, 47, 51, 52, 57, 58, 69, 71, 72, 75, 76, 77, 79, 82, 83, 85, 87, 88, 89, 91, 92, 93, 94, 95, 96, 97, 99 104, 105, 109, 111, 115, 120, 121, 129, 130, 131, 135, 136, 138, 146, 151, 152, 160, 164, 168, 172, 173, 175, 182, 185, 186, 187, 193, 194, 198, 199, 201, 202, 205, 208, 213, 214, 216,

218, 221, 222, 223, 224, 225, 226, 230, 231, 233, 234, 236, 240, 241, 243, 244, 245, 251, 252, 253, 255, 256, 258, 260, 264, 265, 267, 268, 269, 270, 273, 284, 285, 295, 298, 300, 302, 303, 310, 313, 314, 315, 316, 317, 318, 319, 320, 322, 323, 324, 325, 326, 328, 329, 330, 331, 332, 333, 334, 335, 336, 337, 352
Ordinary level 153, 161, 224, 228, 246
ORT 351, 259, 262, 305, 306
Oxfordshire 96, 99, 101, 114, 120, 124, 126, 258, 280, 316, 340, 356

P

parental choice 138, 236, 237, 238, 251, 284, 287, 288, 293, 251, 284, 287, 288, 293, 309, 341, 352, 309
Parliament 39, 40, 44, 46, 49, 51, 76, 91, 96, 123, 142, 178, 202, 203, 205, 213, 219, 223, 240, 251, 259, 265, 285, 290, 295, 296, 301
partnership 41, 145, 212, 213, 214, 216, 248, 306, 326, 345, 351
payment by results 39, 280
pendulum 1, 7, 8, 9, 18, 19, 20, 21, 22, 27, 28, 29, 30, 31, 33, 252, 267, 303, 313, 317, 322, 323, 328, 331, 335, 353
pensions 69, 229
per capita 295
policy of exclusion 8, 322, 327, 334, 336
poor attendance 198
poor children 37, 39
poor performance 198
primary 13, 28, 30, 31, 32, 35, 38, 41, 42, 47, 50, 61, 63, 68, 72, 73, 76, 77, 83, 85, 90, 96, 98, 148, 169, 180, 191, 202, 218, 219, 240, 242, 255, 256, 258, 275, 276, 281, 284, 287, 290, 298, 305, 308, 309, 310, 314, 315, 342, 343, 349, 351, 352, 355
private funds 194, 222, 239, 240, 295
private money 24, 242, 244, 249, 325
private schools 14, 241, 242, 293
privatisation 229, 235, 238, 239, 241, 245, 248, 249, 352, 354, 361
progressive methods 6, 195, 196, 201, 202, 207, 209, 218

R

responsibility 13, 14, 13, 14, 13, 14, 13, 14, 26, 34, 48, 60, 67, 71, 77, 91, 104, 145, 153, 185, 229, 239, 241, 249, 272, 284, 293, 294, 295, 324, 326, 327
Robbins report 205, 226, 228, 246, 350
Roman catholics 64, 66

S

scholastic attainments 193, 324
school boards 35, 40, 41, 42, 45, 52, 314
school leaving age 50, 63, 68, 76, 80, 161, 167, 217, 223, 314, 355
School-based management 15, 32, 345, 349
school-leavers 211
Schools budget 296
Second world war 18, 51, 57, 229, 252
secondary education 5, 8, 11, 24, 30, 31, 35, 36, 41, 42, 43, 45, 46, 47, 50, 52, 53, 54, 57, 68, 69, 70, 71, 72, 73, 77, 83, 84, 87, 90, 92, 93, 96, 98, 99, 100, 101, 102, 104, 105, 106, 107, 108, 110, 112, 113, 116, 118, 120, 121, 122, 123, 125, 126, 127, 128, 138, 139, 140, 141, 142, 143, 147, 151, 152, 154, 162, 163, 164, 166, 174, 177, 178, 179, 180, 181, 182, 184, 187, 189, 190, 191, 192, 195, 196, 197, 198, 205, 213, 214, 219, 221, 226, 259, 304, 305, 314, 315, 317, 319, 320, 322, 335, 340, 344, 346, 347, 348, 351, 352, 353, 354, 356

selection 6, 84, 87, 88, 89, 100, 103, 106, 108, 141, 143, 145, 148, 152, 169, 170, 171, 172, 173, 174, 175, 177, 184, 186, 187, 190, 193, 195, 199, 200, 201, 202, 203, 206, 208, 211, 272, 284, 285, 293, 294, 307, 311, 315, 318, 320, 321, 322, 324, 335, 342, 346, 352, 354, 356
self-determination 8, 171, 184, 186, 321, 335, 337
self-discovery 263
self-fulfilling prophecies 197, 198, 255, 197, 198, 255
Self-government for schools 285, 296, 297, 309, 345
self-image 280, 281
service-oriented culture 290, 291
sixth forms 318
skilled workers 45, 226
small is beautiful 240, 249, 292, 353
social system 22, 23, 27, 33, 351, 352
specialist schools 282, 286, 301
Spens 69, 72, 87, 109, 352
stability 9, 27, 28, 329, 330, 332
Staffordshire 175, 356
standards 6, 9, 14, 27, 28, 31, 42, 47, 52, 64, 79, 82, 85, 90, 93, 96, 97, 109, 111, 115, 118, 121, 123, 124, 125, 154, 155, 156, 157, 161, 162, 173, 184, 185, 193, 194, 195, 196, 199, 200, 201, 202, 203, 204, 205, 206, 207, 208, 209, 210, 211, 212, 213, 214, 216, 218, 220, 222, 230, 234, 235, 236, 237, 251, 252, 253, 254, 255, 256, 259, 260, 266, 268, 270, 271, 272, 273, 274, 2 75, 276, 284, 288, 293, 298, 299, 300, 301, 311, 314, 316, 317, 321, 324, 325, 327, 328, 329, 334, 337, 351, 353, 354
standardisation 19, 20, 21, 28
state control 38, 67
streaming 6, 171, 193, 195, 196, 197, 198, 199, 200, 201, 202, 203, 204, 205, 216, 324
structural transformation 8, 21, 23, 27, 30, 208, 313, 323, 328, 329, 332, 337
Swansea 175
Sweden 17, 18, 20, 261
Switzerland 44

T
Taylor report 239, 248, 351
technical schools 6, 45, 72, 73, 87, 88, 92, 93, 99, 103, 107, 109, 111, 112, 115, 117, 152, 163, 164, 165, 166, 167, 168, 169, 186, 189, 190, 192, 305, 318, 350, 356
TGAT 11, 268, 269, 270, 273, 274, 308
The next steps 289, 290, 310, 343, 348
Theory Y 26
Tory Party 218, 248, 286, 300, 218, 248, 286, 300
tripartite system 6, 8, 51, 52, 87, 88, 94, 95, 103, 106, 107, 108, 110, 111, 113, 114, 121, 140, 151, 152, 162, 163, 165, 168, 169, 175, 176, 177, 178, 179, 180, 182, 183, 186, 285, 302, 316, 318, 319, 321, 322, 324, 326, 327, 328, 330, 336
TVEI 11, 258, 259, 260, 261, 264, 265, 305, 344, 346, 353, 354

U
undermined 183, 187, 206, 234, 261, 318, 338
unemployment 69, 229, 231, 232, 233, 247, 259, 324
United states 14, 32, 84, 307, 352
universities 16, 110, 153, 157, 202, 205, 206, 219, 226, 259

V
value for money 249, 292, 293, 294, 349
Victorian period 229

vocational studies 265, 302, 327
voluntary schools 5, 36, 41, 46, 47, 51, 57, 58, 59, 60, 61, 63, 64, 67, 77, 80, 82, 96, 133

W
Wales 1, 8, 18, 29, 31, 48, 54, 57, 66, 84, 85, 151, 170, 171, 188, 189, 203, 206, 289, 302, 313, 317, 331, 346, 348
Walford 241, 242, 245, 249, 250, 282, 289, 308, 309, 354
welfare state194, 221, 229, 230, 231, 246, 324
West riding 76, 131, 147, 175, 347, 76, 131, 147, 175, 347
Westmorland 96, 100, 113, 119, 124, 356
William tenderly report 209, 218
working classes 40, 43, 189
Wright 206, 219, 355

Index of Names
A
Adler Michael 287, 288, 301, 302, 309, 311, 341, 352
Allison Lincoln 234, 248, 341
Andrew Gamble 231, 232, 234, 247, 248, 346
Archer Margaret S. 19, 32, 341
Argyris Chris 24, 33, 341
Arnold Matthew 45
Auld Robin 220, 341

B
Bacon Alice 178, 181
Bacon William 178, 181, 304, 341
Baker Kenneth 251, 255, 262, 268, 305, 345
Ball Stephen J. 207, 218, 219, 267, 307, 341, 350
Barrett Frank J. 33, 353
Bashi Joseph 253, 304, 341
Batley Richard 133, 135, 141, 147, 148, 341
Beare Hedley 252, 253, 304, 341
Becher Tony 254, 304, 341
Bell Moberly E. 48, 54, 341
Bendix Reinhard 33, 341
Berlak Harold 270, 307, 341
Bernstein Basil 171, 190, 341
Bertalanffy L. Von 23, 332, 341
Black Paul J. 341, 342
Blaug Mark 224, 237, 245, 246, 247, 248, 303, 311, 341, 342
Bolton Eric 242
Boyle Edward 177
Boyson 218, 219, 341, 343, 344
Bradley Ian 247
Bradley Ian 342
Brennan E.J.T. 42, 44, 55, 342
Brighouse Harry 289, 300, 342
Broadfoot Patricia 16, 19, 32, 272, 280, 282, 307, 308, 311, 342, 352
Brooksbank Kenneth 304, 342
Brown R.J. 10, 127, 128, 140, 145, 342, 353
Buckley Walter 34, 337, 340, 343, 359

Bullock A. 220, 298, 343, 345
Butler R.A. 48, 58, 59, 60, 61, 62, 64, 66, 67, 68, 69, 71, 73, 74, 75, 76, 79, 80, 81, 82, 83, 84, 86, 91, 153, 156, 212, 222, 223, 246, 314, 315, 340, 343, 348

C

Cantnach Miss 66, 81, 83
Caldwell Brian J. 14, 32, 253, 338, 343
Callaghan James 194, 196, 208, 210, 211, 220, 343
Cheng, Yin Cheong 253, 338, 343
Chitty Clyde 191, 207, 209, 210, 214, 219, 220, 228, 238, 248, 249, 270, 295, 307, 309, 310, 341, 343
Churchill Winston 57
Clark Colin 247, 343
Clive Griggs 206, 207, 219, 218, 219, 235, 236, 242, 247, 248, 347
Coleman James 252, 304, 343
Couchman Randall 238
Coulby D. 257, 305, 343
Covell Charles 247, 343
Cox C.B. 202, 218, 219, 256, 341, 343, 344
Cruickshank Marjorie 44, 48, 55, 82, 83, 86, 344
Cullingford Cedric 281, 282, 308, 344, 355
Cuttance Peter 253, 304, 344

D

Dale Roger 261, 305, 344
Dalin P. 253, 344
David Miriam E. 344
Davies Andrew 159, 188, 199, 217, 280, 344
Davies R. Peter check with Davies, Andrew
Dearing Ron 265, 306, 344
Dennison W.F. 246, 344
Dent H.C. 42, 54, 73, 76, 85, 344
Dimmock C. 253, 345
Disraeli Benjamin 69, 314
Dockrell W.B. 272, 273, 308, 342, 345
Drake H. 155
Drucker Peter 248, 345
Dyson A. 202

E

Eatwell Roger 233, 248, 345
Eccles David 155, 161, 167, 177, 189, 191
Eloy William 61

F

Fenwick I.G.K. 127, 132, 138, 140, 142, 145, 147, 148, 191, 346
Filer Ann 270, 280, 281, 307, 341, 342, 346, 349, 352
Finegold David 261, 305, 346
Finn Chester 15, 32, 346
Fisher H.A.L 99, 314
Floud J.E 171, 190, 346
Flude Michael 293, 294, 310, 346

Fogarty Michael 229, 247, 346
Friedman Milton 32, 235, 246, 248, 343, 346, 349, 354, 355

G
Gamble Andrew 231, 232, 234, 247, 248, 346
Geiger Theodore 232, 247, 346
Gillborn David 277, 278, 280, 308, 347
Glatter 288, 301, 309, 355
Gleeson Denis 305, 346, 347
Gleick James 33, 347
Golby Michael 257, 347
Goodlad John I. 253, 347
Gosden P.H.J.H. 131, 147, 347

H
Halpin 18, 354
Halsall Elizabeth 147, 148, 347, 355
Halsey A. H. 10, 42, 171, 347
Hamilton Oliver 82, 249, 340, 343, 347
Hammer Merril 293, 294, 310, 346
Handy Charles B. 26, 34, 146, 347
Harris Ralph 247, 347
Havilland Julian 310, 347, 354
Hayek F.A. 229, 234, 247, 248, 347
Hee-Chun Kang 42, 50, 69, 347
Hewitson J.N. 147, 148, 347
Holmes M.G. 75
Hopkins David 253, 254, 304, 305, 348, 353
Hough G.R. 232, 247, 348
Howard Anthony 83, 348

J
Jantsch Erich 33, 34, 340, 348, 352, 362
Jencks Christopher 252, 304, 348
Jennings Robert 132, 348
Joseph Keith 236, 244, 248
Jowitt William A. 74

K
Kay James 38
Kelly A.V. 196, 198, 199, 200, 201, 217, 218, 348, 355
Kelsall R.K. 175, 191, 348
Kemp E.P. 290
Kenway Jane 14, 348
Kesternard Isaac-Henry 132, 138, 147, 148, 348
King Edmund J. 30, 34, 217, 349
Kirp David 288, 309, 349
Kirst Michael W. 15, 32, 349
Knight Kenneth E.33, 349
Kogan Maurice 51, 69, 84, 349

L
Lacelle-Peterson Mark 280, 349
Lamont Norman 290, 291, 292, 310, 349

Langerman Shoshana 32, 349
Lauglo Jon 16, 17, 19, 20, 32, 33, 342, 349
Lawton Denis 153, 154, 188, 212, 213, 220, 283, 305, 309, 310, 349, 350, 351
Leonard Martin 283, 309, 349
Levacic Rosalind 298, 349
Lewin Kurt 34, 349
Liell Peter 77, 349
Lloyd Geoffrey 177, 213
Lloyd George 223
Lord hailsham 213
Lord Rodney 44, 63, 83, 213, 249, 259, 305, 349, 355
Lord selborne 63
Lord taunton 44
Lowe Roy 18, 69, 153, 154, 175, 177, 88, 189, 191, 219, 347, 349, 351
Lynn Richard 203, 204, 218, 349

M

Maclure Stuart J. 54, 84, 181, 248, 254, 293, 304, 310, 34, 349
Macmillan Harold 223
Macrae S. 267, 307, 350
Maslow Abraham H. 350
Maychell K. 350
Maynard, Alan 350
Mays John Barron 350
McCulloch Gray 350
McGinn Noel 350
McGregor Douglas 34, 308, 350
McLean Martin 19, 32, 33, 342, 349
Meyer Marshall W. 333, 334, 350
Morris Estelle 286
Murphy Patricia 351
Murray John 66
Musgrove Frank 206, 219, 351

N

Newbold David 351
Nuttall Desmond 351

O

Olson Mancur 232, 247, 351
O'Sullivan 248, 345
Owen Joslyn 351

P

Parkinson Michael H. 351
Parsons Talcott 22, 33, 34, 329, 351
Part A. 159
Patten Chris 243
Patten John 285
Pedley F.H. 351
Pedley R.R. 203, 218, 351
Peters Thomas 249, 311, 351
Philip James H. 131, 132, 147, 309, 351, 355

Phillips Robert 10, 18, 280, 308, 342, 351, 354
Philpot Margaret 280
Pidgeon Douglas A. 171, 190, 274, 308, 351, 355
Pollard Arthur 204, 218, 280, 342, 352
Power Colin 13, 14, 15, 317, 319, 320, 323, 324, 326, 331, 332, 333, 338, 352, 354
Prentice Reg 213
Prigogine Ilya 23, 27, 34, 352
Pring Richard 10, 241, 242, 243, 244, 245, 248, 249, 250, 352, 361
Pryor John and Torrance280, 352
Pugh Patricia 43, 54, 352

R
Raab Gillian 287, 302, 309, 352
Ramsbotham Herwald 57
Ranson Stewart 18, 77, 85, 302, 311, 352
Reid M. 196, 197, 199, 200, 201, 217, 218, 352
Reynolds David 344, 352, 353
Ribbins Peter M. 128, 140, 145, 353
Rosenthal Robert 353
Rubinstein David 353
Rutter M. 252, 353

S
Saran Rene 128, 129, 130, 132, 134, 136, 139, 140, 145, 147, 148, 353
Schiff Martin 15, 32, 33, 353
Schultz Theodore W. 224, 246, 353
Schumacher E.F. 249, 353
Scruton Roger 233, 248, 353
Seldon Arthur 236, 237, 247, 248, 343, 346, 347, 353
Senker Peter 261, 305, 353
Shils Edward 33, 34, 351
Short Edward 205
Simon Brian 353
Sir geoffrey crowther 212
Slavin Robert E. 20, 33, 353
Sparrow John 205, 219,Spinks 14, 32, 253, 343
Srivastva Suresh 24, 25, 33, 353
Stanton Geoff 265, 266, 306, 353
Stewart Michael 179, 191
Stiglitz Joseph E. 228, 247, 311, 353, 354
Sungaila Helen 33, 338, 354
Swanson Austin D. 20, 32, 354

T
Tawney H.R. 43, 54, 55, 69, 354
Taylor Councillor T. 77, 85, 239, 248, 306, 351, 354
Temple Fredrich 41, 53, 63, 64, 78, 80, 81, 83, 208, 217, 219, 343, 344
Thatcher Margaret 181, 205, 208, 258, 262, 290, 181, 205, 208, 258, 262, 290
Thompson Joan 106, 107, 125, 354
Thorneycroft Peter 223
Tomlinson George 153, 178, 222
Tomlinson John 305, 352, 354
Tomlinson Sally 306, 307, 308, 350, 354

Torrance Harry 280, 281, 346, 352
Tymms Peter 280, 354

V
Vernon P.E. 170, 171, 184, 190, 321, 335, 354
Volansky A. 15, 32, 343, 349, 354, 355

W
Walford Geoffrey 241, 242, 245, 249, 250, 282, 289, 308, 309, 354
Walsh William 205, 219, 354
Ward S. 257, 305, 343
Watts A.E 171, 354
Watzlawick Paul 33, 335, 354
Webb Sidney 43
Wells M.M. 77, 85, 220, 354
Whitty Geoff, 18, 354
Wilkinson Ellen 153, 178
Williams Shirley 210, 214
Williams Vivian 10, 210, 214, 295, 298, 310, 338, 355
Wilson Harold 179
Woodhall Maureen 224, 246, 355
Woodings Val 280, 308, 355
Woods Philip A. 288, 301, 309, 355
Woodward R.J. 355
Wright Nigel 206, 219, 355

Y
Young A.G. 37, 70, 71, 83, 84, 154, 170, 197, 198, 199, 217, 259, 261, 265, 266, 278, 305, 355
young David 259

Z
Zucker Lynne 24, 25, 33, 146, 350